Preparing to Teach Writing
Research, Theory, and Practice

Third Edition

Preparing to Teach Writing
Research, Theory, and Practice

Third Edition

James D. Williams

LAWRENCE ERLBAUM ASSOCIATES, PUBLISHERS
2003   Mahwah, New Jersey   London

Lawrence Erlbaum Associates, Inc., Publishers
10 Industrial Avenue
Mahwah, New Jersey 07430

Cover design by Kathryn Houghtaling Lacey

Library of Congress Cataloging-in-Publication Data

Williams, James D. (James Dale), 1949-
Preparing to teach writing: research, theory, and practice / James D. Williams. — 3rd ed.
    p. cm.
Includes bibliographical references and index.
ISBN 0-8058-4164-4 (pbk. : alk. paper)
1. English language—Rhetoric—Study and teaching—Research.
2. English language—Composition and exercises—Research. 3. Report writing—
Study and teaching—Research. 4. English teachers—Training of. I. Title.

PE1404.W54   2003
808'.042'071—dc21   200340771
                                                            CIP

Books published by Lawrence Erlbaum Associates are printed on acid-free paper,
and their bindings are chosen for strength and durability.

Printed in the United States of America
10 9 8 7 6 5 4 3 2

*This book is dedicated to the memory
of my mother and father,
Jessie and Elmer Williams*

Contents

Preface

My first teaching job many years ago was at a high school just outside San Jose, California. I taught six writing classes and monitored the rest rooms during lunch hours while trying to understand why my students couldn't write. In spite of my English degree and credential, nothing I did seemed to help, perhaps because I really had not been prepared to teach writing. It just wasn't part of the education curriculum in those days. Overwhelmed by how much I didn't know, I began reading everything I could about teaching writing, which wasn't much because there wasn't much available.

Over the next decade, that situation changed. Rhetoric and composition emerged as a field of study, and eventually I completed a PhD in that field. My first university position was at UCLA, where I was asked to teach, among other things, a class in composition theory and methods for young people seeking their teaching credentials. This course determined the direction of my career, and I have been training teachers, with only a few interruptions, ever since. That summer, I reflected on my experiences as a teacher and began planning the course. I quickly realized that most of the materials I had used for my graduate work were inappropriate for prospective elementary and high school teachers, and I started looking for a text or two that covered all the topics that I thought were important for these students. A couple of titles looked promising until I reviewed them. They were either too deep or too shallow. I finally resorted to profligate photocopying, putting together a "course pack" that was expensive and hard to use.

By the end of my first year at UCLA, I decided that I would write my own book that would include all the topics and information that beginning teachers need if they are going to teach writing effectively. *Pre-*

paring to Teach Writing began to take shape during that summer, even though it was not finished until some years later.

From the beginning, I wanted *Preparing to Teach Writing* to be comprehensive because there are so many factors that influence learning to write and thus teaching writing. I wanted to provide a text that truly would prepare future writing teachers for the many challenges they would face in the classroom. The first edition (1989) was positioned firmly in the cognitive approach to composition that dominated the field at that time. It explored writing as a psychosocial action and advocated a "pragmatic" approach to instruction before the ideas of "social constructivism" had fully jelled in the profession.

A bit to my surprise, the book proved popular in spite of the fact that some of the chapters were fairly demanding. After a decade, I was asked to produce a second edition, which was released in 1998. By that time, the field of rhetoric and composition had changed significantly, becoming more political and less concerned about the pragmatics of instruction. The second edition explored some of the ramifications of this change and raised a number of questions associated with the focus in the field on postmodernism.

OVERVIEW

Today, with the publication of the third edition, we have entered what some have referred to as the post-postmodern period, which has been characterized as a time of professional fragmentation. What this means is twofold. First, there is no dominant theory or approach for writing instruction. Second, rhetoric and composition now, more than ever, has separated theory and practice to such a degree that there are very few points of contact between them. This does not mean, however, that we cannot identify the most effective way to teach writing or that we cannot base teaching methods on sound theory. Quite the contrary. It simply means that the field, at least as it is defined by the majority of those who publish in the professional journals, has chosen a different direction.

This third edition, like the previous two, is based on some fairly simple assumptions:

- Literacy, which includes writing as well as reading, is important; it leads to personal growth and success and makes for a better society.
- All children deserve the chance to become fully literate.
- Some methods of teaching writing are measurably more effective than others.

- Our schools and teachers have both a social and a professional obligation to provide the best literacy training possible.

The primary goal of *Preparing to Teach Writing*, therefore, is to give teachers and prospective teachers the knowledge to meet their obligations.

Any new edition of a textbook necessarily combines the old with the new. Most of the pedagogical apparatus that characterized the first two editions is preserved here; research and theory are examined with the aim of informing teaching. Also preserved are discussions and references to foundational studies that helped define the field of rhetoric and composition. The chapter titles listed as follows give a clear indication of the range of topics. For new readers, they map the most essential territory of the field. For those who used the second edition, they should have a comfortable familiarity:

- The foundations of rhetoric.
- Contemporary rhetoric.
- Best practices.
- The classroom as workshop.
- Reading and writing.
- Grammar and writing.
- English as a second language.
- The psychology of writing.
- Writing assignments.
- Writing assessment.

NEW IN THE THIRD EDITION

But there is much that is new in the third edition. Chapter 1, for example, provides a more thorough discussion of the history of rhetoric, from its earliest days in ancient Greece to the first American composition courses offered at Harvard University in 1874. Chapter 2 is almost entirely new, examining the major approaches to teaching writing—current–traditional rhetoric, new rhetoric, romantic rhetoric, writing across the curriculum, social-theoretic rhetoric, postmodern rhetoric, and post-postmodern rhetoric—and considering their strengths and weaknesses. Chapter 3 also has much that is new; it takes the consideration of the strengths and weaknesses of the various major approaches to its logical conclusion and advocates on epistemic approach to writing instruction that demonstrably leads to improved student writing when implemented effectively. Chapter 4 examines how to implement this approach through the classroom workshop, which is predicated on the concept of writing as a process.

Chapter 5 is new insofar as it provides a more detailed account of the phonics–whole-language debate that continues to puzzle many teachers and parents. Chapter 6 has been significantly revised to eliminate the discussion of grammatical analysis found in the previous editions. The focus now is on explaining why grammar instruction does not lead to better writing, the difference between grammar and usage, and how to teach grammar and usage effectively. The chapter summarizes some of the more common problems in grammar and usage that teachers encounter regularly and then offers brief overviews of the four major grammars to help readers understand that the choice of grammar in teaching has significant pedagogical consequences because each has different goals and perspectives on language.

Chapter 7, addressing English as a second language and nonstandard dialects, has an expanded section on Chicano English that now includes a brief discussion of Spanglish. Chapter 9 also has been expanded to provide more information on outcome objectives, which have become increasingly important since the publication of the second edition. To help public school teachers plan and set viable outcome objectives, the chapter includes a summary of the learning outcomes statement developed by the Counsel of Writing Program Administrators for first-year composition courses. This summary will help public school teachers have a clearer view of what they need to do to prepare high school students for university writing, and it will help those in graduate programs prepare for teaching assistantships in first-year composition. Finally, chapter 10 has been thoroughly revised to provide a more comprehensive analysis of assessment. It considers such important factors as the validity, reliability, predictability, cost, fairness, and politics of assessment. The revisions also include a discussion of state-mandated testing and its effect on teaching. Finally, the section on portfolios is greatly expanded, with an examination of the pitfalls of abandoning standard protocols and the influence on evaluation of such factors as gender, socioeconomic status, and ethnicity.

Overall, the third edition of *Preparing to Teach Writing* is clearer and more comprehensive than the previous edition. I consciously aimed to provide the most thorough consideration available of the numerous disciplines that inform the effective teaching of writing. Doing so entails a certain risk. The book is, admittedly, challenging in some parts, especially for those readers who are hoping for a cookbook approach to teaching writing. Nevertheless, those who accept the challenge will come out on the other end with the knowledge necessary to take the first steps toward becoming a first-rate writing teacher.

ACKNOWLEDGMENTS

I owe much to my many students over the years who regularly have taught me new things, and I thank them. I also thank my colleagues around the country who used the first edition and then the second edition and who were kind enough to send me notes detailing their successes and failures with the book. This information has been invaluable. I would like to thank the many great teachers I had in school, especially Lou Waters, Hans Guth, and the late Phil Cook, all of San Jose State University, and Ross Winterowd, Jack Hawkins, and Steve Krashen of the University of Southern California. Sharon Gibson Groshen of Towson University, Clark Jones of State University of New York at Cortland, and Ralph Voss at University of Alabama provided many useful suggestions for this new edition, and I am grateful for the time and effort they invested in this project. A special thanks goes to Erika Lindemann for being my colleague, mentor, and friend for many years at the University of North Carolina at Chapel Hill and who encouraged me to apply many of the ideas in this text when I was director of the UNC Writing Program. Finally, thanks to my wife, Ako, for everything: *Anata-wa boku-no taiyo desu.*

—James D. Williams
Chino Hills, California

1

The Foundations of Rhetoric

WHAT IS RHETORIC?

Rhetoric is a term that people use all the time, but not everyone knows what it means, in part because *rhetoric* has several different meanings. One sense of the word is speech that doesn't convey anything of substance. Politicians who make appealing, but ultimately false, promises to voters in campaign speeches, for example, are said to use "empty rhetoric." Then there are those books that purport to teach people how to write. Called "rhetorics," they represent another meaning of the term.

The Greek philosopher Aristotle defined rhetoric as "an ability, in each [particular] case, to see the available means of persuasion" (Kennedy, 1991, p. 36). Developing this ability, however, typically involved studying the structure of effective arguments, psychology, proof, and so forth, as well as practicing how to deliver a speech. In this text, *rhetoric* is defined in two ways—first, as a field of study that examines the means by which speakers and writers influence states of mind and actions in other people; and second, the application of those means. Thus, the discussions that follow explore rhetoric as something that people study and something that they apply to influence others. This definition treats rhetoric as an intellectual discipline as well as an art, skill, or ability that people may possess and use.

Contemporary rhetoric is characterized by several specialties, such as public speaking and the history of rhetoric, but composition is by far the largest of these. The importance of composition is so great that many professionals today commonly refer to the field of rhetoric as "rhetoric and composition." Note, however, that those who specialize in "composition" are not characterized as "writers" or "authors," although many of them are, but as "teachers of composition." This distinction is central to the field and to this book, which is not intended to help readers become better writers but *is* intended to help them become better teachers of writing.[1] Also worth noting is that the pedagogical foundation of composition necessarily links it to such fields as education, linguistics, and psychology.

The multifaceted nature of rhetoric and composition causes many people to be suspicious of broad definitions like the ones just mentioned. They argue that the question "What is rhetoric?" is meaningful only in relation to the cultural characteristics of a given society in a specified period. There is much truth in this argument, especially insofar as rhetoric can be applied to garner support for a given position. In classical Greece, rhetoric was viewed primarily as the use of language for purposes of persuasion. But almost from the very beginning there existed different emphases and purposes, and thus slightly different notions not only of what rhetoric did but of what it was. These notions certainly changed over time, but through all the changes there was at least one constant—the focus on examining how people use language to attain certain ends.

In my view, this focus is crucially important today. American society is more diverse than ever, and the need to train young people to be leaders who can weave the many strands of this diversity into a cultural fabric is especially acute. Historically, leadership has been predicated on the ability to communicate effectively, yet over the last several decades, we've seen the oral and written communication skills of our students decline precipitously. Growing numbers of young people use what is called "restricted code"—language characterized by a limited vocabulary and an inability to communicate abstract ideas—that is painfully unsuited to conveying anything but the most shallow concepts. Restricted code does not inspire—it alienates and fails to serve as the common currency of leadership.

HISTORY AND THEORY

Teachers who are concerned about helping students become better writers tend to be pragmatic. They want ideas and suggestions that

---

[1]Some scholars differentiate *writing* from *composition*. They argue that *writing* is a broad term that usually refers to fiction and journalism, whereas *composition* refers to academic writing, particularly the sort of writing that students produce in an English or composition class. Although this argument has some merit, I generally use the terms interchangeably throughout this book for the sake of convenience.

they can use immediately to improve student performance. Although this trait is admirable, it can make discussions of the history and theory of rhetoric seem like obstacles that delay grappling with practical issues.

Teaching writing, however, has become a complex endeavor, informed not only by state or district curriculum standards but also by a huge body of research and competing aims. All have a significant influence on methodologies. Focusing on methods without understanding the historical and theoretical foundations of rhetoric and composition would be shortsighted for at least three reasons. First, not all curriculum guides are based on sound principles. In California, for example, the state curriculum standards for language arts give little attention to skills sequencing, with the result being that students in sixth-grade classes and students in 10th-grade classes are asked to perform essentially the same tasks. Moreover, the skills-based nature of this curriculum emphasizes a "bottom-up" approach that does not accurately reflect how people master writing, a point that I discuss in several chapters that follow. Any teacher without some understanding of the history of rhetoric will find it harder to recognize these deficiencies and will have a more difficult time developing methods and assignments that serve to compensate. Second, students and classes differ so much that no one method works for everyone or in all situations. Knowledge of the historical foundation of rhetoric enables teachers to evaluate techniques and strategies more effectively and then make adjustments to classroom activities to meet student needs. Finally, there are social, political, and ethical dimensions to language instruction that cannot be ignored. How we prepare students to use language matters; our instruction shapes not only who they are but also who they become. Knowing some of the history of rhetoric helps us better understand the influence we exert.

Because a large part of current theory and practice is based on ideas developed in ancient Greece, it seems appropriate to start our voyage of discovery there. Then, in chapter 2, we look at more recent issues.

CLASSICAL GREEK RHETORIC

The origins of rhetoric are difficult to determine. Tradition holds that the formal study of rhetoric began around 467 B.C. in the Greek city of Syracuse on the island of Sicily after an aristocrat named Thrasybulus seized control of the government and set himself up as a tyrant. He either executed or banished his enemies, who were many, and then confiscated their property and that of their friends and relatives, giving it away to his supporters as rewards. More rash than wise, the tyrant was overthrown within a year, and the citizens of the newly established democracy faced the problem of taking back their property in a time when public records were inaccurate, incomplete, or perhaps even nonexistent. They turned to the courts for help.

A teacher named Corax (which translates into "crow"), after observing several trials, noticed that successful litigants used certain techniques in speaking that their adversaries did not. He used his observations to develop a "system" of rhetorical study and began teaching classes on how to win in court. Corax took on a student named Tisias (which translates into "egg"), who, being a clever person, negotiated a contract with Corax for his tuition that specified that he would not have to pay until he won his first trial. After completing his training, Tisias declined to practice law and refused to pay the tuition under the terms of the contract. Corax took his student to court, where he argued that he had given Tisias the best education in rhetoric that he could. Moreover, if the court ruled in favor of Tisias, he would have to pay the tuition because he thereby would complete the terms of the contract, whereas if the court ruled against Tisias, he would have to pay by order of the court. Either way, Corax would get his money.

Tisias, being equally inventive, reportedly replied that if the court ruled against him it would demonstrate that Corax had failed to teach him rhetoric very well and that he thus should not have to pay, whereas if the court ruled in his favor, it would demonstrate that he had mastered rhetoric on his own, in spite of an incompetent teacher. The court dismissed the case without a ruling, declaring *"kakou korakos kakon won"*—"from a worthless crow comes a worthless egg." In spite of an action that satisfied neither party, Corax and Tisias supposedly went on to produce handbooks on public speaking that were very popular, especially in Athens (Enos, 1993; Kennedy, 1980), where democracy was well established and where a less systematized form of rhetoric combined to provided fertile ground for the handbooks.

Democracy ensured a need for rhetoric in the assembly, where civic leaders deliberated on a range of issues affecting the city. The result was the development of *deliberative* rhetoric, which focused on political questions. The litigious nature of the Athenians guaranteed the further development of *forensic,* or legal, rhetoric, designed to sway juries.

It is worth noting that this traditional view has been criticized recently. Schiappa (1999), for example, argued not only that there is no evidence to support the claim that Corax and Tisias ever existed but also that there is no evidence that the term *rhetoric* existed before

Plato wrote his dialogue *Gorgias* around 380 B.C. If Schiappa is correct, his analysis would have significant implications for rhetoric and our understanding of its role in Greek society. We would have to reconsider, for example, the connection between rhetoric and democracy.

Although based on fairly compelling research, Schiappa's view is not yet shared by many. More widely accepted is the view that education, rhetoric, and politics developed a symbiotic relation early in Greek society. Vernant (1982), for example, argued that democracy and rhetoric were simultaneously stimulated in Athens in the middle of the seventh century B.C. when the ruler Draco codified Athenian law, thereby setting limits on aristocratic power and laying the foundation for democracy. In this view, Draco's laws were revolutionary because they articulated a new way of governing: The sword ceased being the sole—or even the primary—means of governing the populace. Vernant also argued that after the seventh century B.C., speech gained increasing importance as a means of exercising political power, in large part because of the spread of literacy that occurred in Athens during this time.

One of the more popular views is that rhetoric began to emerge when a shifting economic base effected changes in politics and education. Patterson (1991), for one, argued that at some point in the seventh century, agriculture in Greece shifted from grain to olives, figs, and wine, which were far more profitable owing to scarcity and higher prices. These crops, however, also required large sums of capital because it took years for the trees and vines to bear fruit. Small farmers and sharecroppers lacked the resources to produce such crops, so they were displaced by the changing economy and moved to Athens in search of work.

The social and economic consequences were complex. Patterson (1991) proposed that the displaced small farmers created a farm labor shortage, and the landowners responded by relying increasingly on slave labor to tend and harvest their crops. Meanwhile, the large number of free but destitute displaced farmers in Athens gained political power by using the threat of revolution as leverage. They sought to blunt abuses of power by the elite and to assert their status as freemen.

The end of the Persian War in 480 B.C. allowed Athens to begin developing an empire, which was accomplished by coercion when possible and by force when necessary. Successful military expeditions turned the conquered into slaves, and as their numbers increased, the value of freedom grew until it was more important to the majority of Athenian citizens than material wealth. In fact, wealth became desirable only insofar as it allowed freemen to enjoy the luxury of their status. Athenian freemen sought to cultivate their minds and souls (and those of their sons[2]) for the benefit of the city-state—hence the explosion of education at all levels.

About 10% of Athenian citizens were wealthy, and by law they were required to use their wealth to erect government buildings, pay for festivals, and field armies and navies in time of war—expenditures that frequently sent families and entire clans into bankruptcy. Poor citizens made up about 50% of the population, and the middle class made up the remaining 40%. Both groups lacked the means to provide material benefits to the city, so, according to Patterson (1991), their contributions came in the form of government service, a happy compromise that saved the ruling elite from revolution while maintaining their general status. Such service, however, required more and better education, greater skill as a speaker, and more democracy. All of these factors combined to create an environment that was ideal for the teaching and practice of rhetoric. When the Sicilian handbooks arrived in Athens, circumstances ensured an enthusiastic reception.

Rhetoric and the Greek Philosophers

Although the socioeconomic argument is fairly compelling, it is not accepted by all scholars. Munn (2000), for example, linked the rise of rhetoric to the pressures and turmoil of the great war between Athens and Sparta that began in 431 B.C. He proposed that victory over the Persians at the battle of Salamis and a growing empire nurtured a sense of pride as well as a sense of manifest destiny among the Athenians that, in turn, led to widespread reflection on the various factors that distinguished Athens from all other cities in the ancient world. One result was a conflation of the ideals of personal excellence with the ideals of civic virtue, both of which were expressed in Greek as *areté*. As Munn stated, "Private identity . . . now openly competed with communal identity" (p. 52).

The oldest subject of study in Athens was poetry, and for many years knowledge of poetry and the ability to produce poetry were linked to ideals of personal excellence. A group of teachers collectively called *Sophists*—from the Greek word for wisdom, *sophia*—taught poetry before the emergence of empire, but the transition to a communal identity attracted them, as Munn (2000) noted, to "the challenge of de-

---

[2]Girls were educated at home rather than in school. Those from families with some means were taught art, music, poetry, cooking, sewing, and household management. Those of lower status probably were trained solely in household tasks.

fining the nature of the political community" so that they "adapted their teachings and writings to the subject of politics and to its medium in another form of artful expression: persuasive non-poetic speech" (p. 78). Thus, the Sophists became the first teachers of rhetoric in Athens.

Little is known about the Sophists because they didn't produce much writing and because what survived the centuries consists largely of fragments embedded in the works of others. Although we refer to them as a group, the Sophists held only a few views in common, which increases the difficulty of reaching any generalizable conclusions about them. We know that many came to Athens from Asia Minor. We also know that the process of adapting their teaching had an effect on the Sophists themselves: The reflection required to understand the nature of *areté* led to further explorations into the workings of nature and society, until the Sophists acquired the status of philosophers. Under their influence, the exclusive focus on forensic and deliberative rhetoric broadened to include examinations of the nature of truth, virtue, and knowledge. In other words, rhetoric became more philosophical as the Sophists began to emphasize rhetoric as a *theory of knowing*. In the dialogues of Plato, rhetoric as a theory of knowing was transformed into *dialectic,* a questioning, philosophical rhetoric that had the aim of discovering truth—and ignorance.

But the hurly-burly of Athenian realpolitik was always present. Political conditions prevented rhetoric from ever moving too far afield from its origins in law and government. We get a glimpse in Munn (2000) of the life-and-death issues that dominated daily life:

> Athens in the 420s was a vortex that sucked in the revenues of far-flung commerce, of a naval empire, and of its own identity. The handling of the people's money, as it was assessed and as it was spent, generated a nearly continuous flow of judicial hearings. Regular audits of officers responsible for public funds were legally mandated. Although testimony from *hoi boulomenoi* was always admitted where there was evidence that crimes had been committed against the public interest, when any hint of financial wrongdoing required legal investigation the state deployed specialists to handle the case. These public prosecutors were the *synegoroi,* or *syndikoi,* who were appointed to assist the financial auditors of the Council whenever a case came before a jury.
>
> Under these circumstances, prominent men involved in the people's business among the Athenians and their subject-allies were liable to find themselves brought under unwelcome public scrutiny, defamed by accusers claiming to act in the public interest, threatened with fines, or worse. (p. 82)

All too often, from 432 to the end of the Peloponnesian War in 404 B.C., the courts were used as political weapons to subvert the authority and popularity of one leader after another. Accusations of wrongdoing frequently lacked any validity but nevertheless required a vigorous defense—if one lost, the state could take all his property and even his life. Accusers and defendants alike used set speeches to sway juries, and Sophists were happy to provide them, for a fee. Many Sophists thereby earned lucrative incomes from their skills with language. However, they also earned something else: a questionable reputation. They soon were criticized for taking money and successfully defending people who did not deserve to win in court. To the dismay of many Athenians, Sophists had the ability to make even ridiculous claims seem reasonable, turning traditional concepts of truth and justice upside down. Their facile cleverness seemed at odds with *sophia*. Many came to believe that Sophists used rhetoric to obscure the truth rather than to discover it. This was the accusation Plato made against them again and again in his Socratic dialogues, and they never were able to free themselves of the taint of pandering to audiences.

Who Were the Sophists?

George Kennedy (1980) described the Sophists as "self-appointed professors of how to succeed in the civic life of the Greek states" (p. 25). We get some insight into their claim that they could teach *areté*, or civic virtue, by considering the Greek concept of law. The Greeks recognized that many laws, such as those protecting property, had no natural foundation but were exclusively the work of men who wanted to live together harmoniously. More specifically, the Greeks differentiated between the laws of nature *(physis)* and the laws of man *(nomos)*. They also saw that these laws frequently were in conflict, making it difficult to know how to behave for the good of society. Laws of nature might move people to punish criminals as a form of retribution for past actions. Laws of man, on the other hand, might move people to punish criminals as a way of discouraging them from future criminal actions. In this case, laws of nature move citizens in one direction whereas laws of man move them in another, and it can be difficult to know which path is better overall. The Sophists claimed to be able to provide this knowledge.

Some scholars have suggested that the very concept of teaching *areté* set Sophists against the Greek aristocracy, who maintained that *areté* was innate, at least among members of their class, and thus could not be taught. Beck (1964) wrote, for example, that the Sophists believed "in the power of knowledge to improve human character. . . . This implies both a theory of the disciplinary value of certain studies . . . and the rejection of the aristocratic theory of 'virtue' as a matter of innate gifts and divine descent" (p. 148). On this account, many have concluded that the Sophists were supporters of democracy,[3] but it may be the case that they merely were responding to social changes associated with the emergence of the empire. The shift from a private identity to a communal one necessarily would involve expanding the concept of *areté* to include those outside the aristocracy.

There is no reason to assume that such an expansion entailed a rejection of aristocratic values. In fact, considering that the Sophists depended on aristocrats for their livelihood, any overt expression of democratic ideals seems unlikely. Isocrates illustrates the difficulty: He had close connections to the courts of various tyrants and was critical of democracy, which put him in a delicate position when civil war erupted between the forces supporting democracy and the forces supporting tyranny. Bluck (1947) argued that Isocrates published *Antidosis* in the hope of defending himself against democrats who were angry about his associations.[4] Thus, it seems far more likely that the goal of the Sophists was not to advocate democracy but rather to get those outside the aristocracy to embrace certain aristocratic values.

The pursuit of *areté*, however, was essentially an effort to develop an outstanding reputation. On the private level, aristocrats could cultivate reputations through athletic competitions, appearance, success as military leaders, and, *ne plus ultra,* success in politics. On the communal level, their reputations were based on lineage and public service in the form of gifts to the city. The common people lacked these opportunities until empire and a more inclusive democracy shifted notions of civic virtue toward the communal. One of Pericles' more important reforms was providing pay for public service, which expanded participation in government, but payment itself precluded any accrual of *areté*. It signified a job, not a civic contribution. In fact, the only means those outside the aristocracy had to pursue reputation was through military service. By distinguishing themselves in battle and expanding the empire, even common soldiers received public recognition (Thucydides, 1986, 6.31.1, 3–4). Thus, *areté* for the common man was restricted to the communal level. This restriction was made more acute by several factors, including the inability of the people to speak with one voice and the tendency for important decisions to be worked out in

---

[3]Jarratt (1991) claimed that, in addition, the Sophists were the first feminists, but this claim seems remarkably far-fetched, given everything that is known about Athenian society during this period and that there are no extant writings that support this notion.

[4]Enos (1993, p. 84) concluded on the basis of a brief reference to Isocrates in Plato's *Phaedrus* that Isocrates was at one time Plato's student. This would explain much about Isocrates' attitudes toward democracy, but Enos' conclusion appears to go far beyond any evidence present in *Phaedrus*.

secret among the wealthy and influential of the city. The common people therefore were forced to turn to those among the aristocracy willing to serve as leaders and to speak on their behalf. This situation gave rise to demagogues (from *demos,* "people," and *agogos,* "leading") who nearly always used the people to advance their own ambitions and dreams of power.

Unfortunately, shared notions of civic virtue did not lead to harmonious relations between aristocrats and the common people. The opposite was true. Even as the common people adopted aristocratic notions of excellence and civic virtue, the aristocracy's resentment toward them, already sore because of democratic reforms pushed through the assembly by Pericles years earlier, became sharper. For their part, the common people became intoxicated with their growing power and wanted more. It was the people and their leaders, for example, who urged the conquest of Sicily so as to expand the empire, ignoring completely those who advised caution and restraint. The resulting tension between the supporters of democracy and the supporters of aristocracy defined many of the calamities Athens suffered during the Peloponnesian War.

A society in transition often sees traditions challenged, and the three most well-known Sophists—Protagoras (approximately 490–420 B.C.), Gorgias (approximately 480–375 B.C.), and Isocrates (approximately 436–338 B.C.)—clearly appear to have played a part in this regard. Whether their challenges to tradition were conscious or unconscious, we can never know.

Each of these Sophists argued that truth is relative, a disturbing notion that still has the power to upset many. In their view, if a question arises regarding the truth of a matter, each person involved is "right," because each sees one facet of the truth. This position has led many scholars to propose that rhetoric for the Sophists was a tool for examining the various sides of an issue. Because each side holds an element of truth, in the sophistic view, people who would practice rhetoric are obligated to explore that truth fully in order to understand it. By understanding multiple aspects of truth, or rather by understanding all sides of an issue, one acquires wisdom. To the Sophists, the person who mastered rhetoric also mastered knowledge and could view reality more clearly than someone limited by a single perspective. Some scholars have suggested that this view provides the foundation for Western education, which seeks to examine topics from multiple perspectives as a means to developing an objective understanding.

Looking more closely at the three sophists mentioned earlier— Protagoras, Gorgias, and Isocrates—can shed some light on these ideas. It also helps us understand some of the tensions that arose early in the development of rhetoric, tensions that exist even today.

Protagoras. In keeping with the Sophists' relativistic perspectives on truth and knowledge, Protagoras taught his students to take either side in a legal case. This approach was based on a view of knowledge that was contrary to tradition, which maintained that one side always was right and the other wrong. For Protagoras, there was no such thing as falsehood. According to Guthrie (1971), Protagoras taught that "a man was the sole judge of his own sensations and beliefs, which were true for him so long as they appeared to be so" (p. 267). Although this perspective seems, mistakenly, to deny the existence of evil and the willful lie, it nevertheless is an astute analysis of what constitutes "truth" or "fact" for most people. Contemporary analyses, for example, propose that a fact is "what a majority of people (as members of a given group) agree to call a 'fact' *until they have some reason not to*" (Williams, 2001, p. 127, italics in original).

Related to this view is Protagoras' proposal that all men are endowed with civic virtue, which he defined as a rudimentary sense of justice and respect for others in a society of equals. Proper education refined these basic qualities to enable every man to contribute to the community, a point that some scholars suggest provided a foundation for the democratic reforms of Pericles, whom Protagoras advised. The most significant effect of Protagoras' teachings on rhetoric, however, was to advance it as a means of persuasion. If no objective reality exists, but instead only personal beliefs, a skillful speaker can create truth and reality in the minds of an audience—quite useful in court or government. This view also was a strong affirmation of the value of *nomos* and the pragmatic. Prior to his influence, laws of nature had been held to be absolute, whereas those of man were merely matters of convention and convenience. Patterson (1991) suggested that antidemocratic forces frequently appealed to laws of nature to support their arguments for oligarchy and against democracy. They would point out that in nature the strong rule the weak through inherent superiority; because democracy treats men equally, it is unnatural.

Any argument for the relativity of truth and fact runs the risk of implicitly encouraging unscrupulous and unethical behavior, a point that underlies Plato's criticism of rhetoric and the Sophists. We see the inherent danger even today if we consider recent claims that, for example, the Holocaust never happened, that Cleopatra was black, that the Founding Fathers "stole" the concept of democracy from an Indian tribe, and that America never put men on the moon but instead hired Hollywood to produce a series of theatricals. On this account, Protagoras' argument regarding the nature of civic virtue would be a necessary feature of his philosophy and his rhetoric. Because unethical language is inherently antisocial and because blatantly antisocial behavior is generally abhorred, a relativistic rhetoric must be tightly bound to the cultivation of innate civic virtue.[5]

A fragment from a lost work entitled *Truth* suggests the strength of Protagoras' nontraditional views: "Man is the measure of all things, of the things that are, that they are, and of the things that are not, that they are not."[6] Susan Jarratt (1991, p. 50) concluded on the basis of this fragment that Protagoras deemed "phenomena outside individual human experience" to be insignificant, but more accurate is the idea that Protagoras was a humanist who placed mankind at the center of life. Patterson's (1991) work supports this humanistic reading, as when he wrote: "Implicit in this [statement] is a momentous shifting of the focus of thought from people in their relation with god to people as the basis for all judgment about the world" (p. 149). In this regard, Protagoras was following a tradition that started with Homer, which led Patterson to conclude that Protagoras "finally humanized the Delphic injunction 'Know thyself' " (p. 149).

Athenians probably understood Protagoras' assertion not just in a religious or even a philosophical sense but also in a practical one. "Man is the measure of all things" is an affirmation of the ineffable value of all human beings. Although not overtly political, such an affirmation seems entirely congruent with the growth of democracy that characterized Athens during this period. It was an assertion of man-made law over natural law, and, as such, it gave the supporters of democracy an important theoretical foundation.

Gorgias. Throughout the course of the Peloponnesian War, political power was in flux. Supporters of democracy and supporters of aristocracy vied for control of Athens, often with disastrous results. The great general Alcibiades, for example, who usually spoke as an advocate for the people, was placed in charge of a huge army and fleet and sent to attack Sicily in 415 B.C. As soon as he sailed, however, his enemies among the aristocracy had him indicted and sentenced to death in absentia. Arrested in Sicily, he managed to escape on the return to Athens and promptly went over to the enemy, giving them information that contributed to the total annihilation of the Athenian force.

---

[5]We see evidence of this position in Plato's *Gorgias* (1937b), where Gorgias claims not only that rhetoricians learn what is just but also that the rhetorician who has this knowledge "will therefore never be willing to do injustice" (Jowett, ¶460).

[6]Translation from Guthrie (1971, p. 183).

These were uncertain times that left many confused. Battered by plague and decimated by disasters on the battlefield, the population of Athens dropped drastically. Munn (2000) noted, for example, that "As a political presence, the poorest class of Athenians that twenty years earlier had roughly equaled the numbers of citizens of middling or better means was now reduced to virtually nothing" (p. 139).

Gorgias' treatise titled *On the Nonexistent,* which has survived in outline form, seems to reflect the confusion of the times. Here Gorgias stated that truth and ideas do not have any essential existence; if they did they wouldn't be knowable to man; and even if they were knowable they couldn't be communicated to anyone. Usually, these statements are interpreted philosophically to mean that the world always is changing so that any essential existence is impossible, or if it is possible, people wouldn't be able to understand its nature because they are part of the ever-changing reality, which limits their ability to perceive anything outside or different from their changing universe. However, they also can be interpreted as a summary of Athenian reaction to the loss of social, political, and economic stability that had prevailed for more than 50 years. In Gorgias'statement, we see a declaration that the notion of absolute truth that governed political and intellectual life in Athens until this time is meaningless because it is incomprehensible. Gorgias' statement therefore is indicative of an important change in the ways of knowing and rhetoric.

For an advocate in the courts or the assembly, it would be easy to conclude on this basis that man-made laws are fundamentally superior to natural laws. In addition, as Enos (1993) suggested, the philosophy inherent in Gorgias' statement is related to a view of rhetoric and reality that understood individual concepts as being comprised of "dichotomies." Enos noted, for example, that "the nature of rhetoric [for Gorgias] depends upon the proportion of 'truthfulness' or 'falsehood' it exhibits at any given time" (p. 78). Gorgias' philosophy suggests a chaotic view of the world that is contrary to the pragmatic goals of legal rhetoric and leads to what has been called "sophistic rhetoric" (see Enos, 1993; Kennedy, 1980).

Sophistic rhetoric did not deal with truth but rather with the complex interplay of dichotomies, with the uncertain mixture of what was true and what was false that made up reality. The only course available to the sophistic rhetorician, therefore, was to argue *probability.* Such a chaotic worldview was not entirely incongruent with the workings of Athenian courts, where eyewitness testimony was suspect owing to the prevalence of bribery and influence peddling. In lieu of such testimony, those presenting their cases (there were no attorneys) commonly relied on argument from probability, not from fact. The indictment of Alcibiades mentioned earlier, for example, was based in large part on the general perception among Athenians that he was arrogant and therefore *capable* of committing certain crimes, which led to the conclusion that he *probably did* commit them. This probability led (along with significant political intrigue) to a guilty verdict.

In most instances, there exists a range of probabilities from which arguments can be constructed, so rhetoric in this account becomes not only a means of persuasion but also a means of discovering probable arguments based on what normal people do under normal circumstances. Gorgias' *On the Nonexistent* took this notion to its logical conclusion.

Although these ideas influence law and philosophy even today, among Athenians Gorgias was more famous for his rhetorical style, in part because argument from probability was already fairly well established. Gorgias favored an ornate style full of parallel constructions, attention to clause length, and striking images. When he arrived in Athens from Sicily around 427 B.C., he became wildly popular, attracting fans much in the way that a rock star does today, and he apparently earned large sums of money giving demonstrations. Gorgias was infatuated with the power and beauty of language, and he unabashedly claimed to be able to turn any argument around. He apparently would argue a point vigorously in his demonstrations and then argue the opposite just as vigorously, a feat that astounded his audiences.

Eventually, the ornate style that Gorgias practiced and promoted drew much criticism (even though it continued to be taught in many schools of rhetoric for a thousand years). The emphasis on style necessarily subordinated substance, and it frequently resulted in highlighting the cleverness of the speaker—two issues that already were becoming problematic for Athenians. Critics began to disparage rhetoric that aimed simply to entertain audiences through linguistic acrobatics or that aimed obviously to play on the audiences' emotions.[7] These features came to be viewed as tricks that were dishonest and ultimately meaningless, which led to the expression, "empty rhetoric" that we hear frequently today. In his play *The Clouds,* produced in 423 B.C., Aristophanes lampooned the Sophists and their ability to confute creditors and spin nonsense, indicating that these teachers and the rhetoric they advocated had quickly become objects of ridicule.

Isocrates. Many Sophists during this period traveled from city to city giving demonstrations for a fee and taking on students. Even when they remained in one city for years, as Gorgias did after arriving in Ath-

---

[7]Because so many Sophists came from Asia, the ornate style came to be known as "Asian rhetoric."

ens, they taught rhetoric largely through an apprenticeship method. A few young men would follow their teacher around while he gave demonstration speeches. They would meet more or less informally at someone's home to receive instruction. Isocrates, however, established a school of rhetoric in Athens, around 390 B.C., which gave his teaching a sense of stability and formality that was lacking among other teachers. There he lectured on philosophy and the structure and nature of rhetoric. The apprenticeship method continued, but in a more formal setting.

Isocrates was a student of Gorgias, but he was highly critical of other Sophists and their methods. He argued, for example, that they outrageously claimed they could teach anyone to be a successful speaker, even those who lacked native ability. In his view, formal training can help those with natural aptitude and practical experience, but it can do little for those without ability, except give them some general knowledge of the subject. More striking is the fact that Isocrates did not claim to teach civic virtue, although he did maintain that the study of rhetoric could improve a student's character. Ever practical, Isocrates viewed the teachings of Plato, his contemporary, as metaphysical abstractions that had little value in the hard world of Greek political life.

Isocrates is sometimes characterized as the most successful teacher in ancient Greece, and certainly he earned wealth and an outstanding reputation. His school provided a model for all others in the ancient period, and it influenced formal education throughout Western history to such an extent that Isocrates occasionally is referred to as the founder of humanism (Kinneavy, 1982). Some features of the curriculum can be seen even in our own schools, such as the inclusion of music, art, and math. Isocrates also was the first rhetorician who wrote all of his speeches; he never delivered any through public demonstrations as his contemporaries did. We can assume that writing was an important part of the curriculum throughout the 50-year life of the school. If so, the influence of Isocrates was significant, indeed. As Welch (1990) noted, "part of the intellectual revolution of the second half of the fifth century and the fourth century B.C. involved the centrality of writing" (p. 12). In addition, Kennedy (1980) suggested that writing was an important step toward shifting rhetoric from purely oral to written discourse, a process that he described as the *"letteraturizzazione"* of rhetoric, or the shift in rhetorical focus from oral to written language. This process underlies our own emphasis on composition in public schools and colleges.

Finally, Isocrates proposed that three necessary factors make a good rhetorician: talent, instruction, and practice. Of these three, talent was the most important. Isocrates had no hesitation in affirming that his teaching was the best, and he gave students ample practice, but he admitted that he could not provide anyone with talent. This view dominated Western schools until modern times, resulting in higher education that was primarily for the intellectual elite.[8] When American universities began adopting open admission policies in the 1960s, the role talent plays in education, regardless of level, became a hot topic. It continues to be important in composition studies because so many teachers, students, and parents believe that good writing is the result of talent rather than effort.

Socrates and Plato

Although many people have never heard of the Sophists, just about everyone has heard of Socrates and Plato, even though they may not have read any of their work. Both are cultural icons who exist in our collective consciousness, often without any clear reference. Plato was a student of Socrates, and most of what we know about Socrates comes from Plato's dialogues, especially *Apology, Gorgias, Protagoras,* and *Phaedrus.* Another notable source of information are four works by Socrates' friend and contemporary, Xenophon: *Oeconomicus, Apologia, Symposium,* and *Memorabilia.*

Separating the historical Socrates from the literary isn't easy, but several characteristics emerge that most scholars agree on. Like the Sophists, Socrates was concerned about the nature of truth, reality, and virtue. He taught that wisdom was the greatest good, and he advocated soundness of mind and body through philosophic inquiry, exercise, and moderation in food and drink, although reportedly he himself was quite overweight.

Rather than give public speeches and lectures like the Sophists, Socrates used a question-and-answer approach—or *dialectic*—that has come to be known as the "Socratic method." Apparently, Socrates never committed anything to writing, and in two of Plato's dialogues, *Gorgias* and *Phaedrus,* he displayed outright hostility toward writing, arguing that it dulls the senses and destroys the memory. Furthermore, Socrates was an elitist who distrusted democracy. He decried the growth of democracy in Athens, but he wasn't directly involved in politics.

---

[8]It is worth noting that Scottish higher education took a more democratic approach until it finally was restructured on the British model in 1858. Scottish universities recognized the uneven preparation and abilities of their students and provided what we might think of as remedial classes for those who needed extra help.

Unlike the Sophists, Socrates did not consider himself to be a teacher, yet he had many students who held him in the highest esteem. Socrates thought of himself as a social critic. He saw his mission as being to demonstrate the ignorance of those around him and to explain why the changes that Athens had undergone during his lifetime in the areas of education and politics were bad. He described himself as a "gadfly" ever ready to challenge the increasing pride and self-satisfaction of his fellow citizens. In *Apology,* for example, Plato (1937a) had Socrates state: "And so I go about the world, . . . and search and make inquiry into the wisdom of any one, whether citizen or stranger, who appears to be wise; and if he is not wise, then . . . I show him that he is not wise" (p. 23).

When Sparta defeated Athens in 404 B.C., the Spartan king Lysander empowered a group of 30 men to take control of the government. Known for their sympathies toward Sparta, their aristocratic values, and their antipathy toward democracy, the Thirty Tyrants, as they came to be called, began a campaign of terror that led to the murder or execution of at least 1,500 of the most notable men in Athens. To silence critics, the Thirty banned the teaching of rhetoric and declared that anyone making public speeches would be arrested. The abuses of the Thirty Tyrants reached such an extreme in 403 B.C. that civil war broke out, resulting in defeat for the Thirty and their supporters. Reestablishment of democracy followed, as did a purge of the leaders of the Thirty and their sympathizers. This purge eventually led to the arrest, trial, and execution of Socrates in 399 B.C.

Plato recorded these events in three dialogues, *Apology, Crito,* and *Phaedo,* which he may have composed as much as 50 years after the events occurred. The image of Socrates that emerges from these dialogues is that of an innocent man executed by the rule of a mob that was incapable of recognizing his wisdom and virtue. Historically, however, we know that Socrates' arrest and trial were part of the struggle between aristocracy and democracy that had turned the Greek world upside down for three decades. According to Plato, Socrates was charged with corrupting the youth of Athens through his teaching, but, if so, Socrates had been doing that for years, which raises the question of why he was arrested and tried at this time.

Most likely, three factors converged. In his teaching and at his trial, Socrates displayed utter contempt for politicians, civic leaders, and the common people, all of whom he considered not only ignorant but stupid. To drive this point home, Socrates reminded the jury at his trial that the oracle at Delphi had proclaimed that no one is wiser than Socrates (*Apology,* Plato, 1937a, p. 21). Not surprisingly, he ignored warnings to moderate his unorthodox views when speaking in public and when teaching. Socrates insisted that he answered only to his personal spirit or divinity *(daimonion),* not to the people, not to the politicians, not even to the law. In doing so, he flouted every principle of Athenian society. Moreover, in the final analysis, Socrates' teachings appeared to be something less than innocent. Several of his students, such as Critias and Alcibiades, were guilty of truly horrible acts, and no doubt the jury saw Socrates as the spiritual leader of the Thirty. His fate was sealed.

On the whole, Socrates and Plato stand in contrast to the Sophists. In fact, these two philosophers apparently disliked just about everything associated with the Sophists, although the reasons aren't entirely clear.[9] In *Protagoras,* Socrates suggested it is because they charged fees for their teaching, which hardly seems probable because teachers had been charging fees for many years. Moreover, Plato charged students at his school, the Academy.

Numerous writers have proposed alternative explanations for this animosity toward the Sophists (e.g., De Ste. Croix, 1981; Dodds, 1951; Havelock, 1982; Ober, 1989). Some argued that the Sophists were foreigners in a land where all non-Greeks were called "barbarians," and it is possible that the underlying prejudice against foreigners became stronger than the Greek fascination with the rhetoric they employed. Gorgias' rhetorical flourishes were admired by many, but they also left many confused and dazed. His style of rhetoric emphasized the cleverness of the speaker rather than the discovery of truth and led to cynicism with respect to human values. Such cynicism not only was contrary to accepted notions of justice, philosophy, and rhetoric but also was contrary to the primary emphasis of Socrates and Plato.

Another explanation is based on disagreements over politics and philosophy. Although the Sophists probably did not overtly support democracy, they nevertheless argued that *nomos* was superior to *physis* and that at least a rudimentary form of civic virtue was innate. Both views, no doubt, were seen as implicit endorsements of democracy. In addition, the Sophists were advocates for pragmatism and relativism—concepts that Socrates and Plato opposed vigorously. Ostwald (1986) suggested that the political and philosophical positions developed together: "Norms which before . . . [the democratic revolution in Athens] were thought of as having existed from time immemorial now came to be regarded as having been enacted and as being enforceable in a way similar to that in which statutes are decided upon by a legislative

---

[9]Having mentioned *The Clouds,* it's worth noting that Aristophanes identified Socrates as a Sophist, which seems to be a deliberate misrepresentation designed to enhance the humor of the play.

agency" (p. 50). This change in perception placed more authority in the hands of people and less in the hands of the gods; or on the day-to-day level, less authority was held by a ruling aristocracy claiming divine rights. Given the tendency of the Sophists to wander from city to city, it is easy to understand how they would link the supremacy of *nomos* to relativism. They could observe that social norms and laws differed from place to place.

Socrates and Plato, on the other hand, proposed that everything was absolute and that change occurred only at a superficial and ultimately trivial level. In their view, there was an absolute truth, an absolute virtue, and so on. They also argued for an ideal rhetoric, the question-and-answer process of dialectic, which Plato used to great effect in his dialogues. Language in this ideal, Plato maintained, should be used as a tool to separate truth from falsehood—that is, to determine the true and absolute nature of reality. Consequently, those who claimed that truth and reality were relative concepts and who would use language to argue this point were deceivers who should be censored.

Socrates and Plato were not much concerned with legal rhetoric, although Plato was involved in writing laws and a constitution. Moreover, Plato claimed that the rhetoric the Sophists taught was used to trick audiences into believing that the worse argument was the better, which he saw as inherently evil because it masked the truth and hindered justice.

In addition, Plato may have distrusted rhetoric (legal or otherwise) because it was intimately linked to the rise of democracy. He was, after all, a conservative aristocrat who characterized democracy as the rule of the mob. Not surprisingly, Plato viewed the Sophists' advocacy of *nomos* over *physis* as a profound mistake that threatened society with chaos because it elevated uncertain man-made law over natural law. Given the connection between democracy and rhetoric, it is revealing to note that Plato and his students visited the courts of tyrants frequently, behavior that the democracy-loving Athenians probably did not appreciate. Plato supported the Thirty Tyrants. He also was intimately involved in a messy coup attempt in Syracuse that temporarily replaced a relatively benevolent tyrant, Dionsyius II, with the austere and haughty tyrant Dion, who was one of Plato's students.[10]

From a political perspective, it is easy to see how Plato's conservative views would bring him to oppose the Sophists and rhetoric. The

---

[10]In a letter to Dion's supporters, Plato (1961) lamented how, under the democracy that overthrew the Thirty, Athens "was no longer administered according to the standards and practices of our fathers" (Letter VII, 325d). Given the murderous behavior of the Thirty, Plato's statement is fairly appalling.

Sophists' rhetorical instruction gave anyone with the means to pay the fee the ability to influence others. The power of language, as already noted, came to replace the power of the sword and to a certain degree the power of money and position. However, the power of the word in the hands of someone lacking virtue was relatively weak in a society that placed great weight on personal character and honor. The Sophists overcame this fundamental problem by claiming that they could teach *areté*, or civic virtue. This claim may have been a response to the sociopolitical conditions of the time, but it nevertheless seems to have been perceived as a threat by the aristocracy because it implicitly suggests political equality for all citizens. Anyone who believed in natural superiority and social stratification would resist these ideas as an act of self-preservation.

Aristotle

Aristotle exerted more influence on rhetoric than any other person in history. He was born in 384 B.C., and in 367 he traveled to Athens to study with Plato. The curriculum of Plato's Academy included philosophy, political theory, math, biology, and astronomy. At the time of Aristotle's arrival, rhetoric may have been taught as an object of study rather than as a subject; that is, students may have studied what the Sophists taught but did not practice giving oral presentations. After completing his studies, Aristotle stayed on as a teacher for almost 20 years. Kennedy (1991) suggested that, along with other classes, Aristotle began teaching rhetoric of some kind in the late 350s: "The course seems to have been open to the general public—offered in the afternoons as a kind of extension division of the Academy and accompanied by practical exercises in speaking" (p. 5). When Plato died in 347, Aristotle left Athens and taught in various places before returning in 335 to start his own school, the Lyceum.

Aristotle was a prolific writer, producing works on natural science (which includes astronomy, meteorology, plants, and animals); the nature, scope, and properties of being; ethics; politics; poetry; and rhetoric. Kennedy (1980) indicated that rhetoric was not a major interest for Aristotle and that he "taught it as a kind of extracurricular subject" (p. 61). If rhetoric was merely a hobby, it was one that Aristotle pursued actively. He produced *Gryllus* around 360 B.C., a lost work that examined the artistic nature of rhetoric. Another lost work, *Synagoge Technon,* was a lengthy summary and analysis of the rhetorical handbooks that Aristotle knew. The work that did survive, *The Art of Rhetoric* (Aristotle, 1975), analyzes rhetoric in great detail and offers views that continue to be useful today.

Aristotle called rhetoric an art because it can be systematized and because it results in a specific product, not because it was related to literature or painting or because it drew on some romantic notion of inspiration. Unlike Plato, Aristotle accepted the practical nature of rhetoric and was not overly concerned about the prospect that speakers might use it for ignoble ends. However, he did criticize the Sophists because in his view they advocated an irrational approach to language that focused on style and emotion rather than substance. In the first part of *The Art of Rhetoric,* for example, Aristotle defined rhetoric as a theoretical system for discovering the available means of persuasion on a given topic. He then used this definition to dismiss sophistic rhetoric because it did not provide a theory of knowing and because it did not deal systematically with the "proof" necessary for persuasion to occur. We see in this work the beginnings of empiricism and a reliance on objectivity, both of which have come to dominate discourse in the Western world.

But there are notable differences between argument in Aristotle's world and ours today. "Proof" is a central feature of Aristotle's rhetoric; consequently, it is important to avoid a common tendency—confusing our modern notions of scientific proof with what Aristotle meant when he used the term. In Aristotle's rhetoric, proof does not consist of factual evidence that leads to an incontrovertible conclusion. Instead, it consists of the *reasons* that speakers give their audiences for accepting a claim. Over the centuries, factual evidence has become far more available than it was in Aristotle's time, and there is a much greater reliance on such evidence to support claims. Argument from reasons has not disappeared, however. Reasons have come to be recognized as "rhetorical proofs" that are fundamental to rhetoric. Many legal arguments, for instance, continue to revolve around rhetorical proof even in light of strong factual evidence. One of the more graphic examples in recent times is the O. J. Simpson murder trial, in which the jury discounted solid DNA evidence that linked Simpson to the crime and instead accepted the defense team's emotional reasons for acquittal.

Pragmatic rhetoric in ancient Athens dealt with questions that needed a quick decision, either in court or in government. A speaker had to propose a decision and persuade others to accept it. A typical argument might have had a basic structure similar to the following: "We should build a road to Corinth, and here are the reasons why." This basic structure still governs arguments.

Aristotle outlined several different kinds of rhetorical proof in *The Art of Rhetoric,* but he deemed three to be so important that he devoted about 20 chapters to them. They are *ethos, pathos,* and *logos.* Ethos usually is translated as "character." A speaker or writer has to project a "good character" to audiences, a character that is, say, kind, considerate, intelligent, and reasonable. A good character simply is more believable than one who isn't, and audiences want to accept what he or she has to say.

Consider the following two modern examples that illustrate the operation of ethos: citations in academic texts like this one and athletes' endorsements. At work is the principle of association. Citations associate writers' ideas with those of published scholars, which makes those ideas seem more credible. They also have the effect of displaying writers' intelligence and knowledge because of the projected implication that the writers have read all the works they cite. Something similar happens in advertising. When athletes appear on cereal boxes or when they endorse a brand of sneakers, consumers of those products feel as though they are associating with (perhaps even being like) their sports heroes, even if it is in the most marginal way.

Pathos usually is translated as "emotion." Emotion can be a powerful proof in language because it circumvents reason. Advertising and sales offer ready examples. Ads soliciting donations for children's aid programs commonly picture woe-begotten children who tug at our heart strings. Many car salespeople urge prospective buyers to take a test drive to "feel the excitement" of the new car. They know that a test drive bonds people emotionally to the car, making it harder to walk away from the purchase. It is easy to adopt a negative view toward such blatant emotional manipulation. However, emotion does not have to be negative. A positive use of emotion is exemplified in Martin Luther King's "I Have a Dream" speech, which decades after it was delivered still has the power to move audiences to tears.

Logos, Aristotle's third rhetorical proof, usually is translated as "reason" but may be better understood as "analysis" or "information." It often consists of facts, common knowledge, specialized knowledge, or statistics. Consider a continuation of the earlier example about the road to Corinth: Building such a road would make it easier to transport goods to and from Athens, which would benefit trade.

After treating proof extensively in *The Art of Rhetoric,* Aristotle took up the psychology of the audience, examining not only the range of psychological states that a speaker might encounter but also how to identify them. In each case, Aristotle identified the associated emotion, the state of mind that leads to it, and the focus or direction of the emotion. This discussion of psychology is the earliest one known, and it is particularly important in understanding how rhetoric from the beginning was linked to the characteristics of particular audiences. This connection has become a central feature of current rhetorical theory.

JOURNAL ENTRY

Classical Greek rhetoric is commonly linked to the development of individualism and democracy. Reflect on the relations that you see among rhetoric, individualism, and democracy. What factors do you see that link them so strongly? Then reflect on our society, giving special attention to what you know about the current state of rhetoric, individualism, and democracy. Are there any similarities between the relations in the past and the relations in the present?

ROMAN RHETORIC

As Rome grew from a small village to a major power, it begrudgingly adopted much of Greek culture and civilization, including rhetoric. The Romans perceived the Greeks as weak and effeminate, a people too attached to unproductive intellectual pursuits like philosophy. The Greek influence, however, was unavoidable. Most of Sicily and nearly all of southern Italy had been colonized by Greeks and was dotted with prosperous, well-populated cities. With regard to rhetoric, Sicily was considered to be its birthplace, and southern Italy became an intellectual center, as teachers from both Greece and Sicily opened numerous schools of rhetoric there. The growth of Rome naturally attracted Greeks from these southern cities, including teachers of rhetoric.

Rhetoric in Rome was different from rhetoric in Athens, however, because the cities had different sociopolitical agendas. Like Athens, Rome shifted to a slave economy fairly early, and it experienced many of the same difficulties, particularly the threat of revolt by freemen displaced when they could not compete in the new economy. But the outcomes were quite different. In Athens, laws and customs required citizens of means to contribute to the city's infrastructure. This amounted to a tax that essentially kept the wealthy on the brink of bankruptcy. Consequently, when the poor and displaced threatened revolt in Athens, the ruling aristocracy was not in a position to appease them by redistributing wealth. They chose instead to redistribute power, which resulted in a more democratic government.

There were no similar laws or customs in Rome, and by the time the poor threatened to revolt, a state of continual warfare and expansion was channeling the wealth of the Mediterranean into the coffers of the ruling elite, who were able to buy off the rabble through an elaborate system of patronage, doles, and entertainment that quickly came to be viewed as entitlements. Thereby they preserved their power. The poor and displaced, meanwhile, seemed quite willing to give up any demands to participate in government as long as their entitlements weren't threatened. As Grant (1992) stated, "The very root of Roman society was the institution of a relatively few rich patrons inextricably linked with their more numerous poor clients, who backed them in return for their patrons' support" (p. 50).

In this climate, rhetoric could not have a significant link with democracy because democracy never existed. The ruling elite, in fact, viewed rhetoric with such great suspicion that the Roman Senate twice banned the teaching of rhetoric and closed all the schools, first in 161 B.C. and then again in 92 B.C. (Enos, 1995). Although these efforts were in part motivated by strong anti-Greek sentiments among the Romans, it is clear that the major motivation was to eliminate a powerful tool for democratic change. As Enos stated, underlying the Senate bans was fear that rhetorical education would enable the poor to "express attitudes contrary to patrician interests" (p. 47).

The bans, however, could not last as long as Rome invested the court system with some measure of justice and fairness. The pragmatic need for rhetorically trained legal advocates was so strong that the bans were lifted and, for a time, rhetoric flourished, producing such great rhetoricians as Hortensius, Cicero, and Quintilian. In addition, entitlements reduced the threat of revolution, and schools modified their methods to make them more congruent with Roman, rather than Athenian, values. The result was a renaissance of Roman rhetoric that began toward the latter part of the Republic. Space constraints make it impossible to look closely at Roman rhetoricians, but we can't leave this important period of classical rhetoric without looking at the greatest of them, Cicero.

Cicero

Cicero's parents were of modest means, but they nevertheless managed to provide him with a good education.[11] He studied rhetoric with various Greek tutors and then was apprenticed to the most important lawyer of the time, Mucius Scaevola.

Success came quickly. At the age of 26, Cicero argued his first significant case, defending Sextus Roscius, who was accused of murdering his father. The case was complicated by politics: Some of Rome's most influential families supported Roscius, whereas the man who accused him was a Greek ex-slave who also happened to be a favorite of the dictator

---

[11]For an excellent biography of Cicero, see Everitt (2001).

Sulla. Cicero won the case by skillfully appealing to both of the powerful factions interested in the outcome and by offending neither, displaying characteristics that he would use repeatedly throughout his career.

Famous from this success, Cicero began a legal practice that flourished. After only a few years, however, he decided to take time off to travel to Athens for further training in rhetoric. His studies lasted two full years, and when he returned to Rome, he decided that he would run for public office. Friends in high places, as well as his skill as a speaker, ensured that he won the election for *quaestor,* or magistrate. This position offered two significant advantages to an ambitious young man: It opened the door to more important political offices, and it granted the holder lifetime membership in the Roman senate. Cicero solidified his position about this time by marrying Terentia, the daughter of a wealthy noble.

With his future now assured, Cicero began cultivating his alliances. One of the more important was with Pompey, who had become the most powerful man in Rome. As Jimenez (2000) noted, "[Cicero] had just been elected a *praetor,* and he knew that when he stood for the Consulship in two years, the support of Pompey would be crucial" (pp. 36–37). Cicero defeated Lucius Catilina for the consulship in 63 B.C., becoming one of the youngest men to hold the office. Catilina, however, did not take his loss lightly: He attempted to assassinate Cicero and take over the government by force with the help of several ambitious but reckless senators. The plot was discovered, and Cicero denounced Catilina on the floor of the senate in a series of speeches that stand out as being among the more widely known from the period. Catilina fled immediately and raised an army in the hope of defeating the forces of the senate, but the army was crushed, and he was killed in battle. His coconspirators had been arrested a few days after the plot was discovered, and over the protests of Julius Caesar, Cicero had them executed without trial.

Although he believed that he had saved the country, Cicero's hasty action earned him lifelong enemies whose power and influence far surpassed his own. Roman law provided that accused persons were to receive due process, and 5 years after the executions, the tribune Clodius managed to convince the senate that Cicero had denied due process to the conspirators in 63 B.C. Cicero went into exile rather than face a jury, and the senate quickly passed a bill declaring him an outlaw and confiscating his property. In addition, one of those whom Cicero had executed was the stepfather of Marc Antony, trusted lieutenant to Caesar. Marc Antony never forgave the orator.

After 2 years of exile, the political winds changed, and Cicero was able to return to Rome. His property was returned, and he resumed his duties in the senate. He also began a very dangerous game—juggling his allegiance between Pompey and Caesar, who along with Marcus Crassus made up the First Triumvirate. When the Triumvirate began to unravel and it became clear that Caesar would respond with force to perceived slights, Cicero gave his support to Pompey. He urged Pompey to bring his army to bear as soon as possible, and he wrote numerous letters urging all to take up arms against Caesar. As it turned out, of course, he was backing the wrong horse. Pompey abandoned Italy rather than confront Caesar in battle, and Cicero was left stranded in a small town on the Italian coast, with no means of escape. Fearing for his life, he hoped to appeal to Caesar's well-known policy of *clementia,* or clemency. As Jimenez (2000) noted, "Cicero sent [Caesar] a fawning (and misleading) letter, praising his wisdom and kindness and assuring him that 'when arms were taken up, I had nothing to do with the war, and I judged you therein to be an injured party' " (p. 81).

The fact that Cicero survived the bloody civil war that ensued is testimony to his skill and intelligence, but to a certain degree he was under the protection of Caesar. When Caesar was assassinated, Cicero's days were numbered. Marc Antony quickly asserted himself and took control. He despised Cicero for ordering the execution of his stepfather 20 years earlier, and his feelings were intensified by the knowledge that Cicero had witnessed Caesar's assassination and done nothing to help the man who had treated him with great kindness. Also, Cicero had immediately proposed a general amnesty for the assassins, which infuriated Antony. Blind to this own danger and filled with satisfaction a month after the assassination, Cicero (1978) wrote that "Nothing so far gives me pleasure except the Ides of March" (*Letters to Atticus,* 14.6.1).

By the summer of 43 B.C., however, Antony and Octavian had joined forces and were systematically tracking down and executing everyone who had conspired to kill Caesar. Cicero learned that his name was on the list of those to be executed and, in a panic, tried to flee, to no avail. He was found before he could escape. We see his end described in Plutarch (1958): "He was all covered with dust; his hair was long and disordered, and his face was pinched and wasted with his anxieties—so that most of those who stood by covered their faces while Herennius was killing him. His throat was cut as he stretched his neck out from the litter" (*Cicero,* 48).

It is impossible to describe fully Cicero's influence on rhetoric. Suffice it to say that his influence on rhetoric, as well as on literature and philosophy, was equal to or perhaps even greater than the influence of Plato and Aristotle until the modern period. Although Aristotle was known to the Romans, Cicero was held in higher esteem. After the Empire collapsed, Aristotle was lost to the West until the 13th century, and throughout this time Cicero was considered to be the greatest rhetorician. Many of his speeches have survived, as well as more than 900 letters and several works on rhetoric, such as *On Invention (De Inventione), On Oratory (De Oratore),* and *Brutus.*

On Invention is a technical handbook that focuses on discovering ideas and topics. In many respects it reflects a contemporary emphasis on form that had its roots in the early Greek handbooks. *On Invention* also seems to be consistent with how rhetoric was being taught in the Roman schools, where there was little consideration of philosophy, psychology, or truth and where rhetoric was not deemed to be a theory of knowing. By Cicero's time, rhetoric had been divided into five "offices": *invention,* analyzing a topic and finding material for it; *disposition,* arranging the speech; *elocution,* fitting words to the topic, the situation, the speaker, and the audience; *delivery;* and *memory. On Invention* describes these offices and thereby reflects much of the rhetorical teaching of the time, which tended to reduce rhetoric to a rigid system for producing certain kinds of discourse. *On Invention* presents a rhetoric that consists of form without content, in spite of its stated aim of helping readers discover ideas and topics.

On Oratory, on the other hand, is much closer in spirit to Plato and Aristotle, so much so that many modern evaluations criticize it for being derivative. The work, a dialogue, begins with a discussion among friends about the value of rhetoric. Crassus, one of the key speakers, states his view that rhetoric is the foundation of government and leadership, for without it government has no direction. In addition, Crassus proposes that the ideal rhetorician will be a philosopher statesman. After being challenged to elaborate these claims, Crassus outlines a course of study for the rhetorician that includes information on such topics as the duties of the rhetorician; the aims of speaking; the subjects of speeches; the division of speeches into invention, arrangement, style, memory, and delivery; and rules for proper language use. Following Isocrates, Crassus notes that talent, an appropriate model, and practice are necessary in a person who would become an orator and that talent is the most important requirement. Style is discussed at length and is classified into grand, middle, and plain.

Today, we have ready access to the works of Plato and Aristotle, which give us a better perspective on Cicero than was possible in the past. We can see, for example, that *On Oratory* offers interesting insights into Cicero's views on Roman rhetoric, views that probably were representative, but that it contains little original material. Cicero borrowed extensively from Plato and Aristotle, as well as from the Sophists. In Book I, XIII, for example, Crassus notes that "the accomplished and complete orator I shall call him who can speak on all subjects with variety and copiousness" *(De Oratore,* Cicero, 1970), an observation that is strikingly similar to the view of Gorgias. Cicero acknowledged his debt to the Greeks throughout the work, but in Book I, XXXI, he also suggested that there was nothing new in *On Oratory.* Crassus states that "I shall say nothing . . . previously unheard by you, or new to any one." Cicero exerted tremendous influence on rhetoric throughout the Middle Ages and the Renaissance, but, as a result of this lack of originality, his value today may lie largely in his speeches, which provide important historical information and also illustrate an excellent practitioner at the height of his craft.

THE EARLY CHRISTIAN PERIOD

Richard Enos (1995) argued that Cicero's death marked the end of rhetoric as a "political force" in Rome. This evaluation is based on the perception that the courts of law were arenas in which litigants fought political, not just legal, battles. Such battles were not possible under the Empire, so there was little need for the sort of rhetoric that Cicero practiced. In this environment, the focus of rhetorical study shifted. Schools concentrated increasingly on technical matters of form and less on pragmatic applications. Students studied texts, such as Cicero's speeches, and wrote analyses that defended an interpretation. Kennedy (1980) described this shift as being from *primary* (oral speeches intending to persuade) to *secondary* (written interpretations of texts) rhetoric.

In this context, there was another shift that was growing more powerful and influential every year: Christianity. Although Hollywood depictions of this period usually portray the early Christians as peasants downtrodden by the nobility and the government, history offers a different view. Brown (1987) noted that the majority of Christians in Rome were members of the middle and upper classes, were well educated, and were imbued with a sense of morality that was entirely compatible with Christianity. They were sophisticated and cultured to such a degree that the pagan stories of the gods borrowed from the Greeks failed to satisfy their spiritual needs. One such citizen was Augustine. Born in North Africa, Augustine exerted a tremendous influence on the development of the Church as well as on the development of rhetoric.

St. Augustine

The story of St. Augustine's influence on rhetoric is perhaps one of the more interesting in history, and to my knowledge it has not yet been fully told. Born in 354 A.D., in what is now Algeria, Augustine was an intelligent, curious, complex man driven to excel. He was significantly influenced by his mother, a devout Christian who struggled to ensure that Augustine received a good education. Augustine flirted with various philosophies and religious sects before embracing Catholicism, and he is known as one of the more important Founding Fathers of the Catholic Church.

In his comprehensive biography, Brown (1967) noted that Augustine was educated in a tradition that valued memorization, mastery of Latin literature, and the ability to move audiences through oratory heavy with pathos. He could recite, for example, all of Virgil and much of Cicero from memory. Like other intellectuals of the time, he considered the works of Virgil to be perfect, a view that he later applied to the Bible. After finishing his basic education, Augustine went to Carthage at age 17 to complete his training in rhetoric. The next 2 years were a time of change: His father died, and he acquired a mistress and had a child. Toward the end of this period, he began taking steps to establish himself as a professional rhetorician. Another significant—and ultimately more lasting—change occurred when he read one of Cicero's works, *Hortensius*.

In this work, Cicero asserted not only the immortality of the human soul but also the need to attain wisdom so as to facilitate one's ascension to heaven. Wisdom for Cicero was to be found in philosophy, but for Augustine, raised in a thoroughly Christian environment, it was to be found in the Bible. He was disappointed, however, when he went looking for this wisdom. As Brown (1967) wrote:

> [Augustine] had been brought up to expect a book to be "cultivated and polished": he had been carefully groomed to communicate with educated men in the only admissible way, in a Latin scrupulously modelled on the ancient authors. Slang and jargon were equally abhorrent to such a man; and the Latin Bible of Africa, translated some centuries before by humble nameless writers, was full of both. What is more, what Augustine read in the Bible seemed to have little to do with the highly spiritual Wisdom that Cicero had told him to love. It was cluttered up with earthy and immoral stories from the Old Testament; and, even in the New Testament, Christ, Wisdom himself, was introduced by long, and contradictory, genealogies. (p. 31)

This experience with the Bible seriously dampened Augustine's enthusiasm for Christianity, and the Church's strictures on behavior dampened it even further. Although far from being a libertine, Augustine enjoyed a number of common human pleasures condemned by the Church. In his autobiography, which came to be known as *The Confessions of St. Augustine* (1962), he noted how these pleasures kept him from turning to Christianity during his youth, stating that his prayer was: "Make me chaste and continent, but not yet" (p. 174).

Nevertheless, Augustine, like other intellectuals of this period, hungered for spirituality, seeing it as the only way to find meaning in life. He experimented with several sects, especially Manicheaism. Nearly 400 years had passed since the Crucifixion, but the Catholic Church was hardly the bastion of doctrine and faith that it is today. Various sects vied for followers and power in the newly Christianized West, such as the Pelagians, who denied the doctrine of original sin, and the Donatists, who believed that the sacraments were invalid unless administered by priests who were without sin, a requirement that had the unfortunate consequence of threatening to bring religious services to a complete halt.

Manicheaism was one of the more important sects, its influence stretching from the west coast of North Africa to China. It was founded by Mani, a third-century Persian from southern Iraq who proclaimed himself the last prophet in a succession that included Zoroaster, Buddha, and Jesus. The fundamental doctrine of Manichaeism was its dualistic division of the universe into contending realms of good and evil. Followers believed that God was perfect and that, as a perfect being, he could not be associated in any way with evil. To explain the existence of evil in the world, the Manichaeans proposed that evil, in the form of Satan, was a separate entity that was as powerful as God. God ruled the realm of light, whereas Satan ruled the realm of darkness; the two were in perpetual conflict, and out of this conflict mankind was created. Human life, in fact, was a microcosm of the great struggle between good and evil, for the body was seen to be material and evil, whereas the soul was seen to be spiritual and good. Until his conversion to Catholicism, Augustine was a forceful advocate of Manichaeism who delighted in using his rhetorical skill to confuse priests and bishops.

By 382, Augustine had established himself as a teacher of rhetoric, but he was weary of the unruly students in Carthage and their small fees. Ambition motivated him to look to Rome, where he believed he could be more successful. Traveling to Italy in 383, Augustine used his Manichaean connections to attract the attention of Symmachus, the prefect of Rome, who at that time was charged with selecting a professor of rhetoric for the city of Milan. This was an important position largely because the imperial court was in Milan, not Rome, and because the duties involved offering public lectures and demonstration speeches that provided direct contact with the Emperor and the nobility. Augustine's intelligence and ability were never in question; nevertheless, as Brown (1967) suggested, Symmachus may have chosen Augustine for this important post primarily for political reasons. The bishop of Milan was Ambrose, cousin to Symmachus, who had been instrumental in convincing the Emperor Valentinian II to abolish paganism against the prefect's advice. Having a very intelligent anti-Catholic Manichaean serve as Milan's professor of rhetoric potentially could influence the Emperor to reverse his decision and preserve paganism in the face of an increasingly intolerant Church.

If that was Symmachus' plan, it failed. Under the influence of Ambrose, Augustine began to develop a new perspective on Christianity, one that emphasized the immaterial rather than the material. After much prayer and reflection, he was baptized by Ambrose in 387. Only 4 years later, he returned to North Africa and was ordained. He became bishop of Hippo (now Annaba, Algeria) in 395, an office he held until his death.

After his conversion, Augustine determined not only to spread the Word but also to help others understand Christianity and Catholicism better. He faced several challenges. His biggest was paganism, even though the ancient beliefs were increasingly derided by the Church and attacked by the government. In the fourth century, Christianity was still a minority religion, albeit a very powerful one (see Brown, 1987; Chauvin, 1990). Moreover, several thousand years of pagan culture ensured that pagan beliefs and ways of thinking permeated the lives of Christians, bringing them into frequent conflict with Church values. For example, upper-class Romans generally were highly moral, a characteristic that made Christianity attractive to them, and they viewed sex as a civic duty imposed upon married couples for the express purpose of begetting children for the Empire (Brown, 1987). But this solidly Christian antipathy toward sex was compromised by the widespread pagan belief that only "a hot and pleasurable act of love" experienced both by the male and the female could guarantee conception of a child with a good temperament (Brown, 1987, pp. 304–311). This belief stood in stark contrast to the position of the Church, which maintained that sexual pleasure even among married couples was a sin.

Another challenge emerged when Church leaders began attacking rhetoric and the schools throughout Italy for espousing pagan ideals (Murphy, 1974). Increasingly, education was viewed as an obstacle to faith. "The wisdom of man is foolish before God" became a favorite expression of those who sought to discredit Roman education and learning. Matters reached a crisis point when the Fourth Council of Carthage in 398 A.D. issued a resolution forbidding bishops from reading pagan texts.

In this context, Augustine set about defending the Bible and rhetoric, although he approached the latter with an ambivalence caused by his training in rhetoric on the one hand and Christian distaste for anything pagan on the other. *On Christian Doctrine (De Doctrina Christiana)* reflects his efforts at reconciling these opposites. In this work, Augustine (1958) argued that rhetoric could be put to use in preaching and, more important, in interpreting the Bible. In addition, he proposed that rhetoric was a critical tool for discovering scriptural truths and explaining them to the misinformed and the unenlightened, thereby possibly gaining new converts. He also used rhetoric to analyze the Bible in ways that illuminated its literary merit.

Augustine's success on all fronts can be measured by the fact that, over a relatively short time, texts other than the Bible became the subject of much rhetorical analysis. Furthermore, a vast array of pagan myths and writers were assimilated into the Christian cosmology. The most notable example is Plato, whom Augustine studied assiduously and whose work came to be embraced as a precursor of Christian values, with the result that Plato's influence on the Middle Ages was greater than Aristotle's until the 13th century (Artz, 1980). Cicero was likewise rehabilitated by Christians, who (mistakenly) turned to him as model of conscious disengagement from society, not as a model or teacher of oratory (see Conley, 1990).

Augustine's importance in the history of rhetoric cannot be overestimated. He is a pivotal figure in the shift from primary to secondary rhetoric. Before Augustine, rhetoric focused on public discourse, on speeches in the law courts and the assemblies. After Augustine, rhetoric focused on analyses and interpretations of texts. In addition, Augustine proposed a view of human history that came to have a significant influence on Western thought. The classical world generally saw human history as a process of gradual decline from a supposed "golden age." In *The City of God,* Augustine argued the reverse—that the story of mankind was one of progress that brought humanity closer to God. This view provided a clear demarcation between the ancient, pagan world and the new, Christian one. Moreover, it laid the foundation for modernism.

Admittedly, we cannot separate Augustine from his time or place; his world was in turmoil and decline, even though the general population either did not know or would not admit that the Empire was in trouble. Most believed that the Empire was stable and would last another thousand years, or more—while the imperial armies were being defeated by Teutonic barbarians and the Vandals controlled part of North Africa. Under these conditions, there was little use for deliberative rhetoric. Litigation shifted away from argument on the merits toward the cultivation of influence among patrons who would support one's case. Thus, in the late Empire, the teaching of rhetoric changed; schools could not realistically prepare students to use deliberative or forensic rhetoric. Students increasingly concentrated on "declamations" on set themes as rhetoric became more literary. The content of these speeches grew ever more abstract and irrelevant; what was important was style and delivery.[12] As Bonner (1977) noted, "Many teachers of rhetoric . . . under the Empire did not have . . . [Cicero's] practical experience, but were content to transmit the precepts [of rhetoric] in stereotyped and compact form, and to make their students learn them by heart" (p. 288). Bonner also pointed out that these declamations became "more bizarre and artificially contrived, [and] the exercise was especially associated with the *scholasticus* or 'schoolman,' and was called a 'scholastic theme'" (p. 309).

Although Augustine condemned sophistry, the rhetoric he espoused was grounded in literature. A literature-based rhetoric is ineluctably tied to matters of style, a fact that made Augustine's condemnation of sophistry ring hallow. Furthermore, this rhetoric emphasized the search for biblical truth, which was deemed to be universal but which also was highly abstract. These factors combined eventually with others to create, for the first time since Plato, significant interest in dialectic. This interest grew as the West moved into the Dark Ages and opportunities for primary rhetoric diminished. In time, the focus on literature and the concurrent emphasis on style led to the gradual reduction of rhetoric, until Peter Ramus, in the 16th century, stripped it of all but two of its traditional offices, style and delivery.

JOURNAL ENTRY

Ancient Athens and Rome have influenced greatly who we are today, and some of those influences are examined in the previous pages. Consider some other ways we have been influenced by these ancient cultures.

FROM THE MIDDLE AGES TO THE
NINETEENTH CENTURY

The Middle Ages strike many people as being dull and relatively uneventful. When the Empire fell near the end of the fifth century A.D., what Poe (1962) referred to as the "grandeur that was Greece and the glory that was Rome" (p. 23) faded from the world scene, along with

---

[12]Most historians refer to this period as the "Second Sophistic," indicating a connection with the sophistic rhetoric of ancient Greece. Although in most respects there is little connection, it is the case that both forms emphasized highly ornate style and rhetoric as a demonstration. *Lives of the Philosophers,* by Eunapius (1922), provides numerous interesting insights.

the sense of purpose and direction that had characterized Western civilization for a thousand years. Although the Roman Empire was plagued by internal conflicts throughout its history, it nevertheless manifested a political unity and civilizing influence that were profound. Both disappeared with the last Emperor, Romulus Augustulus. In its place emerged a hodgepodge of petty dictators and self-proclaimed kings who engaged in warfare so relentless that war, along with religion, became the cultural signature. The now separate parts of what had been the Western Empire began developing their own histories, not just because they were ruled by separate groups of barbarians but because the universal culture that had defined the Empire was shattered. In a remarkably short time, Latin evolved into the Romance languages—Spanish, Portuguese, Italian, French, Romanian—each distinct, each mutually unintelligible. Even handwriting, which had been uniform under the Empire, evolved into independent forms: Visigoth script, Beneventan script, and Insular script, as well as numerous scripts peculiar to various monasteries—each essentially unreadable to anyone untrained in that form.

In this environment, rhetoric became, in certain respects, more complex than ever before, which makes it difficult in a short space to address the many developments that occurred during the Middle Ages. However, two fairly distinct trends in rhetoric are visible, trends that persist even today. The first is Aristotelian, the second Platonic.

Many of Aristotle's ideas about rhetoric survived through translations and commentaries on Cicero. Cicero had made frequent references to the writings of Aristotle and Plato, and after the fall of the Empire, scholars relied on Cicero to become acquainted with the opinions of these philosophers without any knowledge of or access to the actual philosophical systems. One of the more important was Aristotle's emphasis on the practical nature of rhetoric.[13] Rhetoric as a pragmatic tool was preserved during the Middle Ages, but in ways that Aristotle would not have recognized. The art of letter writing *(ars dictamenis),* for example, can be viewed as one manifestation of this pragmatism. The most significant feature of Aristotle's rhetoric, however, was logic, which became a vital part of rhetoric in the Middle Ages.

The situation with Plato was quite different. He had not fared well among the Romans. He was too philosophical, and his rejection of practical rhetoric in favor of dialectic simply didn't meet Roman needs. Only one of his works, *Timaeus,* was widely known in the Empire. Ro-

---

[13]Aristotle and Cicero, however, differed in other respects. For example, Aristotle emphasized argument and proof, whereas Cicero emphasized eloquence.

man interest in Plato did not emerge until the third century, when an Egyptian Greek named Plotinus drew on a variety of sources to re-create Plato's philosophy.[14] However, it was not until the fourth century, when scholars like Augustine and Ambrose began to see elements of Christianity in this philosophy, that Plato became a significant figure.[15] By the Middle Ages, the Church Fathers had so thoroughly assimilated Plato into Christianity that, as Artz (1980, p. 181) indicated, he was the spiritual and philosophical "guiding star" of Catholicism.

Plato's popularity led to a general reevaluation of dialectic, most notably in the work of the philosopher and statesman Boethius. In his most important work, *Topics (De Differentiis Topicis),* Boethius set out to explain the work of Aristotle and Cicero, but what he ended up with was a treatise on the relation between rhetoric and dialectic. Dialectic had played only a small role in rhetorical education or practice until the Second Sophistic, but Boethius argued that dialectic was prior to and inherently *superior* to rhetoric. He based this argument on the perception that rhetoric deals with the immediate concerns of daily life whereas dialectic deals with universals—which can easily be turned to support Christian ideals. As Conley (1990) noted, this distinction led Boethius to conclude that "rhetorical topics derive their force from the abstract propositional rules provided by dialectic. Dialectic therefore governs the genus of argumentation, and rhetoric becomes a subordinate part of dialectic because it is a species of that genus" (p. 80).

During the years after Boethius, rhetoric continued to change in ways congruent with the needs of the Church, particularly the monastic influence that always had been strong. Two new strands of rhetoric emerged: the art of letter writing *(ars dictaminis)* and the art of preaching *(ars praedicandi).* Grammar and logic became important as fields of study, with logic increasingly connected to dialectic, which Bishop Isidore of Seville described in the seventh century as that discipline "which in the most exacting controversies distinguishes the true from the false" (quoted from Isidore's *Etymologia* in Murphy, 1974). By the ninth century, the study of grammar had replaced the study of rhetoric, leading the writer Rabanus to define grammar as the science of speaking and writing correctly. By the end of the 12th century, most

---

[14]Plotinus made Plato's philosophy available to educated readers, but according to Brown (1967) Plotinus was "one of the most notoriously difficult writers in the ancient world" (p. 86). Thus, the philosophy was available but not readily accessible. In addition, reading Plotinus meant that Plato's philosophy was transmitted through a filter, and it did not provide the same experience as reading the original works of Plato.

[15]We now refer to these scholars as "neo-Platonists."

schools in Europe weren't teaching rhetoric at all but instead were teaching grammar and dialectic (Murphy, 1974).

Interest in rhetoric revived significantly in the 13th and 14th centuries, when numerous classical texts were discovered and made available to scholars. Gerardo Landriani, bishop of a small town just outside Milan, found the complete text of Cicero's *On Oratory* in a cellar. Poggio, who happened to develop the font that came to be known as Roman, discovered Quintilian's *Instituto Oratoria* in the basement of a monastery. As these manuscripts became widely disseminated, Renaissance readers grew curious about the Greek authors the texts cited so regularly. Their curiosity was more easily satisfied after 1453, when Constantinople fell to the Turks; Greek scholars fled west in droves and were able to teach Greek throughout Europe.

Soon, classical texts were systematically integrated into higher education, which had the inevitable effect of motivating scholars to analyze and criticize the rhetorical precepts of Aristotle, Plato, Cicero, and others. It appears that these criticisms were grounded in a significant change that was altering the way Europeans looked at the world. The ancient Greeks and Romans interacted with the world on a qualitative basis and did not concern themselves much with exact measurements. Although they used hours to calculated duration, they did not use minutes. In addition, they divided a day into 24 hours, but they assigned 12 hours to day and 12 to night, even though the lengths of day and night vary with the seasons and geography. During the Middle Ages, people throughout Europe became increasingly concerned with accuracy of measurement, and the end result was that, as a group, Europeans shifted from a qualitative to a quantitative worldview. In rhetoric, this view finds expression in the emphasis on grammar and logic, which are more quantitative than the general rhetorical principles of Plato and Aristotle.

Peter Ramus

Peter Ramus was one of the more influential scholars who benefited from adopting a quantitative approach to rhetoric. The son of poor parents, Ramus nevertheless managed to attend college and earn a master's degree. The title of his thesis, "All of Aristotle's Doctrines Are False," signaled the start of a very difficult and turbulent life. He held teaching positions at the College de Mans and then at the College de l'Ave Maria until his written attacks on Aristotle so disturbed other scholars that King Francis I removed him from his teaching position and forbade him from teaching or writing philosophy. Ramus then took up mathematics, only to return to philosophy and rhetoric after the plague created so many teaching shortages that in 1547 the Cardinal of Lorraine petitioned the king to lift the ban on Ramus that had been in place for 4 years. The king complied, and Ramus promptly renewed his written attacks on Aristotle, stirring up a new storm of resentment and anger among intellectuals. In 1562, Ramus left the Church and converted to Calvinism just before religious wars broke out in France between Catholics and Protestants. He fled Paris but returned in 1570 under the protection of the king. This protection did not save him, however. In 1572, hundreds of Protestants in Paris were killed in the Massacre of St. Bartholomew, and Ramus was among them.

Although most contemporary scholars opposed his ideas, Ramus argued that rhetoric should be limited to style and delivery. He proposed that syntax was the proper domain of grammar and that invention, memory, and arrangement were part of dialectic. In addition, Ramus argued that dialectic should subsume other features of discourse that in the past had been part of rhetoric. Dialectic was not merely a means of determining truth and falsehood; in Ramus' view it also was the art of speaking decisively on matters that were in question. However, real-world applications never figured into Ramus' consideration. Neither rhetoric nor dialectic was related to law or politics at that time, and both primarily involved writing, not speaking, which made the issue of delivery moot. In making this shift, Ramus expanded the role of dialectic to include forensic and deliberative language.

If Ramus had not died as a martyr, his ideas might never have survived the 16th century, but martyrdom ensured that his books were reprinted throughout the Protestant countries of Europe, where they were immensely popular and influential. This influence is felt today in several ways. Ramus' approach to rhetoric finished the long decline of primary rhetoric. In addition, his attacks on Aristotle took a toll. As Kennedy (1980) noted, there were no Aristotelian rhetorics developed during this period or for many generations after. Plato's notions of rhetoric and dialectic came to dominate the schools, especially in Germany (Conley, 1990), and we already have seen that Plato was not a friend of rhetoric. Also, by equating rhetoric with style, Ramus provided what may be viewed as the natural evolution of St. Augustine's work in literary exposition. He thereby set the stage for the belles-lettres movement of the 18th and 19th centuries that continues to influence notions of what constitutes good writing even today.

Later scholars refined and elaborated Ramus' rhetorical propositions, but generally they did not challenge them. Hugh Blair, for example, was following in Ramus' footsteps when he argued in the late 18th century that invention was beyond the scope of rhetoric. Invention, the process of discovering things to say about a topic had, since ancient times, provided the *content* of discourse. What was left if there was no content? Style. About a hundred years later, Alexander Bain (1866) made the same point, stating that content was beyond the scope of rhetoric, leaving nothing to teach or learn but style.

ART OR SCIENCE

Bain stands out because he was the first to articulate the logical result of the shift from primary to secondary rhetoric, the elevation of dialectic, and the reduction of rhetoric to style. He proposed that *rhetoric was composition*. His book *English Composition and Rhetoric,* published in 1866, was remarkably popular and went through numerous editions in the United States. Part of its appeal may have been Bain's attempts to provide a psychological foundation (Bain was a psychologist) for rhetoric and style, but most of the appeal probably lay in how Bain's views simplified teaching. From classical times, teachers had stressed the role of talent in rhetorical training, and where there was no talent there could be little education. Plato, for example, complained about the lack of talent that he saw in the young tyrant Dionysius II of Syracuse. Teaching students how to think is so difficult that not even someone of Plato's genius could get ideas to germinate in barren soil. Bain implicitly provided a rationale for not trying. If the content of rhetoric, or composition, is irrelevant, and if all that remains is style, instruction can focus on imitation. The rich (and demanding) education that Cicero had described in *On Oratory* becomes irrelevant.

As Crowley (1990) argued, the focus on style ended the centuries-long emphasis in rhetoric on generating knowledge—its epistemic function—and rhetoric became a vehicle for merely *transmitting* knowledge, what was already known. Crowley stated that "the best to be hoped for from writing was that it could copy down whatever writers already knew. What writers knew, of course, was the really important stuff—but this was not the province of writing instruction" (p. 160). Matters were further complicated by the widespread perception that students did not really know much of anything, so writing in the classroom took on the characteristics of an empty exercise.

These views were grounded in the emergence during the 19th century of modern curricula throughout Europe and the United States, as well as the establishment of modern departments and disciplines. These developments had the unfortunate consequence of further eroding the status of rhetoric. Goggin (2000) provided a critical analysis when she wrote:

> To claim disciplinary status for an academic subject, scholars had to demonstrate that their field was a *Wissenschaft* (a science) rather than an art. The root *wissen* means knowledge. A *Wissenschaft* created theory and knowing, whereas an art was understood as a practice and a doing. A *Wissenschaft,* in other words, accomplished the research ideal of creating knowledge. Moreover, those seeking disciplinary and departmental spaces could not just claim any old *Wissenschaft;* they had to show that their field was a *naturwissneschaft* (a science dealing with that made by nature) rather than a *geisteswissenschaft* (a moral science dealing with that made by humans). The former was understood to render universal truths and the latter was understood to render contingent truths subject to human whim. (p. 14)

For rhetoric, the question of status—whether is was an art or a science—was hotly debated, but in reality, the outcome was predetermined by the fact that rhetoric was housed in English departments. Clearly, rhetoric was not a *naturwissneschaft,* and as it had come to be practiced in English departments, it was not a *Wissenschaft,* either. The majority of academics therefore viewed it as an art by default.

Rhetoric nevertheless had the potential to establish itself as a viable academic discipline, but a number of factors ensured that it did not. One of the more important: The goal of higher education in America, at least until 1870, was to discipline the minds of unruly students, not to provide content (Geiger, 1999, p. 48).[16] When Adams Sherman Hill developed and implemented the first composition courses at Harvard in 1874, he was responding, in part, to the perception that Harvard undergraduates were largely illiterate. The university had initiated a writing exam in 1872, and only about a third of first-year students were able to pass it. Thus, unlike other "arts," composition placed sole responsibility for product in the hands of students—from the faculty's perspective, ignoramuses all.

The First Composition Courses

These 19th-century views affect us today. Looking briefly at the nation's first composition courses helps us understand why. Harvard's composition courses required students to write themes daily with longer themes due once a week. These writing tasks covered a range of topics, but the majority involved literary analysis, which ostensibly

---

[16]It is widely assumed that higher education in America was reserved for the wealthy until the democratization of the 20th century. Geiger (1999), however, reported that "many students [in the nation's premier universities] clearly came from . . . humble circumstances, chiefly sons of farmers" (p. 42).

provided content. The university hired several readers to handle the huge paper load, and these young men marked the papers for errors and provided suggestions intended to help the writers improve.

However, because both the teachers and the readers saw their students as intellectual midgets with little knowledge of and even less appreciation for literature, there was no expectation that students would actually produce anything resembling *Wissenschaft*. They simply were deemed incapable of creating knowledge. Thus, the "content" of literature was largely a charade to mask the fact that the teachers themselves were incapable of providing any other content and that they really wanted to be teaching literature, not writing. Moreover, this approach established a contradiction that English departments, which have maintained responsibility for writing instruction, either ignored or found impossible to resolve: As literature teachers succeeded in claiming "scientific" status for literary studies, composition increasingly was viewed as neither fish nor fowl. Scholars could debate whether rhetoric was an art or a science, but in the everyday reality of the university, *composition* quickly became identified as a service course without any academic standing. Its purpose was merely to remediate illiterate undergraduates until the public schools could be prodded into doing their job of teaching students how to communicate.

Meanwhile, literature faculty successfully positioned literary studies as a "scientific endeavor; that is, a theoretical and explanatory one that created knowledge rather than an artistic or practical one" (Goggin, 2000, p. 22). Although Adams Sherman Hill was one of the chief advocates of the rhetoric-is-art position, he was unable to raise composition above the level of a service course. The course at Harvard was predicated on the notion that learning how to write is an inductive process (moving from particulars to generalizations) that involves focusing on individual features of texts, such as spelling, punctuation, word choice, and sentence structure. As readers marked papers for errors in word choice and sentence structure, they were exercising the view that writing skill could be assessed and evaluated on the basis of form rather than content. Today, few writing teachers question this view, but in the 1870s, it was a novelty because prior to the advent of the modern curriculum, writing was assessed largely on the basis of content—what students had to say about a topic, not their punctuation. Under Hill's influence, classroom instruction involved discussions of inspirational models, drawn primarily from literature, and drills and exercises in grammar, which were believed to improve the style of student writing.

This model for composition instruction spread very quickly to other universities. Within two decades, it had been incorporated into the first year at nearly all of the nation's institutions of higher education (Goggin, 2000). Meanwhile, the pressure on public schools to do a better job of teaching writing did not abate but actually increased. High schools that hoped to send their graduates on to university were compelled to modify their curricula to meet increasingly strict admission requirements. They therefore implemented the Harvard model, reducing the number of writing assignments owing to the higher student–teacher ratio and increasing the amount of time devoted to drills and exercises. Ironically, the number of students entering schools like Harvard with unsatisfactory writing skills did not drop significantly.

Today, we find that conditions have changed very little. If anything, they have become worse. Large numbers of first-year college students have very poor writing skills. For example, about 70% of first-year students in the California State University system have remedial writing (as well as reading) skills. Colleges and society blame the public schools, which are seen as failing to provide meaningful training in composition. In response, most states now require credential candidates to take at least one course designed to prepare them to teach writing, even though most do not require such students to take any writing courses beyond first-year composition, which many exempt on the basis of SAT scores. Unfortunately, most new teachers appear to abandon nearly everything they learned about writing pedagogy after 2 years or less of full-time teaching. In addition, mandatory testing has been implemented in nearly every state over the last several years as a means of holding public schools and teachers accountable, of forcing them to teach what students need to know. Although scores on these state-mandated tests have shown modest increases, results on other measures, such as the National Assessment of Educational Progress (NAEP), indicate that skills continue to decline—raising the question of what the state-mandated tests are actually measuring. Thus, by any objective standard, the Harvard model of composition instruction has failed.

2

Contemporary Rhetoric

APPROACHES TO TEACHING WRITING

A commonplace in education is that most teachers teach the way they themselves were taught. Education classes are designed, in part, to provide an alternative based on research and theory, but they are not always successful in moving teachers away from methods based on their own experiences. In composition studies, several factors influence teaching, including philosophical perspectives on the relation between language and mind, the role of individuals in society, the goals of writing, and the nature of education. One consequence is that there are multiple approaches to writing instruction—some overlapping, some in conflict. Teachers often find it difficult to work their way through the resulting noise and therefore elect to hold to the approach that feels most comfortable—the one they experienced as students— regardless of whether it is effective or theoretically sound.

The several perspectives that influence writing instruction today yield different rhetorical approaches and teaching methods. Although none of these approaches might be called "ideal," there are clear and well-researched variations in their effectiveness. James Berlin provides a good starting point for examining some of the more widely used approaches. In 1982, he discussed four major pedagogical influences on contemporary rhetoric: *classical rhetoric, current–traditional rhetoric, new rhetoric,* and *romantic rhetoric.* Several other influences exist that Berlin did not consider, such as writing across the curriculum, and they are included in this chapter.

First, it is important to note that Berlin's classification raises some issues. For example, there are elements of classical rhetoric in each of the other three, and neither new rhetoric nor romantic rhetoric is completely free of the influence of current–traditional rhetoric, and vice versa. Elements of romantic rhetoric are particularly prevalent in current–traditional classrooms. Nevertheless, these terms have significant merit because they allow us to explore various educational, methodological, and philosophical positions that shape the ways writing is taught today. Because so few teachers or textbooks employ anything even remotely resembling a fully elaborated classical rhetoric, I do not discuss it here.

CURRENT–TRADITIONAL RHETORIC

Current–traditional rhetoric is rooted in the 19th century. Its assumptions and methods were implemented in the first composition courses offered at Harvard in 1874. As Berlin (1982) noted, current–traditional rhetoric is characterized by certain fundamental assumptions about the world and about writing. One assumption, for example, is that the world is understood only through the senses; another is that understanding and knowledge come through induction (reasoning from the specific to the general) rather than through deduction (reasoning from the general to the specific). Commenting on current–traditional rhetoric, Hillocks (2002) suggested that yet another assumption is that "the truth is somewhere waiting to be discovered, that it exists independently of the investigator" (p. 221).

These assumptions yield a specific rationale and methodology for writing instruction. The rationale is often expressed in terms of "writing as thinking," which leads to a focus on teaching students how to think. Although thinking of the reflective, critical kind is certainly a worthy goal, there is some question as to why critical thinking should be the special province of writing instruction and whether writing teachers are qualified to teach it. The usual response is that the study of literature is especially efficacious in developing critical-thinking skills. Thus, from third grade through high school, language arts classes are primarily about reading and discussing literature. There is no evidence, however, that years of contact with literature develops critical thinking. Seniors may demonstrate higher skill levels than sixth graders, but this most likely is the result of maturation, not exposure to literature. The notion that studying literature somehow improves critical thinking therefore seems to be at best teacher's lore and at worst sheer myth.

What we know for certain is that a majority of writing tasks in language arts classes involve book reports that merely summarize the reading. The goal is to determine whether students can provide the names of characters and plot summaries. This goal has the unfortunate effect of turning the act of writing into a form of examination. With the exception of Advanced Placement (AP) and honors English, interpretation commonly does not surface until the college level, even though the act of interpreting does, indeed, require critical thinking. Some college composition classes are actually introductions to literature, with the course divided into units on poetry, fiction, and drama, but where the emphasis on form typically de-emphasizes interpreting. As literacy skills have declined over the last several decades, many curriculum guides in our public schools also have de-emphasized the essay (and even summary book reports), on the grounds that it is too difficult for our students, and have shifted the focus to personal and business letters. This shift has become so pervasive in the public schools that letter writing is introduced in many districts as early as first grade. Because letters tend to be highly pragmatic, they are not conducive to developing critical thinking. Thus, writing instruction overall in the current–traditional approach is unable to actualize its most pervasive rationale.

Bottom-Up Methodology

The focus on induction results in what is known as a "bottom-up" approach to teaching. Instruction moves from small units—words, sentences, and paragraphs—to larger ones, defined not by audience, aim, or even essay, but by "rhetorical modes"—description, narration, exposition, and argument. In many current–traditional textbooks and writing classes, argumentation is dropped, and the focus is on description, narration, and exposition, with exposition divided into definition, classification, comparison/contrast, process event, and cause/effect.

We should expect teachers and textbooks implementing current–traditional rhetoric to point out that these modes typically exist only as *parts of whole essays*. We are likely to find a definition, for example, in an expository essay on, say, education, in which a concept such as "zone of proximal development" is defined for readers. By the same token, we are likely to find comparison and contrast in an expository essay on, say, the causes of the Civil War, in which the North's and the South's views on slavery are analyzed. A discussion of part-to-whole is consistent with the bottom-up approach to learning that characterizes current–traditional rhetoric. However, teachers and textbooks rarely take this step. Instead, they present the modes as independent rhetorical entities, and they ask students to produce a "definition essay" or a "comparison–contrast essay" or a "process–event essay," as though

there really are such things in the world outside the classroom. Instruction includes little, if any, attention to audience and the reasons
for writing but instead focuses on the form of writing, as though composition somehow exists outside a social context.

What gets ignored in this approach is that language is only partially—and in some respects only slightly—about words, sentences,
and paragraphs, or stated another way, *structure*. It is primarily about
intention and meaning, audience and purpose. Nearly all writing
teachers have been trained to read literature, so it is understandable
that they typically point out that poetry—some of it, anyway—is most
certainly about structure. Be that as it may, the assertion that language is primarily about intention and meaning, audience and purpose
is fairly easy to test: In the middle of a conversation, stop listening for
a moment and try to recall the structure of the last two or three sentences uttered. Very few people can do this successfully. The same is
true of written texts. After completing a paragraph, readers can easily
summarize the meaning, but they find it nearly impossible to say much
at all about the structure of the individual sentences that make up that
paragraph. Even readers with extensive knowledge of grammar cannot
recall the structure of sentences they have not memorized. Thus, by focusing on bits and pieces of writing—sentences, paragraphs, and grammar—the current–traditional approach ignores most of what writing is
about. Moreover, telling students about the structural features of writing has little, if any, effect on writing skill because as soon as students
actually start composing, they quite naturally focus on intention and
meaning.

Grading Student Papers

Another very visible pedagogical feature of the current–traditional approach lies in how teachers grade student papers: They edit them as
though they are preparing manuscripts for publication, even though
students never have the opportunity to correct mistakes, then assign a
grade at the end of the paper followed by a written comment justifying
the grade. Typically, the errors—ranging from punctuation and spelling errors to errors in subject–verb agreement—are deemed to be the
result of students' deficiencies in grammar, so teachers spend a great
deal of time drilling their classes on mechanics, in a self-perpetuating
cycle of failure—failure to teach and failure to learn. These drills never
seem to improve students' writing, so they are repeated year after year
from grade to grade. A review of any state curriculum guide for language arts shows that students study grammatical terminology, punctuation, and sentence/paragraph structure from third grade through

high school. That's about 9 years of study for a subject that is not only easy but also just marginally related to what writing is about.

Pervasiveness of the Approach

Given these serious shortcomings, it should not be surprising that, in his meta-analysis of composition research, George Hillocks (1986) concluded that the current–traditional approach is not very effective in teaching students how to write. Nevertheless, it is the most influential and widely used approach to teaching writing today. The massive amount of scholarship and research that has accumulated over the last 40 years in composition studies has produced only a single modification in current–traditional pedagogy—the incorporation of some features of what is known as "the writing process."

Because current–traditional rhetoric is largely incongruent with literacy development in general and writing development in particular, its pervasiveness can be understood only in terms of the comfort level it provides. Bottom-up pedagogy lends itself to curriculum guides and syllabi, providing the means to describe orderly, sequenced learning that has a complete essay as the end goal. In other words, it is concrete. Also, this approach seems intuitively correct because so much human activity—from building automobiles to constructing skyscrapers—involves putting pieces together to make a whole. Numerous textbooks (and the teachers who use them) indeed treat writing a paper as though it is like building an automobile or baking a cake. They offer recipes such as "seven easy steps to composing," "the funnel introductory paragraph," and "the five-paragraph essay." For theoretical validation, they frequently turn to a taxonomy of behavioral objectives that proposes that all learning moves from the cognitively simple to the cognitively complex. Language in general and writing in particular, however, are more complex than either the recipes or the taxonomy can adequately describe. Moreover, they operate on different principles. Thus, a cookbook approach to writing and teaching writing is destined to fail. The five-paragraph model not only has no real counterpart outside the classroom but also inevitably leads to the sort of shallow, unreflective writing that we all decry as the plague of American public education.

NEW RHETORIC

World War II marks a pivotal moment in the history of rhetoric and composition. The war laid the foundation in the United States for a reorganization of society through democratization, which, in turn, affected rhetoric and composition. Desegregation and the civil rights movement, as well as the women's movement, emerged out of wartime social conditions that forced the nation to reexamine its concepts of democracy, equality, and freedom. The war disrupted established social patterns as women replaced men in many areas of the workforce, taking on jobs and pay rates that had not been available to them prior to the war; and although segregated in the ranks, blacks became a major part of the war effort. When the war was over, few were willing to return to the status quo.

Roger Geiger (1999) correctly noted that the Servicemen's Readjustment Act of 1944, more commonly known as the GI Bill, essentially redefined American colleges and universities. By 1947, the number of students enrolled in higher education had almost doubled from just before the war: In 1940, the total student population was 1.5 million, but in 1947, enrolled servicemen alone totaled 1.1 million (Geiger, p. 61).

In a recent work, Richard Lloyd-Jones (2002) described how this influx of veterans affected campuses, suggesting that the ex-GIs were a pragmatic bunch who were used to writing battlefield reports that needed to be clear and detailed and that did not have much room for stylistic niceties. A majority were interested in earning degrees in science and business, areas that emphasized content, not style. Lloyd-Jones noted that many universities responded by developing writing programs that were themselves pragmatic, or rhetorical, adjusting curricula and syllabi to this new type of student.

The turn toward the pragmatic had important consequences. One was a shift away from fuzzy ideas of inspiration-based composing toward consideration of what writers actually do; another was significantly more interest in and attention to pedagogy. As Lloyd-Jones (2002) noted:

> At the 1948 annual meeting of the National Council of Teachers of English (NCTE), a regular convention session intended for collegiate members chaired by John C. Gerber was devoted to conferring about problems of running a composition program. It was jammed. When participants were supposed to give up the room to another group, those present simply weren't done talking. They asked Gerber to arrange a meeting in the spring of 1949 to explore the problems more fully. That meeting was intended to serve the functions now taken on by the Council of Writing Program Administrators (WPA), and it brought together a number of people who had major vocational reasons for wanting more knowledge about the subject matter they were responsible for and to pick up ideas about running programs. (p. 16)

This conference laid the groundwork for publication of *College Composition and Communication,* the first issue appearing in 1949.

Those responsible for teaching composition and running writing programs at the nation's colleges faced a major disadvantage. They could look to other areas for ways to administer their programs, but there were few sources available on how to teach writing effectively. In addition, there were no theoretical frameworks in which to situate rhetoric and composition other than what had been in place since the 19th century—current–traditional rhetoric—and it had proven ineffectual.

The Influence of Linguistics

Then, in 1957, Noam Chomsky published *Syntactic Structures,* a work that redefined linguistics and provided a tremendous stimulus to rhetoric and composition. Prior to Chomsky, linguistics had been almost purely empirical. It was rooted in anthropology, and its primary agenda for more than 50 years had been recording and preserving American Indian tribal languages. Chomsky insisted that any legitimate study of language must include a theoretical component, and he proposed a new grammar—transformational-generative grammar—as the means of improving our ability to describe language while simultaneously providing a theory of language (and ultimately of mind). One of Chomsky's more important proposals was that language acquisition among children involves developing an internalized grammar of the language. The mind is predisposed to developing grammar, in this view, so children do not have to learn terminology or rules consciously; they simply have to be immersed in a natural language environment and they will, over a relatively short period, produce grammatically correct utterances. For many of those teaching writing, Chomsky's work provided a theoretical framework as well as exciting new directions for teaching and research.

New directions were sorely needed, owing to the significant social changes that were beginning in the early and mid-1960s. The civil rights movement and the Civil Rights Act of 1964 opened universities to historically marginalized groups. College enrollments swelled, and large numbers of the entering students lacked the writing skills necessary to succeed. Much of the emerging research aimed to understand the problems these students brought to academic discourse and how to solve them. With interest in rhetoric and composition stirring, teachers and scholars began asking questions about writing and learning that no one had considered for generations. The National Council of Teachers of English (NCTE) organized various workshops and discussions about writing and then formed a committee to assess the state of knowledge about composition. The committee's results were published in 1963 as *Research in Written Composition,* a seminal book by Richard Braddock, Richard Lloyd-Jones, and Lowell Schoer that traced several lines of research in composition and suggested new areas for investigation. This book essentially redefined rhetoric and composition by posing a very straightforward question—"What is involved in the act of writing?" (p. 53). Shortly thereafter, Wayne Booth (1965) asserted that "we need a new rhetoric for a new rhetorical age" (p. 140).

Drawing on Chomsky's work, Kellogg Hunt (1964, 1965) began examining writing maturity in children. Prior to Hunt's investigation, maturity was commonly deemed to be related to sentence length, and the surest way to increase sentence length among children was thought to lie in having them read works of literature, in which long sentences abound. Hunt's findings, however, were at odds with both of these widely held perceptions. Among the students he studied, there was some increase in sentence length as the children became older, but sentence length was not the most significant variable related to maturity. Instead, it was clause length—more specifically, independent clauses, which for the purposes of his study Hunt termed *T-units,* short for *minimal-terminal units.* Hunt also found that T-unit length tended to increase as the result of embeddings, usually of dependent clauses. This second finding was important because narrative-descriptive writing, which commonly holds a prominent place in current–traditional rhetoric, tends to be characterized by relatively short T-units but relatively long sentences. Sentence length in narration and description, however, increases through the addition of *phrases,* not embedded clauses.[1] Hunt seemed to be on to something.

John Mellon (1969) saw in Hunt's research the seeds of a pedagogical opportunity. Clausal embedding is accomplished through grammatical operations that allow us to take two or more short clauses and combine them into a single unit, usually a sentence. Hunt's study indicated that, unfortunately, it takes students years to internalize these operations, which shed light on the common observation that the process of becoming a better writer is slow and laborious but which did not seem to provide much help for writing pedagogy. It occurred to Mellon, however, that schools might be able to shorten the road to writing maturity if it were possible to teach students directly the grammatical operations necessary to combine short sentences into longer ones. He therefore taught students in his study the various transformational-grammar rules associated with embedding, which gave them the ex-

---

[1]If sentence length increases through the addition of phrases in narration and description, it should be fairly clear that sentence length increases through embedded clauses in exposition and argument.

plicit tools for combining short sentences into longer ones. Because short sentences generally have just one clause, the effect of combining is longer clauses and, ostensibly, more mature writing. Then Mellon asked the students to write essays so he could determine whether the result was *improved* writing.

In theory, this program should have worked, but it didn't. The essays that the students produced were not any better than those they wrote before the study. Some actually were worse. But why?

Frank O'Hare (1972) thought he saw a flaw in Mellon's approach. Keep in mind that, according to Chomsky, grammar is internalized at a fairly young age. O'Hare therefore recognized that students do not need to have formal knowledge of grammar to combine short sentences into long ones because every native speaker of English already knows the grammatical operations implicitly. Teaching students the grammar raises tacit knowledge to a conscious level in ways that interfere with the efficient language processing necessary in writing. In other words, students in Mellon's study probably were thinking more about the grammar rules than they were about writing, with deleterious effects. O'Hare therefore altered the focus of Mellon's research so that students did not spend any time studying rules but instead focused simply on combining sentences. The results were impressive. At the end of the study, students produced essays that were judged far better than the ones they had written before training. Sentence combining was born. It became, in just a couple of years, a pervasive technique for improving student writing, and teachers and students from coast to coast began combining sentences.

The work of Hunt, Mellon, and O'Hare should be seen as a response to the changing educational climate of the time. Almost contemporaneous with Hunt's work on writing maturity, for example, William Labov (1966) published an extensive study of Black English and social stratification, research that recast the nature of Black English and prompted serious consideration of what constituted "Standard English." Ironically, the influx of college students from working-class homes simultaneously led to calls for greater emphasis on grammar as a means of "improving" student writing. Grammar and logic had been mainstays of composition for generations, and many people believed that if teachers just offered more of both, the barbarians pouring through the gates of academe would become civilized.

Experience should have made it clear to everyone that grammar instruction and drills did nothing to improve writing, but in this case experience was a poor teacher. The belief was unshakable. Indeed, it persists even today. District and curriculum guides across the country specify grammar instruction from third grade through high school, and nearly all link such instruction to writing. Some scholars and teachers, however, saw the question of grammar instruction as an empirical issue, to be determined by research. Braddock et al. (1963) examined numerous studies of the relation between grammar instruction and writing and summarized their findings in a statement that became highly controversial largely because so few accepted it: "The teaching of formal grammar has a negligible or, because it usually displaces some instruction and practice in actual composition, even a harmful effect on the improvement of writing" (pp. 37–38). In his meta-analysis of an even larger number of studies on this same issue, Hillocks (1986) also found that teaching grammar has no measurable effect on writing performance.

Such studies were problematic for those who saw linguistics as a powerful tool for studying writing. Equally troubling, however, was the growing body of evidence indicating that transformational-generative grammar is fundamentally flawed (see, e.g., Williams, 1993, 1999). By the mid-1980s, most composition specialists had abandoned linguistics, particularly grammar, although a few still saw some promise in the applied areas of psycho- and sociolinguistics. Stephen North's (1987) influential assessment of writing research did not even mention linguistics as a subfield of rhetoric and composition. This omission effectively closed the book on what initially had seemed to be an area of rich opportunities.

An Emerging Field

Throughout the 1960s, interest in rhetoric and composition grew, and scholars began investigating writing from several perspectives, not only linguistics but also philosophy and psychology. Numerous researchers adapted empirical designs and methodologies from the social sciences to tackle the many thorny questions inherent in studying writing. Prior to about 1965, the overwhelming majority of articles dealing with composition were anecdotal accounts by teachers reporting some particular assignment that had worked for them with a given group of students. Now a shift was under way. Increasingly, articles began appearing that attempted to explore underlying issues in composition that could be generalized to whole populations of students. A common goal was emerging: *discovering what differentiated good writers from bad ones and helping bad writers become better.*

Although we can look back now and see that the work of scholars during the 1960s was laying the groundwork for what became the field of rhetoric and composition, this was not clear to most people at the time. Indeed, the term *rhetoric* appears in a minority of these early publications. One reason was that the scholars involved were from university English departments, where hostility toward rhetoric had been strong since the 19th century, leading rhetoricians finally to pack their bags and move to speech communications departments around 1915 (S. Miller, 1982). There was a knowledge gap that made it difficult to link linguistic and psychological studies of writing to the rhetorical tradition that extended to ancient Greece. This situation changed in 1971, when James Kinneavy published *A Theory of Discourse: The Aims of Discourse,* a complex but clear analysis of the relations between composition and classical—specifically Aristotelian—rhetoric.

A Theory of Discourse affected the field in several ways. It suggested that anyone who would be serious about composition needed to go back to the roots and study the classics, particularly Aristotle, and it provided a historical and theoretical rationale for viewing composition as part of a rhetorical tradition 2,500 years old. In doing so, *A Theory of Discourse* helped legitimize composition as a field of study. Scholars (particularly those in literature) had denigrated composition for generations, but they couldn't denigrate the classics so easily, and *A Theory of Discourse* illustrated how composition and classical rhetoric were intertwined.

In addition, the book's subtitle suggested not only rich associations but also a revised methodology. Classical rhetoric had been pragmatic and closely tied to concerns of audience, but these features had disappeared from composition; student essays were school exercises that generally focused on literary analysis. Using a "communication triangle" (Fig. 2.1) that included "reality" as one of its points, Kinneavy reminded readers that people generally use language for good reasons and that good reasons—as opposed to writing as a form of examination or as busy work—should underlie school writing. *A Theory of Discourse* also connected composition to important work in the philosophy of language, where scholars like J. P. Austin (1962) and John Searle

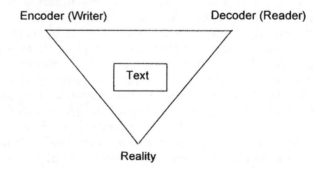

FIG. 2.1. Kinneavy's communication triangle. From Kinneavy (1971). Copyright © 1971 by Norton. Reprinted by permission.

(1969) were describing language as a social action. (See Witte, Naka-date, & Cherry, 1992, for a book-length discussion of the influence *A Theory of Discourse* had on composition.) Kinneavy combined these perspectives with Aristotelian principles and encouraged a reconsideration of the knowledge-generating (or epistemic) function of rhetoric.

An equally important contribution was Kinneavy's argument that the entire essay, not sentences or paragraphs, must be the focus of instruction. If the aims of discourse determine all other features of writing, such as structure, voice, length, standards of proof, and ways of knowing, instruction must begin with the whole essay, not sentences and paragraphs. *A Theory of Discourse* suggested that writing instruction must follow a top-down approach, in contrast with current–traditional rhetoric and its bottom-up approach.

New Rhetoric and Process

The same year that Kinneavy published *A Theory of Discourse,* Janet Emig (1971) published *The Composing Processes of Twelfth Graders,* a work that Stephen North (1987) called "the single most influential piece of . . . [composition] inquiry" (p. 197). The details of the *process approach* that Emig was instrumental in creating are discussed in the next chapter. Nevertheless, a few remarks are pertinent here.

In the process approach, teachers work to change students' behaviors with regard to composing, helping them identify and then emulate the behaviors of successful writers through intensive writing of *entire papers*. Thus, process pedagogy is predicated on a top-down model of language learning and is embedded in the epistemic (or knowledge-generating) view of rhetoric. Students are encouraged to focus first on what they want to say rather than on how they want to say it. This focus leads necessarily to an emphasis on *revision.* Today, it is difficult to understand how revision could *not* be important, which is testimony to the pervasiveness of the idea. Prior to Emig's work, however, revision was not a significant part of writing instruction; in the typical classroom, teachers gave an assignment, and students wrote a single draft. Although teachers encouraged students to proofread, they rarely addressed revision.

Process entails a great deal of close contact among students and teachers because of the emphasis on revision. Instruction is individualized and collaborative, with teachers commonly joining small groups of students or meeting with them individually to show them how to solve rhetorical problems. The degree of contact resembles an apprenticeship. A fundamental principle of this approach is that writing processes themselves are individual. The "universal" features of process are quite limited and fairly general. Stated another way, there are a few behaviors that all good writers share, but many more are particular. The most salient universal features were identified as "stages" of the composing process:

- Prewriting.
- Planning.
- Drafting.
- Revising.
- Editing.
- Publishing.

On this account, "planning" is deemed a universal feature, but how writers actually plan a paper varies from person to person. Some may outline; others may talk about their ideas with friends or classmates; and still others may develop a purely mental plan. The process approach therefore involves helping students adopt and practice the universal features while giving them opportunities to discover their individual processes so they can learn what works best for them.

Another important feature of the process approach is that it de-emphasizes error correction. The current–traditional approach focuses on errors in students' writing; it is common, for example, to find that the instructor's manuals of many current–traditional textbooks are designed to train teachers in the use of error-marking methods. "AWK" is for marking "awkward" sentences; "FRAG" is for sentence fragments; "RO" is for "run-on" sentences, and so forth. The manuals explain how these notations, when placed in the margins of student papers, serve as learning devices, alerting students to serious errors that they then, presumably, can correct. Emig challenged this notion, pointing out that "much of the teaching of composition in American high schools is essentially a neurotic activity. There is little evidence, for example, that the persistent pointing out of specific errors in student themes leads to the elimination of these errors, yet teachers expend much of their energy in this futile and unrewarding exercise" (p. 99).

Since about 1980, nearly all writing instruction at every level has incorporated one or more elements of process pedagogy. As Lester Faigley (1992) noted, "Process pedagogy was extraordinarily valuable . . . because it proved widely adaptable across many kinds of writing courses" (p. 67). This does not mean, however, that all writing instruction is now process oriented. Although Emig's work altered the way composition specialists thought about how we teach writing through a study of high school students, the practical consequences were felt primarily in university writing programs, not in high schools. Teachers in the public schools generally were slow to learn about process pedagogy and even slower to adopt it. For public schools, the central obstacle is the apprenticeship method, which is incongruent with the assembly-line organization of public education. In language arts classrooms with 30 or more students, organizing collaborative work groups can be very difficult, and conducting individual conferences can be a daunting challenge.

Most of the public school teachers who did try to adopt the process approach—encouraged by curriculum guides and the field's commodification of process as "stages of composing" (prewriting, drafting, revising, editing, publishing)—not only eliminated some of the more salient pedagogical features but also fossilized the stages as composing universals. The results were twofold. In many cases, the pedagogical features of process were trimmed so severely that there was nothing left but the effort of implementing a new pedagogy. The preexisting current–traditional approach was left intact, albeit with the token addition of one of the process stages, usually prewriting, which had no effect whatsoever on students' learning how to write. In other cases, fossilization undermined the whole notion of individual composing processes. Students were (and are) told, for example, that they cannot produce a paper without first prewriting, which takes the form of outlining or brainstorming or freewriting or clustering, depending on the individual *teacher's* orientation. Although prewriting was originally conceptualized as invention, or discovering knowledge about a topic, it quickly became a gimmick related almost entirely to structure. In both cases, writing instruction continues to focus on grammar drills and exercises and structural correctness—not on process and not on content.

It is important to stress that, in theory, the process approach offers exciting opportunities for improving student writing by changing the way teachers approach instruction. However, after about 30 years, it seems clear that this approach has not met the expectations of teachers and society for improved writing. The most thorough assessment of writing performance nationwide is the NAEP report published every 4 years. Often called "the report card on America's schools," the NAEP report assesses educational achievement in a variety of areas, such as math, science, reading, and writing. This report card has shown a steady decline in the writing abilities of our students, even though process pedagogy has been incorporated, in one way or another, into language arts curricula for more than two decades. The failure of process pedagogy to improve student writing appears to be related to what Jon Elster (as cited in Callinicos, 1988, p. 78) called "methodological individualism," a powerful presumption in the process approach that all social phenomena are explicable only in terms of individuals. Indeed, this presumption may well underlie—and undermine—each of the four major methodologies identified by Berlin.

An Emphasis on Psychology

If there was one characteristic feature of new rhetoric, it was the emphasis on psychology. Both James Berlin (1990) and Maureen Goggin (2000) traced the emergence of new rhetoric to developments in cognitive psychology. The National Defense Education Act of 1958, passed in response to the Soviet Union's 1957 launch of Sputnik, made improving public school performance a high priority. Educators held numerous conferences over the next several years to develop strategies that would enable them to meet the challenges presented by the Act, and an influential leader in these efforts was Jerome Bruner, one of the foremost psychologists in the country. Drawing on the stage-development theories of Jean Piaget, Bruner articulated curricula that emphasized using process to master the core knowledge of academic disciplines, and his ideas took root. (Efforts to base classroom instruction on psychological principles often are linked to what is known as the "progressive education" movement, which generally attempted to focus attention on schools' role in giving students the cognitive tools to lead well-balanced and productive lives.) Berlin's evaluation of Bruner is worth quoting at length:

> [Bruner stressed the] role of discovery in learning, arguing that students should use an inductive approach in order to discover on their own the structure of the discipline under consideration. . . . The student was to engage in the act of doing physics or math or literary criticism, and was not simply to rely on the reports of experts. . . . The implications of Bruner's thought for writing instruction are not difficult to deduce. Students should engage in the process of composing, not in the study of someone else's process of composing. Teachers may supply information about writing . . . but their main job is to create an environment in which students can learn for themselves the behavior appropriate to successful writing. The product of student writing, moreover, is not as important as engaging in the process of writing. (p. 208)

On this basis, Berlin argued that Emig's work emerged from the cognitive context that Bruner in particular and progressive education in general encouraged.

Cognitive psychology is the study of how people process information, including language, so with good reason it offered fertile lines of research for scholars. Between 1975 and 1985, the majority of influential studies in composition examined the psychological dimensions of writing (Hillocks, 1986). Flower and Hayes (1981), for example, developed a cognitive model of the composing process that was one of the more frequently cited studies throughout the 1980s. Matsuhashi (1981) simultaneously published an important assessment of pausing and planning during writing, suggesting that effective writers use pauses during composing to adjust their plans. Williams (1985) studied micromovements of the articulatory musculature, which becomes active during mental activities, and concluded that good writers think more during pauses than poor ones.

In retrospect, we can see quite clearly that this approach—and with it new rhetoric—was destined to fail, and why. Today, the numerous psychological investigations of writing that characterized new rhetoric can be viewed as merely laying the groundwork for more rigorous and more revealing research into the particular mental operations associated with writing. However, this research was never conducted. The psychological approach was abandoned before it ever reached maturity. The reasons are fairly straightforward.

Many people in composition and rhetoric—indeed, a majority—were uncomfortable with the cognitive approach. Triggered by the emphasis on empiricism, the debate over whether rhetoric is an art or a science, which had lain dormant for some time, resurfaced with more acrimony than ever. Ken Macrorie, editor of *College Composition and Communication* in 1964, for example, spoke out strongly against the influence of linguists and empirically oriented rhetoricians: "If their efforts diminish the attention paid to art in composition, the teaching of writing may become too analytical and mechanical to tap all the human powers of freshman students" (np). Those on the other side of the issue responded by establishing their own journal, *Research in the Teaching of English (RTE),* in 1966, with Richard Braddock, whose training was in education, not English, as the first editor. For many in rhetoric and composition, *RTE* signaled the beginning of a new era in language research, one in which fuzzy, ill-defined notions of writing were replaced by the rigor of the scientific method. Conflict was inevitable.

By embracing cognitive psychology, new rhetoric had aligned itself with science, yet nearly all writing teachers, trained as they were in literature, saw their work as an art, albeit a malformed one. Even as curriculum guides, teacher-training workshops, and syllabi rapidly incorporated at least the language of process and new-rhetoric research, writing teachers at every level continued to focus on discussions of literary models and the belleletristic essay. Moreover, the research of new rhetoric was inherently exclusionary. Prior to the turn to empiricism, just about anyone could be a writing "scholar" simply through anecdote; between 1950 and 1965, the vast majority of articles published in *Col-*

lege Composition and Communication (CCC) were conference papers, most of which merely offered reports of successful teaching experiences (Goggin, 2000). This number declined steadily, reaching zero in some years between 1965 and 1977, but for reasons that are examined later, it started to rise again after 1977 and really shot up in 1989.[2]

Under the new paradigm, however, no one could conduct even a fairly simple study without significant training in research methods, design, and statistics. Moreover, simply reading and understanding cognitive studies also demanded serious training. The people conducting this research during the decade between 1975 and 1985 were generally housed in university English departments, where empiricism was (and is) disdained. Unable to understand empirical research and unwilling to accept the validity of empirical data, many English department faculty began suggesting not only that the data were trivial but also that the entire methodology was reductionist.[3] Furthermore, composition and rhetoric scholars were developing graduate programs that were attracting bright students who otherwise might have elected to study literature. These students began writing dissertations that literature-trained graduate studies committees found not only hard to comprehend but also inappropriate for English departments. Gene Lyons (1976) expressed the problem well when, after criticizing English departments for ignoring their social responsibility to teach reading and writing, he concluded that "The business of the American English department is not the teaching of literacy; it is the worship of literature" (p. 34). A backlash emerged as established literature faculty, joined by some manqué compositionists, sought to reassert traditional literary values.

ROMANTIC RHETORIC

The first signs of backlash manifested themselves through what has come to be known as "romantic rhetoric" (Winterowd & Blum, 1994).

---

[2]*College Composition and Communication* did not become a peer-reviewed journal until 1987 (Goggin, 2000, p. 63), which means that, prior to this date, the editors were solely responsible for selecting papers for publication. All science-based journals, of course, are peer reviewed. The fact that *CCC* did not implement peer review until 1987 is indicative of the difficulty those in rhetoric had with the notion that the field could be a science rather than an art.

[3]The most egregious example is Mike Rose. His 1988 article, "Narrowing the Mind and Page: Remedial Writers and Cognitive Reductionism," has been cited frequently by those who advocate rhetoric as art, even though it is filled with inaccuracies and in some cases blatant distortions.

Romantic rhetoric (also widely known as "expressivist rhetoric") is linked to Romanticism, a movement in literature that lasted from about 1750 to 1870 and that is characterized by reliance on the imagination, subjectivity, freedom of thought and expression, idealization of the individual, a search for individual "truth," and rejection of rules. In most respects, Romanticism emerged as a reaction against Classicism, a term used to characterize art governed by conscious restraint, form, and rationality. However, it also was a reaction against two opposites—Rationalism, a system of thought that maintains that reason is the basis for knowledge, and Empiricism, which maintains that all knowledge is based on observation and experience. One of the chief proponents of Romanticism was French philosopher Jean Jaques Rousseau, who expressed many of the movement's tenets when he made a play on Rene Descartes' famous statement of Rationalism, "I think, therefore I am," by declaring, "I felt before I thought." Romantic rhetoric, then, is concerned with individual feelings and a search for personal truth.

Winterowd and Blum (1994) argued that romantic rhetoric developed as a reaction against current–traditional rhetoric. Although there is much truth to this argument, it is not sufficiently comprehensive or accurate. Other factors were involved, particularly the development of new rhetoric and the volatile mix of culture and counterculture that dominated American society during the late 1960s and early 1970s. From a broader perspective, social dynamics made romantic rhetoric possible, and new rhetoric brought it into being. Today, only current–traditional rhetoric is more widely disseminated in American education.

Grounded in the Counterculture

To understand the development of romantic rhetoric, it is necessary to recall that during the 1960s and 1970s colleges and universities in the United States faced significant challenges as a result of social change. The civil rights movement and the Vietnam War created a flood of internal refugees pouring into higher education. Students who in the past never would have sought admission to university because they lacked the money or the motivation suddenly had both as the civil rights movement prompted Congress to make financial aid available on a large scale, and the war prompted countless working-class young men to seek safe haven in college, where they could get a draft deferment that kept them out of Vietnam as long as they were enrolled. The majority of these new students were inadequately prepared for university work. Their reading and writing skills were particularly weak, and teachers and administrators scrambled to find ways to reduce the failure rates (see Coulson, 1996; Shaughnessy, 1977). Many educators were at a loss because there seemed to be no way to advance the nation's social agenda of providing access to quality education to all while maintaining traditional standards of language performance.

Even as colleges and universities were becoming more inclusive and more democratic, students nationwide were criticizing the traditional undergraduate curriculum and were demanding that administrators make higher education more personally meaningful, more "relevant." Protests and demonstrations became commonplace, and although they generally are remembered as protests against the war in Vietnam, more was involved. The campus demonstrations were not led by blacks, even though blacks made up a disproportionate number of the soldiers fighting in Southeast Asia. And they were not led by the blue-collar students who often saw college primarily in terms of a draft deferment. They were led by middle- and upper-middle-class students who, on the face of it, had no reason to protest. Student protesters were, by and large, children of what Beers (1996) called "the blue-sky generation." With comfortable lives and bright prospects, they lacked little in the way of material goods, but the seemingly limitless horizons of the "blue sky" were bounded by the rigid conformity of republican democracy. The demonstrations of the 1960s therefore are best understood as having multiple goals—protesting the war and supporting civil rights by demanding greater pluralism, to be sure, but also expressing a need for greater individualism. At their core was students' assertion of their right to be individuals, who they wanted to be. College campuses saw sit-ins, teach-ins, bra burning, draft card burning, student strikes, a general hostility toward "the establishment," and widespread antipathy toward curricula. High schools faced protests against dress codes, tracking (which grouped students in classes on the basis of ability), discipline, and homework. Outside the campuses, a few cities experienced race riots. Many teachers and most administrators were afraid. Ken Macrorie's (1968) anxiety, for example, is palpable in his assertion that "We have a small chance to keep our students from turning our schools into the shambles remaining after revolutions [sic] in Watts, Newark, and Detroit" (p. 686).[4] In 1970, at Kent State University, school officials requested National Guard help in breaking up a student protest, and the troops complied by shooting dead four students on the campus green. Even so, the tide of individualism was unstoppable. In unprecedented numbers, politicians and ac-

---

[4]What Macrorie was referring to were not "revolutions" at all but rather race riots.

ademic leaders acquiesced to student demands and developed curricula based on what students wanted at the time rather than on any academic principle, educational theory, or vision of the future.

The changes in education were linked to such social factors, but they also were deeply influenced by the reality that many students simply could not master the traditional curriculum, which increasingly was labeled elitist and racist (see, e.g., Lunsford, Moglen, & Slevin, 1990). Also, as I've noted elsewhere (Williams, 2002), the individualism of the 1960s metamorphosed in the 1970s into *extreme individualism*, which identifies the "self" as the center of all actions, desires, ambitions, and goals, while, ironically, sacrificing individuality. Relevance, in this context, translates into a desire to have an individualized curriculum, one that satisfies *personal needs*. The fact that this curriculum may be totally inappropriate for other students or for the benefit of society is quite irrelevant. Then, as well as now, few people recognized that pluralism and extreme individualism are incompatible; it is easier to assume that schools can readily balance the needs of society and the demands of individuals. Unfortunately, this balancing act rarely succeeds in doing anything other than forfeiting the needs of society and groups, usually minorities, within society. The reason is that the tension between the incompatibles—democratic inclusion and extreme individualism—can be attenuated only by abandoning academic standards. This allows schools to validate individual voices regardless of how well they approximate existing standards and, simultaneously, to be completely inclusive.

The Allure of Authenticity

In this context, Ken Macrorie (1968, 1970) and Peter Elbow (1973, 1981) published the foundational texts of romantic rhetoric. Macrorie set the tone in his 1970 work, *Telling Writing*. In the Preface, he wrote:

> [The New English movement] allows students to use their own powers, to make discoveries, to take alternative paths. It does not suggest that the world can best be examined by a set of rules. It does not utilize the Errors Approach. It constantly messes around with reality, and looks for strategies and tactics that work. . . . The program gives the student first, freedom, to find his voice and let his subjects find him; and second, discipline, to learn more professional craft to supplement his already considerable language skills.
>
> And for both teacher and student, a constant reading for truth, in writing and commenting on that writing. This is a hard requirement, for no one speaks truth consistently. (vii–viii)

Many teachers find these views alluring. "Truth" and "freedom" are powerful buzz words. A curriculum based on romantic rhetoric asks students to explore their feelings and thoughts through self-expressive composing, which makes classroom writing tasks, as creative acts, marginally congruent with works of literature. Self-expressive writing also is thought to motivate students to write because it rests on something they know well and are presumably interested in—their own experiences. T. R. Johnson (2001) characterized it as the pleasure principle in action. At the same time, a curriculum based on romantic rhetoric is fundamentally at odds with the educational principles inherent in the cognitive approach, which stresses using writing as a vehicle for learning the core knowledge of disciplines. By their very nature, self-expressive tasks do not deal with academic content but instead reflect a "renegade rhetoric" (T. R. Johnson, 2001, p. 628).

Many feminist rhetoricians have aligned themselves with romantic rhetoric as an alternative to argumentation, which they view as inherently male and adversarial, because they believe that, too often, women's ability to tell their personal stories is suppressed in a patriarchal society. Thus, self-expressive writing offers opportunities to break free of male suppression. By the same token, numerous teachers who believe strongly in the value and stability of the "self" argue that in an increasingly materialistic society only true expressions of the "self" through autobiographical writing can have any real meaning.

The pervasiveness of this latter view is evidenced in William Coles and James Vopat's (1985) *What Makes Writing Good.* Coles and Vopat asked some of the country's top composition scholars to submit a student essay that represented "good writing" and to explain why it was good. Nearly all of the submissions were personal-experience, autobiographical essays. Those who submitted the papers repeatedly used words such as *honest, true,* and *authentic* to characterize the works as "good writing." Erika Lindemann's (1985) comment in this collection seems to sum up the sentiments of all these scholars: "Good writing is most effective when we tell the truth about who we are and what we think" (p. 161). This comment echoes the words of Elbow (1981) from a few years earlier, when he wrote: "That writing was most fun and rewarding to read that somehow felt most 'real.' It had what I am now calling voice. At the time I said things like, 'It felt real, it had a kind of resonance, it somehow rang true' " (p. 283). Romantic rhetoric therefore redefined success in writing was as "authenticity" of expression and having "fun."

There is no question that romantic rhetoric offers a safe solution to the problem presented by students who for one reason or another cannot meet academic standards of literacy. This issue became increasingly important in public schools in the early 1970s as administrators sought to reduce the high failure rates among minority groups. It continues to be important today owing to the huge numbers of English-language learners, or English-as-a-second-language (ESL) students, in our schools. There is no "right" or "wrong" in self-expressive writing; there is only the expression of true feeling. Students who cannot reason sufficiently to write analytical papers or who cannot spell or punctuate nevertheless can receive high grades because assessment becomes determining whether the writing seems "real."

But how are we to understand the preferences of scholars such as Elbow and Lindemann? How are we to address the problem that this fascination with self-expressive writing presents for literacy in general and for the language arts and composition classes that society has mandated will provide literacy education? On a fairly shallow level, the answer is obvious: Narratives are inherently more interesting than academic writing. Most people, including teachers, will prefer an autobiography over, for example, a research report on the mating behavior of guppies. On this account, we might speculate that the contributors to *What Makes Writing Good* may not have been asked to submit samples of good academic writing. Perhaps they simply needed better selection criteria.

On a deeper level, however, we have to understand the complex role that confession—which is the true nature of self-expressive writing—plays in a liberal democracy based on extreme individualism. It provides the primary means of gaining recognition when there is insufficient social capital to gain recognition in any other way. People crave confession because they crave recognition. Intuitively, extreme individualism precludes any real interest in the confessions of others and should result in a high degree of intolerance for autobiography, but reciprocity is necessary to make the act of confession possible. Moreover, as Foucault (1978) noted, confessional activities are regularly used in liberal democracies to instill and enforce discipline; people are encouraged to "divulge their innermost feelings in the presence or virtual presence of an authority who has power to judge, punish, forgive, console, reconcile" (pp. 61–62). But why? The power relations inherent in any confessional act provide a possible answer. They always result in a significant role reversal: The subject of the narrative inevitably becomes the object—the object of our recognition and the object of our pity as the person confessing transforms the autobiographical tale into a story of victimization. Victims draw on one of the few remaining reservoirs of social capital—our sympathy—and thereby increase the level of recognition they receive. On this basis, we can account not only for a common writing assignment in classes based on romantic rhetoric—"Describe the most embarrassing event in your life and explain what you learned from it"—but also the fact that the student papers in *What Makes Writing Good* that received the highest level of praise for being "honest," "true," and "authentic" were those relating the most painful personal experiences.

These factors have made romantic rhetoric popular in public schools and universities alike. Today, even language arts classes based on current–traditional rhetoric generally have a self-expressive writing component. For example, the book report, which in the current–traditional classroom is typically a simple summary of plot, now includes descriptions of how the book made students *feel*. Interpretation—explaining what the book means—is not addressed, nor is argument—taking a position on a topic and providing good reasons for holding that position.

Self-expressive writing is not quite as pervasive in college composition programs as it is in public schools, largely because of the remedial role first-year composition assumed during the 1960s. This course was supposed to provide students with the writing skills necessary to succeed in their other courses. Nevertheless, the approach is still quite widespread at the college level and has, in fact, gained momentum since about 1985. Romantic rhetoric has proved appealing to some university writing teachers in part because it is indeed perceived as, if not a full-fledged "renegade rhetoric," at least a subtly subversive action with respect to higher education's institutional mission.

A full exploration of why college writing teachers might want to see themselves and their pedagogy as either renegade or subversive is far beyond the scope of this text. I would suggest here, however, that the social change that characterized the 1960s, which gave rise to new rhetoric, also set the tone for what rhetoric was to become. As Fleming (2002) noted, "the rhetoric that reappeared at this time was not a general art of practical discourse; it was rather a highly specialized gesture of complaint, suspicion, and irony" (pp. 111–112). In other words, the countercultural influences of the age had their effect on rhetoric, especially when the first generation of new rhetoricians—James Kinneavy, Ed Corbett, Richard Lloyd-Jones, Ross Winterowd, and others—retired and their students, the second generation of rhetoricians, reared in the 1960s, asserted themselves. What many asserted started with romantic rhetoric, but it changed fairly quickly to become something else, postmodern rhetoric.

A Matter of Perspective

We are still left, however, with a basic question: Are there benefits to focusing on self-expressive writing? The answer depends entirely on what one is looking for. From the perspective of advocates, an invaluable benefit of romantic rhetoric is that it gives students the opportunity to explore their own voices and experiences, which leads to "authentic" writing. In the process, students are "empowered" to express themselves and do not have to parrot the knowledge and ideas of teachers, textbooks, and institutions. Moreover, romantic rhetoric offers a solution to the educational problems that pluralism presents, reducing the focus on mastery of academic writing conventions by emphasizing honesty, authenticity, and truth. On this account, advocates have adopted what Fleming (2002) characterized as a "Gorgianic" view of writing instruction: "There is no such thing as writing; if there were, it couldn't be broken down into discrete skills; and if it could, those skills couldn't be taught to first-year college students in one semester in a formal, classroom setting" (p. 117).

Opponents of romantic rhetoric, however, have been quick to challenge these notions. Joe Harris (1987), for example, complained that when good writing is defined as "honest" writing, "it reduces writing to a simple test of integrity" (p. 161). But in practice, such a test may not be simple at all, for teachers have no way of knowing with certainty that any given personal-experience paper is fact or fiction. My classroom observations have shown that teachers who implement the romantic approach typically put pressure on students to make their writing vivid, interesting, and moving, and they overtly or covertly encourage students to reveal intimate information about themselves. Although there is no question that vivid, interesting, and moving writing is better than the opposite in some situations, this pressure ignores the fact that most teenagers have not lived long enough to accumulate many interesting or moving life experiences. Also, from a professional perspective, encouraging students to reveal intimacies is just plain wrong—and students know it. In conversations with students after my classroom observations, many have admitted to me that they "make up" events for these assignments because they know what the teacher wants to read. If these responses are generalizable, and I believe they are, they suggest that any simple test of integrity will fail.

The notion of "empowerment" seems, at first blush, to be less problematic. What teacher would want to "disempower" students? But it is predicated on the assumption that students are suppressed and struggling to break free of the restrictions imposed by a tyrannical society. This kind of 1960s radical thinking is both passé and inaccurate, based on obsolete notions of social change and progress through the overthrow of the dominate political system. Hegel (1956), for example, believed that history and social progress emerge out of the tension between the ruling class trying to preserve and enhance their power, status, and recognition and the working class struggling for some measure of recognition as well as for a bigger slice of the economic pie. Francis Fukuyama (1992), however, argued convincingly that today's liberal democracies have brought an end to history because they satisfy people's needs for material comfort and social recognition. In other words, a liberal democracy meets all the basic human needs that have driven political change, and their triumph at the end of the 20th century signifies the end of political and ideological evolution.[5] Opponents of romantic rhetoric therefore reasonably want to know how teachers are supposed to empower their students and what they are supposed to empower them to do. Advocates have not been able to answer either question satisfactorily.

In their assessment of romantic rhetoric, Winterowd and Blum (1994) noted that one of the biggest flaws in this approach is that it is based on the idea that writing has only one purpose, self-exploration. However, in reality it has multiple purposes. Anyone who would become a better writer must be able to negotiate these multiple purposes. They also suggested that this approach does students a disservice because students need and want to learn how to write academic prose. Certainly, supporters of romantic rhetoric have the freedom to dismiss better academic writing as an educational goal and to claim that self-discovery is more important. In this context, however, Alan France (2000) stated that such a narrow focus "means that our pedagogy idealizes the seemingly untutored ('authentic') expression of personal experience, a 'writer without teachers,' to use Peter Elbow's *koine*" (p. 147). It seems quite clear that authenticity of expression becomes a fiction in any classroom in which teachers give students writing assignments. Indeed, "authenticity" seems suspect whenever we consider the ways in which audiences influence and constrain what we put into writing. France again provided a revealing comment: "The fiction that . . . [student writing] is somehow an authentic expression of personal

---

[5]In *Our Posthuman Future,* Fukuyama (2002) revised his position slightly. He argued that, although the end of history may have arrived in a Hegelian sense, we have not reached the end in terms of human development. In the final chapter, he stated that "We may be about to enter into a posthuman future, in which technology will give us the capacity gradually to alter . . . [what it means to be human] over time. Many embrace this power, under the banner of human freedom. . . . But this kind of freedom will be different from all other freedoms that people have previously enjoyed" (p. 217). Whether such a posthuman future, if it comes to pass, will produce a new political system is an interesting question that can be answered only speculatively. This much we know: We now can see clearly that the United States is moving inexorably toward a two-tiered society of haves and have-nots as uncontrolled immigration changes the character of the nation so that it resembles a Latin American country more and more; in such a society, only those with money will have access to the technology that Fukuyama describes.

experience can only be sustained by resort to suspect formulae" (p. 147).

Also troubling is the difficulty advocates of romantic rhetoric face when they dismiss the claim that they have a professional obligation at least to try to meet society's demands for writing instruction. Society at large expects students to become better writers after studying composition, and it expects teachers to try to help them become better writers. The situation is complicated by the fact that, protestations to the contrary, it is possible to use empirical measures to determine whether romantic rhetoric can improve students' writing skills. In his definitive studies of the effectiveness of writing pedagogy, George Hillocks (1986, 2002) found no evidence that the romantic approach leads to better writing.

JOURNAL ENTRY

Reflect on your experiences in writing classes. How would you characterize the approach or approaches used? In what ways do you believe these experiences will influence how you teach writing?

WRITING ACROSS THE CURRICULUM

Berlin's (1982) description of the four influences on rhetoric discussed earlier was a limited summary of the status of the field at that time. He did not discuss all the existing influences, nor could he foresee others that would emerge in just a few years. One of the more important approaches left out of his analysis was writing across the curriculum (WAC), which even in 1982 was playing a significant role in rhetoric and composition.

WAC can be described as an effort to give writing a more prominent place in classes other than English, and it addresses a remarkable paradox.[6] Writing instruction in the United States is the full responsibility of English teachers, yet only a small portion of the papers students write in school, especially at university, are what might be considered an "English paper." Instead, they are papers about history, philosophy, economics, sociology, business, psychology, biology, and so on. After students leave school and enter the workplace, they never are

---

[6]It's important to note that writing across the curriculum is not really a completely new approach to composition. Colgate College established such a program in the early 1930s, and UC Berkeley did the same in the 1950s (see Russell, 1987). The current approach, which emerged in the mid-1970s, is different in that it is more widespread; WAC programs now exist at the public school level as well as at the college level.

asked to write an English paper. In fact, with the exception of college and university English professors who must publish to be promoted, not even English teachers write English papers. Many English teachers try to set aside this paradox by asking students to write about world affairs or local issues rather than works of literature, but these well-intentioned efforts merely encourage journalistic prose and do not address the underlying issue, which is that most writing is produced for a particular audience, not a general one, and therefore must follow conventions specific to that audience. Neither the English paper nor the journalistic essay will give students the skills to write, for example, a biology lab report or a business proposal.

WAC emerged as a way to address the problem. It is based on a number of observations and assumptions, one of the more important being that writing skill is not monolithic: That is, no single set of skills is applicable in all situations; instead, different kinds of writing for different audiences and purposes require different sets of skills. WAC assumes that writing is situation specific and that good writers are people who can apply different conventions to different writing conditions. From this perspective, practicing self-expressive writing or journalistic writing would not be helpful if a person had to write a lab report—and vice versa. WAC also recognizes that English teachers cannot be expected to master the conventions, ways of knowing, and standards of proof that characterize writing in the many disciplines that make up the curricula of public schools and colleges. Therefore, WAC proposes that all teachers are, in one way or another, language and writing teachers; thus, not just writing assignments but also writing instruction should be a significant part of teaching in all disciplines. WAC thereby eliminates the questionable task of asking teachers trained in literature to know the various discipline-specific writing conventions by putting responsibility for teaching them in the hands of content-area teachers who, it is assumed, know them well.

In addition, WAC recognizes that a fundamental issue in writing classes at all levels is that they are artificial. Real people write for real reasons: Attorneys write motions to get a judge to grant what they want; accountants write financial statements to give clients information about the fiscal well-being of a company; and so forth. Students, certainly at the college level, write papers in history and biology and economics and all other subjects—except composition—to learn more about topics in these disciplines and to master the ways of knowing, the standards of proof, and the language of the disciplines. The typical composition class, as well as the typical language arts class, is quite different. Writing assignments do not involve this sort of learning because all writing instruction is essentially content free. The lack of content is troubling. It allows some teachers to make their students' lives the content of the curriculum, which not only seems inappropriate and pedagogically unsound but which also causes many people in and out of education to view composition instruction as highly suspect. As Fleming (2002) noted:

> The intellectual "thinness" of the first-year [composition] course has become impossible to overlook. By "thin" I mean several things at once. First, the teaching of writing at the post-secondary level is undeniably modest, the entire enterprise typically contained in a single, fifteen-week course. . . . [Also,] the first-year writing class typically lacks substance, as it usually is focused on some abstract process, skill, activity, or form, and, therefore, often lacks intellectual content. . . . [A]nd perhaps most damning of all from an academic standpoint, the course is often just plain easy. . . . (pp. 116–117)

These factors make teaching writing in a language arts or a composition class problematic because few students are motivated to write for no reason.

A central component of WAC, therefore, is its effort to make writing tasks more realistic by linking them to content-area courses. Typically, students view content-area assignments as having a genuine purpose, especially at the college level where many such assignments are linked to students' majors. They consequently take them more seriously, work harder on them than they do on assignments in their composition classes, and tend to view them as more meaningful. To the extent that an English teacher is involved in these assignments, his or her role changes to that of a facilitator or resource, which many find refreshing and validating.

WAC at the Elementary Level

At the elementary level, teachers have more flexibility in implementing WAC than do middle and high school teachers. They are able to build integrated units that link science, social studies, math, and language, in which reading and writing activities work together to build skills. For example, during art lessons, some elementary teachers may have children work in teams. After finishing their artwork, the children can write stories for one another's pictures and then bind them into books. Also at the elementary level, science lessons provide rich sources of writing opportunities. Jim Lee (1987) related how several different writing tasks can be linked to a unit on garden snails. In an assignment that calls for description, students are asked to "Write an account of a day in the life of a snail." For narration, they are asked to "Write a story in which . . . [they] speculate or fantasize about how the snail got its shell." Then, for exposition, Lee offered the following: "Suppose that the sun is moving closer to the earth each day. Using the theories of natural selection and survival of the fittest, project what physical changes might occur in the snail as it attempts to cope with its changing environment" (p. 39).

In each of these tasks, students interact cooperatively in work groups, but the latter assignment better utilizes the potential of collaborative learning. Illustrating the inquiry method in action, this hypothetical situation prompts students to brainstorm ideas as they examine the potential effects of the sun's shift. The writing assignment becomes a stimulus for learning, the social interaction of the work group becomes the vehicle for learning, and the resulting papers represent students' formulation of their learning.

WAC at the Middle and High School Levels

Writing-Intensive Model. The most popular approach to WAC in junior and senior high schools involves designating selected content-area classes as *writing intensive.* This approach has multiple goals. One is to give content-area teachers more responsibility for writing instruction. Another, however, is to use writing as a vehicle for learning about the subject matter of the selected courses. Students in these classes don't just do more writing. They do writing that is focused in ways that help them master content. In the process of writing about the subject matter of a course, students learn more about it and simultaneously gain familiarity with the language and writing conventions of the discipline, with the content-area teacher helping students understand not only the core knowledge of the field but also the ways of knowing, standards of proof, and writing conventions that characterize it.

Writing teachers in this approach serve as resource persons for other faculty, providing suggestions on how to use writing more effectively in the content areas. They commonly conduct training workshops for their colleagues who will be teaching the writing-intensive courses.[7] Writing teachers also offer help throughout the year on how to structure assignments, how to conduct conferences, how to use student work groups to effect collaborative learning, and how to evaluate

---

[7]At some schools (especially colleges and universities), faculty members receive a stipend for attending the training sessions. At the secondary level, in-house writing teachers seldom, if ever, conduct the training when a stipend is available to participants.

papers. The goal is to make teachers in fields outside English better writing instructors. Such training typically includes instruction on how to implement what is known as a *workshop* environment (based on collaborative learning). Rather than lecture on the Civil War, a history teacher might have students work on group projects that immerse them in the material to be covered for a given lesson. A math teacher, on the other hand, might have students, working in small groups, write problems or describe situations that call for application of a newly learned mathematical principle.

Close cooperation among teachers and the nurturing support of administrators allows the writing-intensive approach to work fairly effectively at these levels, and in theory, it has the potential to improve students' writing skills significantly. One of the more important features of this approach is that it puts teachers with subject-matter expertise in charge of writing assignments dealing with that subject matter, which greatly increases the perception among students that their writing tasks are meaningful. However, the writing-intensive approach does have several drawbacks whenever it is applied, as explained later.

WAC at the College Level

WAC at the college level has been implemented in three different ways. Many schools use the writing-intensive approach because it is cost effective and because it offers the most efficient way to distribute responsibility for writing instruction. Unfortunately, the writing-intensive approach has not been very successful overall. Many content-area professors object strongly to the additional work inherent in any writing-intensive class. They are extremely reluctant to increase the amount of writing their students do because additional assignments translate into more time spent grading. Content-area faculty also strongly resist the idea that they are (or can be) writing teachers, claiming not only that WAC instruction takes time away from the substance of their courses but also that they cannot possibly learn enough about composition pedagogy to perform the job well. Some complain that the workshops they attend for their basic training in writing pedagogy are not effective—they are too shallow in some instances and too dense in others. In any case, they rarely feel adequately prepared to provide formal instruction in writing. Some school administrators have responded by mandating WAC, essentially forcing faculty to comply. These efforts are seldom successful because faculty, who are notoriously independent, resist such heavy-handed administration and end up simply going through the motions. A successful WAC program requires more than a halfhearted effort from participants. In addition, those involved in a WAC program too often assume that a single set of workshops is sufficient to implement and maintain the writing-intensive approach. Yet as Walvoord (1996b) and others have noted, the energy and enthusiasm content-area faculty bring to WAC dissipates quickly; within 3 years, writing-intensive classes are indistinguishable from regular classes whenever faculty do not attend regular follow-up workshops to reinforce the principles of WAC.

Generic Model.   The *generic model* for WAC was developed largely to circumvent the problems inherent in asking content-area faculty to take a more active role in teaching writing. This is its strength and its weakness. In this approach, instruction stays in the hands of English teachers who, ostensibly, help students master the conventions of writing in different disciplines. The first-year composition course is usually divided into three parts devoted to writing in humanities, social science, and science, respectively. Students then practice writing in each of the three broad disciplines as a way of mastering the associated conventions. There are no additional costs involved because there is no need for faculty training, and it precludes any anxiety content-area teachers may feel about being asked to teach writing. For these reasons, the generic model probably is the most widely used approach to WAC at the college level. Certainly, it is the only approach for which textbooks have been written.

Nevertheless, the generic model has several inherent deficiencies. The notion that all teachers trained in literature can master the conventions that characterize writing in other disciplines is dubious. They can fairly easily recognize superficial features, such as the fact that the humanities use the MLA (Modern Language Association) format for documentation whereas the social sciences use the APA (American Psychological Association) format. But other discipline-specific conventions are often missed entirely, such as how the humanities reference previously published works in the present tense and how the sciences and the social sciences reference them in the past tense. Furthermore, writing teachers seldom have enough knowledge of other subjects to help students with the *content* of their papers. The rhetorical difficulty is obvious: Writing on a topic one knows very little about is extremely hard. When writing serves as a vehicle for learning, students come to know more about their topics and about the subject matter as a whole, but they benefit from the guidance a knowledgeable teacher can provide. Indeed, this is a fundamental principle of education. Without this guidance, any number of problems can arise. Consider: I once helped a student with his geology paper even though I had no knowledge of the subject; meeting with the geology professor later, I learned that the student's paper was filled with incorrect terms and inaccurate observations that I had no way of detecting because of my ignorance.

The generic model necessarily leads to a focus on style rather than content, and thus it is not far removed from the current–traditional approach to composition. There is, of course, no question that style is important, at least insofar as it is a manifestation of the conventions that govern a particular writing task, but it should not be the focus of instruction or writing. With the exception of certain kinds of journalistic texts, real readers of expository prose are interested in content, not style. I would go so far as to argue that whenever the style of an expository text draws attention to itself, the writing starts to fail. Does this mean that "voice" has no place in student writing? With regard to most academic disciplines, the answer is yes. In fact, the writing conventions of science and social science are intended to suppress "voice" as much as possible.

In addition, the idea that there can be a generic approach to WAC should raise our suspicions. I've noted elsewhere (Williams, 2001) that if the audience of a paper "belongs to an identifiable group, . . . [one] will be writing for *insiders*" (p. 33). But if the audience "does not belong to such a group, . . . [one] will be writing for *outsiders*" (p. 33). Writing produced for insiders is, by its very nature, *exclusive,* whereas writing produced for outsiders is *inclusive.* The most illustrative examples are professional journals (exclusive) and books on science written for people who know little or nothing about science (inclusive). Articles in professional journals use language, concepts, interpretations, and references that only insiders fully understand, so they exclude people who are outsiders. Books on science that are written for nonscientists, however, use vocabulary, concepts, and interpretations that any reasonably intelligent reader can understand. They are designed to be as inclusive as possible.

The generic approach to WAC inevitably focuses on writing that is highly inclusive, not exclusive, because the teachers in these classes lack sufficient content-area knowledge to help students produce texts for insiders. It therefore is at odds with the very concept of WAC because the conventions that govern inclusive texts are "journalistic" in the broadest sense of the term.

The numerous textbooks that have been published to support the generic approach have only exacerbated this problem. They make no attempt to introduce students to discipline-specific features of writing. Most are merely collections of essays with little or no discussion of specific writing conventions. The essays themselves are journalistic pieces that deal with *topics* in science, social science, and humanities. They fail to provide a model of the kind of writing that characterizes the disciplines. Instead, these textbooks suggest that the only factor that differentiates writing in the various disciplines is topic. This suggestion is false.

Linked Model. The *linked model* emerged out of efforts to solve the problems inherent in the writing-intensive and generic approaches to WAC. It involves linking a designated composition class to a content-area class, such as psychology, history, literature, or geology. All the students in the composition class must be simultaneously enrolled in the content course, and the two courses work together. The content-area course is writing intensive, with at least two major assignments, and the composition class is structured such that all of the major writing activities support the work students are doing in their content class. Thus, students submit the two major content-area papers to their content instructor as well as to their composition instructor. These papers receive separate grades, but close collaboration between the two teachers ensures that the grades are congruent. Composition classes necessarily require more than two writing assignments, so the other assignments are related to the topics covered in the content-area class. They become opportunities for students to learn more about these topics while practicing their use of the discipline's writing conventions.

The linked approach presents some obvious difficulties. Coordination between composition teachers and content-area teachers is absolutely critical to the success of the effort; they must do nearly everything as a team—developing syllabi, writing assignments, grading standards, and so forth. Yet such coordination can be challenging owing to conflicting schedules, time constraints, and even different perspectives on learning and writing. The latter factor is often the most vexing because teachers with the best of intentions often have radically different ideas about what constitutes good writing. Many schools have found that the best way to address this issue and ensure smooth coordination is to put all teachers through an intensive training workshop that not only provides common ground for goals, objectives, methods, and grading but also bonds the teachers into effective teams. Unfortunately, these workshops generally require a week of 6-hour-a-day effort, which few teachers are willing to give without compensation. After all, the workshop is above and beyond what they would normally do. Thus, the most serious drawback of the linked model is that it is costly.

The advantages, however, are enormous. Students participating in a linked program find that their writing is more meaningful and, equally important, that their composition class is a valuable resource, not merely a painful requirement. The writing teacher takes on the role of a coach or facilitator who helps the students meet the expectations of the content-area teacher—expectations, of course, that actually were developed jointly by the two teachers. In addition, the value and place of writing are reinforced and elevated via two sources, giving students a fresh perspective on writing. For large numbers of first-year college students, writing is an onerous task to be avoided at all costs because, in their past experience, it was fairly meaningless. But when content-area teachers begin placing the same emphasis on writing as composition teachers, this attitude changes, and we see students taking an interest and actually striving to improve their writing. Most of them succeed. Indeed, there is little debate that the linked model is one of the more effective approaches to improving overall writing skills.

Those schools that have implemented either a writing-intensive or a linked WAC program generally have seen measurable improvement in students' writing, with the degree of improvement varying by the model implemented and the commitment of faculty and administration to make WAC work. Some colleges have combined the three models in hybrid programs that are highly effective. At Soka University in California, for example, students in their first year of study take a one-term generic WAC class in composition; during their junior year they take an advanced composition course that is linked to a course in their major. Meanwhile, all other courses are designated as writing intensive. The result is that writing is taught, practiced, and reinforced throughout the entire undergraduate curriculum.

Implementing WAC

It is relatively easy to implement WAC at a public school because the small staff keeps coordination simple. WAC commonly begins when two or more teachers decide that they want to find effective ways to improve the reading and writing skills of their students (Walvoord, 1996a). Their informal discussions usually lead them to contact a composition specialist at a local university for information, and then they take a proposal to the school principal. A few meetings and a workshop or two later, and all the teachers at most schools will be ready to proceed.

These efforts usually are initiated by English teachers, who must keep in mind that the conventions that govern the typical English essay seldom are applicable to other disciplines. Science reports, for example, have a structure that is quite different from a humanistic essay.

If good writers are flexible writers, students benefit from experience with a variety of composition requirements; they benefit from mastering the conventions that underlie writing in different disciplines. To suggest, even implicitly, that only the belles-lettres essay has any value is to undermine the very foundation of WAC—and it is certain to alienate and frustrate teachers in disciplines other than English.

Above all, successful implementation depends on reaching consensus among colleagues about the role of writing in students' lives and in their education. Ideally, those involved will consider the role of writing in light of pragmatic concerns associated with academic performance in public school and beyond, as well as society's needs for a literate citizenry. The role most definitely should not be limited to considerations of self-concept and personal growth through self-exploration; these issues are important, but they cannot be defining.

On the face of it, such a consensus should be easy to achieve, but in reality it can be difficult because writing has been and continues to be a widely neglected part of most curricula. Moreover, teachers and administrators frequently have conflicting views of writing, which makes consensus building a challenge. In every school that I have visited or reviewed, reading, math, computers, science, and social studies always take precedence over writing, and it is rare to find two educators who agree on the goals and objectives of writing instruction. Matters are made more difficult by curriculum guides that often require teachers to provide instruction that is outdated, atheoretical, or even irrelevant. Large numbers of teachers, for example, teach the three sentence types (declarative, interrogatory, and exclamatory) merely because these items are on a state-mandated test, not because knowledge of these terms has any bearing on writing. There also is the irrational insistence on teaching cursive writing, a 19th-century skill, in a society in which all writing (with the possible exception of family grocery lists) is printed. The point is that without some consensus on the value of writing and on the goals and objectives of writing instruction, any given school will find it difficult to develop a WAC program.

Another criterion for implementing a successful WAC program is that a school must agree to make writing a priority by requiring students to do more writing. As Ackerman (1993) and Walvoord (1996b) noted, the majority if our public schools continue to offer curricula that have few opportunities for writing. The situation is especially troubling at the elementary level, where it is common for students in Grades 3 through 6 to have only one or perhaps two real writing assignments all year—everything else that passes as writing is actually busywork, which does nothing to improve writing skills. As S. D. Miller and Meece (1999) reported in their study of third graders' motivational preferences, children prefer challenging tasks and despise busywork. Children given challenging tasks in this study felt creative and in control of their success, and they worked harder. Children given busywork, which by definition is not challenging, questioned their ability to do the work and felt that the tasks and school were boring.

This problem is multifaceted: Developing meaningful writing assignments is hard, time-consuming work; reading and responding to them can create a crushing paper load; and like parents who use the TV as a babysitter, many teachers use writing as a way to keep students quiet and in their seats. The motivation to keep students quiet is strong, in spite of evidence that getting students talking to one another about their writing is a powerful tool in improving writing performance. Nystrand, Gamoran, Kachur, and Pendergast (1997), for example, reported that in their study of eighth- and ninth-grade English classes, students rarely engaged in discussions, and they concluded that these silent classrooms were a serious obstacle to learning.

School boards and administrators typically are less than helpful. They generally argue that students need to develop reading skills before they begin writing, which has the effect of de-emphasizing real writing tasks. But this argument is hard to support. Scardamalia and Bereiter (1983) showed many years ago that writing skill has strong developmental components that must be triggered early. Recently, partially as a result of state-mandated testing, there has been some movement toward introducing writing tasks earlier and making them more meaningful. SRA/McGraw-Hill, publisher of the widely used *Open Court Reading* program, released in 2002 a K–6 *Open Court* language arts series that includes composition as a major component; a K–6 language arts series that focuses on composition is in press as of this writing. Although both are curriculum driven and include numerous inappropriate features, such as writing business letters in Grade 1, they nevertheless represent a step in the right direction.

The Argument Against WAC

Although WAC has been successful and remains a popular model for composition, it has come under attack in recent years as being an unacceptable approach—not because it fails to improve writing skills but because it stifles individual "voice" and perpetuates what is deemed "institutional" writing. Kirscht, Levine, and Reiff (1994) suggested that hostility toward WAC is the result of incompatible views of what writing and education are supposed to do. They noted that some teachers see WAC as a means of improving learning whereas others see it as a means of mastering discourse conventions specific to given disciplines. Consequently, "writing to learn" just doesn't mean to English teachers what it does to those outside English. For English teachers, writing to learn is related to personal, social, and political growth; for most other teachers it is related to the content knowledge the academy makes available to students. Those who hold these different views supposedly now form two camps, and the hostility toward WAC emerges out of disagreements about the nature of learning.

This analysis, however, misses the mark. As I have already suggested, the real issue is that during the past 15 years or so academic writing itself has come under attack by numerous composition scholars, such as Ann Berthoff (1990), Pat Bizzell (1992), and Peter Elbow, James Berlin, and Charles Bazerman (1991). WAC happens to be a highly visible means by which students are taught how to write academic prose. The argument, perhaps most forcefully articulated in Elbow et al., is that academic writing leads students to adopt the thoughts and views of corporate America, as well as to "detachment." As a result, they are unable to become "liberated" but instead are pawns in what Patrick Courts (1991) characterized as the "military-industrial complex." WAC, therefore, is seen to perpetuate the status quo, so it is at odds with postmodern ideology, at odds with "liberation pedagogy," which aims to get students to resist education insofar as it is a manifestation of the dominant values and institutions of American society. Susan Welsh (2001) captured the flavor of this view when she argued that "Resistance theory commits teachers to hierarchical determinations of the distance that learners have traveled beyond the status quo" (p. 556). Drawing on Henry Giroux's (1983) "Theories of Reproduction and Resistance in the New Sociology of Education," Welsh noted further that as teachers attempt to dismantle academic writing, they can "tolerate compromised oppositional behaviors and . . . seek to understand the circumstances that produce them, but finally . . . [they should] accept little or no incorporation of mainstream culture into the formation of legitimate resistance" (pp. 556–557)

Parents and people in other disciplines have a hard time understanding the argument that students should not learn how to write academic prose, and they have an even harder time accepting the premise that underlies the argument that students are oppressed and need to be "liberated" through resistance pedagogy. They have a hard time believing that students are suppressed and controlled by some "military-industrial complex." From a historical perspective, talk of the "military-industrial complex," "liberation," and "resistance" sounds like a relic of a bygone era that existed before socialism and Marxism lost their allure even for armchair activists. Moreover, it paints an inaccurate picture of society and the power relations that govern society, one in which power is invested in centralized authorities that suppress individual freedoms. A more accurate and revealing analysis may be Foucault's (1979) in *Discipline and Punish,* where he argued that political power is decentered and dispersed throughout a society and that it does not suppress but rather "normalizes" individuals, shaping them from birth to be members of their communities. This process may not seem any less insidious than the Marxist view—until one recognizes that any society that fails to "normalize" its citizens will be faced with, at best, antisocial scofflaws or, at worst, sociopaths and anarchists. Fukuyama (1999) suggested that most Western societies already face this problem. In spite of these criticisms, however, the seriousness with which so many leading composition scholars make this "liberation" argument suggests that it should be acknowledged. What remains inescapable, however, is that formal education inherently is a process of preparing children to take their place in society. When schools fail, and many of them have, society begins to fall apart. Liberation pedagogy seems bent on facilitating the unraveling of society and therefore strikes many as being antithetical to the best interests of both children and the nation.

As for WAC, it grew out of the perception that students can more effectively learn to write when they have a purpose for composing and when they have exposure to the types of writing that people in identifiable communities actually produce. It is difficult to see any overt political agenda in the work of pioneers in the WAC model. It is easy to see, however, great concern for the pragmatic question of how to help students become better writers.

JOURNAL ENTRY

A common observation among experienced writing teachers is that students can learn the Periodic Table of elements in about 30 minutes but can't learn the five major conventions that govern comma use in 7 or 8 years. How would you explain this phenomenon?

THE SOCIAL-THEORETIC MODEL

The rapid rise of WAC as a powerful influence on rhetoric and composition was fueled by work in Aristotelian rhetoric, linguistic pragmatics, and the philosophy of language, each of which encouraged a view of writing as a social action. Increasingly during the late 1970s and early 1980s, writing, like speech, was understood to be a tool to get things done in the world, whether it be a letter asking a telephone company to reverse incorrect charges or a book arguing for a particular interpretation of the causes of the Civil War.

The effect of this view was significant because it altered our understanding of the writer. In his communication triangle (see Fig. 2.1), Kinneavy (1971) designated writer, reader, and reality as the three points that shape text. Although the communication triangle was useful, some scholars recognized that it was a bit misleading. For example, designating "reality" as a point suggests incorrectly that writers and readers exist outsider reality; and depicting "text" in the center of the triangle fails to illustrate how texts influence readers and writers. Even more troubling is that the communications triangle incorrectly suggests that writers exert a great deal of control over a text. It therefore reinforces the erroneous positions of current–traditional rhetoric, new rhetoric, and especially romantic rhetoric, which put the writer at the center of composing and generally ignore the influence of audience. Using Elster's (1988) terminology, it is an example of "methodological individualism."

Discourse Communities

One of the more important influences of WAC was its emphasis on how audience shapes writing. With respect to given disciplines, audiences are understood to be discrete groups who are either insiders or outsiders. By the same token, writers themselves are either insiders or outsiders. Thus, a key to understanding the interaction between writers and groups is the notion of *discourse communities*. Because real writing is always produced for a specific discourse community—even if it is what might be called a "general audience"—writers must decide in advance what their position will be vis-à-vis that community. In other words, they must adopt a particular *rhetorical stance*. There is a very limited number of options: (a) insider writing to insiders, (b) insider writing to outsiders, (c) outsider writing to insiders, and (d) outsider writing to outsiders.

Rhetorical stance, linked as it is to reader expectations, determines nearly all features of a text. The reason is that members of discourse communities share not only values and views but also language and language conventions. To a significant degree, mastering the language of a given group is a basic requirement for admission. People who want to become attorneys have to be able to use the language of law, and those who want to become psychologists have to be able to use the language of psychology. Obviously, more is involved than merely knowing which terms to use. Students have to understand the core knowledge of the discipline and the way members of the discipline view reality.

But these factors are intimately related to language, and in all instances, an underlying pattern is visible—language differentiates insiders from outsiders.

The social-theoretic model of composition recognizes that people belong to a variety of discourse communities, each with its own requirements for membership and participation, its own core body of knowledge, and its own values and ways of looking at the world. It also proposes that writers produce texts in response to the social demands of these groups, not in response to an innate need to communicate or express themselves. It describes writing as an interaction between writers and their environment. Some scholars refer to the model as *social construction* on the grounds that society constructs our realities, our ways of thinking, and even the realities of our texts. The problem with this term is that it is easy to confuse "social construction" with *social constructivism,* which is a stage-based model of cognition and development that rejects innate processes. In this model, children are blank slates who are shaped entirely by society. "Social theory" avoids this potential confusion and has the added advantage of avoiding the Marxist connotations that adhere to "social construction."

The groups writers belong to consist of people with shared interests and goals who will use the finished text in some pragmatic way. Marilyn Cooper (1986), in an important article that was the first fully articulated presentation of the social-theoretic model, characterized this environment as the "ecology" of composing. In this view, groups define their members, giving them an identity and insisting on adherence to certain behaviors and language. Members also define themselves on the basis of their membership in the group, but they simultaneously define the group through their participation in it. The social-theoretic model proposes, as a consequence of these factors, that the texts people produce are governed comprehensively by the writers' membership and participation in a particular group (see, e.g., Allen, 1993).

The interactions of writer, audience, and text are shown graphically in Fig. 2.2. Unlike Kinneavy's communication triangle, this dynamic social-theoretic model places writers, readers, and texts in the context of reality. Writers can be either insiders or outsiders, depending on the writing task, and in a sense they serve as a bridge between the two groups. Most important are the interactive lines of influence, which are reciprocal in all directions. Writers influence their texts, but so does the audience. In addition, the text influences both the writer and the audience. Some of the interactive lines of influence are stronger than others. The audience influences the writer more than the writer influences the audience because the audience controls what the writer can produce and how he or she produces it. That is, the audience con-

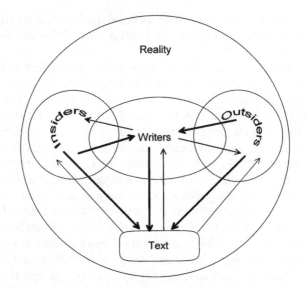

FIG. 2.2.   A social-theoretic model of composing. Writers adopt a rhetorical stance with regard to the audience. They are either insiders or outsiders writing for insiders or outsiders. The arrows indicate the relative degree of reciprocal influence that exists in any act of writing. The darker the
line, the more significant the influence.

trols both content and form. To return to an earlier example, an attor-
ney writing a motion for the court must deal with the matter at issue
and must follow very strict guidelines regarding format. He or she
could not, under any circumstances, submit a motion written in, say,
verse. Necessarily, then, we understand that the audience exerts significant influence on the writer and also the text. The writer's contribution to the text typically is threefold, consisting of his or her knowledge of the subject at hand, any interpretation of that knowledge, and
his or her skill at communicating that knowledge and interpretation
clearly and effectively.

It is possible to view the development of the social-theoretic model as
a correction to approaches to rhetoric and composition that overemphasized the individual writer. None of the most influential approaches—
current–traditional rhetoric, new rhetoric, or romantic rhetoric—describes adequately the way writers work in real situations. Both new
rhetoric and romantic rhetoric emphasize the writer, are predicated on
the assumption that writers have some innate desire to express themselves, and presume that writers are in control of what they produce. In
real situations, however, there are very few people who write because
they want to; most write because they have to. Moreover, they have very

little control over any aspect of the task and often write as part of a team. Professional texts are nearly always collaborations, not individual efforts, and there are very few opportunities for individual expression. Even textbooks like this one are collaborations. They typically are reviewed at least a dozen times by other scholars, each of whom provides suggestions for revision that must be addressed, and they receive further input, often extensive, from the editors. Any published text therefore reflects many voices, not just one.

Although the social-theoretic model is elegant and revealing, it has come under attack for several reasons. J. Harris (1989), for example, complained that the concept of "discourse community" was overly simplified because it usually is presented as cohesive, if not monolithic, because it ignores the fact that some communities have competing discourses, and because it does not adequately define "membership" in a community. Bizzell (1982) criticized the social-theoretic model because it implicitly advocates a neutral pedagogy, one governed by the discourse conventions of specific groups, which necessarily suppresses the political issues that, in her view, should be the focus of instruction. Other writers, such as Gregory Clark (1994), have argued that the emphasis on discourse communities leads to excessive democratic pluralism that silences minority voices and that focuses on human similarities rather than differences. As Clark expressed it: "The problem is that a discourse of pluralism . . . maintains connection and cooperation by excluding the most divisive forces of difference" (p. 64).

J. Harris' (1989) observations are accurate, but they may not provide legitimate grounds for criticizing the model. Most models, but especially those in the social sciences, are simplified descriptions that commonly ignore actions and characteristics that fall outside the mainstream. Psychiatry presents a useful example. There are different branches of psychiatry, and each offers a slightly different method of describing human behavior, resulting in "competing discourses." Within the area of clinical psychiatry, psychoanalysis provides one such method, and it "competes" with the biomedical method. Nevertheless, current models of clinical psychiatry ignore psychoanalysis because it falls so far outside the mainstream of psychiatric treatment, which is based almost exclusively on the use of medications to modify behavior. As for cohesiveness, members of a given community, such as psychiatry, may disagree on many things, but they remain a very cohesive group because they are bound together by training, language, values, goals, and their work. Likewise, the question of defining membership in a community may, upon casual consideration, seem to be problematic, but in most instances, especially with regard to professional communities, membership is defined on the basis of some certificate, degree, or license, which makes determining who is and who is not a member of a given group fairly straightforward (see E. Cohen, 1994; Hertz-Lazarowitz, Kirkus, & N. Miller, 1992; D. Johnson & F. Johnson, 2000; Wiersema, 2000).

Much harder to answer are the criticisms of those who argue against the social-theoretic model, like Bizzell and Clark, on the grounds that it suppresses politics and emphasizes community rather than diversity. They are operating with premises for what writing classes are or should be about that are incompatible with the premises that underlie instruction that aims to improve students' writing skills. The most salient of these antisocial-theoretic premises can perhaps be expressed as follows: (a) all actions are political; (b) the writing class is a venue for creating agents of social change; (c) differences among people and groups are more important than similarities.

The suggestion that all actions are political, however, is not particularly revealing. Because most actions are trivial, their political content is inconsequential. However, is a teacher's failure to engage in radical pedagogy a political statement? Of course. It is a statement that social change, if it is to come, should be in the hands of literate rather than illiterate citizens. Furthermore, the idea that writing classes should be training camps for agents of social change illustrates the tension that currently exists in rhetoric and composition between theorists and practitioners. Teachers who on a daily basis face dozens of students with minimal reading and writing skills may be compelled to concluded that this particular premise seems out of touch with sociopolitical realities of the 21st century and that it also is contrary to the social mandate that created these classes as places where students learn to be better writers.

Few parents are likely to embrace the proposal that our schools should be preparing young revolutionaries. The notion that differences are more important than similarities should be especially troubling because it is completely counter to the spirit of egalitarianism that drove the democratization of education over the last 50 years and because it so easily lends itself to identity politics, demagoguery, and discrimination. The focus on diversity was born of an infatuation with extreme individualism, and it fails to recognize that every person in a society must give up some measure of his or her individualism if that society is to function.[8] The real danger does not lie in a pedagogy that

---

[8]As used in education, *diversity* has come to mean "uniformity" rather than "variety"—uniformity in thinking and ideology. No advocate of diversity in faculty hiring, for example, would support a proposal to hire a feminist as well as a sexist or a fascist as well as a Marxist, even though doing so would certainly increase the ideological diversity on a campus, at least in the traditional meaning of the term.

suppresses political issues or that emphasizes community rather than diversity. The real danger lies in the prospect that some teachers, once they close their classroom doors, are so shut off from the communities they serve that they aim to produce anarchists and scofflaws rather than contributing members of society. In this context, the assessment of Jean Baudrillard (1988) seems cogent: "the people least able to understand America are its intellectuals, who are shut away in their campuses, dramatically cut off from the fabulous concrete mythology developing all around them" (p. 23).

Writing in a Social-Theoretic-Oriented Classroom

From the perspective of the social-theoretic model, writing *does* something. Consequently, people write for a reason. In school, students write because they must demonstrate that they have learned course material, that they can interpret information using what they've learned in class, or that they can work independently or in a group. Underlying each instance is an individual reason for writing, which is called *rhetorical purpose.* Rhetorical purpose includes the writer's personal goals for producing a text. These goals are not the same as the aim of a text, which may be to inform, argue, or persuade. Rhetorical purpose is about the writer, whereas the aim of a text is about the audience and the effect the text should have on readers.

The range of individual purposes is broad but not limitless. Within professional groups, there are three categories of rhetorical purpose: *traditional, innovative,* and *confrontational.* It is common to think of scientists, for example, as people who typically write to create knowledge and then use writing to disseminate it. In such instances, we find an innovative rhetorical purpose. Many scientists, however, replicate experiments to validate work others have performed. They do not create knowledge but rather confirm it. In these instances, we find a traditional rhetorical purpose. Scientists who attempt to overturn established conclusions may be said to have a confrontational rhetorical purpose. In some texts, we may see various combinations of rhetorical purpose, but usually one dominates.

The social-theoretic model is elegant and powerful because it describes accurately the various factors associated with real writing. People do participate in discourse communities, and these communities do determine to a significant degree the "what" and "how" of writing. However, the composing students do in school is usually far removed from real writing, so in practice we see the notion of discourse community applied to students only in marginal ways. True, students belong to several communities, the most obvious one being that of "students," but these groups are amorphous and inclusive, whereas the discourse communities described by the social-theoretic model, like those in WAC, are discrete and exclusive.

In response, some teachers have proposed that the classroom itself is a discourse community. This proposal, however, is based on a misunderstanding of the social-theoretic model, specifically that a discourse community is merely a group of people sharing common experiences (the class). Real communities are complex and are defined by more than the shared experiences of their members. The only theoretically congruent efforts at building a discourse community in the classroom are those that engage students in role playing. For example, a class might take on the role of a business, with groups of students assigned specific roles within that business, such as marketing, accounting, and personnel. But this sort of role playing doesn't work very well at the public school level because it requires a commitment on the part of students to participate. High absenteeism and lack of discipline in the public schools work against such efforts. Furthermore, role-playing activities seldom account for a key factor in the social-theoretic model—individual motivation to become a member of a given discourse community. True, some students, especially by the time they reach college, know what they want to do professionally as adults, which should allow them to assume the role of insider and thereby practice the conventions that govern written discourse in that field. But the suggestion that all students, whether in college or high school, know "what they want to be" should be considered cautiously, and teachers should be concerned about the viability of getting students to take on the role of insider when students have little knowledge or understanding of what constitutes insider status.

POSTMODERN RHETORIC

Postmodern rhetoric began to emerge around 1985. I attended a conference that year at which several presenters argued that new rhetoric lacked any viable theory, and they argued that rhetoric and composition should turn to literary criticism for legitimate theoretical foundations. At about this time, postmodern approaches to literature, particularly deconstruction, were very popular (and had been for several years), and these approaches quickly were applied to rhetoric.

Many factors gave rise to postmodern rhetoric, and it is not possible to examine all of them here. A few, however, stand out as being particularly important. For example, this approach seems linked to the long-standing tension between rhetoric and composition specialists on the one hand and literature specialists on the other. Chapter 1 examined the debate over whether rhetoric is an art or a science and noted that literature faculty successfully positioned literary scholarship as a *Wissenschaft*. From the perspective of higher education, these faculty created knowledge, whereas their rhetoric and composition counterparts did not. But matters became quite complicated when new rhetoric adopted the methods of the social sciences and suddenly laid claim to *Wissenschaft* status.

In record time, from about 1975 to 1985, more than two dozen graduate programs in rhetoric were organized and implemented, and projections indicated that, by 1990, new hires in rhetoric and composition would outnumber those in literature. A hot job market and institutional validity bestowed by the growing doctoral programs made the future look bright, and the confidence of new rhetoricians soared. One consequence of this confidence was that composition specialists on many campuses began efforts (followed by very few successes) to divorce writing programs from English departments.

But it soon became apparent that the future was not so bright, after all. Many people had chosen to ignore the fact that most of the graduate programs in rhetoric and composition required students to take numerous courses in literature. The requirement had been a compromise with literature faculty in most instances, necessary to gain support for the new programs, and few in composition recognized that it was a poison pawn. Departments frequently used the concentration in rhetoric and composition—and the hot job market for composition specialists—to recruit students whose primary interest was literature, not rhetoric.[9] These students finished their degrees and took jobs as composition specialists, but what they really wanted to do was teach literature. They wrote dissertations that had the term *rhetoric* in the titles but that nonetheless were exercises in literary criticism. Students without much interest in literature were frequently pressured into writing dissertations with a literary emphasis, and it was understood that they had to align themselves with literature faculty in one way or another. In addition, owing to their greater numbers, literature faculty could increase the literature requirement essentially at will, weakening the graduate programs in rhetoric in the process.

---

[9]The job market also motivated many people trained in literature to embark on quick reeducation programs—they read the most popular works in rhetoric and composition and then advertised themselves as composition specialists. At UCLA in the late 1970s, Dick Lanham developed the University Writing Programs as a place where, under his tutelage through occasional workshops, PhDs in literature could teach writing while engaged in such reeducation. To be fair, it must be said that many of those who retooled found a real calling in rhetoric and composition and became significant contributors to the field.

The rush that accompanied the growth of rhetoric and composition during this period was quickly followed by dismay in the face of the hard realities of campus politics. Deans and provosts, no doubt encouraged by English departments and seeing an opportunity to add to the bottom line, generally refused to grant full programmatic status to independent writing programs. Teachers would not be tenured faculty but rather adjuncts and/or graduate teaching assistants, all of whom could be hired to teach composition at a fraction of the cost of a full-time, tenure-track faculty member. Yes, many new graduates, doctorates in hand, were being hired all over the country, but in nearly all instances these new hires did not add to a critical mass of composition scholars, nor did they form the foundation of an institutional effort to develop a rhetoric and composition faculty. Instead, they assumed administrative or quasi-administrative roles as directors of writing programs and writing centers; they trained and supervised adjuncts and graduate teaching assistants; and they served as a resource for literature faculty forced to teach composition. In many cases, a writing program would have a director with a PhD in rhetoric and composition who supervised teachers whose training was entirely in literature. In other cases, the new hires were those who had concentrated in rhetoric but who actually wanted to teach literature—the manqué compositionists. Their goal, usually implicit, was to reverse the direction of new rhetoric and to make the study of rhetoric and composition more like the study of literature, which by 1985 had taken a turn toward sociopolitical issues. Thus, from a political perspective that considers the level of control over funding, hiring, promotions, institutional influence, and so forth, rhetoric and composition faculty were in a very vulnerable position made even more tenuous by the fact that so many composition courses were being taught by literature faculty or graduate students who were striving to find places for themselves in literature, not rhetoric.

Another important factor in the development of postmodern rhetoric was English department infatuation, which began in the mid-1970s, with modern French philosophy. The focus of this infatuation were the works of Jacques Derrida, Michel Foucault, and Jacques Lacan, who were instrumental in developing postmodernism.

Raschke (1996) defined postmodernism as everything that "cannot be compressed in the term *modern*" (p. 2), but what exactly does that mean? More than a set of fixed ideas, modernism implies an attitude, a method of thought. On a broad level, the attitude can be described as an abiding self-confidence in the steady progress of Western civilization; the inherent superiority of Western science, technology, social structures, and political systems; the value of formal education; and the value of high culture, represented in standard works of literature, classical music and opera, and art. The method of thought in modernism is dominated by empiricism and rationalism, with special status given to the scientific approach. Although modernism's roots extend to the 18th century, it gained impetus during the early 1900s, until as Docker (1994) noted, it "flowered into a great aesthetic movement, challenging and transforming every received art form, from literature and music to painting and architecture" (p. xviii).

Postmodernism is essentially the antithesis of modernism. It not only devalues all that modernism holds dear but also insists on finding significant political issues in every facet of life. Early converts in the United States borrowed much of their political perspective from Herbert Marcuse, a popular philosopher during the 1960s who advocated leftist politics and who was a severe critic of Western (especially American) society.[10] Marcuse blended Marxism with Freudian psychoanalytic theories and reached the conclusion that Western society is corrupt and repressive. In *Eros and Civilization* (1955) and *One-Dimensional Man* (1964), he argued that in the West the "ruling classes" have established scarcity in lands of plenty by deliberately withholding resources, goods, and services from "subject populations" so as to keep them deprived, downtrodden, and miserable.

Western society, insofar as it is defined as the prevailing traditions and institutions that are deemed to be of historical significance, is fundamentally evil, according to Marcuse, and must be overturned by any means necessary. For example, in 1965, he argued that only those with left-wing views should be afforded the right of free speech. This right should be denied to those with incorrect thoughts by invoking the "natural right" of "oppressed and overpowered minorities to use extralegal means" to silence opposing points of view. The similarity between these sentiments and the political correctness that now dominates American society, especially college campuses, is not mere coincidence. As Seidman (1994) indicated, "the idea of . . . postmodernity has been advanced largely by Western, mostly academic, intellectuals, many of whom are connected to the social rebellions of the sixties and seventies" (p. 2).

---

[10]Seeking refuge from Nazism, Marcuse immigrated to the United States from Germany in 1934. Although later he often seemed to urge the overthrow of the American government, he worked, ironically, for various intelligence agencies during World War II. Postmodern thought is deeply indebted to Marcuse, who introduced the ideal of "transcendence" into his social theory in *Reason and Revolution,* published in 1941. He argued that personal "liberation" involved transcending the archaic social traditions that keep people alienated and unhappy, a thought that has become doctrine in postmodernism.

The antifoundationalism of the 1960s significantly informs post-modernism, giving it a radical—some might even say revolutionary—edge. As it emerged, postmodernism rejected high culture in favor of popular culture, eschewing *Hamlet* for *Frasier,* Mozart for Michael Jackson, Socrates for Bart Simpson. If in modernism all the world's a stage, in postmodernism all the world's a spontaneous carnival, but much less fun (see Eco, Ivanov, & Rector, 1984, for a discussion of the "festive" elements of postmodernism). Although often predicated as "play," the postmodern carnival has a dark side. As Blanding (1997) noted, "In our imagination . . . , the carnival is still the terrain of those who don't fit—of runaways and vagabond teenagers [and] down-and-outs" (p. 2). And Raschke (1996) argued that "Postmodernity is the transcendence, 'overcoming,' of all archaic or 'legendary' orders of significance that have underwritten cultural discourse" (p. 2). In other words, an important goal of postmodernism is to overturn established values, principles, and ways of thinking, which are held in contempt (Norris, 1993; Seidman, 1994).

One factor in this goal is the postmodern perception that modernism insists on assuming a unity in the world where none exists. Instead, society is deemed to be fragmented, chaotic. With regard to language, especially texts, this perception leads to the conclusion that "meaning" does not exist. This position has been most vigorously advanced as *deconstruction,* a philosophical method of inquiry developed by Jacques Derrida.

Defining deconstruction is difficult, even for Derrida. When asked to provide a definition in an interview, he stated (Caputo, 1996): "It is impossible to respond. . . . I can only do something which will leave me unsatisfied. . . . I often describe deconstruction as something which happens. It's not purely linguistic, involving text or books. You can deconstruct gestures, choreography. That's why I enlarged the concept of text" (p. 17). Scholars who have interpreted Derrida have had an equally difficult time. James Faulconer (1998), for example, stated:

> Some words are their own worst enemies. *Deconstruction* is one of them. . . . Coined, more or less, by the contemporary French philosopher, Jacques Derrida, the word *deconstruction* began its life in the late sixties, but it has only become part of the American vocabulary in the last ten years or so. In that time, however, it has moved from a technical philosophical term adopted by literary critics for their related uses to a word that pops up in offhand remarks by everyone from botanists to the clergy. Whatever its original meaning, in its now widespread use, deconstruction has come to mean "tear down" or "destroy" (usually when the object is nonmaterial).

One of the principal features of modernism that Derrida attacked was the idea that words *signify* something, that they have meaning. A paper on *Romeo and Juliet* might argue that the play is primarily about the misfortunes that follow when people can't control their emotions and that it is not primarily about romance. In this framework, the word *romance* signifies a certain meaning; likewise, all the words together signify that the paper is an argument, that the argument reaches a certain conclusion, that the writer advocates this conclusion, and so on.

In his book *Of Grammatology,* Derrida (1976) argued that the question of meaning in writing was meaningless because there is no connection between reason and what words signify:

> The "rationality" . . . which governs a writing thus enlarged and radicalized, no longer issues from a logos. Further, it inaugurates the destruction, not the demolition but the de-sedimentation, the de-construction, of all the significations that have their source in that of the logos. Particularly the signification of *truth.* (p. 10)

Advocates of postmodern rhetoric adopted Derrida's position on meaning as a way to attack traditional notions of language and rhetoric.[11] Derrida denied in this passage (and throughout *Of Grammatology*) the existence of an objective reality, a reality that exists independent of individual acts of mentation. In Derrida's view, if words don't signify anything, determining what they mean is impossible (see Quine, 1960, and Putnam, 1975, for further discussion of signification). This indeterminacy goes beyond replacing objectivity with subjectivity because denying a link between language and logos suggests that not even the speaker or writer of given words can know what they mean. As the term *de-construction* indicates, the result is an attitude that denies the value of creating, of writing. In its place is *reading*. Deconstructive reading, however, cannot focus on what words mean, because meaning is indeterminate. Instead, it must focus on what words *do not* mean.

A perspective that denies meaning, even a subjective one, is hardly conducive to teaching students how to writer better. In *Fragments of Rationality,* Lester Faigley (1992) accurately described one consequence of deconstructionism's influence:

> By the end of the decade [the 1980s], . . . disturbing versions of deconstruction had come to composition studies, questioning the advice given

---

[11]One of the first casualties, however, was professionalism.

in composition textbooks to use thesis statements, topic sentences, head-
ings, and other cues to the reader. Such advice, from a Derridean perspective, gives writers a false sense of confidence that their meanings
can be readily intelligible, and more insidiously, teaches them to ignore
other meanings and other perspectives. (pp. 37–38)

Thus, one of the more salient features of postmodern rhetoric is that
it largely abandoned concern for what differentiates poor writers from
good ones. Indeed, it abandoned any attempt to help improve the writing of students. This position was most recently expressed in *Alt
Dis: Alternative Discourses and the Academy,* edited by Christopher
Schroeder, Patricia Bizzell, and Helen Fox (2002). This book argues
for encouraging "alternative" writing styles among students. Such alt
dis includes the emoticons (= ^. ^ =, :), :o, ^o^, etc.) and abbreviations (LOL, BRB, BTW)[12] that are used by some people in online chat
rooms, as well as alternative graphemic forms like the following,
WhIcH mAKe REadIng vERy DiFFiCuLt, eSPeciAlLY wHEn tHe
WoRDs hAVe MoRE tHaN oNe SyLlaBlE. at tHe cOnFEreNCe oN
TEaCHiNg CoMpOSiTIoN sPoNSoReD by the Southern California
Writing Program Administrators (WPA), held in the spring of 2002,
Andrea Lunsford expressed excitement and enthusiasm at the pros-
pect of seeing alt dis make its way into student papers within 5 years.
More traditional teachers argue that if the proponents of alt dis pre-
vail, students will be unfit to advance academically, and they will be
unfit for the workplace.

By abandoning the goal of improving student writing, postmodern
rhetoric drove much deeper the wedge that already separated theory
and practice in rhetoric and composition, leaving them essentially separate enterprises. Postmodern rhetoric replaced pedagogical concerns
with an abiding but ultimately naive interest in politics, as manifested
in the neo-Marxist writings of Berlin (1992a, 1992b) and others.
Owens (1994, p. 225), for example, argued that freshman composition
as a venue for teaching academic discourse should be abandoned because such discourse imposes "debilitating restrictions" on writers.
Fitts and France (1995, p. 324) opposed " 'writing' in general" and argued that it should be replaced with "cultural studies" that focus on
"cultural critique, even ideological transformation." More recently,
France (2000) argued that the lack of content in composition reduces
writing classes to worthless exercises on "skills":

---

[12]LOL = laughing out loud, which people in chat rooms seem to do quite often.
BRB = be right back. BTW = by the way.

What is there of intellectual substance in composition? Does our teaching subject, our professional claim to expert knowledge, consist merely in an ensemble of techniques adequately represented as "skills" (such as knowing how to correct or avoid dangling modifiers by embedding agency in introductory verbal phrases)? (p. 146)

Institutional realities have prevented calls for abandoning composition from having much effect on first-year writing. Colleges and universities are not about to dismantle writing programs, which not only are an expected part of the college experience but which also generate huge revenues. That so many postmodern rhetoricians ignore the politics of writing programs is, of course, highly ironic. But the calls to dismantle composition as an educational enterprise also are, or should be, disturbing. On one level, we have to recognize that the efforts of postmodern rhetoricians have been amazingly destructive. They have not killed the field of rhetoric and composition but have done something more insidious—made it irrelevant. And there is every indication that the careers of these rhetoricians have likewise become irrelevant, now mirroring those of literature faculty, their work of interest only to a coterie of insiders and of questionable significance. On another level, we have to recognize that colleges have a way of insulating themselves from the workaday world, so we expect a fair amount of idealized theorizing. Yet the ability to communicate well in writing is such a central part of our society that efforts to dismantle a program that tries, however badly, to improve this ability seems particularly out of touch with the needs of young people to succeed once they leave school. The jobs they take have required, for many years now, more writing, not less, and we can be certain that employers who assign this writing will expect it to be readable and to mean something.

POST-POSTMODERN RHETORIC

Currently, rhetoric and composition is a fragmented field. Unlike the new-rhetoric period, no one approach dominates, and both scholarship and pedagogy seem adrift, lacking direction. Many in the field appear to have adopted a perspective similar to the one Jean-Francoise Lyotard (1985) expressed in *The Postmodern Condition:* By splintering culture into a multiplicity of differences, postmodernism has had a "liberating" influence on society. This is the "liberation" that accompanies extreme individualism, however—and it has come at a high cost. In *The Great Disruption,* Fukuyama (1999) described in detail the loss of social capital, increasing levels of crime, changes in family structure, the lack of true intimacy, and the triumph of individualism over community that have characterized the postmodern period. We could easily add to this list the loss of civility, courtesy, service, and professionalism.

Lester Faigley (1992) suggested that much of the postmodern malaise should be blamed on the new globalism:

> Diminishing of spatial barriers has created a world bazaar of products to satisfy an enormous appetite for diversity in consumable form. The middle class eagerly patronizes ethnic and foreign restaurants, listens to an extraordinary range of music, watches films, and buys cars, clothing, furniture, art, and many other products from around the world. The middle class as consumers seemingly cannot get enough diversity and novelty, but the triumph of the world market economy has also changed the nature of social interaction . . . , [and] the demise of stable institutions is for the middle class the dark underside of the joys of consuming." (p. 78)

But this idea seems wide of the mark. It cannot escape anyone's notice that globalism and capitalism are functions of modernism and its belief in progress. One of the more lasting images of postmodernism is the protesters in Seattle, circa 2000, battling police as they demonstrated against a meeting of the World Trade Organization (WTO), whose primary purpose is to promote globalism. It is not America's fondness for ethnic food and German automobiles that threatens to destabilize social institutions and to fragment society but rather the postmodern attack on both.

A more accurate analysis suggests that the consumerism Faigley (1992) described is linked to post-postmodernism and the triumph of liberal democracy (see Williams, 2002). In this context, the WTO protesters are an anachronism, fighting a postmodern battle in a war that has already been lost in the post-postmodern world. The success of liberal democracy is based on its ability to provide ample material goods and sufficient recognition to keep citizens contented, if not happy. Fukuyama (1992) argued that the citizens of the Third World understand this economic reality and are generally willing, if not eager, to sacrifice their insular ways if it means increasing their standard of living. What they want are more VCRs and satellite television, not more native dress.

From this perspective, we can see that America's institutions are not unstable but rather have been reorganized in the new social order along the lines of the service sector, which, of course, provides no service. It is the ultimate oxymoron. Contrary to Faigley's (1992) claim, the only "dark side" of consumerism for consumers is the prospect of diminished buying power—and the inability to find anyone willing or able to fix our electronic gadgets when they break. In post-postmodern America, what drives people is not ideology, not activism, not politics, but economics. Some post-postmodernists, such as Jean Baudrillard (1988), embrace this pragmatic position as well as the idea that the goal in this "new utopia" of liberal democratic capitalism is to accumulate as much wealth as possible. The social implications, as Baudrillard noted, are significant:

> If utopia has already been achieved, then unhappiness does not exist, the poor are not longer credible. . . . The have-nots will be condemned to oblivion, to abandonment, to disappearance pure and simple. The ultimatum issued in the name of wealth and efficiency wipes them off the map. And rightly so, since they show such bad taste as to deviate from the general consensus. (p. 111)

"Empowerment" in a liberal democracy means something completely different from what postmodernists, trapped as they are in a neo-Marxist mind-set, assume it means. It is the right, based exclusively on one's ability, to hold down a good job, with prospects, that affords the nice house, the nice car, and weekend trips to Las Vegas. As Baudrillard (1988) noted, those who lack this ability become "disenfranchised": "You lose your rights one by one, first your job, then your car. And when your driver's license goes, so does your identity" (p. 112).

For those who find these views as distasteful as those of postmodernism, Fukuyama (1999) held out hope that we have turned a critical corner and are on the way toward a "Great Reconstruction" characterized by increased levels of social capital, reduced crime, and a greater sense of community. More and better education lies at the heart of this change. If Fukuyama is correct, we are shifting into a post-postmodern period that will require us to remove postmodernism's fossilized methodology and to develop new research programs to better inform approaches to writing.

This is likely to be difficult. In Goggin's (2000) assessment, we now see a separation of the "activities of knowing from those of doing" (p. 201), in part because a "multidimensional construct" of rhetoric that would combine research, theory, and pedagogy "has been unable to find a stable home within most departments of English and within higher education more generally" (p. 201). On this account, Fleming (2002) argued convincingly that "the two-pronged project of composition-rhetoric seems to have stalled" (p. 114). And again, Fleming:

> Though the relation between teaching and research is tense in every discipline, in composition-rhetoric, it is, I believe, especially unstable and

becoming more so. In the field, there is often a literal separation between the two projects, with part-timers, adjuncts, graduate students, community college teachers, and women shouldering a disproportionate load of "composition," while tenure-track professors at research universities do most of the "rhetoric." This causes problems on both sides: The teachers complain about the irrelevance of theory and research to their day-to-day work; the researchers complain about the inexorable pull of pedagogy in what should be an epistemic enterprise. (p. 114)

Nowhere is this separation more visible than in the professional journals. A review of the literature of the last 5 years indicates that rhetoric has become all about theorizing and dissecting sociopolitical contexts, whereas composition has lapsed once again into anecdotes separated from real research and meaningful theory. Thus we find, as noted earlier, that the number of conference papers published in *College Composition and Communication* that merely offer reports of successful teaching experiences has increased dramatically since 1989. In addition, as the influence of postmodern rhetoric has faded, the rhetoric of science, feminist rhetoric, and workplace rhetoric have emerged as important strands in the field. But these strands focus almost entirely on research. They have no pedagogical component. What has happened, then, to the question that was at the heart of rhetoric's renaissance in the 1960s: How do we improve students' writing?

Many people in rhetoric and composition now argue that this question cannot be answered and that debates about influences and methodologies are useless, which may explain the quiescence that also characterizes the field today. The literature of the last 5 years suggests that those who identify themselves as new rhetoricians, romantic rhetoricians, postmodern rhetoricians, and so on have reached détente. It is rare to find an article actually exploring whether one methodology is better than another at improving students' skills. In fact, the entire issue of improving students' writing is seldom addressed. There simply are no articles in any of the major rhetoric and composition journals that consider the continuing decline in students' writing as documented in the last three NAEP reports. These reports indicate that all the efforts in research, theory, and pedagogy not only have failed to improve student writing but also have failed even to stem the tide of decline. They should be setting off alarms nationwide. Instead, it is as though this huge problem doesn't exist.

Ironically, the research published over the last 5 years deals primarily with public school writing, not college writing. As recently as 1995, the situation was reversed. Quite striking is the fact that this research focuses on small groups of students or individuals, which severely limits the usefulness of the findings because they are not generalizable.

Moreover, few articles published during the last 5 years deal with writing performance. They focus, instead, on social issues and contexts, which teachers generally cannot influence or control and which, therefore, have questionable value to classroom teachers, who may always have seen such scholarship as irrelevant.

At the public school level, the situation has become particularly acute because the "research" conducted by "rhetoricians" has, over the last dozen years, moved further and further away from the realities of teaching young people how to communicate. The typical K–12 teacher isn't paid very much but nevertheless finds great value in making a contribution to society by educating young people. The gratification that comes from making a contribution makes the low pay bearable, even in the face of heavy teaching loads at the junior and senior high levels that result in working with about 150 rambunctious students each day. It is therefore easy to understand why so many public school teachers have little patience with college professors of rhetoric who argue not only that the composition class should be a place to subvert the very institution that provides professional and personal validation but also that the enterprise of teaching writing is absurd. If the separation of rhetorical research and theory from composition pedagogy continues in this post-postmodern period, it seems certain that rhetoric in the broad sense will shift from its current "stalled" status to a moribund state. Quite simply, writing pedagogy without research and theory has no legitimacy. By the same token, rhetorical research and theory without pedagogy is empty and, ultimately, meaningless.

JOURNAL ENTRY

Preparing to Teach Writing argues steadily that writing instruction should focus on helping students meet the demands of writing in content-area courses and the workplace and that most writing instruction is not oriented toward this goal. What is your position on the goal of writing instruction? What is your position on the pragmatic goal of helping students write in content-area courses and the workplace?

Best Practices

HOW DO WE TEACH WRITING EFFECTIVELY?

Rhetoric and composition experienced a significant shift away from ped-agogy after the mid-1980s as the field immersed itself in social issues and cultural studies. Romantic rhetoric, for example, aims to give stu-dents opportunities to engage in self-expressive writing, and as Hillocks (2002) suggested, its pedagogical focus is on getting students to see more clearly the world around them and to describe and share their feel-ings; there is little attention to audience, rhetoric, or structure because this approach privileges the writer and thereby subordinates standard writing conventions and reader expectations. Moreover, romantic rheto-ric commonly demonstrates hostility toward preparing students to per-form the writing tasks assigned in college or in the workplace, which anyone concerned with helping students succeed in life must view as a serious shortcoming. Postmodern rhetoric has even less interest in ped-agogical issues, rejecting the idea that writing instruction has meaning. Indeed, some advocates of postmodern rhetoric have called for the aboli-tion of composition classes and for a focus on cultural and political is-sues, a move that can be characterized not only as antieducational but also as antisocial.

The movement away from pedagogy was led primarily by faculty at large research universities who, if they teach composition at all, have very light teaching loads. In most cases, this movement has not ad-dressed or even considered the needs of teachers at smaller universi-ties, community colleges, and public schools, where the teaching loads are heavy and where unparalleled immigration since about 1980 has resulted in classrooms with ESL populations as high as 90% in many areas. If one is not teaching composition, it is easier to ignore or even dismiss the workaday reality of those who are charged with improving the writing of scores of students each week, and, for many reasons—some of which were examined in the previous chapter—scholarship in rhetoric and composition today is not positioned to offer much support to teachers in these situations. Fortunately, earlier work has already provided important insights into what works and what doesn't in the classroom, allowing us to explore much of what constitutes best practices in writing instruction.

THE PROCESS APPROACH TO COMPOSITION

The process approach has been implemented in writing classes nationwide since the late 1970s. Curriculum guides in most states include some statement about teaching writing as a process. Unfortunately, there is no evidence that this implementation has had a significant effect on student writing skills. Over the last 20 years, during which process has been integrated into instruction nationwide, all NAEP reports have shown a gradual decline in writing performance. The *NAEP 1996 Trends in Writing* report (U.S. Department of Education, 1996), the most current comparative report as of this writing, showed that holistic scores (on a 6-point scale) for fourth-grade writers changed from 2.82 in 1984 to 3.02 in 1996. This change is statistically insignificant. The percentage of run-on sentences actually increased during this period, as did the percentage of sentence fragments. The more recent *1998 NAEP Writing Report Card* (U.S. Department of Education, 1999) does not look at longitudinal data but nevertheless allows us to compare student performance as reported in the 1996 *Trends in Writing* report. The 1998 report examined results for Grades 4, 8, and 12 and found that percentages of students performing at the *basic* (below-average) level were 84, 84, and 78, respectively. The percentages of those performing at the *proficient* (average) level were 23, 27, and 22, respectively. Only 1% of students at each grade level performed at the *advanced* (above-average) level. If we compare the 1998 and the 1984 data, we find that the above-average figure is unchanged for 1998, that the average figure is lower for 1998, and that the below-average figure is higher for 1998.

As woeful as these findings are, the problem appears to lie in the implementation of process pedagogy, not in the concept itself. NAEP data indicate that when the process approach is compared to other approaches, it offers the best chance for improving students' skills. The *NAEP 1996 Trends in Writing* (U.S. Department of Education, 1996) report concluded, in fact, that "the process approach to writing, in which planning, writing, and revision through several drafts are practiced, gives students the opportunity to write more and to employ editing strategies, which in turn affords them the opportunity to improve their mastery of . . . writing conventions" (p. 34). What follows is a detailed discussion of the various features of process pedagogy and the best practices that are associated with it.

Although Janet Emig (1971) is rightly credited with originating process pedagogy in composition, it is important to recognize that the late 1960s witnessed an intellectual shift in many fields toward process, a shift grounded in "process philosophy," a worldview that identifies reality with pure process. Some of the more vivid examples come from art, where process emerged as a new voice in artistic expression. In 1976, for example, the artist Christo made headlines when he ran a nylon ribbon 18 feet high and 24 miles long across a California hillside. The artistry did not reside in two dozen miles of nylon, the art critics noted, but in the *process* of erecting the ribbon in such an unlikely place. The process movement in rhetoric and composition, therefore, can be said to reflect the spirit of the times.[1]

Prior to the advent of the process approach, writing instruction focused on a student's finished product. Certainly, a well-written paper is (or should be) a goal in all composition classes, but most other approaches to composition instruction have either negligible or uninformed pedagogical components, resulting in little real writing instruction. In the current–traditional approach, for example, the assumption is that students improve their writing by reading and discussing works of literature and by studying grammar and topics related to composition, such as "introduction," "thesis," and "transitions." Often, students are asked to follow rigid rules that are assumed to lead to good writing, such as "all paragraphs must have a topic sentence," "all essays have an introductory paragraph, three body paragraphs, and a concluding paragraph," and "all concluding paragraphs

---

[1]Postmodernism, on the other hand, is generally hostile to process, preferring performance, instead. The difference is significant. Whereas "process" connotes communication, "performance" connotes dramatics. In a postmodern performance, communication in the usual sense is not even a goal. As Raschke (1996) noted, postmodernism's aim is to tear down the notion of "language as social interaction" (p. 3). To accomplish that aim, it has redefined "logic as 'aesthetics,' . . . message as medium, communication as dramatics, . . . [and] truth as embodiment" (p. 2). One consequence is that much postmodern writing is difficult to read owing to its performance dimension, which includes putting braces and brackets around words. Another is that even after readers work their way through the peculiarities of form that hinder processing, they discover all too often that there is surprisingly little content because the "message is the medium."

reiterate the information in the introduction." But regardless of which of these rules or activities obtain, the "instruction" remains rooted in the *form* of writing, with unhappy results. Applying rigid rules, studying grammar or composition topics, or reading works of literature does not improve student writing. How wonderful if good writing *could* be reduced to a recipe. Students would just put the necessary ingredients together and have a readable paper.

Instruction in the process-oriented classroom is different. First, it is top-down, not bottom-up, which means that the focus is on producing entire papers, not on grammar or parts of papers. Perhaps more important, however, is that process instruction aims to modify student behaviors to match those of good writers; it does not concentrate on form or rules or literature. These behaviors, identified through observations, interviews, and analyses of good writers at work, are consolidated as the following various "stages" of composing:

- Invention (or prewriting).
- Planning.
- Drafting.
- Pausing.
- Reading.
- Revising.
- Editing.
- Publishing.

It is important to note here that the stages are hypothesized as universals. That is, every writer is assumed to engage in these stages to some degree. However, the process approach recognizes that writing is a very personal activity in numerous respects, which means not only that there are many behaviors that are not universal but also that there is variation within the universals. Thus, invention may take the form of discussion, brainstorming, outlining, and so forth, depending on a given writer's preference and, no doubt, on the writing task at hand.

Student-Centered Instruction

One of the more significant innovations of the process approach is based on the realization that the key to improving student writing consists of three factors: (a) asking students to write often, in meaningful contexts, (b) providing frequent feedback on work in progress, and (c) requiring numerous revisions based on that feedback. Again, the NAEP data pro-

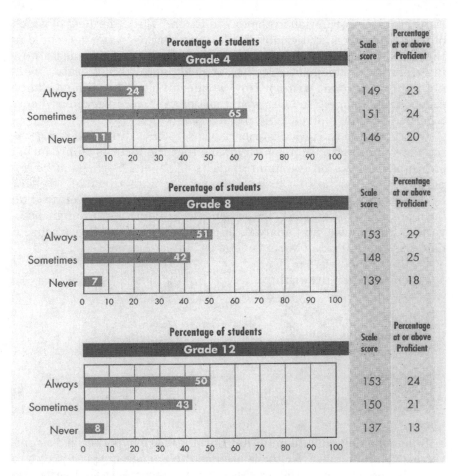

FIG. 3.1. Students' reports on the frequency with which their teachers talk to them about what they are writing: 1998. Percentages may not add to 100 due to rounding. From U.S. Department of Education (1999).

vide compelling insights. As Fig. 3.1 shows, with the exception of Grade 4, performance improves when teachers talk to students about their writing, which is a factor in providing a meaningful context.[2] Figure 3.2 shows, again with the exception of Grade 4, that performance improves when teachers ask for more than one draft of a paper.

In the 1970s, rhetoric and composition as a field adopted a reorganization of writing classes as "writing workshops" in which students

---

[2]The NAEP scale score is based on a total of 300 and a mean of 150. Thus, a student with a scale score of 150 is writing at the average level.

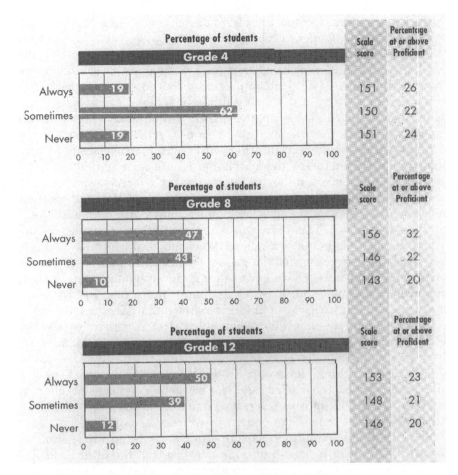

FIG. 3.2. Students' reports on the frequency with which their teachers ask them to write more than one draft of a paper: 1998. Percentages may not add to 100 due to rounding. From U.S. Department of Education (1999).

share their work with one another and teachers intervene regularly as students develop compositions through several drafts. The writing workshop was, and continues to be, seen fairly widely as the most effective way to deliver the three factors listed previously.

To turn a classroom into a workshop, teachers abandon traditional rows of desks and create work groups in which students arrange their desks in small circles. Each work group usually consists of five members. These groups become collaborative teams in which students help one another succeed. The teacher's role in the workshop largely is one of coach or facilitator. As students practice the behaviors that characterize good writers, the teacher offers advice and suggestions that not only guide the drafting or revising process but also model for students the way to read and comment on a text. Activities focus on writing, discussing drafts, and rewriting—not on grammar exercises or discussions of literature. Thus, in the process-oriented class, students do a great deal of writing and revising in class. When discussions of published texts occur, and they do, the texts are not literary but rather are expository works that illustrate how to deal with a topic or ways to solve rhetorical problems. In other words, reading professional texts aims to provide rhetorical models that students can use to develop the discourse and genre familiarity necessary for effective writing.

Language arts classes, of course, are not composition classes. Language arts teachers must engage students in many different activities in addition to writing. This point, although well taken, does not detract from the effectiveness of workshops. Workshops can form the foundation of a class regardless of the lesson or unit. The goal is to use the small work groups to get students talking, thinking, and writing about the given lesson, whether it be on writing or literature. In fact, workshops offer an effective way of linking reading and writing activities.[3]

One result of the workshop approach is that it provides students with the means to assume a more active role in learning. Members of work groups are always busy talking, writing, thinking, researching. Unlike the traditional classroom, in which students assume a passive role as they listen to teacher-talk, the workshop requires teachers to say very little. This approach is referred to as *student-centered instruction,* and it is a central component of process pedagogy.

Educators have paid lip service to student-centered instruction for so many years that it has become a buzzword that too often is misunderstood and misapplied. Large numbers of teachers and administrators, for example, assume that student-centered instruction means simply putting students' concerns and welfare first. This perspective should immediately raise our suspicions, for what teacher would want to put them second or third or fourth? Others characterize student-centered instruction merely as individualized pedagogy. Both conceptualizations are inaccurate. Student-centered instruction actually is quite specific and, for most teachers, a challenge to implement. It consists of shifting the focus of classroom activities from the teacher to the students.

Observations of language arts classrooms have for years shown that our schools employ a very traditional delivery system. Teachers talk,

---

[3]The study of literature, however, should *not* be linked to writing instruction unless it is part of a fully developed WAC program. See chapter 2.

and students supposedly listen. Even when teachers believe that they do not lecture, they often do. For example, when Nystrand et al. (1997) studied a large sample of eighth and ninth graders, they found that teacher-talk dominated the classes they observed. Many participating teachers insisted that their classes were "discussion based," yet Nystrand et al. observed that discussions actually averaged less than *a minute per day per class*. In the few classes in which teachers encouraged dialogic interactions and asked authentic questions rather than questions that served merely to test knowledge, there were higher levels of achievement.

Student-centered instruction also involves using a variety of activities as well as a classroom structure, such as a workshop, that allows and, indeed, encourages student interactions. With regard to composition, activities consist of tasks associated with the composing process. To facilitate invention, for example, a teacher might direct students to brainstorm in their groups for a period of 10 minutes; at the end of this period, each group would report its results, thereby producing a whole-class discussion. Or consider editing. Students exchange papers with their groupmates, and then the teacher might direct them to identify prepositional phrases to reduce nominalization or to combine sentences to increase sentence variety. In all cases, the focus of the class shifts from the teacher to the students and their work. Students are actively engaged in learning, and the talk in the room is student-talk, not teacher-talk. As a general guideline for a truly student-centered classroom, teacher-talk should not exceed 15 minutes in a 50-minute class.

Teacher as Coach

As with most other complex skills, people bring any number of bad habits or poorly learned techniques to the writing process. Weak writers, for example, have a tendency to assume that the only reader of their essays will be the teacher, who already knows what the topic is, so they fail to identify the topic explicitly in their texts. Many of these writers also learned a variety of myths associated with writing that hinder them whenever they compose. For example, they may believe that they cannot begin a sentence with a coordinating conjunction: *and, but, for, nor, or, yet.* They may believe that they cannot use the personal pronoun *I* or end a sentence with a preposition or use contractions. And when more knowledgeable teachers try to help them overcome these myths, the writers may resist.

In most cases, students will adopt more effective writing behaviors when they are encouraged and corrected on the spot. Advocates of the process model therefore propose that effective teachers think of themselves as coaches in a workshop environment. Coaches intervene regularly in the learning process, immediately correcting those things students do wrong and praising those things they do right, giving reinforcement when it is most useful and most beneficial. When teaching writing, the same principles apply. In practical terms, such intervention requires that teachers ask students to produce multiple drafts of an assignment. Class time is devoted to revising drafts on the basis of feedback that the teacher as well as fellow students provide.

Stages of the Composing Process

The process model proposes that a finished paper is the result of the complex interaction of activities that include several stages of development (see Table 3.1). Not every writing task passes through every stage, however. In some situations, a writer may not have an opportunity to do much planning, or an editor may be responsible for editing. Nevertheless, these stages are believed to reflect in a general way how successful writing develops.

TABLE 3.1
Stages of Writing

Writing Process	Definition	Description
Prewriting	Generating ideas, strategies, and information for a given writing task.	Prewriting activities take place before starting on the first draft of a paper. They include *discussion, outlining, freewriting, journals, talk-write,* and *metaphor.*
Planning	Reflecting on the material produced during prewriting to develop a plan to achieve the aim of the paper.	Planning involves considering your rhetorical stance, rhetorical purpose, the principal aim of the text, how these factors are interrelated, and how they are connected to the information generated during prewriting. Planning also involves selecting support for your claim and blocking out at least a rough organizational structure.

(Continued)

TABLE 3.1
(Continued)

Writing Process	Definition	Description
Drafting	Producing words on a computer or on paper that match (more or less) the initial plan for the work.	Drafting occurs over time. Successful writers seldom try to produce an entire text in one sitting or even in one day.
Pausing	Moments when you aren't writing but instead are reflecting on what you have produced and how well it matches your plan. Usually includes reading.	Pausing occurs among successful and unsuccessful writers, but they use it in different ways. Successful writers consider "global" factors: how well the text matches the plan, how well it is meeting audience needs, and overall organization.
Reading	Moments during pausing when you read what you've written and compare it to your plan.	Reading and writing are interrelated activities. Good readers are good writers and vice versa. The reading that takes place during writing is crucial to the reflection process during pausing.
Revising	Literally "re-seeing" the text with the goal of making large-scale changes so that text and plan match.	Revising occurs after you've finished your first draft. It involves making changes that enhance the match between plan and text. Factors to consider usually are the same as those you considered during planning: rhetorical stance, rhetorical purpose, and so on. *Serious revising almost always includes getting suggestions from friends or colleagues on how to improve the writing.*
Editing	Focusing on sentence-level concerns, such as punctuation, sentence length, spelling, agreement of subjects and predicates, and style.	Editing occurs after revising. The goal is to give your paper a professional appearance.
Publishing	Sharing your finished text with its intended audience.	Publishing isn't limited to getting a text printed in a journal. It includes turning a paper in to a teacher, a boss, or an agency.

107

Invention

Invention activities (also known as prewriting activities) help writers generate ideas, strategies, information, and approaches for a given writing task. They are processes that engage the mind with the writing task at hand. From this perspective, invention, in its broadest sense, is the *thinking* and *reflecting* good writers do before they start composing.

The sections that follow describe some of the more effective ways to stimulate student thinking about a topic. It is important to stress that there is not one best way to go about invention. What works well for some students doesn't work so well for others; what works well for one assignment will not work well for another. Some writers use various combinations of invention activities, whereas others are committed to only one. Students should experiment to determine what works best for them.

Discussion.   Discussion provides multiple points of view on a given topic. Teachers usually initiate the discussion by asking the class questions regarding how to proceed. Discussions tend to be most helpful when they occur a day or so after students receive an assignment. The time in between allows students to begin formulating a plan that they can modify and enrich through the discussion. Teachers should urge students to listen as well as contribute and perhaps to jot down notes.

Following is a checklist of questions that students can use to stimulate and guide discussions. Although they are not comprehensive, the questions illustrate the kind of thinking that is part of an effective discussion.

Outlining.   Outlines can be a very beneficial invention device if used properly. Too often, however, the focus is on the *structural details* of the outline rather than its content. That is, students spend much effort deciding whether an A must have a B; whether a primary heading begins with a Roman numeral or an upper-case letter; whether a secondary heading begins with a lowercase letter, a lowercase Roman numeral, or an Arabic numeral, and so on.

Such details aren't important. Outlines begin when writers list the major points they want to address in their papers, without worrying much about order. They become more useful when they acquire more features. In other words, outlines start with *general* points and shift to *specific* ones. It is worth noting, however, that *outlines appear to work most effectively when writers use them to generate ideas about topics and theses that they've already decided on.*

DISCUSSION CHECKLIST

✓ Who is the audience for this paper?

✓ What am I trying to do in this assignment? Interpret? Explain? Analyze? Compare and contrast? Am I writing a term paper that reflects everything I learned during the semester? Am I writing a paper that applies a single principle studied during class? Am I writing a research paper that demonstrates my ability to identify and interpret leading work in the field?

✓ What effect am I trying to produce in those who read my paper? Am I writing as an insider or an outsider? Do I want to show the audience that I understand the topic? Do I want the audience to understand the topic better? Do I want the audience to accept my point of view?

✓ What point or message do I want to convey?

✓ How should I begin?

✓ Where will I get information about my topic? Through library research? Through experience? Through background reading?

✓ When explaining a point in the paper, what kind of examples should I use? How will the examples work to make my paper more readable, informative, or convincing?

✓ If I make a claim in the paper, how do I support it? On the basis of experience? By citing authorities? On the basis of reason? On the basis of emotion?

✓ What's the most effective way to organize the paper, to make sure that the various parts fit together well?

✓ What should the conclusion do?

Freewriting. Freewriting, popularized by Peter Elbow (1973), draws on the perception that, when present too early, concerns about audience, aims, organization, and structure can keep writers from fully exploring potential ideas and meanings for topics. Freewriting is intended to force writers to set such concerns aside while they consider potential ideas. The main goal is to discover things to say about a topic rather than to plan the paper.

This technique involves writing nonstop for 5, 10, or 15 minutes. During this period, students keep generating words, even if they cannot think of anything meaningful to say. The rationale is that, eventually, they will begin producing ideas that they can develop later into an effective paper. Sometimes freewriting is combined with an activity called *looping,* in which students stop freewriting after 5 minutes and reread what they've produced. If they find a good idea on the page, they use it as the basis for another freewriting period, repeating the process for about 15 minutes.

The freewriting sample that follows was produced by Amy, a high school student who had to write a history paper about the Civil War:

Freewriting Sample

[1] I have to write a paper about the civil war, but I don't know much about the civil war yet. I'm only a sophomore so how am I supposed to know anything about it? But the teacher says I have to write the paper and that I can find out information about the war in the library. I hate going to the library—it's so full of books! I feel helpless. How can anyone expect me to know as much as the people who wrote books, for goodness sake. Maybe I can fake it and not really go to the library. This is dumb. I'd much rather be at the lake, but what does my teacher care. He isn't interested in how hard it is to write and how boring the civil war is. I mean, who cares? Seems to me that the whole thing was a mess, so many people dying. Hey, how did I remember that? Oh, yeah, my teacher talked about the civil war in class one day. What did he say? Something like 600,000 people died in the war, more than in any other war in American history.

[2] Hmmm. I wonder about that. I mean, everyday I hear about how the country is so racist and everything, but if America is such a racist place, why did so many white soldiers fight and die to end slavery? That doesn't make sense, does it?

[3] That might make for an interesting paper, though. I remember grandma telling me that her grandfather fought in the war. I wonder if I could work that in. See, I just don't know enough! I guess I have to go the library after all.

Journals. Journals are like diaries: Each entry has a way of helping students reflect on their experiences. They are places where students can filter and process ideas in private. One of the more effective ways to help students plan writing tasks is to have them keep a reading journal, in which they record their reactions to all the reading they do, assessing texts, summarizing their main points, linking them to one another and to ideas. Many teachers encourage students to use their journals as the starting place for writing because it will contain not only a wealth of information but also their reactions to and interpretations of this information, which are central to success as a writer.

Following is an excerpt from a journal that Steve kept for his high school English class in which students were reading *Moby Dick:*

Journal Sample

[1] Ok, I've read so much of this book and it's tough. People don't talk this way. These sentences go on forever. Why in the world do I have to read this thing? How

could anyone think this book is a great work? And the teacher said that the whale was symbolic. Symbolic of what? I guess that's what I'm supposed to figure out. Well, the whale is pretty evil. It ate Ahab's leg and now Ahab wants to kill it no matter what. It's like he's a force for good or something, out to destroy evil. Yeah. And Melville made the whale white to confuse people because white usually is linked to good. But in this case it's linked to evil.

Talk-Write. Another prewriting activity is based on the perception that speaking, listening, reading, writing, and thinking are intimately related and mutually reinforcing. It also is based on the idea that if students can explain a concept or an operation to someone they probably understand it pretty well.

Talk-write involves asking students to construct a plan mentally and to deliver an oral composition to the class. The goal is to have students develop a plan that is as complete as possible, with minimal reliance on writing. Generally, they have a short time for planning—about 20 minutes. They may jot down a few notes initially, but when they deliver the oral composition, they must do so without using any notes. After they finish, classmates provide suggestions and comments designed to help improve and elaborate the plan. The next step is for students to begin writing, using what they learned from their presentation to develop a first draft of the assignment.

An advantage of talk-write as an invention activity is that it forces students to develop fairly elaborate plans very quickly and to internalize their details. The writing itself is usually easier as a result, and it also tends to be more successful. Researchers account for this consequence in fairly complicated terms that come down to a simple principle: A person has to understand a topic to explain it to others. A valuable fringe benefit is that making such oral presentations is likely to increase one's self-confidence about speaking in public (see Zoellner, 1968).

Another version of talk-write consists of having students use a tape recorder to compose a paper orally. They then transcribe the recording to produce a written draft. This technique is particularly beneficial for a special category of students. For reasons that are not very clear, some native speakers of English cannot readily write grammatical sentences. Many people might find this statement amusing because they assume that this is *the* problem with all student writers, but they would be mistaken. The situation is unusual for three reasons. First, nearly all of the problems writing teachers identify at the sentence level as being "grammatical" are not—they are *usage* problems (see Williams, 1999, for a full discussion of the difference between problems of grammar and problems of usage). From a linguistic perspective, for example, the sentence *Fritz and me are going to the movies* is not ungrammatical but reflects a problem in usage—the subject pronoun *me* is in the objective case rather than the nominative, or subject, case. A truly ungrammatical sentence is one that violates English word-order patterns, as in *Fritz the movies and me to are going.* Second, with a few notable exceptions, native speakers of any language do not produce truly ungrammatical sentences unless they consciously try to do so. And third, these students are fully capable of creating grammatical sentences when speaking, although they often use a restricted register, which means that they have a very limited vocabulary and thus have a hard time dealing with abstract concepts and using language precisely. If asked to tell someone what *Romeo and Juliet,* for example, is about, such a student is likely to offer few, if any, details but might describe the play as a love story with "lots of romance, fighting, and *stuff." Stuff* and *things* are two words that figure prominently in the language of these students.

The grammatical problems in their writing are unusual in that they are not like the example of a truly ungrammatical sentence shown previously. Instead, the ungrammaticality is of a different order. The most common problem is that these students tend to link two clauses together that have no real connection, as in the sentences that follow, taken from a student paper on censorship written in a first-year college composition class:

1. Censorship is usually something the right wants to do, and burning books transcends the parents who should control what children read.
2. If parents pay more attention to what their children read, political correctness has gotten out of control.
3. The harmony alleviates when nice people do dumb things because of the good that comes from the enforcement of politically correct thinking into a society of discrimination that Hentoff is a liberal so it must have been painful for him to write.

As these sentences also illustrate, another problem for these students is their use of words that carry no meaning in the context of the work. In Sentence 1, "burning books *transcends* the parents" means nothing. The same is true in Sentence 3, "The harmony *alleviates.*"

Asking such students in conference what they mean in sentences like these isn't helpful because they commonly state that they don't really know. Indeed, reading the students' problematic sentences aloud always evokes a similar response: They express surprise that they wrote something that makes no sense to them. They often will check the sentence on the page to ensure that the teacher read it correctly.

Particularly interesting is that when asked what they wanted to say in a given sentence, these students can produce something orally that is both grammatical and relevant to the task at hand, although, again, it may be in restricted register. This response is what makes talk-write with a tape recorder so potentially beneficial. When they produce an outline to ensure some measure of organization and then *talk* about a topic, these students show significant improvement, with far fewer ungrammatical sentences and inappropriate words. With a working draft in hand that is readable, teachers then can help a student revise and edit in meaningful ways.

Metaphor. The last invention activity discussed here is one that isn't often considered in examinations of prewriting. *Metaphor is a description in which one thing is compared to another.* Following are some simple metaphors that illustrate how the comparison works:

- The car was a lemon.
- The party was a bomb.
- Fred was a real animal.
- The outgoing governor was a lame duck.
- Rita sure is a hothead.

Many discussions of metaphor suggest that it is merely a figurative use of language that helps writers create special images. In this view, metaphor is a feature of style. However, metaphor can be a powerful model-building device that helps students generate ideas and information. Metaphor includes comparisons such as those just mentioned, but it also includes *metaphorical language,* that is, statements that use imagery without the formal comparison associated with true metaphors. For example, consider the following sentences:

- The day I came home from my vacation, several science projects greeted me when I opened the refrigerator.
- It was raining cats and dogs.
- Fritz insisted that he wasn't thin, really, but when he stripped to his swim trunks at Macarena's pool party, I decided that Webster's Dictionary needed to add a new entry under the definition of "toothpick."
- Historians have described American Indians in one of two ways—as noble tribesmen living in harmony with nature on the one hand, or

as vicious brutes caught up in perpetual warfare with their neighbors and then the white settlers on the other—and neither is quite correct. In reality, American Indians were examples of evolution in action, people driven to the brink of extinction when faced with social and technological changes that they couldn't understand, couldn't even grasp.

The novelist Richard Wright left a valuable record of how metaphor can work as an invention technique. Shortly after he published *Black Boy* in 1945, he was asked to write a short essay discussing how other autobiographical narratives had influenced his life and work. In the first draft of this essay, Wright listed a number of books that had influenced him, and then he stated that "these books were like eyeglasses, enabling me to see my environment."[4] In the second draft, Wright expanded this metaphor and changed it from "eyeglasses" to "eyes." He stated, for example, that the books that influenced him were "eyes" through which he could see the world as the authors saw it, enabling him to "understand and grasp" his own experiences. This metaphor continued in the third draft, but again there were changes. The paragraphs that show Wright's revisions illustrate how he used the metaphor to develop his thoughts.

By the time Wright got to the final draft, however, he shifted the metaphor again. Books were no longer "eyes" but "windows." The change is significant, in part because it allowed Wright to become the agent of seeing rather than the beneficiary of others' sight.

Planning

Planning is one of the more effective features of the writing process, although it also can be one of the more challenging. Useful planning involves considering a variety of questions that influence every text: Who is the audience? What is the writer's position with respect to the audience, insider or outsider? What is the aim of the paper; that is, what is it supposed to do? What is the purpose of the paper; that is, why write it? What kind of organization is most appropriate? Which writing conventions will govern the text? Does the paper require research? If so, how much and what kind?

These questions are so straightforward, obvious, and necessary to effective writing and writing instruction that they may seem trivial at

---

[4]Technically, Wright uses a *simile* when he writes "these books were like eyeglasses." Similes are a certain kind of metaphor that normally use the preposition *like* to make a comparison. Differentiating metaphors from similes doesn't appear to provide many benefits, so the term *metaphor* is used here for both.

first glance. Yet many teachers never discuss planning with their students, and most students will not even consider these questions on their own. The *1998 NAEP Writing Report Card* (U.S. Department of Education, 1999) noted, for example, that approximately 30% of teachers in Grade 8 never discussed planning with their students. A remarkable 45% of students never engaged in planning before writing, which suggests that some students failed to plan even when their teachers encouraged them to do so. The figures for Grade 12 students are almost identical. As we should expect, there were significant differences in writing performance between the groups. For eighth graders whose teachers asked students to plan before writing, the average scale score was 163.5 (out of a possible total of 300), whereas for those whose teachers did not address planning the average score was 140.5. For 12th graders, the numbers were similar, 160.5 and 141, respectively.

These figures reveal more than just the benefit of planning. They suggest that process pedagogy, pervasive though it is, has not been implemented very effectively. We have no way of knowing from the data whether all the teachers in the study were trained in the process approach, but it seems reasonable to speculate that those who lacked this training comprised less than 30% of the total. If so, then those trained teachers who did not ask students to plan before writing simply were ignoring their training. In addition, a process-oriented classroom requires teachers to structure and then monitor writing activities closely to ensure that students stay on task and follow through. The fact that 45% of students did not engage in planning suggests that many teachers who encouraged planning for writing tasks failed to provide appropriate structure and monitoring. The differences in the students' writing scores show the consequences of failing to implement process pedagogy appropriately.

Drafting

After students have generated some ideas about topics and developed a working plan, the next step is to begin writing a first draft. Several factors influence a successful drafting process. Discipline is perhaps one of the more important, so students need to be encouraged to budget their time and plan ahead. Flexibility is another factor. The downfall of many student writers is their belief that their first draft should be perfect; they spend far too much time fiddling with sentences and punctuation rather than concentrating on getting their ideas on paper. Some writers, in fact, will get a good idea while writing a draft and will worry so much about how to express the idea that it slips away or becomes strangely less appealing as the frustration level mounts. Students need to understand that early drafts don't have to be pretty or well organized or even highly readable. A first draft simply should chart the territory of the topic. It should be like a road map, marking the general direction the paper will take.

The benefit of producing more than one draft is evident from the NAEP data shown in Fig. 3.2. Although multiple drafts had no measurable effect on the writing of fourth graders, it did for eighth and 12th graders. Students in these grades who produced more than one draft had scale scores of 156 and 153, respectively, whereas students who did not had scores of 143 and 146.

In addition, students should be encouraged to use a computer for all their writing, including drafts. Computers make drafting easy for several reasons. Most people can type faster than they can write by hand, and the work is easier to read, too. Moreover, computers can check for spelling errors, so writers are freed from the worry of whether they are spelling something incorrectly. Having a typed draft is particularly important if the class is divided into work groups. People read more intelligently and efficiently when they have a typed paper rather than one written by hand. As a result, they are able to give better feedback about what works and what doesn't. Perhaps the greatest benefit, however, is that computers allow writers to move text around at will, cutting, pasting, and rewriting with ease.

These advantages seem to translate into better writing. Figure 3.3 shows the 1998 NAEP data for students who produced drafts or final versions of their papers on computers. As we have seen previously, there appears to be no effect on the writing of fourth graders, but for eighth and 12th graders using a computer resulted in significantly better scores, 151 and 155, respectively, compared to 146 and 138 for students who did not use a computer.

In the first century B.C., a Greek author named Longinus recommended that writers who were serious about their work should set a draft aside for 9 years before going back to it and making changes. His idea was that the passage of time would allow writers to see their writing more clearly and to determine whether it was worth improving. Longinus was a bit extreme in recommending a wait of 9 years, but the principle he advocated was right on target. All writers, but especially students, need to allow some time to pass before making changes.

How many drafts should students produce before a paper is finished? There's no answer to this question. Every paper is different; every paper has its own context and requirements. Sometimes a single draft will be sufficient, other times a paper may require 5, 6, or even 10

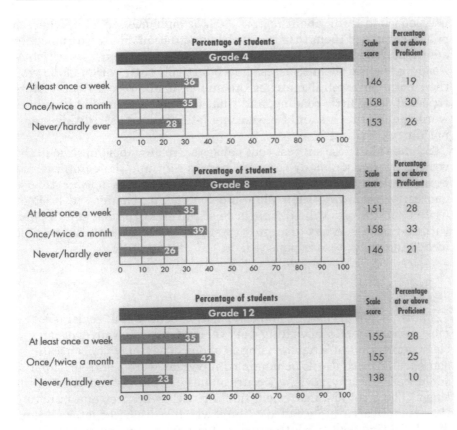

FIG. 3.3. Students' reports on the frequency with which they use a computer to write drafts or final versions of stories or reports: 1998. Percentages may not add to 100 due to rounding. From U.S. Department of Education (1999).

drafts. Unfortunately, many students assume that their first draft is their final draft. Teaching them to think otherwise is a difficult, but necessary, challenge.

Pausing and Reading

Ann Matsuhashi (1981) examined what happens when people write and saw that the scribing of her subjects (the time that they actually applied pen to paper) was interrupted frequently by pauses. Williams (1985) examined pausing in more detail and suggested that pauses are linked to thinking during writing. His data indicated that good writers use pauses to think about factors such as audience and aim, whereas poor writers use them to think about punctuation and word choice. In addition, good writers use pauses to read what they have written. Reading enables them to assess how effectively their work is following their plan, how well it matches the audience, and so on. Poor writers reported doing little reading, and what they did was limited largely to word choice, which should have come later, during the editing stage, not during writing.

Studies like these suggest that pauses serve an important role in the writing process. In many respects, pauses continue the planning that begins before students start writing. Good writers appear to use pauses for reviewing their plan and for making changes in it. Poor writers, on the other hand, appear to stick rigidly to their initial plan, with bad results. A key to improving student writing therefore may lie in helping them to use pauses more effectively.

Revising

Many people in rhetoric and composition believe that revising is the most important part of writing well, yet students generally have an unclear perception of what revising is about. They may concentrate on sentence-level concerns, changing individual words or reorganizing sentences. Actually, revising occurs on different levels and at different times. The level just described, fiddling with sentences and punctuation, is more accurately called *editing,* which is discussed later in some detail. Editing deals with the surface features of writing and is generally performed *after* a paper does what writers want it to do. Revising is more properly what writers do to the writing *before* a paper does what they want it to do.

Good writers appear to revise mentally during pauses in composing, and they tend to focus on "global" changes that are intimately linked to their audience, purpose, and stance. Revising, then, requires that writers consider their role and that of their readers in regard to the topic. In addition, effective revising depends on having knowledge about an audience's motivation for reading a paper. It requires that writers be critical readers (D. Johnson, 1993). They must be able to look at writing that has taken time and effort to produce and see it as it is, not as they wish it to be. They must be willing to cut sentences and paragraphs that don't work. They must be willing to shift sections from one place to another to enhance the overall organization of the composition. Shifting the focus of writing activities to the classroom workshop makes these difficult tasks easier to perform because it is a relatively risk-free environment where making changes in drafts is a given.

Editing and Publishing

During the invention stage, writers generate ideas, and during the planning stage they reflect on how these ideas match the goals of the paper. During the drafting stage, they put these ideas into some rough order. Then, during the revising stage, they hone organization and expression. Finally, during the editing stage, they deal with sentence-level concerns such as spelling, punctuation, and usage.

In some respects, editing is one of the harder parts of writing. One reason is that as malformed ideas about process found their way into composition pedagogy, many teachers were left with the mistaken belief that errors in form don't matter in student writing. As a result, large numbers of students simply are never taught how to edit. Another reason is that editing requires conscious effort. Most students, however, err in assuming that writing should be like speaking—essentially effortless, requiring little if any thought as to form or expression. Applying focused, conscious thought to questions of punctuation, sentence structure, word choice, and so forth is hard work that many students cannot perform consistently or easily. In addition, writers generally have trouble spotting surface errors in their own work because they tend to read for content rather than form, so they will not see an error in, say, spelling, but rather will see the correct form. Providing editing activities that ask students to edit one another's papers in class is an effective way to help them improve the quality of their work while simultaneously giving them needed practice in attending to surface details.

Publishing is used in composition to refer to the act of making a finished paper public. It doesn't suggest that a paper is printed in a journal or book, although many public school teachers often bind student papers into a book because it is motivating for students. Making a paper public may involve simply sharing it aloud with other students, or it may involve posting it on a bulletin board or some other place where people can read the work. There is a popular but mistaken perception among students that writing is private. An important part of teaching writing is helping students understand that writing is a social action and that their work inherently is intended for others to read.

JOURNAL ENTRY

Consider the writing classes you have taken. What approach did they follow? Looking back on those classes with the benefit of what you have read so far in this chapter, what were some strengths and weaknesses of the instruction you received?

It is important that writing teachers be writers themselves. Reflect on your own writing process. How do you go about writing papers? Can any of the information in this chapter enhance your writing?

A Phase Model of the Composing Process

One of the difficulties inherent in most discussions of the composing process is that the stages are presented as discrete steps that lead to the production of a text. The suggestion is that students cannot begin drafting until they have finished prewriting, that they cannot begin revising until they have finished drafting, and so forth. Thus, the stages of the composing process appear to be part of an algorithm—a step-by-step procedure—that should ensure effective writing. In numerous classroom observations and discussions with teachers, I have found great reluctance to move away from this algorithmic approach. The stages have become so fossilized that many teachers are resistant to any suggestion that students might be able to produce a good paper without first going through, say, invention. Yet we know that composing does not consist of discrete stages and that, in fact, there are no stages at all, as such. Although solid evidence is not available, it seems likely that the widespread perception that process stages are part of an inviolable algorithm has been instrumental in the failure of process pedagogy to improve student writing in our schools.

A more effective way of conceptualizing the various activities associated with successful composing is through a *phase model* rather than a stage model. Phase models occur most commonly in science. Water, for example, when described with a phase model, has three dominant states—liquid, vapor, and solid—and it can be understood to be always in a state of flux between states. Thus, water in a liquid state is turning into vapor through evaporation; water in a solid state is turning into both vapor and liquid. The composing process also may be thought of as having dominant states—planning, drafting, revising, and so on—but these states can be understood to be in a state of recurrent flux. On this account, students revise as they draft; they plan as they edit; and so forth. A phase model has the advantage of describing the simultaneous and recurrent nature of the composing process; planning, drafting, and editing may occur more or less simultaneously and in a recurrent manner. The stage model does not readily account for or describe either the co-occurrence or the recurrence. I don't want to suggest, however, that the idea of focus has no relevance in writing. It does. Students should begin editing after their content is fully developed and organized, for example. If they don't, they are likely to lose their concentration on content. All experienced teachers are familiar with the error-free paper that says very little because the writer's attention was on form at the expense of content.

As far as I can determine, few teachers have embraced the phase model, in part because it does not lend itself to print. There is no easy way to represent or describe the phase model graphically. The stage model, on the other hand, lends itself quite readily to both. This unfortunate situation has led to perpetuation of a model that is a bit inaccurate and that is not fully supported by many scholars in the field.

MAKING WRITING MEANINGFUL

As chapter 2 noted, the social-theoretic view of writing is pragmatic and recognizes writing is a social action. Stated another way, real writing actually does something in the world. It follows, then, that a cornerstone of best practices involves making writing meaningful to students. When teachers make writing meaningful, the majority of students still may not be able to see themselves as historians, musicians, accountants, or whatever, but they at least may stop seeing themselves merely as students and start seeing themselves as *writers* who can get things done with written discourse. At the 2002 Conference on College Composition and Communication in Chicago, Irene Clark noted in this regard that writing assignments represent a genre, or role, that students must assume to succeed. "Writing assignments are like stage directions for a play," she stated, "and students are like actors who have never seen a play." I would add that matters are complicated even further by the fact that most students don't want to be in the play.

Helping students see themselves as writers is rewarding and, fortunately, not very difficult. In most situations, the key lies in making certain that writing tasks are related to the world outside the classroom. What does this mean in practical terms? Too often, the answer to this question leads to artificial assignments. Students are encouraged to "write a letter to the editor," "write a letter to a senator," or "write a letter of complaint" to a company that has provided unsatisfactory service or a shoddy product. In fact, reflecting a significant pedagogical shift, letter writing is now a major focus of curriculum guides in a majority of districts in numerous states; students are expected to begin producing business letters as early as Grade 1. Although teachers must comply with the dictates of their districts, it should strike all of us as a bit unsettling that our schools now allow commerce to exert such influence on young lives. This point aside, we surely must recognize that few students of any age are motivated to write letters to editors or senators. Many will not even know what an editor or senator is or why anyone would possibly write to these people. Such assignments, therefore, do not relate writing to the real world.

E-mail Pen Pals

Yet letters can play an important role in writing development, especially in this age of e-mail. Many teachers use the Internet to establish pen-pal programs for their students with children not only from different parts of the country but also from different parts of the world. Corresponding with a peer hundreds or even thousands of miles away is a rich educational experience for most young people. They learn something about different schools, towns, and countries; they learn something about the commonalties and differences among people; and they also learn something about writing.

Some of my classroom observations stand out more than others. A young woman I'll call Rita was a high school junior who was struggling in all her courses and who had below-average grades at a school that treated grade inflation as a professional obligation. Although a native speaker of English, Rita's writing was full of problems that years of writing instruction had failed to solve. Following is a paper Rita wrote on censorship for her language arts teacher. The class had read *Fahrenheit 451,* and the teacher had devoted approximately a week to telling students what the book was about, noting that the book burning that the story describes is a form of censorship. Then, rather than asking students to write about the novel, the teacher asked them to write about censorship. The actual assignment follows: *We noted that Fahrenheit 451 is a book about censorship. Write a five-page paper about censorship.* Rita managed to produce two paragraphs:

> Censership is an important issue. When I hear the word censership it immediately brings to mind. Right winged conservitives are trying to cut us down, they don't let us speak. They don't let us write what we want. Communication is imporant because we have to share that there are important things about life. The government needs to do something to stop this. This is a bad situation. But I think maybe the government is the blam.
>
> And anyways what about other freedoms? How come we can't dress the way we want at school? Isn't this a form of censorship? Doesn't the constatution say that we have all these freedoms? Then why can't I do what ever I want? I think lots of students want to do lots of things and its not right. Anyways, that what I think about all this.

While recognizing that the teacher's assignment is very, very poor, the focus here must be on Rita's response. The problems in Rita's "essay" range from faulty spelling and sentence construction errors to too many rhetorical questions. Perhaps the biggest problem is the near total lack of anything worth reading. Experienced teachers, unfortunately, see this sort of writing regularly, and it is easy enough to assume that students who produce it are simpleminded and uneducable. However, another perspective (albeit one that requires us to ignore for the purposes of this discussion the serious pedagogical issues associated with the lesson on *Fahrenheit 451* and censorship and the resulting writing task) suggests that Rita is merely going through the motions on this assignment because she is not engaged or motivated to do well. She realizes that her teacher is her only reader, that her teacher knows much more about censorship than she does, and that, essentially, this is an empty exercise designed to take up time. From this perspective, the writing assignment does not call for writing that does something, for writing that is a social action, for writing that is meaningful. It is simply busywork.[5]

After attending a workshop on effective assignments, Rita's teacher decided to make some changes in her pedagogy. Two days a week, she arranged to have students meet in the computer lab rather than in their classroom. Through friends, she contacted a high school in Japan and set up a pen-pal program for the students. After 3 weeks of correspondence, Rita's writing had changed significantly, as the following letter shows:

Dear Kumiko,

I enjoyed your last letter, but I was amazed to learn that everything costs so much in Japan. When I read that you pay about $25 for one movie ticket, I was shocked! Even the most expensive movies here are only $9. I don't think I would be able to see many movies if tickets here were so expensive.

I really liked the pictures you attached of your family and your house. I've attached some of my own here. Hope you like them! I couldn't help but notice that your brother's hair is really long. Is he in a band, or is that just the style in Japan? Boys here don't wear their hair long at all. In fact, they keep it very short. Some actually shave their heads. It seemed strange to me to see your brother's hair—it reminded me of pictures I've seen of boys in the 1960s, when everyone was a hippy. You can see my parents in one of the pictures I've sent. Everyone says I look like my mom. I've also included one of my room. If you look closely, you can

---

[5]In my experience, more than 75% of writing tasks in public schools are assigned either as busywork—the students have to be doing *something*—or as punishment. There is no question that student resistance to writing is grounded in this dismal reality.

see my cat, Bruno, lying on my bed. He's a funny thing, likes to hide under the bed and attack my feet as I walk by, and he's really lazy. In fact,
in this picture, he's sleeping—and I think he had been sleeping nearly all
day when I took this.

Well, I will sign off now. I want to hear more about your school. I can't
believe that you have to attend classes on Saturday. Yuck! How do you
stand it?

> Your friend,
> Rita

The first thing we notice about Rita's letter is that it has no surface
errors. The writing is smooth and engaging. For an 11th grader, however, this is just the starting point. Today's curriculum is fairly rigorous: In addition to her English class, Rita was enrolled in history,
Spanish, biology, and economics—all of which required papers. Successful letter writing alone would not allow Rita to succeed on these
papers. Rita's language arts teacher teamed with the history teacher
for the next writing assignment. They agreed that students could submit one paper for both classes. She then assigned Monica Sone's *Nisei
Daughter,* which is a story about life in American concentration camps
during World War II. In their history class, students were studying the
war, so this book greatly personalized the experiences of Japanese-
Americans during that period. In addition, of course, the book provided a starting point for a series of e-mail exchanges with students in
Japan about the war. The unit culminated in a paper about the intern-
ment. A portion of Rita's paper follows:

A few military officials and politicians claimed that the Japanese-
Americans were a threat to the security of America because their loyal-
ties were with Japan. They claimed that they could easily sabotage
power plants, dams, and harbors. But no one ever found any evidence
that this was true. There was not one recorded case of sabotage, and
there was not one piece of evidence to support the claim that the Japanese-Americans were disloyal. Why, then, were they put in concentration camps?

Two factors played an important role. First, and most obvious, was
prejudice. Americans had always been prejudiced against Asians, and the
Chinese Exclusion Act of 1882 was designed to exclude Chinese. The Immigration Act of 1906 was designed to bar Japanese. The second was economic and is less known. But Japanese-Americans produced about 75%
of all the strawberries and fresh vegetables on the West Coast, and white
Americans wanted the land and crops for their own. The war gave them
the means of taking everything for themselves.

Although not perfect, this excerpt illustrates the great improvement that Rita achieved in her writing. Two influences worked to motivate Rita to do better work. The first was her communication with Kumiko, her pen pal in Japan. Kumiko knew almost nothing about the concentration camps but was very interested and wanted Rita to share her research information. This real audience had the effect of making Rita a teacher of sorts, even though she may not have been fully conscious of that role. Because she wanted Kumiko to think highly of her, Rita organized her research material and sent it to Kumiko via e-mail for her feedback. In a sense, she was planning and drafting in meaningful ways that then transferred to the actual writing assignment. The second influence was the link between the language arts and the history classes. Rita no longer was writing merely for her English teacher— she was writing for an audience that included her history teacher and Kumiko, different people with different levels of knowledge and experience. She knew her writing had to be clear to satisfy the needs and expectations of both. In this situation, her language arts teacher could more readily serve as a coach.

Simulation

One of the more effective methods for making writing assignments meaningful is simulation. Simulation consists of asking students to take on roles and to act in character. In history classes, for example, students may take on the roles of soldiers, loved ones, and political leaders in the Civil War; they then write letters, diary entries, and policy statements related to their experiences and the war. In language arts classes, they may take on the roles of characters in books they are reading and write any number of texts that are congruent with their characters. In most instances, students have to research periods, places, and events to engage successfully in a simulation, which enhances the learning experience. Students also seem to enjoy role playing a great deal, and thus they are highly motivated by simulations. A clear strength of simulations is that they offer students reasons to move out of their role of student and into the role of writer.

Even though simulations offer one of the more effective ways of making writing meaningful for students, they are not used widely for a couple of reasons. First, with class sizes hovering around 30 or more, it is very difficult to get all students assigned to individual roles. Second, the amount of planning and organization required is significantly greater than what goes into a traditional class. Although there is no remedy for the second problem, the first one is solved through the workshop structure, which puts students in groups of five. Each group then takes on an individual identity, reducing the number of roles from 30 to 5 or 6.

An example from a ninth-grade English class illustrates how this arrangement can work. The class had just finished reading Homer's *The Odyssey*. During the course of their reading, the class had discussed the historical accuracy of the poem, Heinrich Schlieman's excavations during the late 19th century, his removal of ancient artifacts, and the efforts by the government of Turkey to get these artifacts returned. The teacher assigned a role to each work group, with one representing a team of scholars engaged in studying the connections between the poem and the historical site, one representing Schlieman and his crew, one representing the German government, one representing the government of Turkey, and one representing a philanthropical group working to restore the ancient ruins. Each group began researching information related to its particular role, and the teacher provided a variety of writing tasks that students completed individually in their groups. The group representing the government of Turkey, for example, produced arguments for the return of the ancient artifacts from Germany as well as letters demanding the same; the group representing Schlieman and his crew produced an argument justifying his excavation methods and his removal of artifacts to Germany; and so on. These activities not only led to improvements in students' writing but also put students in control of their own learning, with the result that they knew far more about *The Odyssey* and ancient Troy than they ever would have if they had merely read the poem.

EXPECTATIONS AND STANDARDS

Since the 1970s, researchers have conducted numerous studies into the role of teacher standards and expectations in academic achievement. The results have shown fairly conclusively that teacher expectations—sometimes referred to as *teacher efficacy*—are one of the more important factors in student success (Ashton, 1984; Benard, 1995; Brook, Nomura, & P. Cohen, 1989; Edmonds, 1986; Garbarino, Dubrow, Kostelny, & Pardo, 1992; Howard, 1990; Kohl, 1967; Levin, 1988; Perl & Wilson, 1986; Proctor, 1984; Rutter, Maughan, Mortimore, Ouston, & A. Smith, 1979; Slavin, Karweit, & Madden, 1989; Werner, 1990).

Expectation theory proposes that teachers make inferences about a student's behavior or ability based on what a teacher knows about a student. Willis (1972) found that contact with students leads to the formation of stable (and largely accurate) differential expectations within a few days after the school year begins. The formation of expectations is normal and is inherently neither good nor bad. The critical issues are whether the expectations are accurate and whether the teacher maintains flexibility with regard to modifying those expectations. Inaccurate expectations are extremely problematic and will seriously jeopardize a student's chance of success.

Teachers, like all other adults, respond positively to anyone who appears interested in learning but negatively to those who appear disinterested, disengaged, or antisocial. This natural tendency can have a potentially damaging effect on students and is sometimes referred to as a "self-fulfilling prophecy." Students who appear to be unwilling to learn generally do not, in part because teachers are unwilling to interact with them and provide them with the same level of education that they provide to more engaged students. Cultural factors also influence teacher expectations. Because blacks, Hispanics, and nonnative English-speaking students historically have manifested achievement levels below whites and Asians, expectation theory predicts that teachers will be inclined to expect less from their nonwhite and nonnative English-speaking students. Behaviors in class that deviate from middle-class norms—calling out or talking out of turn, excessive laughing, restlessness, as well as excessive shyness—also result in negative assessments and lower teacher expectations.

Proctor (1984) suggested that for elementary school children, teacher expectations are based almost entirely on classroom behavior, whereas for older students, in middle and high school, expectations are based more on academic performance. Yet these expectations are necessarily linked to the earlier perceptions of children. Proctor described eight dimensions of teacher efficacy. In his view, teachers must:

1. View class work as meaningful and important.
2. Expect student progress.
3. Accept accountability and show a willingness to examine performance.
4. Plan for student learning, set goals, and identify strategies to achieve them.
5. Feel good about teaching and about students.
6. Believe that he or she can influence student learning.
7. Develop joint ventures with students to accomplish goals.
8. Involve students in making decisions regarding goals and strategies.

Based on these factors, Proctor developed a model for teacher expectations, illustrated in Fig. 3.4.

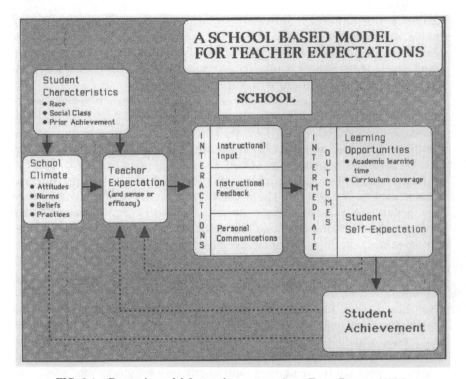

FIG. 3.4.   Proctor's model for teacher expectations. From Proctor (1984). Copyright 1984 by *The Elementary School Journal*. Adapted by permission.

Teachers convey their expectations most commonly through their personal relationships and conversations with students. They look for students' strengths and weaknesses, encouraging the former and working to support the latter. Ashton-Warner (1963), Carini (1982), Curwin (1992), Howard (1990), and others found that performance improved when teachers praised their students for work well done, when they motivated students by telling them that they believed in them and in their ability to do a specific task, and when they challenged students with difficult but manageable assignments. (This sort of encouragement and support is significantly different from the hollow praise associated with the self-esteem movement, which applauded students whether they succeeded or failed and which, consequently, led many students not even to try.)

In addition, teachers convey their expectations by how they engage students in learning. This step is more difficult than it may initially seem. Teachers naturally want to feel that they are successful in the classroom, and one measure of success is the level of student participation in discussions and question–answer sessions. In every class, there are some students who are more outgoing than others. These students tend to dominate all discussions and question–answer sessions, even when teachers make a concerted effort to involve every student. Classroom observations reveal a consistent pattern at all grade levels and subject areas. As a discussion gets started, a teacher is likely to call deliberately on the quieter, less participatory students to bring them into the lesson. Commonly, these students will not respond or will not respond quickly. But few teachers wait more than 5 or 6 seconds for a response before going on because silence is seen as a threat to the dynamics of the discussion. Inevitably, they turn to those active students they know will provide a response, students who by this time have waving hands thrust into the air. This pattern repeats itself three or four times but then changes as teachers start to focus exclusively on the active students and to ignore the inactive ones, often without even being aware that they have abandoned several students and that they are implicitly communicating to these young people that they are incapable of learning.

Teacher expectations take a more insidious form when they involve groups of students. Although we usually associate negative expectations with ethnic groups, they also appear to be influenced by gender and socioeconomic status. In "Identity and Reliability in Portfolio Assessment," for example, Williams (2000) reported that teachers in his study consistently gave boys and students whose papers seemed to reflect a lower-middle-class family background lower scores than girls and students whose papers seemed to reflect an upper-middle-class family background. The 1998 NAEP report likewise showed that girls consistently received higher scores than boys on their writing. Nationwide, boys received a score of 138 on the 300-point scale, which is well below the mean, whereas girls received a score of 158. This gap of 20 points is very significant statistically. What is especially interesting, however, is that when Williams controlled for handwriting, which is a highly visible differential between boys and girls, the gap between their scores narrowed to the point of insignificance. As Good and Brophy (1990) noted:

> Expectations tend to be self-sustaining. They affect both perception, by causing teachers to be alert for what they expect and less likely to notice what they do not expect, and interpretation, by causing teachers to interpret (and perhaps distort) what they see so that it is consistent with their expectations. Some expectations persist even though they do not coincide with the facts. (pp. 441–462)

Finally, in their 4-year study of writing teachers, Perl and Wilson (1986) found that what most distinguished successful from unsuccessful instructors were teacher expectations. The successful teachers viewed students as possessing considerable linguistic and rhetorical knowledge and as possessing language competence. The unsuccessful teachers, on the other hand, viewed students as having little or no competence, as being, in fact, linguistically deficient. Perl and Wilson reported that in classrooms where this latter view was evident, even the most sound teaching methods failed to produce significant gains in performance.

High expectations alone, of course, will not improve students' writing skills. Another factor is appropriate standards. In too many instances, writing teachers have lowered their standards to such a level that any piece of paper turned in with some writing on it is cause for celebration. This observation is not an attempt to disparage teachers but rather a recognition of the difficulties presented by high absentee rates (averaging close to 25% nationwide in high schools), lack of student motivation, heterogeneous classes, disruptive behavior, and increasing numbers of students with limited English-language proficiency. Reversing the trend and taking a firm position on high standards is not easy. Nevertheless it is extremely important.

Lev Vygotsky (1978) called the difference between what a child can do with help and what he or she can do without guidance the "zone of proximal development." This concept is often translated in our schools as "grade level plus one," meaning that students should always be expected to perform beyond their comfort level. With regard to writing instruction, the standard can be set much higher, provided that the classroom is organized as a workshop. For example, teachers can insist on papers that are totally free of surface errors because students have the opportunity in a workshop to revise repeatedly. Of course, the nature of students and our classes does not result in error-free papers. Nevertheless, depending on one's teaching load and number of students, an important best practice consists of grading completed papers and then giving students with grades lower than a C the opportunity to rewrite them one last time. The word *opportunity* here is significant because this final rewrite must be the student's choice rather than a requirement. Furthermore, this best practice works only when teachers refrain from editing papers during grading, a point that is discussed in detail in chapter 10.

Successful teachers communicate their high standards to students on a regular basis, and they adhere to them in the face of student and often parental distress. In addition, they communicate their expectations that all students can meet these standards through discipline and hard work. They then provide the support necessary—including refusing to accept anything less than students' best efforts—to help students succeed.

4

The Classroom as Workshop

STRUCTURING A CLASSROOM WORKSHOP

Most writing intended to be read by others is a collaborative effort. In the workplace, reports and proposals commonly are written by teams. Before academics send their papers out for publication, they ask friends to read the manuscript and offer suggestions for improvement. Sometimes they use the suggestions in their revision, and sometimes they don't, but they always feel grateful to their friends for taking the time to offer constructive comments.[1] Recognizing these realities, the process model led to an important change in the structure of writing classrooms. It transformed them into writing *workshops*.

In a workshop, students sit in groups of three to five. Nearly all of their work begins and ends in the group. For example, a teacher who intends to ask students to write an analysis of a reading assignment might begin by having them do some freewriting on the assignment. The freewriting then might form the foundation for group discussions and brainstorming to help develop ideas for the writing task. Students might use the information from these activities to begin drafting their analysis. Drafts can be read by groupmates or by members of other groups, but they eventually return for revision. As students are revising, the teacher circulates among them and offers constructive comments on their work. He or she may see that several students need intervention for, say, punctuation problems. The teacher interrupts students, gives them brief instruction on punctuation, and then has

---

[1]Feedback of this sort, used to help revise a paper still in draft form, is often referred to as *formative evaluation* (see Huff & Kline, 1987).

them return to their work so that they can apply the lesson immediately. These sorts of interventions have led many in composition to view the writing teacher as a coach.

It is natural to focus on how teachers in workshops respond to errors or problems in students' drafts, but it is a mistake to ignore the opportunities that workshops provide for teachers to offer individual words of encouragement and praise for what students do well. Effective teachers balance advice with encouragement, and they regularly ask students to stop working for a moment so that they can read to the entire class part of a work that is particularly well written. This technique makes everyone feel better about writing, strengthens the bonding in the class, and motivates students to work harder.

Building Community

Because students read one another's drafts and then offer constructive comments, they need to feel comfortable working together. However, one of the biggest obstacles to the success of a workshop is the high level of discomfort students feel when asked to offer meaningful comments on their peers' papers (Bleich, 1995; Bruffee, 1993). Therefore, an important first step toward developing a viable atmosphere for a workshop is to allow students to get to know one another as well as possible on the first several days of class. Each student needs to come to think of the class as a group of friends who can be counted on for help, advice, and support. This kind of relationship takes more than a few sessions to develop, of course, but the goal is clear: Students need time to get acquainted so that they can respond candidly to one another's work. However, they also need some guidance regarding how best to provide constructive comments, and this should emerge from the teacher's comments as he or she is circulating among students. Teachers need to model the behavior they expect from their students.

SETTING UP WORK GROUPS

After students have had time to get acquainted, many teachers attempt to make some evaluation of their writing abilities. The aim is to identify strong and weak writers so as to balance the work groups. It isn't a good idea to have all the strong writers in one group and all the weak ones in another because collaboration thrives on input from different voices. Teachers often ask students to respond in class to a selected topic, after making it clear to them that the essays will not be graded. They then evaluate these responses and use their analyses to group students according to ability.

In most classes, some students will have had richer experiences than others, and the wealth of background material they can draw on will put less fortunate students at a disadvantage when it comes to writing this initial essay. Making the task text based can help level the playing field. Students read a short, selected passage and then use it as the basis for their writing. They do not necessarily write about the reading selection, but the selection is relevant to their writing; it forms the background for the response. For example, a writing prompt might ask for an argument for or against the idea of having students in public schools wear uniforms; the associated passage might be a published article that describes instances in which one student harmed another and stole his or her designer-label clothes.

Many teachers refer to this initial writing task as a "diagnostic" essay, but this seems to be a particularly inapt term, given its medical connotations. Teachers aren't physicians working with diseased patients in need of healing. They work with normal students going through the normal process of mastering the language.

Although writing samples can be useful in forming work groups, they should be used with a high degree of caution. A variety of studies have noted that impromptu writing tasks do not assess student skills with much accuracy (Belanoff, 1991; Haswell & Wyche-Smith, 1994; Livingston, 1980). Sometimes those who produce the worst impromptu responses turn out to be the best writers in a class and vice versa. Teachers should use these initial writing samples as one piece of data and should balance them with others, such as grades from the previous year, comments by other teachers, and their own observations.

Determining the social interaction within groups is often more important than determining the various levels of writing proficiency. Groups composed of close friends usually fail just as surely as groups composed of enemies. Thus, teachers need to be ready to reorganize groups whose members spend more time socializing than working. Many teachers find it desirable to have students respond to a questionnaire that helps identify the social network. Such a questionnaire typically will ask students who is the smartest person in the class, who is the best leader, who is easiest to get along with, who are good friends, and so forth. Even very young students will probably have some awareness of the existing network, and because the questionnaires are filled out anonymously, the responses are generally candid.

Before groups can function effectively, members must go through a bonding process that unites them in a common purpose. Once the bonding is completed, the group will work as a collaborative unit. For these reasons, *groups should stay together for an entire term.* Moving students from group to group appears to offer greater variety in regard to feedback on drafts, but the advantage of variety is significantly offset by the lack of bonding that results from shifting students around. For the true cooperation that characterizes effective work groups, bonding is essential (see Huff & Kline, 1987). Without it, student feedback on drafts will rarely rise above a superficial level.

The size of a group affects how well it functions. In groups of three, two members may take sides against the third. In groups of four, the group may split evenly whenever decisions are called for, so little gets accomplished. The ideal number is five, because it avoids these difficulties and allows for better interaction among members.

Over the last decade, fewer and fewer schools have desks bolted to the floor, and the advantage to group work is significant. With moveable desks, students can arrange their seats into small circles that make working together easier. Bolted desks require arranging students in small semicircles facing the front of the room. Group members sit in adjoining rows, with two students in one row and three in the next. This seating pattern will enable students to see each other as they interact, and it will also allow them to observe the teacher when he or she needs to address the whole class. Finally, it is always a good idea to have an empty desk or two separating the groups, if at all possible. Such separation not only leads to a greater sense of bonding within each group but also creates a sense of privacy. Both are important.

Students should not under any circumstances form their own groups, for it creates problems as friends cluster and end up talking about everything other than class work. In addition, if left to themselves, younger students commonly group themselves by gender. In most classes, students will group themselves by race, gender, or language. None of these membership patterns is desirable. Especially problematic in today's academic environment is the fact that many classes—in public schools as well as colleges—have large numbers of nonnative English speakers. Without instructions to the contrary, these students will often begin talking to one another in their home language, making it impossible for most teachers to monitor their efforts.

Workshops are relatively noisy places. Students are reading papers aloud, asking one another questions about their writing, and offering comments. If a workshop is quiet, it probably is not working. Students are allowed to assume a great deal of responsibility for their own learning, which means that not everyone will be doing the same thing. Some students may be working alone writing a draft, others may be discussing ways to improve a student's paper. Still others may be getting advice from the teacher in a short conference.

Writing workshops may seem chaotic to teachers who have been trained to think of composition pedagogy in a traditional way. The apparent lack of structure and control can feel threatening. But a successful workshop actually requires more structure and planning than a traditional classroom, because students must be kept busy as well as focused without being made to feel that the teacher is hovering over them.

What this means in practical terms is that teachers using the workshop approach need to devise plans that move students through different activities during a lesson. For example, a typical lesson lasts 50 minutes. Students may spend 10 minutes analyzing a writing sample at the beginning of the hour, 25 minutes writing or rewriting, and then the final 15 minutes talking about the work they just finished. Or they may use the first 15 minutes in role playing to enhance audience awareness, with the remainder of the hour devoted to writing and rewriting. It is important to move students through each activity quickly so that their attention does not lapse. Teachers should keep a lively pace. Also, the writing activity should be a part of every day's lesson. No matter what else they do, students should write for at least 20 minutes a day, especially at the elementary level. Hour-long writing activities, however, usually aren't very productive because students will lose their attentiveness. Nesting writing between two brief and related activities will help keep students focused on the task. Some schools are shifting to 2-hour blocks for language arts, but the entire period seldom is devoted to writing. Nevertheless, these block schedules offer teachers greater flexibility, for they can adjust how they divide the time given to writing.

Obstacles to Work Groups

Legislated curricula and district-imposed programmed instruction often thwart even the best teacher's intentions. Many districts, for example, limit writing instruction in English classes to 1 day a week, *or less*. The other 4 days are reserved for literature and traditional grammar instruction. At the elementary level, English instruction commonly is limited to reading, spelling, grammar, and handwriting exercises. Although there is no question that reading skills are crucial to children's education, the absence of writing is remarkable, especially in view of the fact that writing about reading assignments enhances comprehension and critical thinking. Many parents measure the success of elementary English instruction by their children's scores on spelling tests, and they never question the pervasive lack of writing assignments. But the role spelling plays in most elementary classrooms is highly questionable. Students learn lists of words that have no context. One result is that many don't know what the words mean or how to use them. Another is that students receive the lists on Mondays, take a spelling test on Fridays, and have forgotten the words by Sunday.

Grammar instruction usually is just as devoid of context. Reflecting market demands, the typical English text at all grade levels provides lists of sentences that students use to identify nouns, verbs, modifiers, and so forth. Rarely do we see any mention of the fact that grammar is different from usage or that nearly all related problems in student writing are grounded in usage, not grammar. Furthermore, students use these books to complete exercises that never call for any writing. Instead, they underline and circle words in a workbook, which leads them to believe that writing and grammar and usage are totally divorced from one another. Without an appropriate context, most students rapidly forget what little these books have to teach, and as a result, the same instructional goals and lessons appear in state standards and district curriculum guides year after year, grade level after grade level. Students in 10th grade consequently are doing almost exactly the same work with grammar that they were doing in fifth grade. Even worse, when these students graduate from high school and go on to college, they still haven't learned anything about grammar and writing. After 9 years of instruction in nouns, verbs, prepositions, and commas, most first-year college students do not know a noun from an adjective, and they can no more punctuate correctly than they can fly.

Only recently have publishers recognized and started to address the pedagogical problems associated with separating reading, spelling, grammar, and writing. The SRA/McGraw-Hill *Writing and Language Arts, K–6* series (Williams, Gillett, & Temple, 2003), for example, makes a concerted effort to integrate these components, with good results. However, even if this series eliminates the problems inherent in the typical, dissociated approach to teaching writing, there currently is no plan to develop a similar series for Grades 7–12, which means that the achievements students realize in elementary school are likely to be undone in middle and high school.

In light of these difficulties, it is important to keep in mind that curriculum guides are not the absolute arbiters of what teachers do in the classroom. In many cases, they aren't even written by teachers, so they frequently fail to reflect much awareness of the dynamics of instruction. Newly credentialed teachers understandably often feel compelled to follow their guides religiously, never deviating one bit; others simply follow the guides because it is easier than teaching creatively. But guides should be viewed merely as maps for taking students from point

A to point B, which leaves ample room for meeting the needs of individual students, classes, and schools. If a guide does not specifically call for including writing activities in each day's lessons, teachers need to use their own professional judgment to provide them. Likewise, if a guide does not specifically call for using work groups in the classroom, the teacher should, on his or her own initiative, implement them. There may be some subjects that cannot be enhanced through the incorporation of writing activities, but none comes readily to mind.

A more problematic obstacle has emerged over the last several years—attempts to undermine the very concept of collaboration and work groups. A number of scholars have argued that work groups are discriminatory (see G. Clark, 1994; Halloran, 1993; J. Harris, 1989; Kent, 1991; C. Miller, 1993; Young, 1990). They base their argument on the fact that workshops are predicated on democracy, which depends on agreement and cooperation. Students and teachers have to agree on a wide variety of values: what constitutes good writing, what constitutes a meaningful response to an assignment, what constitutes acceptable behavior in the classroom, what constitutes the goals of writing in particular and education in general, and so on. According to these scholars, agreement (and consequently democracy) inevitably silences expression of values contrary to those accepted and endorsed by the majority.

This argument seems flawed. Part of the problem is that it involves questionable underlying premises: that differences are more important than similarities, that agreement is inherently bad, and that middle-class values somehow are tainted and unworthy of endorsement. The idea that democracy and cooperation silence voices at odds with the majority appears to reflect a poor understanding of both democracy and society, suggesting as it does that the majority use some hegemonic form of agreement to keep the minority repressed and that it imposes some social reality that works to the detriment of students.

We must remind ourselves that the "minority" in this context is ideological, not ethnic. Over the last couple of decades, the voices of those advocating some minority ideology or another seem to have grown louder (especially on college campuses), belying the argument that they are being silenced. Indeed, the most persistent complaint of university ideologues is that the majority of students refuse to take them and their shrill attacks on middle-class American values seriously. We also must consider the many different roles cooperation plays in the foundation of society. As Searle (1995) argued, social institutions and social facts require collective intentionality for their very existence. Institutional facts such as money, marriage, property, and even education cannot exist without agreement. There is nothing intrinsic in the pieces of paper that we use for $20 bills that makes them count as money. Their "authority" as $20 bills is the result of a self-referential social reality (Searle, 1995, p. 32). Likewise, in the context of education, there is nothing intrinsic in the person of a teacher that gives him or her the authority to ask students to agree on what constitutes good writing, meaningful responses, and so on. Rather, this authority has been bestowed upon the teacher through a licensing procedure and certain performative acts that are part of a broader social agreement pertaining to education. Both the procedure and the performative acts are designed to ensure, to whatever extent possible, that those who are licensed as teachers reflect a range of values and behaviors that are consistent with the institutional fact of education and the social reality of "teacher."

Although describing these values and behaviors would require more space than is available here, we can reasonably assume that they include such factors as love of learning; desire to help others; fondness for children; and dedication to freedom, honesty, fair play, and hard work. They do not include such factors as marital status, sexual orientation, fondness for gambling, political beliefs, or a variety of values and behaviors that are deemed personal rather than professional—and that in any event are excluded from the classroom by both convention and fiat. Furthermore, the social reality of "teacher," as well as the social responsibility implicit in that role, authorizes teachers to introduce students to a variety of values and perspectives so as to broaden their minds and horizons. But it does not authorize teachers to proselytize an ideology, religion, or sexual orientation. Stated another way, teachers are not vested with the authority to try to undermine the broader agreement that is the basis for education and, indeed, society.

Does this mean that teachers have the authority to silence contrary voices and attack non-middle-class values? Not at all. Nevertheless, one of the defining characteristics of democracy from its beginnings in ancient Greece is that all views are vetted in various venues. Teachers seem to take special delight in this process, often assuming the role of devil's advocate to move students to examine their most cherished beliefs, with the certain knowledge that they are doing students a great service through such challenges.

For their part, students bring experiences, values, ideals, and ambitions to the educational enterprise that necessarily reflect those of the society at large and our schools because they all are members of this society. Is it possible that some of these values are at odds with the middle-class values of the schools? Without question. Some students do not place much value on education, for example. When such values are contrary to the welfare of students and society, it would seem that teachers have an obligation to attempt to modify them. But the real issue for those scholars who have challenged collaboration and work groups appears to be middle-class values themselves, which they hold in contempt.

This attitude does not bode well for students, as is evident from consideration of the *National Household Education Survey* (U.S. Department of Education, 1995), a longitudinal study conducted by the U.S. Department of Education from 1972 to 1994 and one of the more comprehensive longitudinal assessments of students' values available. The data in this study showed that high school students most often identified two life values as "very important" during the 22-year period of the study. More than 80% of male and female seniors stated that "finding steady work" was highly valued and was rated as "very important" by approximately 90% of the 1992 seniors—the highest scores recorded. A related value, "being successful in work," also was rated highly by more than 80% of seniors over the 22-year period and approached 90% in 1992. Obtaining a good education was also ranked highly by more than 70% of students. These are the middle-class values that have been challenged by the intellectual left, which is confused about the distinction between individualism and individuality.

Those teachers who believe that their job is to prepare young people for successful lives in a functioning society have little difficulty recognizing that cooperation and collaboration have social and educational benefits that make work groups an important part of the classroom experience. The act of sharing drafts of writing in progress helps students understand that mastering composition consists in part of becoming aware of how others respond to the work. Another part consists of revising the work on the basis of these responses. In fact, the very nature of group work builds revision into the act of writing, so that young students are more inclined to see revision as a reformulation rather than an indication of failure. In this respect, work groups can be particularly important for very young writers, who, as Scardamalia and Bereiter (1983) showed, just don't do revision on their own.

Summarizing the Benefits of Work Groups

The benefits of work groups are so significant that many teachers have reoriented all their teaching activities—not just writing—around groups. The cooperation required in group activities appears to lead students to work harder and to discover more than they do when they perform tasks on an individual, competitive basis (see, e.g., E. Cohen, 1994; Crawford & Haaland, 1972; Hertz-Lazarowitz et al., 1992; D. Johnson & F. Johnson, 2000; Spear, 1993; Wiersema, 2000). In addition, work in groups tends to improve motivation. Students who are not strongly motivated to perform will be encouraged by those who are, and for all students the level of motivation seems to remain higher when participating in group work (Garibaldi, 1979; Gunderson & D. Johnson, 1980; D. Johnson & Ahlgren, 1976). Groups also provide an effective environment for interaction among mainstream and non-mainstream[2] students (D. Johnson, F. Johnson, & Maruyama, 1983; Villamil & DeGuerrero, 1999).

Work groups emphasize what too often is ignored in the daily routine of classroom assignments: Writing is a social action. This assessment in no way undermines individuality because, as a social action, writing involves the consensual engagement of writers and readers. Groups provide students with frequent opportunities to interact with one another through writing and talking about their writing, allowing for collaborative learning in the richest sense. A key to improving students' writing skills does not lie in simply having them write. They must write and receive meaningful feedback on work in progress, and then they must use that feedback to revise. At the public school level, it is unrealistic to expect teachers to be able to interact with every single student in a single class period, but it is very easy for students to interact with one another. When students understand how to read and comment on a paper, their feedback can complement the teacher's.

It seems difficult to overestimate the importance of peer interaction in a positive learning environment. David Johnson (1980) noted that such interaction contributes significantly to "internalization of values, acquisition of perspective-taking abilities, and achievement" (pp. 156–157). Working through problems in rough drafts together and discussing ways to make writing clearer and more meaningful lead group members to internalize rhetorical strategies and to expand their role-taking ability. Expanded role-taking ability lies at the heart of cognitive growth, because it enables the formation of a repertoire of alternative mental models (Flavell, Botkin, Fry, Wright, & Jarvis, 1968; Johnson-Laird, 1983). Applying these models helps students become better, more critical readers of their own work, which in turn helps them become better writers (Hawkins, 1980; Huff & Kline, 1987).

As mentioned earlier, collaboration on projects provides students an element of realism when they write, and there is some evidence that they may actually learn more when collaborating than they do when

---

[2]*Nonmainstream* is often used to describe students who have learning disabilities. I use the term throughout this text, however, to refer students whose home language is one other than English or whose home dialect is one other than Standard English.

working alone (Crawford & Haaland, 1972; Laughlin & McGlynn, 1967). This finding is especially strong when the collaboration is part of a simulation. Huff and Kline (1987) reported that "students working together on assignments have more success in completing them, remain motivated longer, build a sense of group purpose that provides additional motivation, tend to continue into other, higher tasks in the same subject area, and view the instructor more and more favorably as learning and success rates improve" (p. 136).

JOURNAL ENTRY

It is often said that teachers teach the way they were taught. Consider for a few moments your own experiences with working as part of a group or your lack of such experiences. How might your own training as a student influence your use of groups in your teaching?

SHARING STUDENT DRAFTS

The act of sharing drafts in progress among work group members can present certain problems. The best method is to have students make photocopies of their papers and pass them around to their groupmates. After every group member has read a particular draft, the group talks with the writer about the paper's strengths and weaknesses. Unfortunately, many will resist paying for this, even though the total cost per person seldom exceeds $15 a year. In addition, students commonly find it hard to plan ahead sufficiently so as to get the photocopying completed in advance and thus ready for class.

Teachers whose schools have large photocopying budgets and a relatively reliable copier can make the required copies, but few schools have such budgets. Short of paying for photocopies out of their own pockets, which could be costly and isn't advisable, teachers have fairly limited options. One such option involves having each writer read his or her draft to the group. This method has the advantage of aiding both reading and listening skills, and writers are often surprised at how their writing actually sounds. They commonly will discover errors in logic, support, wording, and punctuation during a reading. The problem with this method is twofold. First, as soon as several students start reading aloud simultaneously, it is hard for listeners to hear clearly. Second, group members find it difficult to offer advice for improving a paper when their perception is limited to hearing it read aloud. At some point they really need to see the paper, which allows them to reflect on it and offer better comments.

Most teachers therefore find that the only way for students to share drafts is for pairs of students in each group to exchange papers. This approach has the advantage of being inexpensive and of providing readers with a hard copy, but it also has some disadvantages. For example, sharing drafts in this way in essence reduces the audience to one. Teachers must try to overcome this disadvantage by having several exchanges, but this does not entirely solve the problem, and it also is time consuming. The limitations inherent in an audience of one make it imperative that teachers direct students through several activities that will help them focus on various features of writing. For example, a teacher might first ask students to determine whether the paper has a claim and then whether there is enough evidence to support the claim. Students make their comments directly on the paper. The teacher then might ask students to examine the details in the draft to determine whether the writer had provided enough to make the paper concrete and specific. Editing tasks could follow, with students looking at punctuation, verb choices, prepositional phrases, and documentation. To keep the pace brisk, each activity would be limited to a approximately 10 minutes.

SOCIAL BONDING IN WORK GROUPS

Collaboration troubles some students and parents because the traditional educational model proposes that "real" learning is something people do on their own. Working with someone else often is seen as cheating. Nothing can be further from the truth, but teachers nevertheless have to be prepared to help students overcome perceptions and beliefs that they have formed from pervious experiences in school.

In addition, it is not easy for students to be candid about a classmate's work when there is fear of hurt feelings. Indeed, the biggest problem with group work at all levels is the reluctance among students to criticize papers and the urge to label even the most atrocious work as "great." Helping students feel more comfortable with one another will help with this problem but will not eliminate it. Teachers need to emphasize that neither comments nor revising is a signal of failure. Achieving this goal involves taking students through three distinct stages of development that mark collaborative learning: the bonding stage, the solidarity stage, and the working stage. The teacher's job is to help students through the first two stages and then to keep them on task throughout the third.

Before bonding can occur, two things have to happen more or less simultaneously. Students have to identify themselves with their particular group, and they have to feel that they are not competing with fellow group members. Establishing this group dynamic requires a degree of skill and ingenuity, because in many cases students in writing classes are reluctant to work together in a constructive fashion. The myth of writing as a solitary act is pervasive, and students may also worry about individual grades. They need opportunities early on that will promote social bonding and a spirit of cooperation.

During the bonding stage, group members are adjusting to the idea that they will be working together closely for the entire term. They are trying to get to know one another, trying to establish a sense of community. During the solidarity stage, the group establishes a social network in response to the dominant and subordinate personalities of the members. Students recognize their strengths and weaknesses relative to their cohorts and make the adjustments necessary for effective feedback during the composing process. For example, some students may have poor organizational skills but may be excellent editors. The result is a natural division of responsibility, with members sharing equal but different tasks. Also during this stage, students experience a growing sense of confidence in their abilities to evaluate one another's papers, which makes them feel more comfortable with their roles in the work groups. During the working stage, students come to see fellow members as a true support group that can be relied on for positive advice that will lead to a better essay. Students often will identify with their groups such that individual success on an assignment tends to be viewed as group success. However, it may take most of a semester for students to reach this stage.

One technique that many teachers use to enhance the bonding process during the first stage involves asking group members to complete projects that require the participation of all members. The members are essentially forced to work together. Such projects can take the form of reports, where students investigate a topic on their campus or community and write a group report; or they can take the form of panel presentations, where members research a topic and then share what they learn with the entire class. Although most teachers think such presentations are appropriate only for older students, this technique also is quite effective with elementary-age children, who approach it with a level of enthusiasm that middle and high school students rarely muster. Periodic checks on student progress will ensure that each group member is taking part in the project and that no one is neglecting his or her responsibility to the other members.

Another effective technique involves competition. In all but a few esoteric cultures, competition serves as a healthy vehicle for bonding when it makes groups of people feel they are engaged in a mutual effort for a common cause. Thus, one effective way to achieve group identity and bonding is to make it clear that the various work groups are competing with one another to produce the best possible writing. The prospect of competing with other classes tends to enhance the group dynamic even more.

In academics, unlike sports, the sheer joy of "winning" does not often work as a motivator, perhaps because of the higher level of abstraction involved. Grades are universal and strong motivators, but they generally fail to solidify the social bonds necessary to make collaboration succeed. Grades are generally individual rewards for achievement that can actually work against bonding. For the bonding stage, therefore, it is important to consider alternative rewards that will motivate students to compete seriously as groups. Ingenuity is invaluable here because the rewards will vary, depending on the personal inclinations of individual teachers and the degree of freedom allowed by districts and principals.

One potential motivator worth considering, devised many years ago by Staats and Butterfield (1965), is a "token economies" system, which has been used very successfully (often with modifications) in numerous classrooms. Students earn tokens of different values for their work; these can then be used like cash to "buy" items provided in the classroom. This system seems to lead to significant improvements in both motivation and performance. It is also readily adaptable to work groups. Rather than individuals earning tokens, groups earn them on the basis of the quality of their projects. In classrooms where students have access to computers but where computer time is generally short owing to the number of students who have to share terminals, computer time is the most popular "item" for groups to spend their tokens on.

Addison and Homme (1965) developed a system similar to the one advocated by Staats and Butterfield, but tokens were used exclusively to purchase free time, during which students could engage in a "play activity." Computers and educational software, of course, now allow students more easily to turn play activities into learning activities.

Token economics seem to be extremely effective as motivators and thus probably would prove quite valuable in establishing a reward system to enhance group bonding. Yet some parents and administrators frown on token economies. They feel uncomfortable with the idea of encouraging competition among students and with the idea of linking education to what they view as classroom consumerism. In addition, token economies tend to provide extrinsic motivation to achieve, and it is widely recognized that real commitment to learning is largely the result of intrinsic motivation. Some teachers therefore avoid token economics while nevertheless using competition and rewards to solidify group identity. For example, several high school writing teachers in Los Angeles take work groups with the best records out for ice-cream cones at the end of each semester. The biannual gatherings have become something of a ritual, and students work hard to stretch their limits, not so much for the ice cream but for the honor of being among a select few. Many elementary teachers get similar results with "homework slips." They give these slips to students who have done exemplary work; then on any given day, the students can use a slip to skip a homework assignment by writing the specific assignment on the slip and handing it to the teacher. The delight elementary children feel when they can skip, say, a math assignment after doing well in a writing workshop is wonderful to see.

COMPUTERS AND WORK GROUPS

Advances in technology have given teachers some amazing tools that can enhance group work. Many schools have computer networks that allow students and teacher to view work in progress, which eliminates the need for photocopies. In such a network, each group member has a computer linked to the teacher's terminal. Members can work on their individual essays, but at the press of a key or a mouse they can see any one of the group's essays on all their screens. Not only can they then read the draft together, they can offer suggestions for revision through their own terminals so that changes appear immediately in the draft, where they can be further evaluated to determine their effectiveness. Of course, work in one group doesn't interfere with work in any of the other groups. Several companies, such as Lotus and Houghton Mifflin, market software that allows teacher and students to place comments in the margins of drafts they are reviewing. In other schools, a similar network is connected to a projector that puts individual essays onto a large screen in the classroom. Although not quite as effective as the other system, because only one group (or the whole class) can use the screen at a time, it still offers a powerful means of sharing and commenting on drafts.

As teachers and students have become more proficient with technology, there has been an increase in the number of instructors using Web sites as places where students can interact with the teacher and other students. In some cases, these individual Web sites are accessed through the school Web site; in others, they are personal sites that teachers have created by taking advantage of free Web space available through several different Internet service providers (ISPs), such as Yahoo! and MSN.

JOURNAL ENTRY

Many teachers are uncomfortable with computers and won't accept papers written on a computer. Consider your own feelings about the role computers play today in writing and how you will deal with students who want to use a computer for their work.

GRADING GROUP PARTICIPATION

Some teachers believe that students need a rubric to work effectively in groups, so they provide "revision guides" for each assignment. Students respond to the guide questions after reading a draft and then return both the draft and the guide to the writer. Revision guides can take many forms, but the following sample seems typical.

Revision guides can be very useful. Their structure helps accustom students to working in groups by giving them concrete tasks and clear-cut goals. Also, because work groups will be doing different things at different stages of a paper's development, revision guides can serve to direct appropriate feedback at each point, such as idea generation, initial draft, second draft, final revision, editing, and proofing. Separate

---

Revision Guide

YOUR NAME:

PERIOD:

DATE:

AUTHOR'S NAME:

Use the following guide to direct your reading of the rough drafts for this assignment. Answer each question fully so that the writer can use your comments to help his or her revising. Write on the back of this sheet if you need more space.

1. What point is the writer trying to make?
2. What specific details and/or support help the writer make a point?
3. Does the writer respond to all parts of the assignment? If not, what is left out?
4. Does the writer have an identifiable thesis? If so, what is it?
5. Is the paper interesting? Does it teach you anything? If so, what?
6. Is the paper well organized and easy to read?
7. Are the mechanics, like grammar and spelling, reasonably correct?
8. What do you like best about the paper?

---

guides should be tailored specifically to each stage of a paper's development, thereby ensuring that group members make the most of each workshop.

A problem with revision guides is that they tend to constrain discussions of papers. Students are inclined to respond in writing to the questions on the guides and to say very little more. Experience shows that even when directed to use the questions as a starting point for discussion, students fail to develop a true dialogue concerning drafts.

Also, many teachers assign grades for students' participation in their work groups, and they rely on revision guides to quantify student involvement. This practice reflects an unfortunate misunderstanding of the process approach to teaching writing. The reasoning is that if the instructional emphasis is to be on process rather than product, then process ought to be graded in some way. Thus, one gives a grade for each completed revision guide, for each rough draft, for each conference, and so on. In other words, formative evaluations become final, or summative, evaluations (Huff & Kline, 1987).

Although group work is extremely important to improving student writing performance, the idea of grading group participation, or more abstractly, "process," can be counterproductive. Writers need high-quality feedback from group members, but grading revision guides or rough drafts emphasizes quantity. The task focus shifts significantly from having a thoughtful draft to having a draft. Because grades are generally considered individual rewards for achievement, not effort, students are likely to treat work groups as meaningless busywork if they are graded on participation. As a result, the effectiveness of group work is seriously compromised.

When students are working well in their groups, when they are engaging in critical readings of one another's drafts and then following through with revision, their finished essays will show it. It therefore seems reasonable to suggest that the grades teachers give finished essays reflect group participation better than any separate or intermediate evaluation. They should serve as sufficient indicators of group involvement. In other words, students in effective work groups should be writing better papers than those in ineffective groups. The motto in the classroom ought therefore to be: "Teach process, grade product."

The idea of student collaboration bothers some teachers who worry about authorship, but there is really no reason to be concerned that essays will no longer be the work of individual students. Real writers simply do not produce in a vacuum; they receive assistance from people whose contributions serve to make the finished piece better than it would have been otherwise. There is really little danger that the group will take over any given paper. In fact, teachers are far more likely to appropriate a student essay, giving so much guidance that the paper becomes something that a student can no longer claim as his or her own. Increasing the amount of group feedback and decreasing the amount of your feedback will help avoid appropriating students' texts.

TEACHER INTERVENTION

Writing workshops are structured to allow students to work together on their compositions, but they also are structured to allow teachers to intervene frequently during the composing process. Such intervention gives guidance during the development of an essay, which is when it is most needed.

Intervention—interrupting the writing process to provide assistance—is an important part of workshops. It normally involves circulating among the work groups as students write and revise initial drafts. Of course, it is necessary to regulate the level of intervention according to students' needs. With some students, teachers may simply want to listen to the group discussion of individual papers. Where appropriate, teachers may add their own suggestions to complement those of the students. Groups also may call the teacher over for advice or to listen to a passage that is giving them problems. With other students, teachers may want to ask to look over a draft, do a quick reading, and then offer suggestions. The aim in this method is to make fast evaluations and to provide concise, positive advice on how to improve the writing. If something is wrong with a sentence, a paragraph, or a whole paper, teachers need to point it out, but then they need to give students concrete suggestions on how to fix it rather than simply saying, "This needs more work" or "This needs revision."

When circulating around the classroom and conferring with work groups, teachers need to be aware at all times of their position relative to the entire class. They should make certain to situate themselves in ways that allow them to talk to one group while monitoring the others. There is no need to be obtrusive about this, of course, but merely keeping the class in line of sight will discourage students who might be tempted to become disruptive when they see the teacher's back is turned.

Moreover, when talking with students about their papers, it is helpful if the teacher pulls up a seat or squats to be on an equal level. As noted earlier, the teacher in a workshop takes on the role of coach, and advice is easier to take when it comes from someone seated nearby rather than from someone towering overhead.

CLASSROOM CONFERENCES

Conferences with students represent the single most effective tool available to writing teachers. Conferences usually are with individual students, but occasionally it may be necessary or desirable to confer with as many as three in a tutorial, if they happen to have similar problems. The goal in conferences is to draw out of students what their intentions are, how they hope to realize them, and what techniques they are using to do so. Teachers should listen to students talk about their papers, then read them to judge how successfully the draft matches what the students have said. Chances are that the match won't be perfect, which leads to the next step—focusing student attention on what the difficulties are and how to overcome them.

Two factors are crucial to successful conferences. First, students have to do most of the talking. Whenever teachers talk more than students, they usually are appropriating the text. The more students talk about what they are doing, the better they will understand it. Second, students get discouraged when teachers recite a list of errors after looking at their papers. Effective writing teachers commonly focus students' attention on just a couple of points, even though the paper has numerous problems. If a student has a draft that lacks support for an argumentative claim, has no transitions between paragraphs, has numerous spelling errors, and lacks sentence variety, it is a mistake to ask him or her to tackle everything at once. Each student should work on a couple of errors until showing marked improvement. In another draft or perhaps on another assignment, the student can deal with other problems. A good guide to follow is this: Focus on global, rhetorical problems first; local, surface problems second. It also is important to keep in mind that writing takes many years to master fully: All students need time to improve their writing, and one conference or even one class won't change this fact.

Telling students about the rhetorical problems in their papers is one way to conduct a conference, but it may not be the most effective. What seems to work better is a questioning strategy that directs students' attention to features that need improvement. For example, if a paper lacks an easily identifiable thesis or purpose, the teacher might ask the writer to state what he or she wants to do in the paper. More often than not, students will have an aim that just doesn't come through.

After listening to an oral statement of purpose, a teacher can ask the student to indicate where the equivalent statement is in the text. If it isn't there, the student will recognize at that moment that an important part of the paper is missing. Because the writer has already formulated an oral statement of purpose, the teacher then can offer advice on just where it might best appear.

Using an approach in conferences that emphasizes questions rather than statements has the advantage of prompting students to think for themselves about what they are doing. It engages them in the processes of critical inquiry and problem solving that are essential to continued improvement in writing performance, because they are discovering things about their writing for themselves. As a result, the revisions they make are their revisions, not the teacher's. In essence, this approach involves students in learning by doing, and that is the best kind of learning.

Another factor to consider is that conferences should be short. Some teachers try to limit them to 5 minutes, but that seems overly brief for most students. Ten to 15 minutes is perhaps more realistic. Even at 10 minutes per conference, it takes several class periods to meet with every student. Consequently, few elementary and high school teachers try to conduct more than three conferences per student per term, even though the benefits are so significant that they would like to conduct more.

Conferences necessarily raise questions about classroom control. Unlike college professors, public school teachers do not have offices and therefore must conduct conferences during workshop or other activities. In this situation, students may be tempted to drift into socializing or horseplay if they sense that their teacher's attention is focused elsewhere. For this reason, it is best to begin conferences several weeks into the term, after students have adjusted to their work groups and are used to the workshop environment. Another useful technique is to plan some structured group activities during conference days. For example, groups can exchange drafts, and then they can read one another's papers and write evaluation summaries of what they read. The papers and comments are returned at the end of the hour. Equally effective is to schedule 5-minute breaks between each conference; the breaks allow opportunities to circulate around the room and monitor group activities.

Finally, in spite of the potential difficulties alluded to in this chapter, it is important to remember that most students are kind, generous young people. Most are eager to please, eager to do well. Most are very responsible, whenever they are asked to be. What they often lack are chances to demonstrate their responsibility. This is just as true of underachievers as it is of college-bound students. For the majority, workshops and group activities are opportunities to experiment with adulthood and to assume more responsibility.

Reading and Writing

THE PSYCHOLOGY OF READING

One of the more fascinating things about children is their ability to grasp complex linguistic relations without much effort, simply by experiencing them. By the time most children are about 3 years old, for example, they have made a remarkable discovery: Abstract "pictures" can represent words and convey meaning. With this discovery, they have taken the first step toward reading, and it isn't long before they are able to match individual written words with the things these words designate. This is no small accomplishment, given the level of abstraction involved in making the connection between symbols and the world.

A dominant characteristic of children's first efforts with language is that they use it to identify specific objects in their surroundings: "Momma" and "Dadda," of course, but also balls, pets, toys, keys, and so forth. Thus, many of their first utterances are names of things. The special significance of names is related to children's efforts to understand and control their environment. Communication requires a background of shared knowledge, and sharing names for things is fundamental to establishing such a background. Infants in the pretoddler stage are very good at conveying their wants and needs through gestures, but once they reach the toddler stage parents expect them to begin communicating through speech, and gestures are no longer as readily accepted as communicative acts. Wants and needs also become more complex. Children will use the name of an object to designate the topic of the communicative act and then will use gestures to convey related information (Foster, 1985). For example, a child may utter the word *ball* and reach toward it, indicating that she wants the ball.

Moreover, to know the name of something is to give it an existential reality that adults frequently take for granted but that children experience quite profoundly. "I name, therefore it is" does not seem too far-fetched in light of the fact that a world full of unknown and unidentified objects must appear chaotic. Naming begins to impose order. Most children, therefore, are excited to discover that names themselves have an existential reality in written form. The visible nature of writing confirms the identity of things in the child's world in a way that speech cannot.

Children are naturally very curious about their own names, and not long after making the connection between words and symbols they take great pleasure in seeing their names in writing. They frequently will ask their parents to write their names for them. Soon, however, they become eager to take up pen and paper themselves and, with a little help initially, will write their name or even the name of a pet or a friend over and over.

Although printing their own name or that of a friend may represent a child's first true act of writing, several investigators have suggested that writing begins earlier, in the form of drawing or making squiggles on a piece of paper (Graves, 1975, 1979; Gundlach, 1981, 1982, 1983; Harste, Burke, & Woodward, 1983; Vygotsky, 1978). Graves (1975), for example, argued that young children use drawing as a rehearsal for writing, and certainly it is not unusual for preliterate children to combine pictures with scribbles as they "compose" notes for friends and relatives. When asked what a note says, they are quite happy to "read" it aloud, as though they recognize that their writing is not yet at a stage where it can be read by others. Having observed her son engage in this kind of writing activity, Bissex (1980) suggested that he used writing as an extension of both speech and drawing to help himself name and organize his world:

> As a five-year-old he was still absorbed in naming, in knowing his world by naming its parts; through his signs and labels and captions he extended this process in writing. In the next year or two, as his reasoning developed and his need to know and control the world around him [increased] . . . this process was reflected in . . . charts and other organizational writing. (p. 101)

Observing young children having their first experiences with the printed word can tell us quite a bit about how reading and writing develop. It appears that the ability to read and the ability to write manifest themselves at about the same time, but usually not at the same pace; language production always seems to lag behind language comprehension, even in adults.

As Adams, Treiman, and Pressley (1998) noted, children have been taught to read for many centuries. The widespread expectation of universal literacy skills, however, is a relatively recent phenomenon. In the United States, literacy instruction begins early, and most children have the ability to develop rudimentary reading and writing skills before starting kindergarten. Scollon and Scollon (1979) and Heath (1981, 1983) demonstrated that parents in many cultural groups engage their children in reading activities as young as 1 month. Parents frequently begin with picture-labeling games and bedtime stories, and it is not unusual for 2-year-olds with such experiences to manifest simple word-recognition skills.

Based on findings like these, Frank Smith (1983) stated that "children do not learn by instruction; they learn by example, and they learn by making sense of what are essentially meaningful situations" (p. 9). On this account, he argued that children should not be taught phonics but instead should be taught individual words in context through a "sight vocabulary" approach. At a supermarket, a parent might use a shopping trip to teach such words as *soup* and *shampoo*. Smith also argued that if a child cannot read and write by the time he or she begins school, the problem lies not in the child but in the parents, who have failed to provide meaningful reading and writing experiences in the home. Unfortunately, this view fails to take into account the abilities and motivations of children, which range from high to low. It also implies that children are blank slates without their own unique personalities and that they are capable of any accomplishment given the right exposure. However, no matter how many meaningful reading and writing experiences devoted parents provide, children with low abilities and/or low motivation will not be reading in any substantive way by kindergarten—or even by second grade. Even very bright children who lack motivation may not begin to show significant gains in reading until late in the second grade. Writing normally will not begin to develop until sometime in the third grade.

In large part, the slow pace of reading and writing skills in these early grades is developmental in nature. David Rumelhart and James McClelland's (1986a, 1986b) work in neural networks suggested that language learning involves neuro-physiological changes. As a child learns a new word, the brain constructs a neuro-pathway that connects the new word to other, similar words that exist in the brain as changes in cell structure. These pathways do not emerge instantly, fully formed, but rather require an indeterminate number of repeated exposures. In the case of reading, it seems certain that the brain must develop pathways that link the sound of a given word to its symbolic form on the page as well as to the instantiations tied to experiences with the word in everyday settings.

It is also important to note that motivation to read and write in the majority of young children seldom is high. Friends and play usually— and rightly—are their first priorities. The brightest child will chose playing with a friend to reading an exciting book. Successful teachers not only recognize but accept this situation as being natural, yet they nevertheless work to make reading and writing more meaningful to children. Many teachers build free reading time into their class schedules, but few build in free writing time. Ideally, children should be able to do both.

JOURNAL ENTRY

All indicators show that reading for pleasure begins to decline when children reach middle school, and by the time they reach high school most students just don't read for pleasure. Yet we know that reading is a crucial factor in writing well. The question is, how will you stimulate your students to read?

THE PHONICS–WHOLE-LANGUAGE DEBATE

Throughout the 1980s and well into the 1990s there was acrimonious debate regarding how people read and thus how children learn to read. Although some vestiges of the debate continue to linger in education, the majority of the issues have been, for the most part, decided and put to rest. The debate focused on two different approaches to reading instruction—*phonics* on the one hand and what is known as *whole language* on the other. Although the debate began as disagreement about which approach was more effective, it became bitter when, for several reasons, the pedagogical questions became politicized. Political conservatives advocated phonics, whereas political liberals advocated whole language, with the result being that each side in the debate quickly demonized the other.

The importance of the debate has nothing to do with the different political factors that led to what amounts to open warfare in education. A cynic might argue that money and power were at the root of the political fighting, but that would be only partially correct. Certainly, huge sums of money were involved when districts shifted from phonics instruction to whole language: Textbook orders alone amounted to a few billion dollars nationwide, and training workshops for teachers to gear up for the whole-language approach probably ran into the hundreds of millions. But this view ignores several other factors, principally the declining reading levels of children from elementary school through high school that fueled renewed interest in reading instruction and what might be called the "culture wars" that started fracturing academia in the early 1980s. In this context, proponents of whole language tended to view phonics as being atheoretical and, even worse, discriminatory. For example, phonics teaches that the word *ask* is pronounced as /ask/, yet in Black English Vernacular (BEV) *ask* is pronounced as /ax/. Instruction that promotes Standard English pronunciation, therefore, was deemed insensitive and disadvantageous to blacks. Proponents of phonics, on the other hand, tended to view whole-language advocates as panderers of identity politics who were willing to adopt an "anything goes" attitude toward education.

The issues in this debate are important with respect to writing because the writer is his or her own first reader. Revising and editing are inextricably linked to the writer's role as reader, and, quite simply, students who cannot read have no hope of writing. (This latter problem is particularly pressing in middle and high schools, where it is not unusual to have eighth-grade or even 12th-grade students reading at a second- or third-grade level.) As Beach and Liebman-Kleine (1986) and Self (1986) noted, how one reads will affect how one writes.

Examining the Theoretical Issues

According to advocates of phonics, reading begins with the print on the page. Readers look at individual letters, combine those letters into syllables, the syllables into words, the words into phrases and clauses, and the phrases and clauses into sentences. Meaning in this account is determined from the meaning of individual words; these individual meanings are then summed to form the meaning of an entire sentence. In addition, individual word meanings are derived on the basis of sound, which is to suggest that there is not only a direct spelling-to-sound correspondence for words but also a direct correspondence between the sound of a word and its meaning.

Phonics instruction therefore consists primarily of teaching children the several sounds of English—vowels, consonants, consonant blends, and so forth. The aim is to give students the tools to "decode" words, to process them correctly so as to recognize them and extract their meaning. This approach is understood to work in part because children's working vocabularies are larger than their reading vocabularies. By being able to "sound out" an unfamiliar word, they often discover that they already know the word but have not seen it in print before. Decoding skill also has the advantage of enabling children to read on their own, without the help and support of an adult.

Phonics has a long history in reading instruction. One of more important modern proponents was Rudolph Flesch (1955), whose book *Why Johnny Can't Read* became a classic work in support of phonics.

Flesch argued that success in reading depends on accurately identifying words and the sounds of words, and this view predominated until the late 1960s. Then, in 1967, Kenneth Goodman proposed a new view of reading based on cognitive processing. His perception that reading is a "psycholinguistic guessing game" generated significant interest in the psychology of reading. Scholars such as Gibson and Levin (1975), Goodman (1973), and F. Smith (1972, 1983), influenced significantly by Goodman's work, argued that successful reading is more complicated than phonics advocates recognize and that it entails predicting and synthesizing meaning on the basis of a broad range of cues, such as syntax, context, intention, and purpose. Smith's (1972) *Understanding Reading,* which advocated a psycholinguistic model of reading based on language acquisition theories and research, was a remarkably successful book that influenced many thousands of teachers. Linguistic research had demonstrated convincingly that children acquire their spoken language by being immersed in a language-rich environment. Smith proposed that children should be able to acquire reading skills by being immersed in a text-rich environment.

The psycholinguistic model is both powerful and elegant, and the various psychological approaches to reading gradually coalesced and came to be known as the whole-language approach to reading. Summarizing the key components of whole language, Diane Stephens (1991) noted that:

- Learning in school ought to incorporate what is known about learning outside of school.
- Teachers should base curricular decisions on what is known about language and learning, should possess and be driven by a vision of literacy, should use observation to inform teaching, and should reflect continuously.
- Teachers as professionals are entitled to a political context that empowers them as informed decision makers. (pp. 24–40)

This summary, however, leaves out many of the more salient—and in terms of the political battles that eventually emerged, more controversial—features of the approach. For example, whole language stressed the reading–writing connection by having students create oral stories and then put them in written form. But it simultaneously de-emphasized correct spelling and error correction, which were deemed to interfere with the creative process and students' reading of their own work. Students were invited to use "invented spelling," which was understood to make writing and reading more fun, creative, and interesting for students. Phonics advocates viewed invented spelling as a perversion—an abandonment of valuable emphasis on correctness and thus an enabler of the further decline of educational standards.

Advocates of whole language, on the other hand, countered that one of the most obvious shortcomings of phonics is the notion that the meaning of individual words can be derived simply on the basis of spelling-to-sound correspondences. The meaning of individual words often depends on syntax and context, not on spelling, as the word *house* in the following sentences illustrates:

1. The *house* needs new paint.
2. The *House* refused to pass the minimum-wage bill.
3. The officials asked us to *house* the refugees.

Also, there is significant research that suggests that the bottom-up processing model does not depict actual language endeavors correctly (Abbott, Black, & E. Smith, 1985; Fodor, Bever, & Garrett, 1974; Kintsch & van Dijk, 1978; Malt, 1985; Schank & Abelson, 1977; Warren & Warren, 1970). Comprehending Sentence 2, for example, involves knowing not just the meanings of the individual words but also something about how government operates. The meaning of *house* in this case depends on this knowledge. Thus, meaning comes not from combining letters into the word (from bottom up) but from applying knowledge of the world to this particular word (from top down). Writers such as Johnson-Laird (1983), Sanford and Garrod (1981), and F. Smith (1983) concluded on the basis of sentences like 1–3 that reading is primarily a top-down process.

A large body of linguistic and cognitive research indicates that, in fact, language in general operates primarily through top-down processes. Philip Johnson-Laird (1983) had this proposal in mind when he suggested that top-down information processing relies on the development of mental models that describe how the world functions. Readers can distinguish the three different meanings of the word *house* in the sentences listed previously because they are able to construct separate mental models for each sentence. These models, developed from and elaborated through experience, necessarily are relatively general, because the experiences of any two people rarely if ever match exactly. With a sentence like "The house needs new paint," even when the house is visible to the person producing the sentence as well as to the person processing it, their mental models of the house may differ. Consider a scenario in which the house in question is up for sale and a potential buyer tells the owner, "The house needs new paint." The mental models for buyer and seller would include a component related to "money saved" for the former and "money lost" for the latter.

In spite of the nonspecific nature of mental models, people comprehend one another because their disparate mental models are sufficiently alike that key features match across participants in a language event. Sometimes there is no match, but when this happens the audience will reject its initial mental model and try a different one until a match is achieved or until it gives up and classifies the discourse as incomprehensible. F. Smith (1972) called this process "the reduction of uncertainty" (p. 18), but perhaps a more descriptive and useful expression is *hypothesis testing*. A reader formulates certain hypotheses regarding the meaning of a text and then tests those hypotheses against the text itself.

A similar, although more complex, process occurs during the course of reading sentences, paragraphs, chapters, and so forth. When a sentence begins with the subject, readers hypothesize that a verb construction will soon follow. Likewise, the topic sentence of a paragraph prompts readers to formulate hypotheses regarding the content of the rest of the sentences in the paragraph. In the event that a verb construction does not soon follow the subject or the paragraph does not elaborate the topic sentence, readers' modeled expectations are defeated; comprehension is then very difficult.

The concept of hypothesis testing suggests that words, sentences, and longer units of discourse have significance only because readers already know a great deal about what the words and sentences mean. It was this concept that led Goodman (1967) to characterize reading as a psycholinguistic guessing game. However, when readers do not know much about the subject matter of a text, comprehension becomes quite difficult. Typical examples are books on physics or economics, or even something more mundane, such as an insurance policy or a tax booklet. A reader may well know the meanings of the individual words in the individual sentences, but he or she cannot figure out what the sentences mean. Drawing on this observation, Sanford and Garrod (1981) concluded that writing consists of supplying "a series of instructions which tell the reader how to utilize the knowledge he already has, and constantly modify this knowledge in light of the literal content of the discourse itself" (p. 8). Thus, a successful writer provides appropriate instructions: An unsuccessful writer does not.

Whole-language advocates raised another argument against phonics—its typical emphasis on error. Most beginning reading in the classroom is done aloud because this allows the teacher to monitor student progress. Such monitoring can be valuable if used properly; the teacher can observe a child's reading strategies and then work individually with him or her to improve comprehension. Too often, however, reading becomes merely a process of accurately pronouncing words, with the teacher correcting children when they make mistakes.

Understanding the consequences of such error correction requires noting that successful reading is about comprehension, which relies a great deal on two strategies: (a) utilizing the cues provided by syntax, context, purpose, and so forth, and (b) speed. Cues operate in a relatively straightforward fashion. Knowledge of English syntax allows native speakers to predict word functions and meaning. In a sentence that begins "The policeman," native speakers can predict that what immediately follows probably will be a verb. Speed, however, often is overlooked as a reading strategy, even though it is a very important part of comprehension. If reading proceeds too slowly, comprehension becomes extremely difficult, and error correction, by its very nature, slows reading down. The reason lies in how the mind processes and stores information.

Cognitive psychologists currently propose that memory consists of three components: short-term memory, working memory, and long-term memory. In regard to reading, short-term memory is where information is stored momentarily while a person decides what to do with it. If one has no need to retain the information, it is discarded after a few seconds, and it cannot be retrieved. If one decides to retain the information, however, it goes into working memory, which is believed to act as a processing buffer between short-term memory and long-term memory. According to most models, one part of working memory stores a limited amount of information for a limited time, whereas the other part processes the information for meaning. Once processing is completed, meaning is stored in long-term memory, often indefinitely.

Reading speed therefore is crucial to comprehension because it is related to information processing. When proficient readers read a sentence, they break it into phrases that shift very rapidly from short-term memory to working memory. The phrases are held momentarily in working memory, where they are processed into propositions that are stored in long-term memory (Shankweiler & Crain, 1986). (A proposition may be considered to be the meaning conveyed in a construction [see J. Lyons, 1977a, 1977b].)

Because short-term memory has a limited capacity, it is easily overloaded. Few people can hold more than seven bits of information in short-term memory without some deterioration. Consequently, if reading proceeds on the basis of words rather than phrases, if attention is on words rather than meaning, each word will be held in short-term memory until its capacity is reached, at which point an incoming word will displace one of those being held. This sort of overload has been demonstrated to severely impair comprehension (H. Clark & E. Clark, 1977; Malt, 1985).

To prevent an overload, information must be transferred to working memory at a rapid pace, which can be accomplished only if readers process clusters of words (phrases or clauses). Books for beginning readers strive to overcome this problem by using short sentences that do not overtax short-term memory. As children gain more experience with texts, they start processing clusters of words, thereby increasing their speed. Large numbers of children, however, do not take this step. They continue to process words one at a time, soon overloading short-term memory and thus prohibiting integration into sentence or discourse meaning. Although poor readers may be able to pronounce every word in a passage, and if queried can provide the meaning of the individual words, they are quite unable to summarize the meaning of what they have just read. They are processing words, not meaning. In this regard, Shankweiler and Crain (1986) argued that reading problems are actually working-memory problems.

Something similar occurs with children reading aloud whom a teacher interrupts in order to correct an error. The child's attention becomes so focused on individual words that comprehension is sacrificed to accuracy. As a result, reading speed slows, making comprehension even less likely because short-term memory becomes overtaxed, which in turn results in working-memory dysfunction.

Note also that reading aloud without practicing the passage in advance is quite difficult. Even experienced readers make errors of various sorts, errors that Goodman (1973) termed *miscues* (also see Watson, 1985). Miscues can be classified into the following four types, listed in descending order of frequency of occurrence and with corresponding examples:

Type	*Printed Text/Uttered Text*
(1) substitution	the beautiful woman/the pretty woman
(2) omission	a cold, rainy day/a rainy day
(3) insertion	gave her a kiss/gave to her a kiss
(4) scramble	the girls left/they all left

When children read aloud, miscues commonly are seen as evidence of unfamiliarity with a word, so the child is corrected and asked to re-read it. Several studies have shown, however, that most such miscues preserve the meaning of the passage, as in Sentence 1 just listed, so such error correction seems of limited value (see Gibson & Levin, 1975; Weber, 1968). Gibson and Levin, for example, reported that 90% of substitution errors preserve the meaning of the text. If meaning is preserved, there seems no reason to make a correction. In the event that the miscue does not preserve meaning, some evidence suggests that children will stop and reread the passage, making the correction themselves if given the chance (F. Smith, 1983). (Phonics advocates, however, viewed the lax position that whole language took with regard to miscues as further evidence of a lack of standards.)

To illustrate the principles involved, whole-language proponents turned to language acquisition. When parents correct certain features of their children's speech, there is no effect. From this perspective, error correction in reading and speech are related not only in their intent but also in their effectiveness, or lack thereof. H. Clark and E. Clark (1977) offered an example that illustrated the typical result of a parent's attempt at correcting the speech of her child:

CHILD: My teacher holded the baby rabbits and we patted them.

MOTHER: Did you say your teacher held the baby rabbits?

CHILD: Yes.

MOTHER: What did you say she did?

CHILD: She holded the baby rabbits and we patted them.

MOTHER: Did you say she held them tightly?

CHILD: No, she holded them loosely. (p. 333)

Problems in Theory and Research

The various theoretical arguments against phonics seem quite sound, and certainly they are grounded on solid research. For example, there is little question that language in general operates primarily—although not exclusively—through top-down processes rather than bottom-up. The difficulty is that this general principle does not seem to govern all, nor even the most basic, facets of children's language acquisition. There is no evidence to support the theoretical assumption that young children rely primarily on top-down processes. In fact, evidence *against* a primary reliance comes from work on language change.

Children are largely responsible for language change, but until recently the mechanisms where hard to understand. Change occurred most frequently on the level of sound (phonemic level), yet there was, and is, some controversy regarding the nature of the change. Is change tied to individual words, or is it tied to individual phonemes (sound units) without regard to lexical items (Hayes, 1992; Hoenigswald, 1978; Labov, 1980)? If the latter, then the process is bottom-up.

After a lengthy investigation, Labov (1994) argued convincingly that change is broad based and limited to individual phonemes. He stated that "Sound change is a change in the phonetic realization of a phoneme, without regard to lexical identity" (p. 603). The realization occurs on a word-by-word basis as children are acquiring language. On this account, language change is the result of a bottom-up process that affects phonemes and thus words.

We can better understand this process by examining an important feature of language acquisition: children's mastery of new words. As Williams (1993) and others have suggested, language acquisition involves "an elaborate, interactive matching procedure that connects linguistic input and output with internalized models of reality" (p. 557). When children hear a new word uttered by their parents, they commonly repeat it aloud as they try to match their articulation with the parents'. Parents, in turn, commonly correct children's pronunciation to facilitate the match. Many times, however, children and parents alike have to be satisfied with an approximation, or "best fit," because the child's articulation does not exactly match that of the parent. Correction efforts typically last through three turns per incident. In addition, as the child becomes older, the number of incidents decreases rapidly, falling off to near zero by the time a child is around 6 or 7. The principle of behavioral efficiency precludes an indefinite give-and-take with respect to any one word or even any set of phonemes, thus opening the door for slight variations in phonetic realizations. Once parents stop correcting errors in pronunciation, a child will accept his or her phonetic realization of a phoneme as a match and then will generalize it across lexical items.[1]

Consider the following real-life scenario: A father and his 3-year-old child are seated at a park when a sea gull flies overhead. The child has never seen a sea gull before, but he has seen other large birds, such as eagles, ducks, and geese. Moreover, he has never heard the expression *sea gull* before. The father points to the gull and says, "Look at the sea gull." The child attempts to match the relevant utterance and produces "See girl." Both *see* and *girl* are in the child's lexicon; they are quite close phonetically to *sea gull*, so this is a reasonable attempt at achieving a match. The father corrects the child by repeating "sea gull," stressing the vowel in *gull*. The child makes another attempt and comes a bit closer. After a couple more attempts, the parent ac-

---

[1]Social factors also influence this mechanism. Children, more so than adults, are highly motivated to bond with peers, which involves a process of identification, largely through language. Hence, individual variations in phonetic realizations of phonemes will gravitate toward a mean established among peers.

cepts the child's utterance, even though it is not an exact match. It nevertheless is a best fit that becomes established as modified cell structure in the child's brain.

From this perspective, the sentences on page 157 that illustrate the operation of top-down processes are of limited explanatory value because they are not generalizable except insofar as they show the role context plays in language and meaning, which does not have much bearing on the question of teaching phonics. As Williams (1993) suggested, meaning and language processing involve "linking words with mental representations" (p. 557). In the previous scenario, the child's phonetic representation of *gull* was linked by experience to his mental representation and to his father's mental representation. This point is key to the question of meaning because the child's best-fit articulation of *gull* was meaningful for him and for his father. Furthermore, as Labov (1994) suggested, people and language adjust to "preserve meaning in general" (p. 596). They do so by allowing a certain degree of flexibility in syntax and phonology, with the result, for example, that speakers of West Coast dialects and speakers of Southern dialects generally are able to understand one another, even though their phonetic realizations for most words are quite different.

After the link is established between a mental representation and its corresponding phonetic representation, meaning is conveyed whenever the phonetic representation is invoked. Thus the articulation of *gull,* even if it does not exactly match a more generally accepted articulation of that phonetic representation, will count as signifying the appropriate mental representation in speaker and hearers. Additional encounters with utterances of *gull,* furthermore, will modify the child's existing phonetic representation, shifting it closer to the adult representation (although in some cases it never will match exactly). In the case of a word like *house,* which has more complex levels of meaning, there will be a primary mental representation signified by certain semantic features associated with a building of a certain kind used for certain purposes. The other meanings of the word must develop over time and are unlikely to be part of any child's mental representations because children below the age of, say, 10, don't have any meaningful experiences with bicameral forms of government or with situations in which the noun is used as a verb. Nevertheless, when children see the words *gull* and *house* without a context, they are able to assign a meaning to these words, although the meaning will be linked to the associated mental representations, which are the most generic meanings available—what Langacker (1990) referred to as "prototypical" forms. In this case, the meaning of individual words does not depend on syntax and content per se but exists as mental representations that are drawn on to match the demands of syntax and content. Finally, the concept of hypothesis testing mentioned earlier, on this account, does indeed depend on the knowledge and experiences people bring to any language event, but all this means, ultimately, is that well-read adults are capable of making richer interpretations of texts and of better exploring their complexities than are children.

A similar process is at work with respect to error corrections. H. Clark and E. Clark's (1977) report of an attempt to correct a child's tense error was discussed earlier, and the implication was that error correction fails to provide any meaningful input or to effect any change in language. In their example, the child applied the past-participle suffix to the irregular verb *hold*. Clark and Clark, like many others, argued that this example illustrates a characteristic of child-language development, in which children consistently attempt to regularize irregular verbs. However, Rumelhart and McClelland (1986a, 1986b) showed that this error is far from consistent. Sometimes children use the regular and irregular forms correctly. Over time, with additional input, errors become fewer, indicating that some form of error correction, largely implicit modeling, has a positive effect. Excessive error correction, of course, is not desirable because it induces performance anxiety. But some error correction appears to be a natural part of language—and thus literacy—development, especially when it takes the form of natural modeling characteristic of language acquisition. It therefore seems reasonable to propose that error correction with regard to grammatical features such as tense is fundamentally different from error correction with regard to phonemic representations. The difference is understandable when we consider that people process language for meaning and that certain grammatical distinctions, such as the correct past-tense form of irregular verbs, have no bearing on meaning. The fact that the past-tense form of *hold* is *held* rather than *holded* can be attributed to historical accident, and no one listening to the child in the Clark and Clark scenario would fail to comprehend the child's statements. Correct pronunciation, on the other hand, is critical to understanding. The child in the sea gull scenario had strong motivation to get the pronunciation right, and the parent had a similar motivation to provide error correction. Failure to do so would seriously affect the child's ability to communicate with others. How we understand the importance of intervention with regard to phonemic realizations is a mystery, yet we do, implicitly. As a result, this form of error correction works.

The arguments against phonics instruction also fail to account adequately for the real need students have for a method of decoding words for which they have not yet established mental representations of sound-to-symbol correspondences. This need is especially acute for function words. Teachers who rely on sight-vocabulary approaches or learning in context, as though these provide students with all the tools they need, are not recognizing the role bottom-up processes play in reading development. Indeed, any approach that relies on everyday experiences for word mastery is severely limited by the fact that such experiences do not provide a transportable decoding method that students can depend on. Phonics does. A trip to the supermarket, which F. Smith (1983) suggested offers a rich environment for context-embedded, whole-language literacy acquisition, is unlikely to provide any exposure to the word *because,* yet a child encountering *because* in a text must be able to decode it or reading comes to a stop.

In the end, we have to recognize that language acquisition and literacy acquisition are not exactly the same and do not proceed on the basis of identical mechanisms. The elegance and power of the psychological model that underlies whole language are undeniable; however, the model itself is neither completely accurate nor appropriate when applied to literacy. This does not mean that we should abandon whole language, only that we need to understand that it cannot form the basis for teaching children how to read. The movement away from whole language over the last decade gives the appearance of being politically driven, and there is no question that whole language was failing pedagogically. But this movement would not have been possible without the clearer understanding of literacy acquisition summarized previously, and, indeed, nearly all responsible reading teachers and scholars now advocate a view of reading instruction that draws on whole language to support phonics-based programs. They understand that most children need multiple tools to become proficient readers.

CONNECTIONS BETWEEN READING SKILL AND WRITING PROFICIENCY

Teachers have long speculated on the relation between people's reading habits and their ability to write, perhaps because classroom experience shows us that good writers usually are good readers. Various scholars have attempted to explain the connection, and one of the more interesting efforts came from Steve Krashen (1981a, 1985). He approached the question from the perspective that composition skill is similar to second-language skill: Mastery requires comprehensible input over an extended time. In his view, writing skill develops on the basis of the psycholinguistic principles that govern language acquisition. By now, this argument should sound familiar.

Linguists have long noted that "acquiring" language is different from "learning" it. Acquisition involves the unconscious assimilation *of* language, whereas learning involves the conscious mastery of knowledge *about* language. In the early stages of language development, children only occasionally repeat sentences they hear; they tend to generate their own expressions. This phenomenon suggests that children do not learn a particularly large set of expressions or phrases that they repeat back under appropriate conditions. Instead, they seem to internalize the features of language that enable them to produce unique utterances. The process is unconscious and is based on comprehensible and meaningful input, from which a child makes generalizations regarding form, function, intention, and meaning.

Krashen (1985) proposed that writing ability is acquired through reading rather than through listening. In his view, we gain competence in writing the same way we gain competence in oral language, by comprehending written discourse and by internalizing, after much exposure, the numerous conventions that characterize texts. He stated, for example, that "if second language acquisition and the development of writing ability occur in the same way, writing ability is not learned but is acquired via extensive reading in which the focus of the reader is on the message, i.e., reading for genuine interest and/or pleasure" (p. 23). Along these lines, Irene Clark (2002) suggested that genre familiarity is the result of being exposed to different types of writing.

Krashen (1981a) called this proposal the *reading hypothesis,* and he argued the following: (a) "all good writers will have done large amounts of pleasure reading" (p. 3); (b) "good writers, as a group, read and have read more than poor writers" (p. 3); (c) "reading remains the only way of developing competence in writing" (p. 9). Drawing on self-report reading surveys, he further argued that good writers are not only active readers, but self-motivated readers who read intensively during adolescence.

The reading hypothesis is an elegant way of explaining the differences in writing ability in students, and it is entirely accurate insofar as it proposes that reading is a crucial factor in internalizing the various conventions of written discourse. However, reading may be a necessary factor in writing skill, but it is not a sufficient factor. Many extremely well-read people are poor writers. In fact, some of the very worst writing comes from university professors, all of whom are well read. Teachers should encourage students to read and should help them discover the joy in reading and acquiring knowledge through reading, but it is a mistake to assume that in so doing they are directly helping students become better writers. Students will always need significant practice and instruction in writing if they are going to become proficient.

MODELS AND WRITING

Students have been studying models of good writing since the days of ancient Greece, when grammar school teachers introduced students to literature to help them improve their own language and to provide moral edification. Currently, the use of models in writing instruction remains very popular in spite of the emergence in the 1980s of an emphasis on students' own writing rather than that of professionals. Models therefore figure significantly in writing instruction in junior and senior high schools as well as colleges.

There is no question that students must study models to become successful writers. Without models, they have few means of understanding the conventions that govern written discourse. Determining what constitutes an effective model, however, is a point of real controversy (Lindemann, 1993a; Tate, 1993). It isn't surprising that most writing teachers assume that literary models are best; after all, they are trained in literature and have an intrinsic love of great books. Even in ancient Greece the models were largely literary, at least at the initial levels, with Homer esteemed above all others. Historically, the rationale for using literary works has rested on the notion that literature represents the very best writing that exists, which automatically makes it ideal for teaching good writing. More recently, some teachers have justified literary models on the grounds that the study of literature entails high-level critical thinking that is transportable to a range of intellectual activities. Others have suggested that literature introduces students to humanistic values, whatever they might be, that are necessary for a civilized life (see S. Green, 1992).

These rationales appear to be insupportable. The goal of getting students to imitate works of literature in any explicit way has failed. If it had not, written language would not have changed, and readers would have a hard time differentiating between the writing of, say, Melville and Hemingway because both would use similar language. Although works of literature generally convey solid values, their civilizing influence is questionable. Compulsory education and near universal teaching of literature in the Western world has done nothing to reduce crime rates, child abuse, or war.

A more viable rationale for using literary models is rooted in motivation. Many years ago, Sandra Mano (1986) reported a case study of a teenage boy, a mediocre student and poor writer, who went to see the first *Star Wars* movie and had his life changed. He saw the movie again and again, and he determined that he wanted to write screenplays just like *Star Wars*. He began using the library to get books about writing, and he wrote on his own. His grades improved, as did his writing. Literary models probably work in much the same way. They have the *potential* to touch students in ways that make them want to produce writing that has a similar effect on others (see Theresa Albano, 1992). The resulting motivation is remarkably strong. Unfortunately, the number of students who are touched in this way proves to be quite small, which makes the *reliance* on literary models pedagogically unsound.

In addition, there is a tendency among those who use literary models to confuse object with artifact. Students and teachers talk about the model, discussing such features as theme, character, setting, plot, and so forth. One result is that the focus of the class or the lesson is on reading rather than writing. Students clearly need to practice reading and writing, not just reading. Moreover, at the end of the discussion teachers ask students to write a paper about the work, and a few days later they collect an assortment of essays. What's missing is a model of an effective literary-analysis paper and any meaningful instruction in how to go about writing literary criticism. The work of literature, the artifact, has become the object, although the true object of instruction should be the critical essay. The piece of literature should be simply a tool for helping students focus on the object. On this account, attention to the literary model could be justified *only if* students were being prepared to write something similar to the model, which with the possible exception of some poetry is never the case.

During the late 1970s and through the 1980s, criticisms such as these prompted numerous advocates of process pedagogy to abandon professional models entirely and to replace them with students' own writing. There were other factors underlying this shift: an effort to distance new rhetoric from literature and literature faculty; an effort to validate and empower students; an effort to strengthen the sense of community in individual classes; and an effort to focus on writing rather than reading. These are worthwhile goals, but this approach always was open to criticism as well—the most damaging, perhaps, being the assertion that asking students to use one another's writing as a model is the equivalent of asking the blind to lead the blind.

Almost as troubling was the level of student resistance to the effort. Models show students what they should do, but they also show what they should avoid, and the negative comments that inevitably arise during a discussion of any given model are hard for students to take. As a result of these criticisms and of the pressure postmodern rhetoricians have exerted to shift composition back to literary moorings, large numbers of teachers who used student models during the height of the new-rhetoric period have returned to professional, and usually literary, models. This is an unfortunate turn of events insofar as it greatly limits the opportunities students have to study a variety of genres. In literary models, students will not find analysis, interpretations, and argument—the very basis for most writing beyond public school.

READING AND WRITING WITH COMPUTERS

Integrated approaches to reading and writing instruction have been enhanced by the availability of computers, the software that makes them function as word processors, and printers. Often working in small groups, children develop oral narratives that they then type into a computer or word processor. If the classroom also has a printer, students can "publish" their papers with ease, thereby making it possible to share their writing in a meaningful way. With more sophisticated equipment, students can even add illustrations to their work, a feature that younger children especially appreciate.

Another advantage to computers is that they allow writers to edit their drafts with ease, inserting or deleting words, sentences, and paragraphs at the touch of a button. Word processors also allow writers to reorganize without much effort; any element of the text can be moved and inserted elsewhere. Students can run spell check, which helps them learn correct spelling. In spite of these obvious advantages, many public school teachers—for reasons that will forever remain occult—will not accept student papers that are not written in cursive, and they actually will force students to copy by hand a printed paper. The consequences of these actions are painful even to contemplate. The affected students are certain to resent the teacher and are equally certain to have a negative view of writing—all because of a desire to impose an 18th-century skill on students in the 21st century.

When word processors initially became widely available in classrooms, few teachers saw their potential for integrating reading and writing; they were regarded primarily as a means of improving writing through drafting and revision. At the secondary level and the college level, computers continue to be viewed exclusively as a means of making revision less onerous, but there have been some important changes over the last few years.

Some of these changes were no doubt stimulated by the fact that the early expectations teachers had concerning improved revision and improved writing have not been fully realized. A range of studies showed that the mere act of using a computer to produce a text does not affect the quality of students' writing, except insofar as a printed text is much easier to read than one produced by hand (Beesley, 1986; Gilbert, 1987; Hawisher, 1987). Most of the changes, however, are the result of how the Internet has, over the last few years, become an increasingly important tool for writers and teachers of writing. The amount of research that writers now can perform online is staggering, especially considering that only a few years ago serious research online was more a dream than a reality. So many texts and journals are now available online that visiting a library to conduct research may soon become obsolete for all but the most serious scholars. What is currently available online clearly meets the research needs of the most demanding elementary or high school teacher, and even those of undergraduate professors. There remains the ever-present danger that students will not be able to recognize credible information, but this danger has always been present, regardless of the medium, and addressing it is part of the learning objectives of any research unit and is easily managed.

In addition, the ease with which students and teachers can communicate via e-mail has significantly altered both writing and writing instruction. Students can e-mail questions and attach drafts of work in progress that teachers then can review. Some software, such as Lotus WordPro, is specifically designed for team writing and editing, and it allows a teacher to post colored notes on a draft with suggestions for revision. In other words, the Internet has the ability to help teachers reconfigure their classrooms and to reexamine their pedagogy in exciting and innovative ways. It extends and enhances the apprenticeship experience that lies at the heart of effective writing instruction. More enterprising teachers can now develop Web sites for their classes where they can post information about assignments and where students can post and exchange messages regarding their work. Anecdotal evidence suggests that these Web sites have a measurable benefit: Students spend more time working on their writing, reading the work of other students, and engaging in discussions about their writing. The Internet has indeed proven to be one of the more effective tools in integrating reading and writing.

Grammar and Writing

WHY IS GRAMMAR IMPORTANT?

Most English and language arts instructors are required to teach grammar at some point, yet few credential programs require them to take a grammar course as part of their degree. Too often, those programs that do require such a course have housed it in an English—rather than a linguistics—department, which typically lacks the resources to teach any of the developments in grammar that have occurred since the 19th century. As a result, large numbers of newly credentialed teachers are unprepared to teach grammar effectively. The situation is made more acute by the fact that administrators and parents often judge what students are learning about language on the basis of what they consider to be "the basics": nouns, verbs, prepositions, adjectives, and adverbs. "The basics" are deemed especially important when reports surface periodically of students' difficulties with writing. Even more problematic is the widespread failure to differentiate between grammar and usage, for most of the errors in writing that are decried by back-to-basics advocates are not related to grammar at all but rather are errors in *usage*.

Grammar is about how words fit together in patterns to communicate meaning. The most common patterns in English are Subject + Verb + Object (SVO) and Subject + Verb + Complement (SVC). Examples of these patterns are shown as follows:

- Macarena baked the cake.
- Macarena looks pretty.

Usage, on the other hand, is about the words we choose to communicate meaning, not about how they fit together. Consider the following sentence:

- ?I ain't got no money.[1]

Although many people view this sentence as ungrammatical, by the previous definition it is completely grammatical because it has a subject (I) followed by a verb construction (ain't got) followed by a noun construction (no money). In other words, it follows the SVO pattern. But this sentence does not conform to the usage conventions of Standard English, which do not accept the use of *ain't* or the appearance of double negatives in most instances (see Williams, 1999, for a comprehensive discussion of the difference between grammar and usage).

A knowledge of grammar is important to teachers for several reasons, but one of the more significant is that it helps them differentiate between the problems of usage and the problems of grammar that they find in student writing. Without this knowledge, the tendency is to lump everything under the heading of "grammar," with unfortunate results.

In addition, it is important to recognize that who people are and what they do are largely determined by language. People define themselves and are defined by others through language. Daily interactions are based on language, as are careers. All class work involves language. There is no evidence that an explicit knowledge of grammar will advance anyone's career—unless he or she is a language teacher—but knowing as much as possible about something so integral to our lives can provide insight into the mechanisms at work, which in turn can offer us greater understanding of ourselves and others. Language is highly complex, and it is an area of endless discovery and exploration. Even seemingly simple sentences, such as "It's me," present complexities that few people consider but that can be fascinating. Grammar is the tool people use to explore the complexities of language, and without that tool they are limited to superficial analyses of what is nothing less than the foundation of human culture.

More difficult to accept, perhaps, is the assertion that grammar can be great fun, provided it is taught properly. When teachers move away from drills and exercises and begin engaging students in studying the language that is all around them, they open doors that students find interesting and exciting. It is the equivalent of studying psychology, teaching students not only about themselves but also about others. A

---

[1]Sentences that violate usage conventions are preceded by a question mark.

lesson on case, for example, comes alive when students are asked to listen to the conversations of adults and to pay special attention to the use of inflections. Students always discover that even very well educated people have significant errors in their speech, which delights them and motivates them to learn more.

On a more practical level, the combination of expectations and curriculum requirements makes a compelling case for the importance of grammar—at the end of the day, we have to be able to say that we have at least acknowledged the curriculum guide. In addition, when teachers and students discuss writing (as well as reading), it is far more efficient if they share a common vocabulary. Punctuation, for example, is easier to understand when teachers can explain that a comma and a conjunction combine two independent clauses. Students who do not know what a conjunction and a clause are, however, will be at a disadvantage. Nevertheless, it is important at the very outset to recognize that the study of grammar does not lead to improved writing.

WHY TEACHING GRAMMAR DOES NOT WORK

The last statement of the previous section is difficult for most people to accept. Grammar has been taught for generations on the assumption that a knowledge of grammar helps students write better. Teachers, parents, administrators, politicians—all are convinced that students must know grammar to improve their writing, yet few have examined the underlying assumption or have reflected on their own experiences. If they did, they might ask how it is that so many students can do well on grammar exercises but cannot write well at all. Or they might ask why grammar instruction in the third grade is almost identical to grammar instruction in the 10th grade—a sure sign that after 7 years of studying the same terms and concepts students still don't get it—yet writing performance generally improves during this period. Or they might ask how it is that nonnative speakers of English, particularly foreign students from Asia, can know English grammar as well as, or in some cases better than, their English teachers but still cannot write English well.

These questions should drive any discussion of grammar. But no doubt the most pressing questions teachers face are these: What role does grammar *really* play in writing performance? And how does one teach grammar *effectively?*

The answers to these questions make sense only when one understands that there is a broad concept of "grammar" linked to language acquisition and related to how words fit together to form sentences.

This broad concept has been described in various ways, resulting in several different types of grammar, not just one. The major types are discussed in more detail later in the chapter, so brief summaries suffice here. *Traditional grammar,* for example, is what is taught in most schools. It is highly prescriptive, based on Latin rather than English, and does not do a very good job of describing our language. Its only real usefulness lies in the fact that all the grammatical terms we use to talk about language come from traditional grammar. This grammar was abandoned by linguists in the 19th century because of its prescriptive rather than descriptive characteristics, and there is a certain irony associated with the fact that our schools continue to teach something that has been out of date for more than a hundred years. Linguists replaced traditional grammar with what came to be known as *phrase-structure grammar.* Highly descriptive, it is, in the view of some scholars, the most effective grammar we have. In the mid-1950s, however, phrase-structure grammar was criticized for lacking a theoretical component, and it was replaced by *transformational-generative grammar.* Transformational grammar has dominated linguistics for 45 years, but this is not necessarily good (see R. Harris, 1993); it does, however, emphasize the fact that the grammar taught in our schools is almost totally out of touch with the actual study of grammar and language. Although transformational grammar initially seemed to offer exciting prospects for writing instruction, the excitement soon waned, and now it is of interest only to linguists. Even some linguists are unhappy with transformational grammar, which explains why, in the late 1980s, an alternative grammar was proposed that offers more insight into the psychological foundations of language. Called *cognitive grammar,* it helps us understand some of the issues writers face when producing text, but it has no connection whatsoever with improving writing.[2]

Considering the Research

Even though the assumption that grammar instruction leads to improved writing has a long history, reliable evaluations of the connection are fairly recent. Examining summaries of some of the more important studies begins to shed light on the problems. In 1963, for example, Braddock et al. summarized the early research when they stated:

> In view of the widespread agreement of research studies based upon many types of students and teachers, the conclusion can be stated in

---

[2]See Jackendoff (2002) for a detailed discussion of additional alternatives to transformational grammar.

strong and unqualified terms the teaching of formal [traditional] grammar has a negligible or, because it usually displaces some instruction and practice in actual composition, even a harmful effect on the improvement of writing. (pp. 37–38)

Even after this assessment, however, various researchers continued to investigate grammar instruction and writing performance, in part because the assumption of a connection was so strong. Whitehead (1966), for example, compared a group of high school students that received no grammar instruction in writing classes with one that received instruction in traditional grammar, with an emphasis on sentence diagramming. The results showed no significant difference in writing performance between the two groups. R. White (1965) made his study more complex, using three classes of seventh graders. Two of the classes studied grammar, one traditional, the other transformational, and the third class spent the same amount of time reading popular novels. At the end of the study, White found no significant difference in terms of writing performance.

Gale (1968) studied fifth graders, dividing them into four groups: One received instruction in traditional grammar, one in phrase-structure grammar, one in transformational-generative grammar, and one received no grammar instruction. The students who studied phrase-structure and transformational-generative grammar ended up being able to write slightly more complex sentences than students in the other two groups, but Gale found no measurable differences in overall writing ability.

In a much longer investigation, Bateman and Zidonis (1966) conducted a 2-year study that started when the students were in ninth grade. Some of the students received instruction in transformational-generative grammar during this period; the rest received no grammar instruction. Students who studied transformational grammar were able to write more complex sentences than those in the no-grammar group, but there was no significant difference in overall writing performance.

Elley, Barham, Lamb, and Wyllie (1976) began with a relatively large pool of subjects (248), which they studied for 3 years. Because some critics of the earlier studies had suggested that the lack of any measurable differences might be the result of different teaching styles, the researchers were particularly careful to control this variable.

The students were divided into three groups. The first group, composed of three classes, studied transformational-generative grammar, various organizational modes (narration, argumentation, analysis, etc.), and literature. The second group, also of three classes, studied the same organizational modes and literature as the first group but not transformational-generative grammar; instead, they studied creative writing and were given the chance to do additional literature reading. The two classes in the third group studied traditional grammar and engaged in reading popular fiction.

At the end of each year of the investigation, students were evaluated on a range of measures to determine comparative growth. These measures included vocabulary, reading comprehension, sentence complexity, usage, spelling, and punctuation. Furthermore, students wrote four essays at the end of the first year and three at the end of the second and third years that were scored for content, style, organization, and mechanics. The students also were asked to respond anonymously to questionnaires designed to assess their attitudes toward the various parts of their English courses.

No significant differences on any measures were found among the three groups at the end of the first year, with one notable exception. The students who had studied transformational-generative grammar seemed to like writing less than students in the other two groups. At the end of the second year, the students who had studied traditional grammar produced essays that were judged to have better content than the students who had not studied any grammar, but the raters found no significant difference between the traditional grammar and the transformational-grammar groups. In addition, other factors, such as mechanics and sentence complexity, were judged similar for all groups.

The results of the attitude questionnaire at the end of the second year indicated that the students who had studied transformational-generative grammar not only continued to like writing less overall than their counterparts but also felt English as a whole was more difficult. Nevertheless, in regard to expository writing and persuasive writing, the students who had studied transformational-generative grammar and those who had studied no grammar had a significantly more positive attitude than the traditional-grammar students. They also seemed to enjoy literature more.

At the end of the third year, the various factors related to writing were evaluated a final time. A series of standardized measures showed that the students who had studied grammar performed better on the usage test than those who had not. No significant differences on the other measures were found. On the final attitude survey, the transformational-grammar students indicated that they found English "repetitive," which is understandable considering that each year they studied the same grammatical principles. The traditional-grammar group indicated that they found their English program less "interesting and useful" than the other two groups.

More significant, however, is the fact that even after 3 years of work and effort, the actual writing of the students who had studied traditional grammar or transformational-generative grammar showed no significant differences in overall quality from that of students who had studied no grammar. Evaluations of the three groups' essays failed to reveal any measurable differences at all. Frequency of error in spelling, punctuation, sentence structure, and other mechanical measures did not vary from group to group. As far as their writing was concerned, studying grammar or not studying grammar simply made no difference.

Such studies make it clear that grammar instruction has no demonstrated positive effect on the quality of students' writing. This is not to suggest that it has a negative effect, nor should anyone dismiss the possibility that grammar instruction may have some as yet unspecified effect on students' general language skills. But the data do suggest that teaching students grammar has no measurable effect on writing performance.

On this account, we have to examine the enthusiasm with which so many teachers engage students in grammar drills and exercises that not only have no observable influence on student writing but that also are quickly forgotten. Large numbers of college freshmen have no more knowledge of English grammar than fifth graders. The difficulty in identifying the real substance of writing instruction may make grammar attractive as instructional *content*. As Fleming (2002) noted with regard to college composition, the "intellectual 'thinness' of the first-year course has become impossible to overlook. . . . Unlike most other disciplines, composition . . . has no real multicourse curriculum, no undergraduate major, no four-year program of study leading to knowledge, skill, or virtue . . ." (p. 116). With all due respect for the yeomanlike work of our teachers, writing in our public schools is even more intellectually thin than it is in our colleges. Seeking out and marking errors in grammar (or more accurately, usage) thus could easily become a measure of what is taught and what is learned. Writing in *College Composition and Communication*, T. R. Johnson (2001) noted in this regard that "Although we rarely detect the errors that dot the texts of professionals, we actively seek them out in student texts, and when we find them, we figuratively slash them, often with 'bloody' red ink: that is, we expose the texts as unclean, impure, and thus unfit for full membership in the academic community . . ." (p. 632).

Internalized Language Patterns

The fact that the most important studies of grammar and writing were conducted many years ago indicates that scholars are no longer interested in this issue because the earlier results are conclusive. What the studies do not really tell us, however, is why teaching grammar does not lead to improved writing. The most widely accepted reasons are straightforward.

First, every native speaker of a language already knows the grammar on an implicit level. We don't have to be linguists to understand this point; evidence is all around us. With the exception of certain ungrammatical expressions such as "The reason is because . . ." and errors in usage, such as "Me and Fred went to the movies," native speakers of English do not produce ungrammatical sentences when speaking. An ungrammatical sentence violates English word order, as in the following sentence:

- *The barked postman dog at my.[3] (My dog barked at the postman.)[4]

This internalized grammar begins developing at birth because children are immersed in the language, have strong motivation to communicate, and possess a brain that is genetically designed to identify, store, and use the regular patterns of language in adult speech that we describe as grammar.

The language patterns consist of both grammar and usage, and they duplicate closely the language of a child's home and community. If they are not immediately automated (which means that we rarely have to think about the structure of what we intend to say) they become automated very quickly. We do not observe children thinking about sentence structure. Automation is necessary not only because it makes communication more efficient but also because the focus of communication is meaning, not structure. These patterns become deeply embedded in the brain as part of the neural network and are very difficult to change.

For many students, the language of school is different from the language of home and community in several ways (see Heath, 1983, for a

---

[3]Ungrammatical sentences are marked with an asterisk.

[4]A less egregious example is "The reason is because. . . ." We call *is* a "linking verb." Linking verbs can be followed only by adjectives, nouns, and prepositional phrases, as in the following sentences:

The girl is tired. (adjective)
The girl is the winner. (noun)
The girl is in the market. (prepositional phrase)

Because is a subordinating conjunction; thus, the expression is ungrammatical because it violates the word-order patterns just described for linking verbs. The correct form of this expression is "The reason is *that*. . . ." The word *that* here is a complementizer, and it joins the clause that follows it as a complex noun construction.

full discussion of the various dimensions of difference). The language of school is commonly used in analysis and discussion, whereas the language of home is more commonly used to maintain social bonds. Also, the dialect of teachers is sometimes different from that of students. We see this difference most often with regard to black and Hispanic students who have white teachers. Nevertheless, an important function of our schools, historically, has been to normalize language across social and ethnic groups. Conflicts arise when students arrive at school with language patterns that do not conform to school language—which is much of the time.

Although speech and writing draw on the same internalized language patterns, they are different in some interesting ways. Unlike speech, writing lacks context. This explains why the first paragraph of essays and newspaper stories always sets the scene—it provides a context. In addition, writing is more formal than nearly all speech, and it affords people the luxury of returning to statements and examining them closely. Speech, of course, tends to be ephemeral. As a result, the form of expression is often just as important as the content. We praise Shakespeare not just for the content of his plays and poems but also for how that content is expressed. Yet few students have much exposure to formal discourse; fewer still have any experience producing it. The conventions that govern academic writing are relatively unknown to them, and they know well only the conventions of speech. Furthermore, those speech conventions have not failed them; they have been able to communicate their needs and understand the needs of others for years.

Grammar instruction necessarily operates on two planes. The first involves raising students' knowledge of grammar to the conscious level. The second involves giving them the vocabulary of grammar. The grammar–writing connection is predicated on the idea that with a conscious knowledge of grammar and the requisite vocabulary, students will be able to recognize grammar and usage errors in their own writing and repair them. However, conflicts emerge as soon as most students begin writing.

The nature of language motivates students to focus on the content of their writing rather than the structure. As a result, they do not pay much attention to their explicit knowledge when composing. At the same time, their unfamiliarity with the conventions of academic writing forces them to rely on what they do know—the conventions of speech. Many years ago, Williams (1985) reported that the less experienced the writer, the more likely he or she was to rely on the conventions of speech when composing. But these conventions are rooted in the language of the home and community and do not conform to expectations for academic writing. Consequently, a student whose home language does not mark pronouns for case will be inclined to produce the following type of sentence regardless of how much instruction he or she has had in the usage of pronouns:

- ?Me and Fred went to the movies.

One way to reduce the conflict between form and content is to separate composing from editing. But this technique does not completely solve the problem because students have a hard time recognizing these kinds of errors in their writing, which they tend to *read for meaning* rather than for form. Students can easily identify and correct these types of errors in drills and exercises not only because the target sentences are decontextualized but also because the sentences in such exercises have no personal connection. As far as we know, no amount of direct instruction in grammar can readily reverse these behaviors in children. Indeed, it is very likely that the cognitive operations involved in completing grammar drills and exercises are quite different from those involved in composing.

TEACHING GRAMMAR AND USAGE

The studies reviewed earlier have prompted different responses from those involved in education. Many teachers, administrators, and parents have discounted the research and proceeded as though the findings don't exist, putting students through exercises and drills year after year. Others have seen them as a rationale for ignoring grammar instruction. Neither response is appropriate. Students deserve an opportunity to learn about the language they speak. Given the right approach, students are as interested in grammar as they are in social sciences, and for many of the same reasons: Both reveal much about students themselves and about those around them. The real issue is how grammar should be taught, not whether it should be taught.

Teaching usage is equally important. When people complain about the quality of student writing, they focus on such factors as faulty agreement between subject and verb, faulty punctuation, faulty word choice, errors in number, and so on. Although these flaws are labeled as grammar problems, they actually reflect errors in usage, not grammar. Effective teaching, therefore, must differentiate between grammar and usage. Grammar has to do with the structure of language, not with its production. Usage, on the other hand, has little to do with structure but very much to do with production.

Usage and Error

In some respects, teaching grammar is easier than teaching usage. Numerous handbooks are available that we can draw on for grammar lessons, but only a few books seriously address usage. *The Teacher's Grammar Book* (Williams, 1999) is one notable exception. Also, grammar instruction typically consists of mastering terminology and completing exercises. Students already use language grammatically, so there is little problem with applying lessons to language, at least on paper. With usage, however, the goal is to identify errors that are embedded in the patterns of everyday speech and then to eliminate them on the basis of newly learned conventions. Few people can do this easily because it requires the development of a meta-cognitive awareness of how one actually uses language. The process is slightly easier (but only marginally) when it comes to writing because the composing process is slower than speaking and students can call up learned conventions during the editing phase.

One of the more important steps toward teaching usage effectively involves understanding something about the nature of usage errors. Usage is based on conventions that vary across time, geography, education, socioeconomic status, and situation. As a result, usage is in a state of flux. More important, usage is linked to and ultimately governed by what are known as *appropriateness conditions*. A simple example helps explain this concept: Most newly credentialed teachers know that they should wear a suit rather than a T-shirt and shorts when they go for their job interview. Likewise, the language they use during the interview will be different from the language they use when they are having pizza and beer with a group of friends. The T-shirt and shorts, as well as the language used among friends, would not be appropriate for the job interview. Our knowledge of appropriateness conditions is based on what Dell Hymes (1971) called "communicative competence," which begins developing simultaneously with language but which requires many years to reach maturity. When we comment that "kids say the darnedest things," we are really commenting on their lack of mature communicative competence and their lack of full awareness of appropriateness conditions.

A significant part of writing instruction necessarily focuses on helping students expand their awareness of appropriateness conditions. They bring to the classroom the language and conventions of home and community, which are incongruent with the language and conventions of academic discourse. Thus, the language students are familiar with and use on a daily basis is appropriate for communicating with friends and family, but it is not appropriate, generally, for school and writing.

The focus of instruction should therefore be on helping students understand the difference. Because even young children already have developed a rudimentary communicative competence, simulations and role-playing activities work well to reinforce appropriateness conditions for usage. A special note seems justified here: Earlier chapters examined the contention that students have a right to their own language and that conventions of Standard English should be abolished because they are elitist and/or discriminatory. Although well intentioned, advocates of this position seem to miss the point entirely. Students need to expand their repertoire of language skills and conventions, not reduce them, which surely would be the outcome of any serious effort at abolishing academic conventions. The reason is straightforward: Standard English is deemed appropriate and acceptable in the widest range of situations.

Because usage in academic discourse is governed by convention, there are few absolutes, and the concept of "error" is fuzzy and subject to change. But who establishes the standards? They are established by scholars, editors, and writers who periodically are brought together in "usage panels" prior to the publication of dictionaries and handbooks. They review a wide range of usage issues and reach consensus on whether a particular element of usage is appropriate or acceptable. This process ensures that any change in the standards occurs very slowly, which is important for the sake of continuity.

All people make numerous mistakes with language, not just students or the uneducated. In fact, with regard to some usage conventions, the more educated a person, the more likely he or she is to make a mistake. Women tend to be more careful about correctness in language, so they generally produce fewer usage errors than males do. Most people usually ignore the usage errors they hear in speech, unless the errors are truly egregious, repetitive, or simply humorous, as in the case of Mrs. Malaprop, the character in Sheridan's play *The Rivals,* who regularly used the wrong word. The reason is that in oral discourse, the message is the focus of attention, so mistakes tend to be less distracting. The following sentences, from student papers, might have attracted little attention if they had been spoken, but because they were written, the usage errors stand out like a bright light on a dark night:

- The lesson I learned was that I should never take anyone for granite.

- On my trip to the Florida everglades, I saw an allegory that was at least 12 feet long.

- The author makes an interesting illusion to Shakespeare's *Romeo and Juliet.*
- It is a mistake for people living today to except people living in the past to share our values; criticizing the ancient Greeks for not being feminists is like criticizing them for not speaking English.

The preceding errors are most likely the result of students' pervasive lack of reading experience. Too many students simply have not seen even commonly used words in print. One of the more frequent and revealing examples of this phenomenon is the way large numbers of students expand the contraction *could've,* which they represent as "could of." Other usage errors, however, are the result of the inappropriate application of speech patterns. For example, in conversations, the expression "a lot" appears frequently, as in "We know a lot about the ancient Egyptians." Written discourse deems "a lot" to be inappropriate and requires the expression "a great deal." Grammar instruction has no bearing on these issues.

Common Usage Problems

Examining some typical errors in usage illustrates the nature of the problem that students and teachers face; it also lays the foundation for developing pedagogical strategies to help students master the conventions of academic writing. The sentence that follows, for example, uses the object-case pronoun *me* in the subject position and uses the singular *was* as the auxiliary of the verb phrase, creating an error in subject–verb agreement. Both these forms appear widely in various dialects of English but are unacceptable in the standard dialect that governs writing:

- ?Fritz and me was going to the ball game.

Patterns of this type are prevalent in many spoken dialects. Two factors underlie the errors: First, case is a vestige of an older form of English in which word order was not as rigid as it is today. We might even say that it is an obsolete feature of English because today word order, not case markers, determines the function of words in sentences. Whether the pronoun is in the objective case or the nominative case is irrelevant to the grammatical structure here because word order indicates that *me* is functioning as a subject pronoun. In addition, many languages do not mark verbs for number because it is redundant and adds nothing to aid understanding of utterances. Note that in the example sentence *Fritz* and *me* are functioning as a single grammatical unit—the subject. From this perspective, it is understandable that the auxiliary might be marked as singular rather than plural.

The surest way to help students correct these usage errors is to engage them in focused reading activities followed by discussions of the form of writing, not the content. The goals are twofold: to expose them repeatedly to texts to help them internalize the patterns and conventions and to discuss and explain those patterns and conventions to raise their meta-cognitive awareness. After each lesson, students should engage in writing activities that give them opportunities to apply and practice what they are learning. Drills and exercises involving case and subject–verb agreement, however, will be of limited usefulness.

Although we can reduce the number of usage errors through reading and talking about form, eliminating them is a harder task that may take many years, in part because of the powerful effects of word order in English. Consider the following sentence, which came from an administrator at a major research university:

- ?Our catalogue of courses and requirements baffle students.

The plural terms, *courses* and *requirements,* dominate the verb because of their proximity, leading to the error. If educators with PhDs cannot write sentences of this type correctly on a consistent basis, imagine the difficulties students face.

The same can be said of the punctuation errors that cause fragments and run-on sentences and of the numerous faulty word choices that characterize student writing. Students consistently confuse *affect* and *effect* because the words are not usually distinguished in speech and because they have not read enough to note and then internalize the distinction. These words have caused so much grief that many people have tried to replace both with *impact* in an effort to avoid the problem:

- ?The change in leadership had a big *impact* on us all.
- ?Our new coach *impacted* the team in unpredictable ways.

Unfortunately, this replacement does not solve anything because it creates its own usage problems. As a noun, *impact* generally means "collision," or the striking of one body against another, which makes the first example sentence questionable. As a transitive verb, the word generally means "to pack firmly together," which makes the second one funny as well as questionable.

Other problems abound in speech as well as writing, such as the pervasive confusion of *lay* for *lie, that* for *who* and *whom,* and *each other* for *one another.* And though politicians and parents call for increased emphasis on grammar, we have witnessed a growing tendency to discount usage distinctions or to ridicule them as being elitist. Often "language change" is cited as a rationale for sanctioning the acceptance of *impact* in place of *affect.* The situation is paradoxical.

Teaching standard usage requires a knowledge of usage errors. Some of the more common are reviewed in the following subsections.

This and the Problem of Reference. The demonstrative pronoun *this* does not always work with a noun, as in *This book is interesting.* In certain situations, it replaces an entire sentence, as in the following:

- Fritz opened another beer. *This* amazed Macarena.

Here, *this* refers to the fact that Fritz opened another beer, and in this kind of construction it usually is referred to as an *indefinite demonstrative* pronoun. Because the two sentences are side by side, the relationship between them is clear. Inexperienced writers often do not link the indefinite demonstrative with the word it refers to; they may have several sentences separating the two, which makes comprehension difficult. Consider the following student example:

> I liked *Cannery Row* a lot. I especially like the part where Doc gets conned out of a quarter for a beer. Doc probably was the best educated of all the characters in the story. But that doesn't mean he was the smartest. All of the characters seemed smart in their own way. This is one of the funniest parts of the story.

The word *this* in the last sentence should refer to Doc getting conned in Sentence 2, but it doesn't. The intervening sentences make the connection hard to see. Using the indefinite demonstrative in this instance is not appropriate. The sentence would have to be moved upward to be successful. Moreover, many experienced writers object to any usage of *this* in such a broad way, arguing that an alternative, more precise structure is better. They recommend replacing the indefinite demonstrative pronoun with an appropriate noun.

Each Other/One Another. *Each other* and *one another* do not mean the same thing, so they are not interchangeable. *Each other* signifies two people or things, whereas *one another* signifies more than two. In this respect, the usage of *each other* and *one another* is identical to the usage of *between* and *among.*

Reflexive Pronouns.   Reflexive pronouns are used two ways: when someone does something to him- or herself or as *intensifiers.* Consider the following sentences, which illustrate both forms of usage:

- Fred cut *himself* with his razor.
- Macarena *herself* couldn't believe how good she looked.

Large numbers of people are confused when it comes to the case of pronouns: They do not know whether to use nominative or objective case, whether to say (or write) "Fred gave the money to Macarena, Raul, and me" or "Fred gave the money to Macarena, Raul, and I." They know there is a difference because they have been taught it in school, but they really do not know what the difference is. To avoid the entire problem, at least with respect to the pronouns *I* and *me,* they will use a reflexive pronoun in either the subject or object position, as in the following sentences:

- ?Buggsy, Fritz, and *myself* went to Las Vegas.
- ?Buggsy took Fred, Macarena, and *myself* to his new casino.

Using a reflexive pronoun to replace a personal pronoun, however, simply creates another problem because there is no reflexive action. Replacing a personal pronoun with a reflexive is a violation of standard usage.

Lie and Lay.   One of the more widespread usage problems involves the verbs *lay* and *lie. Lay* is a transitive verb, so it requires an object; it has to be followed by a noun. *Lie,* on the other hand, is an intransitive verb and does not have an object; it is not followed by a noun. Nearly everyone is confused by this difference, with the result that they use *lay* intransitively, as in the following example:

- ?I'm going to *lay* down for a while.

Standard usage requires the verb *lie:*

- I'm going to *lie* down for a while.

For years, some teachers have tried giving students a mnemonic to help them remember the difference: "Dogs lay but people lie." The mnemonic fails, however, because it is wrong. Both dogs and people lie.

Subordinating Conjunctions and Semantic Content.   English has many function words, and some of the more interesting are subordinating conjunctions. These words, such as *if, whereas, since, although, even though, because, while, until, before, after,* and so forth, link subordinate clauses to independent clauses, as in *Maria liked Raul because he was kind.* Not all function words have semantic content, or meaning, at least not in the way that a word like *cat* has meaning, but most of them nevertheless do have some sort of semantic content. The semantic content of subordinating conjunctions is related to the type of information they supply to the construction they modify. For instance, in the example sentence, *Maria liked Raul because he was handsome,* the subordinate clause, as a result of the semantic content of the conjunction *because,* supplies information of reason to the independent clause. In *Fred stopped the car when the engine started to smoke, when* is a temporal subordinator, so the subordinate clause supplies information of time. Standard usage requires a match between the semantic content of the subordinating conjunction and the modification provided by the subordinate clause.

Growing numbers of people ignore this usage principle. In conversation and published texts, we find incongruence with respect to time, causality, and contrast, with a temporal subordinator being used where a causal and/or contrastive subordinator is required. Consider the following sentences:

- ?Macarena rode her bike *since her car was broken.*
- ?Toni Braxton wanted to wear her white jumpsuit, *while her manager wanted her to wear her white dress.*

In the first example sentence, the relation between the two clauses is one of reason, not time, so standard usage requires the following:

- Macarena rode her bike *because her car was broken.*

In the second example sentence, the relation between the two clauses is contrastive, not temporal, so standard usage requires:

- Toni Braxton wanted to wear her white jumpsuit, *whereas her manager wanted her to wear her white dress.*

Who and Whom. *Who* and *whom* are relative pronouns, and as such connect a relative clause to an independent clause. *Who* is in the nominative case, which means that it serves as the subject of a relative clause, and *whom* is in the objective case, which means that it serves as the object of a relative clause. The two functions are illustrated as follows, with the relative clauses set in italics:

- Fritz knew the woman *who won the lottery.*
- Macarena spoke to the woman *whom I knew* from the party.

Like all other pronouns, relative pronouns refer to noun anteced-
ents. Thus, we can see that the underlying structure of the first relative clause above is "the woman won the lottery." The underlying
structure of the second is "I knew the woman." By looking at the underlying structure, we can easily see how "the woman" functions as
the subject and the object, respectively, of each relative clause. What
makes matters complicated for most people is the fact that a relative
clause must have a relative pronoun at the beginning to connect it to
the independent clause. Consequently, object relative pronouns are
not at the end of the clause but at the beginning.
These two relative pronouns have caused so much confusion among
modern speakers of English that few know which form to use. Large
numbers of people now use *who* for both subject and object. Even
larger numbers have tried to eliminate *who* and *whom* altogether by
replacing them with the word *that. That* can, indeed, function as a relative pronoun. *The problem is that standard usage does not allow it to be
used as a relative pronoun designating people.* Thus, both of the following violate standard usage conventions:

- ?Fritz knew the woman *that won* the lottery.
- ?Macarena knew the woman *that I knew* from the party.

Grammar Problems

The number of true grammar problems in student writing is quite
small. In addition, many people do not recognize them when they occur
because the errors have become so pervasive in speech. The most common problems are reviewed as follows.

The Reason Is Because.   The most widespread grammar error occurs when people provide reasons for things. Even well-educated and influential people produce this error regularly. Consider the following remarks from former President Clinton, provided during an unscripted
press conference: "Of course we need campaign finance reform, and I'm
going to work very hard to see that we get it. The American people want
action on this, and *the reason is because things are in such a mess.*"
If we look carefully at the italicized part of the remarks, we see that
it consists of a noun-phrase subject *(the reason),* the linking verb *is,*
and a subordinate clause that begins with the subordinating conjunc-

tion *because.* Yet linking verbs cannot be followed by subordinate clauses; they can be followed only by nouns, adjectives, and prepositional phrases, as shown in the following:

- Macarena was tired. (adjective)
- Macarena was the winner. (noun phrase)
- Macarena was in the bedroom. (prepositional phrase)

To make President Clinton's statement grammatical, we would have to change the subordinate clause to a noun construction called a "complement clause," which always begins with the word *that:*

- The American people want action on this, and *the reason is that things are in such a mess.*

Particles. English has a special category of verbs that take what are called *particles,* words that function quite a bit like adverbs. Perhaps the most interesting feature of particles is that, because they are linked in subtle ways to objects, they can appear in two places in a sentence, as the following examples illustrate:

- Fritz put down the book.
- Fritz put the book down.

However, when the object of a sentence is a pronoun, the particle *must* shift positions; it cannot remain attached to the verb. Keeping the particle with the verb creates an ungrammatical sentence, as illustrated in the following:

- Fritz looked him up.
- *Fritz looked up him.

Where and At. Another type of problem occurs when people add words to sentences unnecessarily, as in the following sentence:

- *Where is he at?

Questions of this sort are based on the understanding that the subject *(he)* is somewhere, either here or there, but the word *at* doesn't figure at all into this understanding. It simply appears and is unrelated to the structure or the meaning of the sentence; thus, the sentence is ungrammatical.

Miscellaneous Errors. Ungrammaticality also occurs when people use function words in ways that English does not accept. The error usually involves prepositions and articles, and it may arise from using an unacceptable preposition or article or from having no preposition or article where one is needed, as illustrated in the following sentences:

- *Fred put the shoes *in* her feet.
- *Macarena went the market.
- *A trouble with Fritz is that he never arrives on time.
- *Fritz saw dog walk across the lawn.

Most people associate this type of error with nonnative speakers, yet they nevertheless occur among native speakers with some regularity.

Direct and Indirect Instruction

When students know grammar and usage on an explicit level, they possess shared concepts and vocabulary for talking about language and thus can discuss their writing more easily and effectively with their teachers and among themselves. This kind of knowledge can be taught directly, but without reliance on workbooks and exercises. Given the presence of language everywhere, such workbooks and exercises seem redundant, at best. Effective direct instruction immerses students in their own language. It explains basic concepts and then asks students to use those concepts to analyze their own language, always taking care to distinguish between grammar and usage. Students usually get excited about grammar and usage when they have opportunities to apply their knowledge. One of the more effective activities along these lines consists of asking students to become language researchers by having them listen to others speak with the goal of identifying and recording variations in usage and grammar. Students quickly become astute observers. Becoming more aware of how others use (or misuse) language has the effect, over time, of making students more aware of their own use.

Engaging students in this activity should begin by reviewing with them some of the common errors in usage and grammar summarized previously. A review of certain usage and grammar conventions also can be helpful. These reviews give students the research tools they need to succeed. The activity can be more interesting if students conduct their observations in teams of two or three. Also, the lessons to be learned seem to be easier for students to grasp if they embark on a series of observations, breaking the list of usage and grammar errors down into small units. For example, during one observation, students might collect data only on case and relative pronouns. Another observation might focus on agreement or use of *lay/lie*. Over the last several years, *like* has become ubiquitous in the speech of young people, who use it as filler, signifier, and punctuation. When I have asked students to observe others using *like*, record the types of uses, and count the frequency of use, I have noticed that the students sharply reduce their own use of the word.

Direct instruction works best when complemented by indirect instruction, which links the study of grammar and usage to some other subject as an integral part of daily activities. Reading is particularly appropriate, and the rationale is straightforward. Discussions of reading inevitably involve questions of meaning as students and teacher explore what a given author means in a text; questions of "what" lead quite naturally to questions of "how," which is where issues of structure and usage come in.

In this way, grammar instruction becomes part of an overall analysis of how good writers achieve the particular effects they do. Such analyses are important from any number of perspectives, beginning with attention to detail and craftsmanship. This approach works best when teachers read with their students and periodically make a comment that focuses students' attention on a particular word or phrase. Such indirect instruction reinforces concepts in ways that direct instruction cannot. Remarking that a certain word is an "interesting adjective" draws students' attention to the word, models for them the idea that some words are more interesting than others, and reinforces for them the concept of an adjective. Above all, grammar and usage instruction should give students tools for discovering language in all its varieties. It should not be the basis for busywork and mindless drills.

JOURNAL ENTRY

What was your experience with grammar in public school? Chances are that you are an English or an English Education major, and if you are going into teaching, you will be asked to teach grammar. But just how much grammar do you know? Have you taken a grammar course since public school?

EXAMINING THE MAJOR GRAMMARS

The beginning of this chapter identified the four major grammars as *traditional, phrase structure, transformational-generative,* and *cognitive.* Each grammar represents not only a particular way of describing language but also a particular view of language. Thus, the grammar a teacher chooses to study and teach will influence how a teacher responds to student errors. As Martha Kruse (2001) noted:

> Confronted with a statement such as "Me and my father didn't get along," the prescriptive grammarian will attribute the construction to carelessness, illogical thinking, or a chink in the venerable distinctions between subjective and objective cases of pronouns. Adherents . . . [to] phrase-structure grammar, on the other hand, regard such a sentence as grammatical (because native speakers produce such utterances regularly) but nonstandard. Along with the instructor's responses to departures from Standard English, her preferred theory of grammar may also shape, however subtly, her very perception of her role in the classroom. The transformational-generativist might . . . consider herself the facilitator of her students' efforts to translate their linguistic competence into acceptable performance. The cognitive grammarian engages his students with print in the hopes of creating or strengthening certain neural pathways in the brain's cellular structure. (p. 140)

Before one can make a choice, however, one must know something about what the choices are. Otherwise, the only option is to follow blindly whatever textbook or guide is at hand. The sections that follow offer brief overviews of the four grammars mentioned earlier.

Traditional Grammar

School grammar is traditional grammar, which focuses on prescription and which is based on Latin. It is concerned primarily with correctness and with the categorical names for the words that make up sentences. The idea is that students who speak or write expressions such as "He don't do nothin' " would modify their language to produce "He doesn't do anything" if only they knew a bit more about grammar. Traditional grammar instruction, which often begins as early as third grade and may end as late as 12th grade, follows a routine. Students use workbooks or handouts to complete exercises that ask them to identify nouns, verbs, adjectives, verbs, and so forth, and that ask them to correct errors in decontextualized lists of sentences.

Handbooks and exercises are not recent phenomena. In the Roman Empire and late in the Middle Ages, grammatical treatises became manuals on how to write, and great Latin masters like Virgil were used as models of correctness because Latin was considered the normative language. The prescriptive nature of traditional grammar has a long history. During the Middle Ages, scholars made a significant shift in rhetoric when they connected grammar and logic. The aim was to make language more orderly by linking it to the rules and principles established for logic. Violation of these principles was seen not only as incorrect but also as illogical.

During the 18th century, two other factors increasingly influenced work in grammar: prestige and socioeconomic status. This change resulted largely from the spread of education and economic mobility, which brought large numbers of people from the middle class into contact with the upper class. In England, for example, although both upper-class and middle-class people spoke the same language, there were noticeable differences in pronunciation, form, and vocabulary—what we term *dialect*—much like the differences we notice in the United States between speakers from Mississippi and California. Because the upper-class dialects identified one with prestige and success, mastering the upper-class speech patterns became very desirable, and notions of grammar became more normative than ever.

Language scholars during this time suffered from a fundamental confusion that clearly had its roots in the notion of linguistic decay first formulated by the Greeks. They noted that well-educated people wrote and spoke good Latin, whereas the less educated made many mistakes. Failing to see that reproducing a dead language is essentially an academic exercise, they applied this observation to modern languages and concluded that languages are preserved by the usage of educated people. Those without education and culture corrupt the language with their deviations from the established norm. Accordingly, the discourse forms of books and upper-class conversation represented an older and purer level of language from which the speech of the common people had degenerated (J. Lyons, 1970).

From this analysis, a significant part of traditional grammar is the distinction between what some people do with language and what they *ought* to do with it. The chief goal appears to be perpetuating a historical model of what supposedly constitutes proper language. Prescription, however, demands a high degree of knowledge to prevent inconsistency, and few people have the necessary degree of knowledge.

One of the more interesting examples of widespread inconsistency involves the verb form *be* and case, that feature of nouns and pronouns that marks them as being subjects (nominative case) or objects (objective case). English no longer changes nouns according to their case, but it continues to change pronouns, as in the following:

- *I* stopped at the market.
- Fritz asked *me* a question.

I is the subject of the first example sentence, and it is in the nominative case, whereas *me* is an object in the second, so it is in the objective case. Traditional grammar therefore labels as ungrammatical any instance in which an objective case pronoun is in the subject position or in which a nominative case pronoun is in the object position, as in the following sentences:

- *Me* stopped at the market.
- *Fritz asked *I* a question.

Sentences like these rarely if ever occur among native speakers, but a variety of factors make people confused when there is more than one noun or pronoun in any given construction, with the result that sentences like the following occur regularly, even among well-educated people:

- ?Fred handed out invitations to Fritz, Macarena, Raul, and I.
- ?Fritz, Macarena, Fred, and me went into the city to see the new art exhibit.

Now consider a common situation in which *be* serves as a *linking verb,* a special kind of verb that links the subject to either a noun phrase or an adjective phrase, as in:

- Fritz was *the winner.*
- Fritz was *tired.*

In sentences like these, the word *was* is a linking verb and is the equivalent of an equals sign, a fact that led those who espoused a relationship between grammar and logic to propose that such sentences can be expressed symbolically as $x = y$, where x represents the subject and y represents the construction after the linking verb. The logical equality of x and y requires that they share the same case, which means that in "Fritz was the winner," both *Fritz* and *the winner* are in the nominative case.

This creates a problem for an everyday expression:

- It's me.

The pronoun is in the objective case, and traditional grammar therefore would label this sentence as being both ungrammatical and illogical. Nevertheless, the number of people who actually use the "correct" form is quite small:

- It's I.

The point here is straightforward. Teachers who would criticize sentences like "Fritz, Macarena, Fred, and me went into the city to see the new art exhibit" for being ungrammatical need to make certain that they don't produce sentences like "It's me." If they do, they are inconsistent and are giving mixed signals to students.

English is a Teutonic language and is not based on Latin, which raises one of the more troubling difficulties with traditional grammar—it doesn't fit English very well. English tense illustrates part of the problem. *Tense* is a technical term that describes a change in the verb stem to indicate when an action took place. A moment of reflection will reveal that there are only three possibilities for locating an action in time: past, present, and future. Even in the most accurate discussions, traditional grammar proposes that English has all three tenses. In less accurate discussions, such as those that appear in handbooks published by major companies such as St. Martin's, Prentice-Hall, and HarperCollins, the number of tenses proliferates to include three "perfect tenses" and three "progressive tenses," raising the number immediately to nine.

English, however, has only two tenses: past and present. This fact becomes clear if we compare English with a Latin-based language such as Spanish. Let's consider the Spanish word *hablar,* which means "to speak." The first-person forms would be:

	Spanish	*English*
Present	hablo	I speak
Past	hablé	I spoke
Future	hablaría	Ø

In Spanish, the verb changes in each instance. Yet there is no corresponding change in the verb for future tense in English. Rather, we must use the auxiliary *will* to create a future *verb form.* Verb form is not the same as tense. It also is useful to note that the future in English actually can be signified in several different ways. Consider the following sentences: "Fritz can leave in the morning"; "Raul is going to go to the mountains next week"; and "Fred swims on Saturday." Each has a different verb form, but each indicates a future action.

Likewise, perfect and progressive are not tenses but are verb forms that indicate what is called *aspect,* which signals the duration or ongoing nature of an action. Consider the verb *jump.* The present tense is simply *jump,* whereas the past tense is *jumped.* The future verb form is *will jump. Is jumping* and *has been jumping,* progressive and perfect forms, respectively, signify in the first instance that an action is in progress and in the second that an action is ongoing over time.

However, the most problematic feature of traditional grammar is its focus on prescription. It is this focus that makes so many people cringe when introduced to someone they learn is an English teacher. "Oh, better watch what I say," they usually remark, or "You know, English was always my worst subject." Given what is now known about language, we are long past the time when ideas of appropriateness should have replaced ideas of correctness.

JOURNAL ENTRY

Has anyone ever corrected your language? If so, how did it make you feel? Is there any lesson in your experience that you can apply to your students?

Phrase-Structure Grammar

Until the 19th century, Latin grammar was deemed universally applicable to all languages, not just to English and related European tongues. Contact with "exotic" languages like those spoken by American Indians, however, presented insurmountable problems for traditional grammar that led scholars to replace it with a new grammar that was descriptive rather than prescriptive and that focused on phrases rather than individual words. This new grammar came to be called *phrase-structure grammar.*

The American Indian tribes were more or less ignored after the period of the great Indian wars, but during the last years of the 19th century, they became the focus of scholarly attention as anthropologists like Franz Boas came to recognize that the distinctive characteristics of these indigenous people were quickly vanishing. Researchers began intensive efforts to record the details of their cultures and languages.

Some records already existed, made years earlier by missionaries. But it became increasingly clear during the beginning of the 20th century that these early descriptions failed to record the languages adequately. In fact, in his introduction to the *Handbook of American Indian Languages,* Boas (1911) stated that the descriptions were actually distorted by the attempt to impose traditional grammar on languages for which it simply was inappropriate.

The issue of tense again provides an interesting illustration. English grammar distinguishes between past tense and present tense, but Eskimo and some other related languages do not. In Eskimo, "The husky was running" and "The husky is running" would be the same. As more data were collected, the number of such incompatibilities grew. Within a few years, it became apparent that the goal of traditional grammar, prescription based on a literary model, was out of place in the study of languages that lacked a written form.

Led by Boas, and later by Leonard Bloomfield (1933), anthropologists and linguists abandoned the assumptions of traditional grammar and adopted the view that every language is unique, with its own structure and its own grammar. Known as the *structuralist view*, this approach and the grammar that grew out of it saw the objective and scientific description of languages as a primary goal.

Phrase-structure grammar dominated American language study for many years. Students completing their doctorate in linguistics, for example, commonly spent time on reservations studying aspects of tribal languages as part of their graduate work. Moreover, it remains in wide use around the world, although in the United States it was supplanted in the early 1960s by transformational-generative grammar, which is the topic of the next section (R. Harris, 1993).

A detailed analysis of phrase structure is beyond the scope of this book, but it is important to note that its emphasis on description means that questions of correctness in keeping with arbitrary grammar rules are not germane to analysis. What matters is usage. On this account, grammaticality judgments are linked to attested utterances, which has the effect of focusing on word order in naturally occurring expressions. Native speakers seldom violate word order in any egregious way. This perspective means that according to phrase-structure grammar both of the example sentences that follow are grammatical because both appear regularly in speech:

- I saw Harry last night.
- ?I seen Harry last night.

Phrase-structure grammar developed a notation system for writing grammar rules that makes it easier to describe sentences and their constituent parts. This system is based on the perception that sentences have subjects and predicates and that subjects consist of noun phrases and that predicates consist of verb phrases. Thus, the first rule of phrase-structure grammar states that a sentence, *S*, can be rewritten as a noun phrase *(NP)* and a verb phrase *(VP)*, as indicated in the following, where the arrow means "is rewritten":

$$S \rightarrow NP\ VP$$

This grammar rule, along with supplemental rules for the components of noun phrases, verb phrases, and so forth, allows a detailed description of the language. For example, noun phrases consist of nouns plus determiners (such as *the, a,* and *an*) and any adjectives. Verb phrases consist of verbs plus any modifiers and any noun phrases that represent objects. For a sentence such as "The woman kissed the man," phrase structure would provide the following grammar rules to describe the structure of the sentence:

The woman kissed the man.
$S \rightarrow NP\ VP$
$NP \rightarrow determiner\ N$
$VP \rightarrow V\ NP$
$Det \rightarrow the$
$N \rightarrow (man,\ woman)$
$V \rightarrow kissed$

Each level of this analysis is called a *phrase-structure rule,* and the result is a grammar for this particular sentence. To make the rules more general so they can describe more sentences, it is necessary to make changes in the rules, expanding them to include prepositional phrases, additional determiners and other function words, and modifiers. The range of nouns and verbs would include all nouns and all verbs, not just *man, woman,* and *kissed.*

Phrase-structure grammar is superior to traditional grammar because it isn't prescriptive and because it provides a more accurate analysis of language. In addition, phrase-structure grammar developed conventions that allow most people, especially students, to understand better how the various parts of a sentence work together. Traditional grammar relies on Reed–Kellogg diagrams for analyzing sentences. These are horizontal figures with various types of lines whose shape indicates the functional relationship of any given part. Subjects are identified by one type of line, predicates by another, subordinate clauses by yet another. Students commonly spend so much effort figuring out what the lines mean and then remembering them that they have little mental energy left over for understanding the construction of any sentence they have to analyze. The diagramming convention in phrase-structure grammar, on the other hand, draws on the generalization noted previously, that the basic sentence pattern in English is noun phrase plus verb phrase. It involves using a *tree diagram* to depict how phrases are related within a sentence. Tree diagrams give us much more information than Reed–Kellogg diagrams.

Transformational-Generative Grammar

Transformational-generative grammar is synonymous with Noam Chomsky, who proposed it as an extension of and an alternative to phrase-structure grammar in his book *Syntactic Structures* (1957).

Since 1957, transformational-generative grammar has gone through many changes, and the current version, known as the Minimalist Program, has only a few features in common with the original (Chomsky, 1957, 1965, 1972, 1975, 1979, 1980, 1981, 1986, 1988, 1992, 1995). It is difficult to overestimate Chomsky's influence on modern language study. His work in linguistics is generally considered revolutionary. In *Syntactic Structures,* Chomsky argued that phrase-structure grammar was inadequate because it failed to explain and describe even simple sentences and because it failed to provide a theory of language. In other works, he explored a wide range of linguistic features, particularly the connection between language and mind, but underlying it all is his abiding interest in grammar.

Chomsky's idea that a grammar should provide a theory of language is important, and in many respects it was novel. A theory is a model that attempts to describe a given phenomenon regardless of situation. For example, the theory of gravity proposes that gravity is a force associated with the mass of objects; the more mass an object has, the stronger its gravitational attraction. This theory describes equally well the operation of gravity on Earth and the operation of gravity on the Moon; it isn't limited to earthly observations. Phrase-structure grammar was based on a body, or corpus, of sentences for a particular language. The corpus typically was collected through field studies in which structuralists spent time observing the speakers of a language and recording a wide range, though finite number, of its sentences. The emphasis on observation and on methods for compiling a corpus reflected the structuralist orientation away from notions of universal grammar. Stated another way, the focus was on languages rather than language. Consequently, phrase-structure grammar is highly situation-specific, a result, in part, of structuralists' negative experiences with traditional grammar.

Although trained as a structuralist, Chomsky disagreed with many of the principles of structuralism, but the orientation toward empiricism and the rejection of any notion of a universal grammar were particularly problematic for him because they led to a general lack of theory.[5] It should be noted that structuralists never were particularly concerned with theory, so when Chomsky criticized phrase-structure grammar on this ground he was being a bit unfair. Nevertheless, in his view, reliance on a corpus was fundamentally unsound because it lim-

---

[5]The scope of Chomsky's influence is evident even in the term *phrase structure.* Structuralists called their grammar *immediate constituent analysis.* Chomsky renamed it *phrase-structure grammar,* and the new name stuck (R. Harris, 1993).

ited what one could know about language. He argued that the number of possible sentences in any language is infinite because language allows for endless expansion, much in the way that math does. No corpus, therefore, can ever be "complete." Chomsky also argued that a grammar that concentrates on describing simply a list of attested sentences, even a very long one, will be concerned with only a small portion of the language. The grammar will account for only the sentences in the corpus, and it will not account for all the possible sentences a speaker of the language can produce. It is the equivalent of having a theory of gravity that applies only to the earth.

By criticizing the structuralist reliance on method, Chomsky laid the foundation for a powerful argument: A viable grammar is only one that provides universal rules that describe the sentences people produce and *all of the sentences that they potentially can produce*. It must have a "generative" component, which Chomsky characterized as "a device of some sort for producing the sentences of the language under analysis" (1957, p. 11).[6] Thus, Chomsky proposed a break with structuralists and a return to some of the principles that underlie traditional grammar. Grammaticality, he argued, cannot be determined merely by asking native speakers to make a judgment, which was the structuralist approach, but must be determined on the basis of an utterance's adherence to the rules of grammar.[7]

In addition, Chomsky argued that phrase-structure grammar could not adequately explain language, even with respect to simple sentences. He noted that phrase-structure grammar assigns different analyses to certain sentences that intuitively seem closely related, such as actives and passives, and that its lack of an apparatus to illuminate their relatedness was a serious weakness.

Transformations

To meet the theoretical, explanatory, and descriptive requirements that he saw as necessary to a grammar, Chomsky proposed a new set of rules that operated in conjunction with phrase-structure rules. He argued that each sentence uttered or read has a history, so the new rules

---

[6]What Chomsky meant by "producing" has been a matter of significant debate. As R. Harris (1993) noted, "Chomsky proposed his grammar to model a mental *state,* but many people took it to model a mental *process*" (p. 99).

[7]It would be a mistake, however, to link transformational-generative grammar too closely with traditional grammar. Chomsky's concern for universal rules was part of a goal that traditional grammar never considered and that phrase-structure grammar never seriously articulated.

must allow an analysis that reveals that history. Consider the following two example sentences, which illustrate active and passive voice:

- Fritz kissed Macarena.
- Macarena was kissed by Fritz.

Intuition indicates that these sentences are related, but the grammar, according to Chomsky, should explain the nature of their relatedness. He therefore proposed that all sentences have two states, an *underlying form* (or "deep structure") and a *surface form* (or "surface structure").[8] Pinker (1994) wrote that "Deep structure is the interface between the mental dictionary and phrase structure" (p. 121), which reflects Chomsky's early view that transformation rules are a bridge between the mind's representation of related propositions and the ultimate articulation of those representations in a grammatical sentence. In early versions of the grammar, the underlying form always is an active sentence, which is reasonable because most sentences that people construct are active rather than passive. In this case, the underlying form of "Macarena was kissed by Fritz" is "Fritz kissed Macarena." Stated another way, all passive sentences begin in the mind of the speaker or writer as active sentences. The question Chomsky had to answer, therefore, was how passive sentences are derived from active sentences.

In the early versions of the grammar, Chomsky proposed a transformation rule that changed actives to passives. He proposed a variety of other transformation rules that dealt with other types of sentences. Some of the rules were obligatory, whereas others, like the one for passive sentences, were optional. These rules used phrase-structure notation, but they were by nature more general. That is, any given transformation rule is essentially a statement of conditions. In the case of actives and passives, the rule specifies that any sentence that has the form of a noun phrase + an active verb + an object can be transformed

---

[8]For many years, linguists wrestled with the concept of deep structure because it appeared to contain the meaning, or semantic content, of a sentence. The question of meaning became so problematic that many linguists eventually rejected the very notion of deep structure. The term used here, *underlying form,* is intended to acknowledge the shift away from deep structure and to avoid some of the connotations inherent in the word *deep*. Chomksy, reluctant to give up a concept that is central to his psychological view of language, used the term *d-structure* in his 1981 revision of the grammar known as *Government-Binding Theory*. The Minimalist Program finally eliminated deep structure, which proposes that syntactic structures are the result of combining lexical items into phrases and then combining the phrases.

into its corresponding passive. One effect of such general rules is that an analysis of any passive sentence, for example, requires an analysis of its corresponding active form.[9] The analysis therefore delves into the history of the sentence.

Grammar, Language, and Psychology

Chomsky's argument that grammar was a theory of language opened avenues that linguists had not explored in great detail. Psychologists like Vygotsky (1962), Piaget (1955, 1974), and B. Skinner (1957), on the other hand, had studied language fairly extensively. Although Chomsky disagreed vehemently with the stimulus–response model of language that Skinner proposed, he nevertheless declared that the study of grammar and thus language necessarily involved the study of psychology.

Chomsky's rationale for this view was linked to his interest in linguistic universals. From his perspective, the obvious differences in languages masked underlying similarities. All languages have subjects, verbs, objects, modifiers, and function words. Most languages have at least one tense, and they all are based on phrases. In addition, children learn language in about the same way and at about the same pace in every culture. They acquire it easily on the basis of relatively little input. Adults use language fluently and efficiently to convey information and ideas and as a means of social bonding and cultural dissemination. All languages make use of logical implications, such as "If I fall into the water, I'll get wet."

These facts had long suggested that language is organized in keeping with how the brain is structured or with how it operates. A viable theory of grammar—and correspondingly a viable theory of language—would have to address the relations between brain and language. Chomsky turned to rationalism as a foundation for his argument that language is innate, genetically determined. Work by Broca (1861) and Wernicke (1874) lent some empirical support to this argument. Their investigation of language among patients with brain injuries had revealed that specific areas of the brain are responsible for different types of language processing. This high degree of cerebral specialization made a strong case for the idea that the brain evolved centers whose sole task is language processing.

Research involving people with severe brain injuries has confirmed the concept of innateness (Lenneberg, 1967; Restak, 1979; Wittrock,

---

[9]The rule described for passive here has been replaced by a much more general rule that is beyond the scope of this text.

1977). The brain is divided into two hemispheres, and mental and physical functions tend to be dominated by one hemisphere or the other. Physical movements on the right side of the body involve primarily the left hemisphere; movements on the left side involve primarily the right hemisphere. In most people, the left hemisphere controls language, so when adults suffer damage to this part of the brain, language almost always is permanently impaired. This phenomenon suggests that an innate, physiological basis for language exists, that the left hemisphere is genetically programmed to control language function much in the same way that the occipital region of the brain is genetically programmed to control vision.

But in cases of preadolescent children who experience damage to the left hemisphere, the uninjured right hemisphere in most instances somehow manages to take over language function intact without measurable impairment. Although this phenomenon does not invalidate the innateness proposal, the effect is to weaken it, because language takes on characteristics of learned behavior. Moreover, it suggests the existence of a critical period during which brain function and language development are plastic and can shift readily from the left hemisphere to the right. The idea of innateness required evidence that some features of language are specifically and nontransferably located in the left hemisphere.

Such evidence was found in studies of children who at birth were diagnosed as having one diseased hemisphere that would lead to death if left alone. The children were operated on within a few days of birth (Day & Ulatowska, 1979; Dennis & Kohn, 1975; Dennis & Whitaker, 1976; Kohn, 1980). In some cases the entire left hemisphere was removed; in others the entire right hemisphere was removed. (This procedure causes serious intellectual deficits, but children who undergo the operation develop normally in many ways.) The children were studied as they matured, with particular attention to language development. Tests of vocabulary and comprehension showed no significant differences between those with right hemisphere or left hemisphere removed. Both also seemed equally able to carry on a normal conversation.

Closer examination, however, revealed several important differences. Dennis and Kohn (1975) found that children with the right hemisphere removed could process negative passive sentences, but those with the left hemisphere removed could not. Dennis and Whitaker (1976) found that children with the left hemisphere removed showed an inability to deviate from subject/verb/object word order. They could not understand or produce what are called "cleft" sentences, such as, "What the teller wanted me to do was deposit more money." Nor could they process sentences that use *by* in any way other than indicating location. They could understand "The book was by the lamp" but not "The cake was made by my sister." On the basis of such evidence, most scholars have concluded that some grammar-related features of language are indeed exclusively part of left-hemispheric function. Chomsky's intuition about linguistic innateness was substantially correct.

Language Acquisition

One consequence of the innateness hypothesis was that the question of how children acquire language became a matter of understanding cognitive development. Chomsky observed that young children are not taught grammar, yet they manage to produce grammatical sentences at a fairly early age on the basis of often distorted input ("baby talk"). Moreover, their sentences cannot be viewed merely as parroting of adult speech, because their utterances are not repetitions of what they hear. Chomsky maintained that such facility with language would be impossible without some innate *language acquisition device* (LAD) that induces grammatical rules from very little data.

The standard account of language acquisition proposes that children begin receiving linguistic input at birth.[10] This input is severely limited because of the nature of parent–adult linguistic interactions. Adults just don't speak to infants the same way that they speak to other adults. Their baby talk, or *motherese,* deletes function words, focuses on nouns, and commonly abuses normal word order. Nevertheless, children begin producing intelligible speech within a year or two, speech that conforms in significant ways with adult language.

In this account, the LAD is considered to be a subsystem of the language mechanism, with the sole role of inducing the grammar rules of the child's home language. Fodor (1983), Johnson-Laird (1983), and others have argued that these rules are explicit but inaccessible; they can be described but not consciously altered. The LAD hypothesizes the rules on the basis of input, and the hypotheses are accepted or rejected on the basis of their ability to enable processing of the sentences children hear. Hudson (1980) and Slobin and Welsh (1973), noting that children face a major problem because they must induce accurate rules on the basis of inaccurate and distorted data, argued that the LAD has an innate knowledge of the possible range of human languages and

---

[10]Pages 210–213 present an alternative to the standard account.

therefore considers only those hypotheses within the constraints imposed on grammar by a set of linguistic universals.

In support of the standard account of language acquisition, many scholars (H. Clark & E. Clark, 1977; Krashen, 1980; Pinker, 1994) have turned to an overgeneralization phenomenon involving regular and irregular verbs. During their early stages of language development, children use only a small number of past-tense verbs, but they often use present-tense verbs to indicate a past action. Most of the past-tense verbs they use are irregular and high frequency. For example, a child's lexicon of past-tense verbs might consist of *ate, got, shook, stopped, did, went,* and *kissed.* Because the lexicon includes regular as well as irregular verbs, there is no evidence that the child is using a past-tense rule. The regular and irregular verbs simply appear to be separate items in the lexicon.

Many observers have noted that a change occurs at about 2.5 years. Children start using more past-tense verbs. The number of irregular verbs grows, but not significantly. However, in the standard account, two new linguistic behaviors emerge. First, children develop the ability to generate a past tense for an invented word. If a parent (or researcher) can persuade a child to use, say, the word *bloss,* they will say *blossed* to describe whatever action this might be when it occurred in the past. Second, children now incorrectly attach regular past-tense endings to irregular verbs that they used correctly earlier. As H. Clark and E. Clark (1977) noted, children add *ed* to the root, as in *comed* or *goed,* or they may add *ed* to the irregular past-tense from, as in *wented.*

After about 8 months, the regular and irregular forms come to coexist. Children begin to use the correct irregular forms of the past tense and to apply the regular form correctly to new words they learn. These developments have led many to view the process as strong evidence for the successful induction of grammar rules, for children appear to be using the rules to compute the appropriate output for both regular and irregular verb forms. The rules operate more or less automatically from that point on, in a manner that Fodor (1983) characterized as a reflex. Thus, it is widely accepted in linguistics that children's overgeneralization of tense formation is representative of the entire range of grammar rules.

According to Chomsky's analysis, the grammar rules that the LAD induces are transformational-generative rules, and the suggestion that such rules are internalized led early researchers to attempt to determine whether they had a "psychological reality." The research question was simple: If language users actually apply transformation rules to underlying structures, do they take longer to process transformed sentences? G. Miller (1962) attempted to answer that question through what came to be known as the "click experiments." He compiled a list of sentences, gave subjects a device that made a click sound, and then directed them to use the device as soon as they understood each sentence. Passives and actives were of particular interest because the passive transformation has such a significant effect on the structure of the active form. Miller's data indicated convincingly that transformed sentences like passives took subjects longer to process (also see G. Miller & McKean, 1964). Only much later did it become clear that other factors may have caused the longer processing times. Passives, for example, generally are longer than their corresponding actives, which influences time.

Competence and Performance

The standard account of language acquisition raised a problem. If the LAD induces correct grammar rules, why is human speech full of errors? People have many slips of the tongue that jumble up their language. They often use prepositions incorrectly, saying that someone "got *in* the bus" rather than "*on* the bus," and so forth. Many utterances are ungrammatical, as in the case of a person who fails to shift a particle behind a pronoun. Sometimes speakers are aware of the flaw and will stop in midsentence and begin again, repairing the problem. Other times they may not be quite so attentive, and the flaw will slip by undetected.

As Chomsky formulated the grammar, however, it will not produce ungrammatical sentences under any circumstances. Thus, the generative component of transformational-generative grammar was not congruent with actual language use. To account for the apparent inconsistency, Chomsky distinguished between the sentences generated by the grammar and the sentences actually produced by language users. The terms he used to make this distinction are *competence* and *performance*. Linguistic competence may be understood as the inherent ability of a native speaker to make correct grammaticality judgments. Performance is what people actually do with the language, subject as they are to fatigue, distraction, and all the many psychosocial factors that prevent optimal language production. All native speakers possess linguistic competence, but only an ideal speaker, a mental construct, would be able to translate competence into error-free performance.

The competence–performance distinction was deemed quite useful because it accounts for the occurrence of ungrammatical sentences and also for the occasional inability of listeners to analyze grammatical sentences. Such difficulties are due to errors of performance, errors made somehow between the application of the rules and the articulation of an utterance. They are not due to errors in the grammar.

During the 1960s, many people reasoned that the competence–performance distinction could be turned into an instructional agenda: One need simply provide students with the means for turning tacit knowledge on the level of competence into explicit knowledge on the level of performance. Numerous efforts were made at teaching transformational-generative grammar to raise performance to the level of competence (see Gale, 1968; Mellon, 1969; O'Hare, 1972; R. White, 1965). Although not terribly successful in a direct sense, these efforts had an indirect and substantial effect on studies of style (see Bateman & Zidonis, 1966; Mellon, 1969; O'Hare, 1972; Winterowd, 1975). The stylistic device of sentence combining arose out of attempts to increase writing maturity by teaching students transformational-generative grammar.

Many people were confused by the notions of competence and performance. They reasoned that if students already knew everything about language, teachers had nothing to teach. Others could not understand, as writing skills deteriorated more every year, how students who presumably had such extensive knowledge of English could write so terribly.[11] The problem was—and is—that competence is a slippery term. In everyday language, the term has two meanings: It refers to skill level or to potential ability. In the first case, a person may be a competent pianist if he or she can play a tune on a piano. In the second case, a person may be competent *to play the piano* if he or she has arms, hands, fingers, legs, and feet. The person may not be able to play at all but is competent to do so. Moreover, there is no promise that this level of competence has any real connection to actual performance. Even with training there is no assurance that a person ever will be competent in the first sense of the word.

When composition studies adopted the competence–performance distinction, the tendency was to ignore the technical definition of competence in favor of the popular one related to *potential ability*. Matters were confused further by notions of innateness, until *writing competence* came to mean for many teachers something along the lines of "the innate ability to write." So for many teachers, competence suggested a classroom environment where students have ample opportunities to write, where they have the chance to practice *what they already know how to do* (Berthoff, 1981, 1983; Elbow, 1973; Graves, 1981; Murray, 1982; Parker, 1979). In a peculiar twist, transforma-

---

[11]Whitaker (March 1984, personal communication) expressed the puzzlement of many when he compared the writing of college freshmen to the speech of aphasics.

tional-generative grammar served to support the agenda of romantic rhetoric.

JOURNAL ENTRY

Reflect on your feelings about language and students' abilities to draw on some innate potential to produce "correct" language. How do those feelings compare with the preceding discussion?

Cognitive Grammar

Transformational-generative grammar became popular for many reasons, but two stand out. It was simple and elegant, and it promised new insights into the psychological mechanisms that underlie language. As the grammar matured, however, it lost its simplicity and much of its elegance. The role of meaning in transformational-generative grammar always had been ambiguous. In *Syntactic Structures,* Chomsky (1957) noted that his grammar "was completely formal and non-semantic" (p. 93). Nevertheless, discussions of deep structure suggested that it represented the meaning of a sentence, which led many people to suspect that Chomsky really was interested in meaning after all. A flurry of activity followed in which scholars attempted to develop a way to bring grammar and meaning together successfully in one theory, a move that Chomsky alternately supported and opposed for many years (R. Harris, 1993). But Chomsky's theories of grammar kept changing. Moreover, they grew more and more abstract—and in many respects more complex—until they no longer were easily accessible to anyone without specialized training in linguistics. In time, these factors combined with the growing perception in composition studies that "competence" had been incorrectly applied. Students did not appear to have any innate ability to write. Interest in transformational-generative grammar began to fade.

Cognitive psychology deals with human knowledge and how people use it (A. Clark, 1993; Glass, Holyoak, & Santa, 1979; Kelso, 1995), and cognitive psychologists were among the earliest supporters of transformational-generative grammar because they saw it as a means to better understanding the mind. A certain irony was inevitable. Chomsky was (and is) notoriously antiempirical, whereas cognitive psychology is grounded in empiricism and experimental method. Nevertheless, psychologists ignored the irony, largely because the grammar was congruent with the computational, rule-governed model of mind that had dominated psychology for decades. In this model, explicit, inaccessible rules compute input and output of all types: logic, decision making, reading, and so forth. With respect to language, computation in part involves combining small units to create larger ones.

As noted earlier, one of the first attempts to apply experimental methods to Chomsky's theory was made in 1962, when George Miller set out to evaluate the psychological reality of transformation rules. He hypothesized that transformed sentences would require longer processing times than nontransformed sentences, and he developed an experiment to measure the differences in processing rates. If the rules were psychologically real, if they truly existed in the brain, then transformed sentences indeed would take longer to process. Negatives would take longer than positives, passives longer than actives. Sentences with multiple transformations would take even longer.

Miller's results confirmed his hypothesis, and initially psychologists and linguists alike were excited to have empirical validation of Chomsky's intuition-based model. For several years, the psychological reality of transformation rules was deemed a given. But problems began to emerge when some researchers noted that passive sentences generally are longer than their corresponding active form and that sentence length could have accounted for Miller's results. Then a range of studies that took into account such factors as sentence length and subtle changes in meaning showed that transformations had no effect on processing time (Baker, Prideaux, & Derwin, 1973; Bever, 1970; Fodor et al., 1974; Fodor & Garrett, 1966; Glucksberg & Danks, 1969). Neither transformations nor deep structure seemed to have any psychological reality whatsoever, and transformational-generative grammar failed to lend itself to empirical validation.

Chomsky was unfazed. After all, he developed transformational-generative grammar in part as a rationalist reaction against structuralism and its empirical basis. Psychologists, however, generally saw the lack of experimental validation was a mortal blow for the grammar. Transformational-generative grammar became widely viewed as an interesting theory that had no measurable support, and by the late 1970s most cognitive psychologists had abandoned it. Because language is a fundamental component of cognitive processing, psychologists began searching for a new theory that was experimentally verifiable. What emerged is known as *cognitive grammar* (Langacker, 1987, 1990).

A characteristic of rule-driven systems is that they consistently produce correct output. They are deterministic, so after a rule is in place there is no reason to expect an error. Transformational-generative grammar is rule driven to the core. On this account, we should expect the following: After a person has induced the rule for passive transformations, whenever he or she intends to produce a passive sentence the rule is invoked unconsciously, and it necessarily must produce the same result each time. However, the frequent errors in speech suggest that the rules in fact do not produce correct output, which is why Chomsky's concept of competence and performance was so important to early versions of transformational-generative grammar. Without it, the grammar fails either to describe or explain language in any principled way.

Cognitive grammar simplifies matters immensely by rejecting the rule-governed model of mind and language, replacing it with an association model based on the work in cognitive science by Rumelhart and McClelland (1986a, 1986b) and others working in an area known as *connectionism* (also see Searle, 1992). Although an in-depth analysis of connectionism is not possible here, the model is easy to understand. Connectionism describes learning in terms of *neural networks*. These networks are physiological structures in the brain that are composed of cells called *neurons* and pathways—*dendrites* and *axons*—that allow neurons to communicate with one another. This basic structure is illustrated in Fig. 6.1. When a person learns a new word or concept, the brain's cell structure changes, literally growing the network to accommodate the new knowledge.[12] The more a person learns, the more extensive the neural network.

Rule-governed models like Chomsky's assume that mental activity or thought is verbal—any given sentence begins as *mentalese*. Some of the early versions of transformational-generative grammar attempted to capture the nature of mentalese in the underlying structure. The following example sentence illustrates this principle:

- Fritz loved the woman who drove the red Porsche.

This surface structure contains an independent clause ("Fritz loved the woman") and a relative clause ("who drove the red Porsche"). But the sentence has an underlying structure that consists of the following:

- Fritz loved the woman. The woman drove the red Porsche.

This underlying structure supposedly represents how the sentence exists as mentalese, only to be altered through the application of a transformation rule.

Connectionism, however, suggests that it is a mistake to assume that cognitive activities are verbal just because everyone reports hearing a mental voice when thinking. Instead, it proposes that mental activities are primarily (though not exclusively) imagistic, based

---

[12]Sometimes the network contracts.

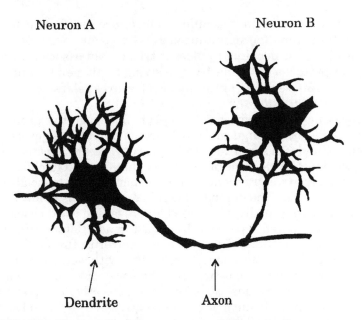

FIG. 6.1. Neurons, dendrites, and axons. Each neuron has numerous dendrites that connect it to other neurons via connecting pathways called axons. From Carlson (1994). Copyright © 1994 by Allyn & Bacon. Adapted by permission.

on images. This point is important for a number of reasons, but one of the more relevant is that it allows language processing to be understood as a matter of matching words with mental representations and internalized models of reality. No rules are involved. Instead, language is governed by patterns of regularity (Rumelhart & McClelland, 1986a, 1986b).

These patterns begin establishing themselves at birth (see Kelso, 1995). As Williams (1993) noted, when children encounter the world, their parents and other adults provide them with the names of things. They see dogs, and they immediately are provided the word *dog*, with the result that they develop a mental model related to "dog-ness." On a neurophysiological level, this model consists of modifications to the cerebral structure: Cells change. The network grows. A child's mental model for "dog-ness" includes the range of physical features that typify dogs, and these features are connected to the mental representation as well as to the string of phonemes that make up the word *dog*. Rumelhart and McClelland (1986a, 1986b) argued convincingly that the connection is via neural pathways. Over time, or owing to some other factors, such as interest, the connection becomes stronger, like a well-worn path, until the image of a dog is firmly linked to the word *dog*. From that point on, the child is able to process the image of "dog-ness" and the word *dog* simultaneously. Stated another way, "Hearing the word [*dog*] or deciding to utter it triggers an association between one set of patterns of regularity, the string of phonemes, and another set that contains subsets of the various features related to 'dog-ness'" (Williams, 1993, p. 558).[13]

In rejecting the rule-governed model of mind, cognitive grammar also rejects the idea that language is computational and rule governed. Conventions still play a significant role, but rules do not because syntax is determined by the patterns of regularity that develop in childhood. (To an extent, cognitive grammar is quite congruent with social-theoretic views of language.) The number of acceptable patterns in any given language is relatively small and is based on prevailing word order. In English, the many sentence patterns that exist in addition to SVO and SVC are essentially variations of the two major patterns. Production consists of selecting a given pattern and then filling it with words that match the mental model of the proposition that the speaker wants to convey. On this account, the grammar itself has no generative component—it is purely descriptive. The high degree of creativity observed in language is the result of an essentially limitless supply of mental propositions and the flexibility inherent in English word order. The grammar involves no special rules to explain the relationship between, say, actives and passives because it simply notes that these two sentence patterns are alternative forms available for certain propositions. The forms themselves are described as being linked psychophysiologically in the neural network, coexisting simultaneously.

In this view, grammar is a system for describing the patterns of regularity that are inherent in language; it is not specifically a theory of language or of mind. Because mental activities are deemed to be imagistic rather than verbal, cognitive grammar does not need an underlying grammatical form for sentences. The free association of images makes the question of underlying structure irrelevant. Surface structure is linked directly to the mental proposition and corresponding phonemic and lexical representations. A formal grammatical apparatus to explain the relatedness of actives and passives and other types of related sentences is not necessary because these patterns coexist in the neural network. The role of the grammar is merely to describe surface structures. Given the emphasis on description, phrase-structure grammar provides the most effective set of descriptive tools.

---

[13]Although the emphasis here is on intentional activities, clearly other factors can have a similar effect. Most people have the experience of encountering a certain fragrance or hearing a certain song that evokes detailed images from the past. The process of association is similar, if not identical, to the account here.

Another advantage of cognitive grammar and its associated cognitive theory is that they explain errors in language without recourse to notions of competence and performance, which at best are highly artificial, ad hoc. Errors occur because each person has other, similar patterns of regularity with many overlapping features. For example, cats and dogs have four legs, tails, and fur. They are pets, require a great deal of care, shed, and so forth. When an association is triggered, the connecting pathways become excited. Thus, whenever a person's intention causes a phoneme or phoneme sequence to become active in a particular utterance, all the words in the lexicon that are similar to the target word become active as well. These words compete with one another on the basis of their connecting strengths to their corresponding mental representations. Normally, the target word has the greatest connecting strength; there is a match, and the person's intention is realized. Sometimes, however, on a probabilistic basis, an incorrect match, or error, will occur. When it does, the person may replace the word *dog* with the word *cat,* or using an example that parents are very familiar with, a child may call "Mommy" *Daddy,* or vice versa (see Goldrick & Rapp, 2001). Figure 6.2 illustrates a schematic rendering of a developed neural network.

Age increases the connecting strengths within the network, so as people grow older they produce fewer errors. However, this model predicts that, statistically, errors always will occur on a random basis regardless of age. This prediction is born out by the fact that everyone produces errors of one type or another while speaking. Analysis shows that people produce similar errors while writing. In addition, the model provides a more accurate explanation of the phenomenon of tense overgeneralization. Contrary to the standard account of language acquisition, children do not apply the past-participle affix to irregular verbs consistently. Sometimes they use the regular and irregular forms correctly, sometimes incorrectly. As Williams (1993) noted, this "inconsistent behavior is almost impossible to explain adequately with a rule-governed model" (p. 560). However, this behavior is easily understood in terms of competing forms: The connecting associations related to past-tense forms are insufficiently developed to allow one form to dominate.

Although cognitive grammar provides explanations of language that are simpler and more elegant than any other grammar, it faces strong opposition from orthodox linguistics, where there is a powerful vested interest in preserving transformational-generative grammar. For a time during the late 1980s and early 1990s, those working in cognitive grammar attempted to share ideas and theories with those working in mainstream linguistics, with disappointing results. Rumelhart indi-

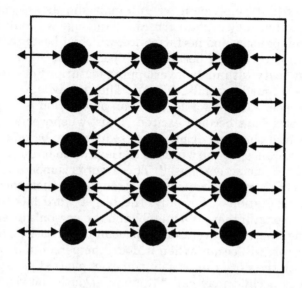

FIG. 6.2. Schematic of neural network. This schematic representation-
ally shows neurons and their corresponding pathways. Note how the neurons are interconnected.

cated that orthodox linguists as a group finally turned away from cognitive grammar and connectionism and wanted nothing more to do
with it (July 1990, personal communication). Many years later, it appears as though the situation has not changed. In the field of cognitive
science, however, connectionism provides a powerful and well-
accepted model of cognitive and linguistic processing.

English as a Second Language and Nonstandard English

BILINGUAL EDUCATION

According to census figures, the U.S. population has more than doubled since 1960, and immigration has contributed significantly to this growth. Some states have been affected more than others. In California, for example, between 1990 and 2000, 9 out of 10 new Californians were Latino or Asian immigrants. In Orange County, south of Los Angeles, the population rose from just over 1 million in 1970 to more than 2.5 million in 2000. Ninety percent of the increase was the result of immigration from Mexico and Asia.

Over the next 40 years, the U.S. population will more than double again, and estimates are that 85% of the increase will be through immigration from Asia, Mexico, and Africa as the world experiences a great movement of people from the undeveloped to the developed world known as the South–North migration. The social consequences of this mass immigration are significant, for it quite literally has altered the state of the nation and figures into nearly every question associated with public policy—from education and health care to housing and employment. For this reason, bilingual education always has been—and is likely to remain—primarily a political issue rather than a pedagogical one.

Mainstream English speakers feel apprehension when they consider the level of immigration that has occurred over the last several decades. The status that English enjoyed after World War I as the dominant language in American society is no longer secure. The sheer number of Spanish speakers now in the United States, the majority of whom speak little or no English, is reshaping the linguistic character-

215

istics of the nation. For example, there are now about 300 Spanish-language newspapers in the United States, more than 300 radio stations, and several television networks. In many areas of the Southwest, Spanish is the first language of the majority of the population. Nearly half of the states in the country, including California, have passed legislation declaring English to be the official language, and many others are considering similar legislation. Such legislation, in turn, makes nonnative English speakers feel apprehensive. The resulting tension seems to escalate each year.

Bilingual education programs are intended to serve a variety of students. Los Angeles, for example, has very large Chinese and Korean immigrant populations, and various schools in Los Angeles Unified School District (LAUSD) provided, until recently, bilingual education in Chinese and Korean. Nationwide, however, when we talk about bilingual education, we essentially are talking about Spanish-speaking students, who vastly outnumber all other non-English-language groups. In LAUSD, approximately 60% of enrolled students speak Spanish as their home language.

The politics of bilingual education are highly polarized. On the one hand are those who advocate assimilation into the English-speaking mainstream. They argue convincingly that assimilation is necessary if non-English-speaking children are to have any hope of enjoying the socioeconomic benefits available to those who have access to higher education and professional jobs, for which fluency and literacy in English are fundamental requirements. Less often heard, but nevertheless salient, is the argument that language is the thread that binds diverse people into one nation and that the welfare of the country is enhanced through monolingualism. One of the more visible proponents of this argument is Richard Rodriguez, whose 1982 book *The Hunger of Memory: The Education of Richard Rodriguez* described Spanish, his home language, as private and English as public. In a 1997 interview, Rodriguez elaborated on this view in response to a question about the role the home language plays in personal identity: "It was not my teacher's role [in elementary school] to tell me I was Mexican. It was my teacher's role to tell me that I was an American. The notion that you go to a public institution in order to learn private information about yourself is absurd."

On the other hand are those who advocate linguistic and cultural pluralism. They argue not only that people identify who they are, individually and culturally, on the basis of the language they speak but also that to ask children to assimilate into the English-speaking mainstream is to ask them to lose their identity and their cultural heritage. In addition, they argue that the nation is enriched by the linguistic and cultural diversity inherent in bilingualism and that the country would be well served if native English-speaking children were required to learn a second language. The arguments of the two camps are convincing because both contain many elements of truth.

In the end, however, the linguistic diversity argument may be moot. The nation's overall goal, expressed clearly in the Bilingual Education Act of 1968, is assimilation, not diversity. States with large immigrant populations, such as California, Arizona, Colorado, Texas, and Massachusetts, have been struggling with low academic performance among their limited English proficient (LEP) students for years, and critics have regularly blamed bilingual education programs as part of the problem. Many districts in these states have LEP populations of 60% or more, and a large number of schools have nearly 100% LEP enrollment. For several decades, California set the standard for progressive bilingual education, but in 1998, voters passed Proposition 227, a measure that essentially dismantled the state's bilingual education programs. Large numbers of educators were dismayed, but parents were generally delighted. In 2000, Arizona voters followed California's lead with Proposition 203, which dismantled that state's bilingual education programs. Several other states, encouraged by these measures, are considering similar legislation.

Problematic Test Scores

Advocates for ending bilingual education programs noted that participating children had uniformly low test scores, even though testing was conducted in Spanish for the majority Hispanic students. Reading scores were particularly low, with only about 7% of LEP students enrolled in bilingual programs reading at grade level. Thus, after the passage of California's Proposition 227, many people were interested in examining test results under the new educational paradigm. Statewide scores released by the California State Board of Education in 2000 for the 1998–1999 Stanford Achievement Test, Version 9 (SAT 9) showed a substantial increase in LEP performance, which many touted as evidence that dismantling the state's bilingual education programs was beneficial.

These test results, however, have been challenged from several quarters. Orr, Butler, Bousquet, and Hakuta (2000), for example, noted that the results are inconclusive because SAT 9 scores rose for all California students during this period. In analyses that I conducted of elementary schools in LAUSD for the U.S. Department of Education (OBEMLA Grants T290U70130, T290U60140, T290U70150, T290U50160), I found that SAT 9 scores for LEP students actually *de-*

clined during the period from 1997 through 2000, even while the participating schools were reporting success in their LEP enrichment programs. Equally troubling is that the results reported by the California Board of Education show a simple linear analysis by year, even though a cohort analysis is more revealing. For example, the fact that third-grade reading scores in 1999 are higher than third-grade reading scores in 1998 is not particularly meaningful. Scores can only be interpreted accurately if we know what the third-grade cohort's scores were in second grade. Otherwise, we end up comparing scores for different groups of students.

PLACEMENT AND CLASSIFICATION IN BILINGUAL PROGRAMS

Most districts today require parents to identify the home language when they register their children for school. On the basis of these reports, schools will test nonnative English speakers either just before or shortly after classes begin, using any one of a variety of available instruments. Under Title I of the Elementary and Secondary Education Act, 2002, all states are now required to draft rules and procedures for assessing nonnative English-speaking students (even if they do not have a bilingual education program), and Section 1111 requires states to present assessment plans to the United States Department of Education by 2004. Since 2001, California schools have been required by the State Board of Education to use the California English Language Development Test (CELDT) to identify and assess the language proficiency of entering students. On the basis of such tests, students are classified as either English proficient or limited English proficient (LEP).[1]

Students classified as LEP generally go into an *immersion program*. Immersion provides dual instruction in the home language (L_1) and English (L_2), until students are proficient in both languages. In ideal situations, *proficiency* includes literacy as well as oral skills, yet in many districts literacy in both languages remains a nagging problem that receives inadequate attention. One result is that large numbers of nonnative English speakers fail to become literate in either L_1 or L_2 (Williams & Snipper, 1990).

The goal of immersion can be bilingualism or monolingualism, and the approaches of Canada and the United States offer illustrative ex-

---

[1]Note that some states, such as California, have changed the designation to "English language learner," or ELL.

amples. In Canada, the goal is bilingualism, so students whose home language is English take content classes in French, whereas students whose home language is French take content classes in English.[2] The Canadian approach is intended to reduce, if not eliminate, the stigma attached to "minority languages" by treating both equally in the schools. A handful of American schools have experimented with the Canadian model, but resistance is strong because the goal of bilingual policy in the United States is monolingualism, not bilingualism. Consequently, immersion in this country is unilateral rather than bilateral. Nonnative English speakers take classes in English, but native English speakers do not take classes in, say, Spanish. Those schools that offer Spanish classes to native English speakers do so as part of a foreign-language program, not as part of a bilingual-immersion program.[3]

After classification, most schools place LEP students in English-only classes that rely on bilingual aides to translate the course material; such students also attend a course on English as a second language (ESL). Some schools, however, place these students in content classes conducted in L_1 and provide them with a supplemental ESL class.[4] In either case, the goal of assimilation results in efforts to reclassify LEP students quickly as English proficient, so the overall approach often is described as reflecting an orientation toward *language shift*. Nearly all LEP students are reclassified within 1 year, and many of them are reclassified within 6 months.

Those educators who strongly disagree with the assumptions underlying both assimilation and language shift advocate an approach to bilingualism that strives not only to preserve but to enhance existing skills in L_1, particularly literacy skills. This approach usually is referred to as *language maintenance*. Compared to their counterparts in language-shift programs, students take content classes in L_1 much longer, with a corresponding increase in the attention given to literacy. Teachers in all classes regularly focus on factors that reinforce stu-

---

[2]Students actually rotate their courses every couple of years so that they do take classes in L_1 periodically.

[3]During the 1970s and early 1980s, foreign-language programs expanded in most districts to include early instruction at the elementary level. During the late 1980s and into the 1990s, budget difficulties prompted many schools to reduce or even eliminate their foreign-language programs.

[4]Several studies show that parents and students value assimilation more than maintenance, although, as Shin (1994) reported, parents often are ambivalent about programs that keep students in L_1 content-area classes for a significant time. In addition, Luges (1994) reported that students in ESL programs view ESL classes negatively owing to their perception that such classes act as obstacles to assimilation.

dents' home culture, such as celebrations of native holidays and reports of important news events in the home country.

Advocates of language maintenance recognize that helping students develop better L_1 skills can have a positive effect on self-confidence, and they argue that the resulting linguistic and cultural diversity offers benefits to the whole society. Cummins (1988), for example, supports policies that would transform American monolingual society into a multilingual one and has argued for greater efforts at maintenance. Although the goals of language maintenance are worthy, Williams and Snipper (1990) correctly noted that proponents frequently fail to consider the numerous social factors that make them impractical. Because so many Americans and permanent residents speak native languages other than English, it is possible to argue that the nation already is multilingual to a certain degree, but official multilingualism of the sort envisioned by scholars such as Cummins would have to satisfy a fundamental sociolinguistic reality: People learn another language only when they have a reason for doing so. Currently, such a reason does not exist for most Americans.

Immersion and Spanish-Speaking Students

The overwhelming majority of nonnative English-speaking students in the nation's schools speak Spanish, and the majority are from Mexico. Immersion has proven stubbornly unsuccessful in helping them master English, prompting some educators to assert that immersion is more accurately *submersion*. The failure of immersion to develop English literacy and oral proficiency among native Spanish-speaking students probably contributes to the high dropout rate among Hispanics, which has hovered around 35% for decades.

Some scholars attribute the failure to the proximity of Mexico and the widespread belief among many Mexican-Americans, even second and third generation, that they someday will return permanently to Mexico (Griswold del Castillo, 1984; R. Sanchez, 1983). Others attribute it to the size of the Hispanic community. With their own subculture of shops, newspapers, radio stations, businesses, and so on, native Spanish speakers experience less socioeconomic pressure to master English than, for example, an immigrant from Iran would feel. Because socioeconomic factors are the principal motivators in mastering another language, in this case English, the lack of such pressure would significantly diminish efforts at second-language acquisition. Still others argue that Spanish speakers have been systematically excluded from America's mainstream economic community, kept at the lowest end of the socioeconomic scale for so long that they lack hope of entry and therefore lack motivation to master English (Griswold del Castillo, 1984; Penalosa, 1980; R. Sanchez, 1983). Graff (1987) argued that such exclusion has been deliberate and that the nation's schools have perpetuated illiteracy among Hispanics so as to maintain for the nation a large pool of unskilled labor to perform menial tasks.

Recent research suggests that a key to improving the success of immersion programs lies in discovering ways to get the parents of native Spanish-speaking students more involved in their children's mastery of English, not an easy task because parents who do not speak English are often reluctant to interact with teachers who do not speak Spanish. Parator et al. (1995) reported gains, however, when parents participated more actively in bridging the home–school environments.

My own work evaluating the outcomes of DOE Title VII grants to LAUSD elementary schools was not congruent with the findings of Parator et al. The enrichment efforts at these schools spanned 5 years, pre- and post-Proposition 227, and included after-school programs that involved students, parents, and teachers; parenting classes; and bridge programs that brought parents into the classroom and involved them in school decision making. The results were disappointing: None of these efforts resulted in any measurable improvement in student test scores either before or after 227.

Sandra Stotsky's (1999) meta-analysis of the pedagogical features of several popular basal readers for Grades 4–5 suggests that other factors may outweigh any potential benefits of enrichment programs. She developed qualitative and quantitative indices that allowed her to assess the pedagogical apparatus of these texts and to compare them to readers published decades earlier. Stotsky reported a serious decline in the number of complex words taught in the readers and an overall limitation of vocabulary. In other words, the texts had been dumbed down significantly and did not aim to teach Standard English. She concluded that the dumbing down of texts may be the primary cause for the poor academic performance among minority students. If this assessment is accurate, after-school programs and parental involvement will have little effect on academic achievement or graduation rates.

ADDRESSING THE NEED
FOR BILINGUAL EDUCATION

The Bilingual Education Act of 1968 was designed to make school districts more responsive to the special educational needs of children of limited English-speaking ability. The nation's schools have responded admirably, for the most part, considering the size of the task, but it is the case that many teachers and administrators are ambivalent about bilingual education. As the legislation in California and Arizona showed, voters are adamantly opposed to such programs. One reason is that they are very costly. LAUSD estimated that it spent approximately $50 million on programs in 1998, the last year of its bilingual education efforts. Critics argue that bilingual education has grown into a bloated industry that caters to publishers, consultants, and other special-interest groups and that costs taxpayers several billion dollars each year—taxpayers who increasingly do not have children enrolled in school as a result of the graying of the white, taxpaying population and the influx of the young, Hispanic, nontaxpaying population.[5]

Matters are complicated by the fact that there are few qualified bilingual teachers, especially for the less common languages, such as Korean, Vietnamese, Taglog, and so on. Though most teachers have studied some foreign language, they are far from being bilingual. Moreover, if the language they studied was French, Italian, or German, it is essentially useless in the classroom. The situation is so extreme that most districts are unable to hire enough teachers who speak the most widely distributed language, Spanish, because the demand exceeds the supply. The consequences of this situation are felt by almost every teacher at the elementary and secondary level, whether one is teaching a designated bilingual class or not. Increasingly, teachers are asked to view their classes as being multilingual because they are likely to work with nonnative English-speaking students at some point, regardless of what grade level or part of the country they teach in. The tendency to reclassify LEP students as English proficient before they are ready adds to the teacher's problems because it usually places LEP students in classes with native English speakers, making uniform assignments and grading difficult. In addition, the writing teacher will be confronted with linguistic patterns that he or she has not been adequately trained to handle.

At this point, it seems as though our schools cannot adequately meet the needs of LEP students, in spite of everyone's best efforts. The numbers are simply overwhelming. The entire question of bilingual education increasingly appears to be a public policy issue that cannot be adequately addressed through efforts like California's Proposition 227 or Arizona's Proposition 203. If demographic projections are accurate and 85% of America's population growth over the next several decades will be the result of immigration from Asia, Africa, and Mex-

---

[5]About 75% of the funds for public education comes from homeowner property taxes. Immigrants typically are renters, and renters do not pay property taxes.

ico, every facet of education, from teacher credentialing to classroom goals and objectives, must change. The problems and challenges are national in scope and cannot be solved, as they have been in the past, at the community level. Unfortunately, the vision necessary to chart a course for public policy and education has never been found in great abundance in the nation's capital.

BILINGUALISM AND INTELLIGENCE

For many years, the two political camps in conflict over bilingual education have argued a presumed relation between bilingualism and intelligence. A variety of studies have shown that monolinguals outperformed bilinguals on intelligence tests (Anastasi, 1980; Christiansen & Livermore, 1970; Killian, 1971), and advocates of monolingualism have used these results to argue for rapid assimilation into the linguistic mainstream. Typically, the claim has been that mental processes become confused and slower when children use two languages rather than one, and often the appearance of *code-switching* (a term used to describe shifts back and forth from one language or dialect to the other during a conversation) is cited as evidence of cognitive confusion.

Advocates of bilingualism, for their part, have criticized these studies soundly. Peal and Lambert (1962), for example, determined that researchers who found monolinguals outperformed bilinguals on intelligence tests were studying dissimilar groups. The bilinguals in the studies were not fluent in L_2, which presumably influenced their test performance. Following this line of thought, numerous researchers conducted additional studies and ensured that they used similar groups of subjects. Under these conditions, the bilinguals performed as well as or better than the monolinguals (Bruck, Lambert & Tucker, 1974; Cummins, 1976; D. Diaz, 1986; Duncan & DeAvila, 1979).

Garcia (1983) noted that many studies failed to account for a factor that historically has correlated significantly with intelligence—socioeconomic status (SES). He showed that, in the studies that found monolinguals outperforming bilinguals, the bilingual subjects characteristically were from lower SES levels than their monolingual counterparts. In the studies conducted with fluent bilinguals, the bilingual subjects came from higher SES levels. Garcia's work seems to confirm the link between SES and academic performance.

Hakuta (1986) recognized the political nature of the debate when he pointed out that the majority of the studies that showed that bilingualism had a negative effect on intelligence were conducted in the United States. The majority of those that showed a positive effect, on the

other hand, were conducted in Canada. Hakuta interpreted his findings as reflecting the different sociopolitical agendas the two countries
have with respect to language policy. In addition, Hakuta hypothesized
that bilingualism may have *no* effect on intelligence. To test this hypothesis, Hakuta and R. Diaz (1984) and Hakuta (1984) examined intelligence and language skill in 300 bilingual Puerto Rican children
but did not compare their performance on intelligence measures to
monolinguals. The premise in this research was that bilingualism is a
performance continuum, which means that some subjects would be
more bilingual than others. This premise makes it reasonable to propose, then, that any relation between intelligence and bilingualism can
be evaluated within a group. Although the design of these studies was
sound, the results were inconclusive. Nevertheless, Hakuta (1986) asserted that "bilingualism . . . bears little relationship to performance
on [intelligence tests]" (p. 40). This conclusion has been supported by
additional studies. Jarvis, Danks, and Merriman (1995), for example,
found no relationship between the degree of bilingualism and performance on nonverbal IQ tests among third and fourth graders. At this
point, it seems certain that bilingualism per se has no measurable correlation with intelligence.

JOURNAL ENTRY

Consider what you would think and feel if your classes suddenly were conducted in a language you don't know. Are there any lessons to be learned
that you might take with you to your own teaching?

REVISITING LANGUAGE ACQUISITION:
THE EFFECT ON ESL

On a day-to-day basis, the question of bilingualism and intelligence,
and indeed of nonstandard English and intelligence, is ever-present as
a pedagogical issue in the classroom. It is especially pressing for writing teachers, because grammatical, or surface, correctness is the criterion by which society generally evaluates the success of written discourse. Eliminating errors therefore takes on a sense of urgency for
both students and teachers.

   With nonnative and nonstandard speakers alike, however, instruction proceeds with great difficulty. Lessons that have taken long preparation and that have been taught with diligence and care frequently
seem to make no difference. The Hispanic child, for example, who uses
Spanish grammar in designating the negative and produces "Maria no
have her homework" may continue to do so even after work with the

English verb form *do* ("Maria doesn't have her homework"). Many teachers find this lack of change extremely puzzling, and even the most conscientious may begin to doubt the intellectual ability of their nonmainstream students. The only way to solve this puzzle is to understand that in the process of language acquisition linguistic patterns become deeply ingrained and therefore difficult to alter.

Language in Infants

The process of language acquisition begins shortly after birth. Halliday (1979) reported that a 1-day-old child will stop crying to attend to its mother's voice; this response is generally viewed as a precursor to actual language. Because the infant's response is not yet language, a more flexible term to describe its behavior is *communicative competence,* which specifies, among other things, the ability to make clear a topic of interest, the ability to produce a series of relevant propositions, and the ability to express ideas in a way that is sensitive to what the speaker knows about the hearer (Foster, 1985; Hymes, 1971).

The development of communicative competence seems to be a fundamental component of the parent–child relationship. Halliday (1979) noted that, just as a child will stop crying to listen to its mother's voice, a mother, "for her part, will stop doing almost anything, including sleeping, to attend to the voice of her child. Each is predisposed to listen to the sounds of the other" (p. 171). This predisposition reflects the innateness of language, but it also reflects the importance of early parent–child interactions, which have a deep and powerful influence on language development.

The complexity of these interactions is visible within a few weeks of birth. A parent and child will actively engage in an early form of conversational turn taking that consists of ongoing exchanges of attention. The child attends carefully to the sounds and the movements of the parent, moving with him or her in a dance of body language. To capture this turn taking, Trevarthen (1974) used video cameras to record mother–child interactions, which showed mother and child in animated mutual address. The child moved its entire body in a way that was clearly directed toward the mother; in addition, it moved its face, lips, tongue, arms, and hands, in what seems best described as incipient communication. At the same time, the mother was addressing the child with sounds and gestures of her own that mirrored her baby's actions. The two did not appear to imitate each other; rather, the gestures and vocalizations appeared to be communicative (though nonlinguistic) initiation and response. When viewed in slow motion, the movements of the child were slightly ahead of the mother's, suggesting that he or she was the initiator, not the mother.

The amount of meaning conveyed in such exchanges is open to argument, but these gestures and movements are clearly important precursors to recognizable words and expressions that begin to emerge typically between 12 and 20 months. Prespeech exchanges may not have a propositional meaning, but they are meaningful from the standpoint of communicating attention and developing pragmatic (e.g., turn taking) competence. As a result, when children do begin to produce language, they already have been engaged in meaningful communication for a long time.

Most of a young child's preverbal communication is related directly to his or her world, composed of toys, pets, parents, and so forth. Children work at communicating particular needs and desires within the context of their environment. Their first communicative efforts are highly pragmatic and functional, bound tightly to their immediate surroundings and their parents, as evidenced by the fact that parents seem to interpret their children's preverbal vocalizations accurately, whereas a stranger cannot.

By the age of 1, and perhaps even earlier, children have a broad range of knowledge about the way the world operates. They know, for example, that cups are for drinking, knives and forks are for eating, beds are for sleeping, that cars take them places, that knobs or remotes turn on TV sets, and so on. Moreover, their pragmatic awareness gives them an understanding that includes knowing that their environment can be manipulated. A reaching gesture made to a parent will result in being lifted and held; crying attracts attention and usually results in the elimination of some unpleasantness, such as a wet diaper, hunger, or the need for a hug. Such pragmatic knowledge appears to be universal across cultures and languages, for identical behavior appears in children everywhere (H. Clark & E. Clark, 1977).

The first verbal vocalizations children make are about the world around them, regardless of the native language involved. Animals, food, and toys were the three categories referred to most frequently in the first 10 words of 18 children studied by Nelson (1973). The people they named most often were "momma," "dadda," and "baby." By age 18 months, children typically have a vocabulary of only 40 or 50 words, but they are able to use single-word utterances to accomplish a great deal of communication by assigning them different operational roles, depending on the communicative context and the relevant function. "Cookie," uttered in the context of a market (where the child knows, apparently, that cookies can be obtained), can mean "I want some cookies." Uttered in a high chair with a cookie on the child's plate, the same word can simply be an act of identification. Uttered in the act of tossing the cookie on the floor, it can mean "I don't want a cookie."

Within a few months of their first single-word utterances, children begin combining words into two-word utterances, such as "Jenny cup" ("This is Jenny's cup") or "Car go" ("I want to ride in the car"). In each case, these two-word phrases seem to represent a natural progression toward more complete verbal expressions. Language acquisition is a continuum, with children moving from preverbal gestures to single words, two-word utterances, and finally complete expressions.

Home Language

The source of children's initial utterances is the family, but children do not simply repeat the language of those around them. Many utterances are novel, and they characteristically are designed to manipulate and organize a child's environment. Infants spend their first 12 months, approximately, listening to language and experimenting with sounds before producing recognizable utterances, but all research in this area indicates that first words cannot be linked to specific input provided by parents (H. Clark & E. Clark, 1977; Hudson, 1980; Slobin & Welsh, 1973). Instead, they are linked to the whole universe of discourse uttered in the baby's immediate environment and directed toward the baby, which explains why children's initial utterances include "kitty" and "dadda" but not "taxes," "groceries," and "furniture."

Nevertheless, what emerges as child language is a very close replication of the language used in the home. Children, their parents, and others in the immediate community share vocabulary, grammar, dialect, and accent. After about age 5, the community exerts more influence on the shape of a child's language than the parents do (but the language children develop still is referred to as the *home language*). As a result, when parents from the Northwest move to the South, they generally will not begin speaking with a Southern dialect and accent, but their children normally will. Parents who differentiate between *lie* and *lay* will typically discover that their children do not if the people in the neighborhood do not.

The home language is very strong and resistant to change. The reasons appear to be psychophysiological. People define who they are through language, and most definitions are linked in one way or another to the home and family. Also, early mental patterns are more firmly established than later ones, evidenced in part by the observation that Alzheimer's patients lose their childhood memories last.

Conflicts Between Home and School

The home language is very resistant to change, and the consequences for teaching are readily apparent. Direct language instruction commonly has a modest effect on student performance, and even this modest effect is slow to develop. Direct instruction involves language *learning*, the conscious mastery of knowledge *about* language. It also involves cognitive processes quite different from language *acquisition*, the unconscious assimilation *of* language. When teachers strive to get ESL students to use English or when they strive to get nonstandard speakers to use Standard English, they are asking students to apply language learning to supplant language acquisition.

This task is very difficult, especially for young children who cannot understand explanations of linguistic principles and therefore require teacher modeling of the target linguistic behavior. Such modeling is insufficient in most cases for two reasons: (a) A classroom teacher cannot compose a linguistic community of the sort necessary to offer an alternative source of acquisition; (b) Students generally have little motivation to emulate the classroom language.

Krashen (1982) argued that direct instruction in later years provides a "monitor" that helps bridge the gap between learning and acquisition. For example, a child who has grown up using *lay* ("I want to lay down") when Standard English usage calls for *lie* ("I want to lie down") can potentially benefit from direct instruction. The teacher can point out that *lay* is a transitive verb in Standard English and therefore is always followed by a noun, as in "I will lay the book on the table." *Lie*, on the other hand, is an intransitive verb and is not followed by a noun, as in "I will lie down for a nap." With this rule at their disposal, students can monitor their speech and writing to avoid the nonstandard intransitive use of *lay*. Unfortunately, Krashen's analysis works infrequently in practice. Application of the monitor is difficult because speakers and writers focus on meaning rather than form. Direct instruction therefore proceeds slowly because it requires asking students to apply conscious procedures to unconscious processes.

Although intelligence may be important in grasping and applying the content of direct instruction, it is not a significant factor in language acquisition. Even children who are severely retarded develop language and are able to use it in most social situations. Furthermore, as already suggested, motivation is an influential factor in modifying the home language. Students must have compelling reasons to change the way they speak. *Most do not.* It therefore is important to recognize that effective language instruction must proceed over several years to produce measurable results. If these results are to have any chance of becoming permanent, they must be reinforced throughout public school because of the power of the home language to attenuate the effects of instruction. Any gaps in instruction run the risk of causing students to regress. At the end of high school, college opens new linguistic possibilities for the 65% of graduates who go on to higher education, where separation from home and immersion in a different linguistic community serve to strengthen skills in Standard English.[6] Language change, like language development, requires constant stimulation and interaction, which suggests that schools should offer more courses in English rather than fewer.

JOURNAL ENTRY

Encouraging the parents of nonnative English speakers to become involved in school activities is one way to help reduce the conflict between home and school language. What are some others?

SECOND-LANGUAGE ACQUISITION IN CHILDREN

There is evidence that second-language acquisition proceeds along the same lines as first-language acquisition (Gardner, 1980, 1983; Hakuta, 1986; Hatch, 1978; Krashen, 1981b, 1982). Hakuta offered a case study that typifies the process for children who are immersed in an L_2 environment: Uguisu, the 5-year-old daughter of Japanese parents who moved to the United States for a 2-year stay. Both parents knew English, but they talked to their daughter exclusively in Japanese. When Uguisu was enrolled in kindergarten shortly after the family's arrival, she spoke no English.

Over the next several months, Uguisu continued to speak Japanese. Although she did pick up a few words of English from her playmates, these were generally imitations of expressions the playmates uttered, such as "I'm the leader." The kindergarten teacher knew no Japanese and therefore was not in a position to provide formal language instruction. Thus, with the exception of classroom activities, Uguisu's exposure to English was informal and consisted of playtime with peers. It closely resembled a child's exposure to his or her first language, except for the obvious lack of parental input.

Seven months after arriving in this country, Uguisu began to use English suddenly and almost effortlessly. Over the next 6 months,

---

[6]It is worth noting, however, with respect to dialects, that the differences between home and university appear to be growing smaller, perhaps as a result of persistent attacks on Standard English.

English became her dominant language. She used it when talking to her parents, who continued to respond in Japanese, and when playing by herself. Hakuta (1986) stated that "within eighteen months after her initial exposure to English, only a trained ear would have been able to distinguish her from a native speaker" (p. 108).

It appears that during her initial months in the United States, Uguisu was unconsciously sorting through the linguistic data she received on a daily basis, using her innate language abilities to master the grammatical, lexical, and pragmatic patterns that govern English. Once she had grasped these patterns, she was able to begin using the language. English input from her parents was unnecessary in this case because Uguisu, like all other 5-year-olds, was linguistically mature and had already developed a high level of communicative competence in her first language.

This example indicates that second-language acquisition, like first-language acquisition, relies largely on meaningful input, *not formal instruction*. The primary difference between the two lies in the role of parental input: It is crucial in L_1, but incidental in L_2, because children can draw on their already developed L_1 competence. The role of peers or playmates is powerful, perhaps even more so than for the child's first language.

Contact with English-speaking peers is an important underlying assumption in bilingual education. The model of second-language acquisition is similar to the one just outlined: The children are expected to participate in the larger English-speaking community and acquire the language on their own outside the classroom. But many nonnative English-speaking children live in neighborhoods where their primary language dominates and English is heard rarely. Schools in these neighborhoods will be linguistically dominated by the "minority" language, so they provide little or no opportunity for children to interact with English-speaking peers. For many years, busing was viewed as a means of alleviating the problem; unfortunately, in the majority of schools where students were bused in from other neighborhoods, the children segregated themselves outside the classroom along racial, linguistic, or socioeconomic lines, again leaving little chance for natural acquisition to occur.

DIALECTS

Up to this point, "Standard English" has been used loosely to describe the prestige dialect in the United States, without any effort to be more specific. A dialect is a variety of language that is largely determined by geography and/or SES (Haugen, 1966; Hudson, 1980; Trudgill, 2001; Wolfram, Adger, & Christian, 1999). Although race appears to be related to dialect, it is not. Tannen (1990) and Lakoff (1987) showed that women use language that differs from how men use it, but the variation is insufficient to count as a separate dialect. Southern dialects are recognizably different from West Coast dialects. They differ not only with respect to accent but also with respect to grammar and lexicons. A person in Oregon, for example, is highly unlikely to utter "I have plenty enough," whereas this utterance is fairly common in parts of North Carolina. By the same token, someone from the upper third of the socioeconomic scale would be likely to utter "I'm not going to the family reunion," whereas someone from the lower third would be more likely to utter "I ain't goin' to no family reunion." A "standard dialect" will be the one with the largest number of users and the one with the greatest prestige owing to the socioeconomic success of those users.

Standard English meets both criteria. It is the dialect of government, science, business, technology, and education. It is the dialect associated with success, as evidenced in part by the number of young actors and actresses in Los Angeles who take voice lessons to lose their regional dialects. It also is the language of the airwaves. More important for the purposes of this text, Standard English is the language of academic and professional writing.

Factors Underlying a Prestige Dialect

Standard English is often criticized for being a "prestige" dialect or an "elitist" dialect. Certainly it is a prestige dialect, but there is nothing elitist about it. Indeed, there is much about Standard English that is fundamentally democratic.

The United States does not have a monopoly on a prestige dialect. Countries like France, Germany, and Mexico have their own standard versions of their respective languages. In most cases, sheer historical accident led to the dominance of one variety of a language rather than another. If the South had won the Civil War, had then developed a vigorous and influential economy and a strong educational system, and had become the focal point for art and ideas, some Southern dialect might be the standard in the United States rather than the current Western-Midwestern dialect.

Haugen (1966) suggested that all standard dialects undergo similar processes that solidify their position in a society. The first step, and the one apparently most influenced by chance, is selection. A society will select, usually on the basis of users' socioeconomic success, a particular variety of the language to be the standard. At some point, the chosen variety will be codified by teachers and scholars who write grammar books and dictionaries for it. The effect is to stabilize the dialect by reaching some sort of agreement regarding what is correct and what is not. Next, the dialect must be functionally elaborated so that it can be used in government, law, education, technology, and in all forms of writing. Finally, the dialect has to be accepted by all segments of the society as the standard, particularly by those who speak some other variety (Hall, 1972; Macaulay, 1973; Trudgill, 2001).

Nonstandard Dialects

People who do not normally use Standard English use a nonstandard dialect. Although regional variations abound, nonstandard dialects are increasingly identified with SES. Wolfram et al. (1999) reported a leveling of regional differences. The reasons for this leveling are not very clear. Some scholars suggest that television is spreading Standard English to regions where it was not heard frequently in the past, but this proposal is based on the mistaken notion that people respond to the presence of language that isn't interactive. An infant placed in front of a TV and lacking normal contact with people using language interactively would not acquire language. The sounds from the TV would be noise, not meaningful sounds. More likely, the changes Wolfram et al. reported are linked to the increased mobility of Americans. People relocate more frequently today than ever before, and the result is an unprecedented blending of various dialects, especially in the South, which has seen tremendous population growth owing to an influx of Northerners looking for jobs, lower taxes, and better weather.

Another, related factor in the issue of dialect leveling that does not receive much attention is the measurable shift of Black English Vernacular (BEV) toward Standard English. This shift is surprising because in many respects segregation today is stronger than since the early 1950s. But affirmative action has been successful in increasing the educational and economic opportunities among African Americans to such a degree that BEV speakers have more contact with standard speakers than in the past. Herrnstein and Murray (1994) reported that the black middle class has been growing steadily, which provides a compelling incentive to shift toward Standard English. Although the white middle class has been shrinking during this same period, the incentives to adopt a nonstandard dialect, to shift downward, are not strong among displaced adults. They are strong, however, among their children; as a result, we see more white preadolescents and adolescents adopting features of nonstandard English than at any other time in history. The popularity of gangster rap and the associated pop-culture glamorization of gangbangers and "prison chic" may also be exerting an influence.

Because SES is closely tied to level of education (Herrnstein & Murray, 1994), nonstandard speakers tend to be undereducated, and they also tend to be linked to the working-class poor. Education, however, is not an absolute indicator of dialect: Some evidence suggests that colleges and universities are more tolerant of nonstandard English than they used to be, and the students' right-to-their-own-language movement has made public schools more sensitive to, if not more tolerant of, nonstandard English. As a result, it is fairly easy to observe college graduates—and, increasingly, college faculty—uttering nonstandard expressions such as "I ain't got no money" and "Where's he at."

The plummeting literacy levels in the public schools and in higher education also exacerbate the problem. Chall (1996) and Coulson (1996) reported serious declines in language and literacy levels for students in all age groups. Chall, for example, described her experience at a community college where the "freshmen tested, on the average, on an eighth grade reading level. Thus, the average student in this community college was able to read only on a level expected of junior high school students" (p. 309). And findings like these are not limited to community colleges. Entering freshmen at a major research university in North Carolina, ranked among the top 25 schools in the nation, are tested each year for reading skill, and their average annual scores between 1987 and 1994 placed them at the 10th-grade reading level.[7]

JOURNAL ENTRY

Most people speak a dialect that moves along a continuum ranging from nonstandard to formal standard. How would you characterize your dialect? Do you think it is important to model Standard English in your classes? Why or why not?

BLACK ENGLISH VERNACULAR

For many decades, serious study of Black English Vernacular (BEV) was impeded by myths and misconceptions. Dillard (1973) summarized many of these misconceptions quite succinctly. He reported, for example, that until the 1960s it was often argued that BEV was a vestige of a British dialect with origins in East Anglia (also see McCrum,

---

[7]During this period, students took the Nelson–Denny reading test, which was administered by the university's learning skills center. I reviewed the data regularly in my capacity as director of the writing program at the school.

Cran, & MacNeil, 1986). American blacks supposedly had somehow managed to avoid significant linguistic change for centuries, even though it is well known that all living languages change ineluctably. Dillard also described the physiological theory, which held that Black English was the result of "thick lips" that rendered blacks incapable of producing Standard English. More imaginative and outrageous was Mencken's (1936) notion that Black English was the invention of playwrights:

> The Negro dialect, as we know it today, seems to have been formulated by the songwriters for the minstrel shows; it did not appear in literature until the time of the Civil War; before that, as George P. Krappe shows . . . , it was a vague and artificial lingo which had little relation to the actual speech of Southern blacks. (p. 71)

Mencken didn't mention how blacks were supposed to have gone to the minstrel shows so that they might pick up the new "lingo"—nor why in the world they would be motivated to do so.

Today, most linguists support the view that BEV developed from the pidgin versions of English, Dutch, Spanish, and Portuguese used during the slave era. A pidgin is a "contact vernacular," a mixture of two (or possibly more) separate languages that has been modified to eliminate the more difficult features, such as irregular verb forms (Kay & Sankoff, 1974; Slobin, 1977). Function words like determiners (*the, a, an*) and prepositions (*in, on, across*) commonly are dropped. Function markers like case are eliminated, as are tense and plurals. Pidgins arise spontaneously whenever two people lack a common language. The broken English that Johnny Weissmuller used in the Tarzan movies from the 1930s and 1940s (which still air on TV) reflects fairly accurately the features of a pidgin.

European slavers developed a variety of pidgins with their West African cohorts to facilitate the slave trade. The result must have been a potpourri of sounds. Although many slavers came from England, the majority came from France, Spain, Portugal, and Holland. Their human cargo—collected from a huge area of western Africa, including what is now Gambia, the Ivory Coast, Ghana, Nigeria, and Zaire—spoke dozens of mutually unintelligible tribal languages. McCrum et al. (1986) suggested that the pidgins began developing shortly after the slaves were captured because the traders separated those who spoke the same language to prevent collaboration that might lead to rebellion. Chained in the holds of the slave ships, the captives had every incentive to use pidgin to establish a linguistic community. More likely, however, is that the pidgins already were well established among the villages responsible for capturing and selling tribesmen and women to the European slavers, and the captured people began using a pidgin almost immediately out of necessity.

Once in America, the slaves had to continue using pidgin English to communicate with their masters and with one another. Matters changed, however, when the slaves began having children. A fascinating phenomenon occurs when children are born into a community that uses a pidgin: They spontaneously regularize the language. They add function words, regularize verbs, and provide a grammar where none really existed before. When the children of the pidgin-speaking slaves began speaking, they spoke a Creole, not a pidgin. A Creole is a full language in the technical sense, with its own grammar, vocabulary, and pragmatic conventions.

Why, then, is Black English classified as a dialect of English rather than as a Creole? True Creoles, like those spoken in the Caribbean, experienced reduced contact with the major contributory languages. Papiamento, the Creole spoken in the Dutch Antilles, is a mixture of Dutch, French, and English, and although Dutch has long been the official language, the linguistic influences of French and English disappeared about 200 years ago. The influence of Dutch has waned significantly in this century. As a result, Papiamento continued to develop in its own way rather than move closer to standard Dutch. In the United States, the influence of Standard English increased over the years, especially after the abolition of slavery. The Creole that was spoken by large numbers of slaves consequently shifted closer and closer to Standard English, until at some point it stopped being a Creole and became a dialect. It is closer to English than to any other language, which is why speakers of Standard English can understand Black English but not a Creole.

BEV nevertheless has preserved many features of its Creole and pidgin roots, which extend to the West African tribal languages as well as to Dutch, French, Portuguese, and Spanish. The most visible of these features are grammatical, and for generations Black English was thought to be merely a degenerate version of Standard English. Speakers were believed to violate grammatical rules every time they used the language. Work like Dillard's, however, demonstrated that Black English has its own grammar, which is a blend of Standard English and a variety of West African languages seasoned with European languages.

There is a strong similarity between BEV and the English used by white Southerners because blacks and whites lived in close-knit communities in the South for generations, slavery notwithstanding, and the whites were the minority. White children played with black children, who exerted a powerful influence on the white-minority dialect. As Slobin (1977) indicated, language change occurs primarily in the speech of children, and throughout the slave era white and black children were allowed to play together.

Ebonics

Since the late 1960s, some educators and politicians have argued for what is known as "students' right to their own language." The focus has been almost entirely on Black English and its place in education (see Robinson, 1990). The argument is that BEV should be legitimized in the schools to the extent that it is acceptable for recitation and writing assignments. Some schools during the early 1970s actually issued specially prepared textbooks written in Black English rather than Standard English. In 1996, the superintendent of the Oakland, California, schools issued a policy statement declaring Black English to be a separate language and giving it the name *Ebonics,* a neologism from the words *ebony* and *phonics.* The statement attributed the differences between Standard English and Ebonics to genetic factors and proposed that African-American students be taught English as though it were a foreign language while content courses be taught in Black English. Although the efforts of the Oakland administrators and teachers were well intentioned, even those who were sympathetic to the difficulties faced by students reared in a Black-English environment had a hard time seeing this policy statement as anything more than political posturing.

The idea that Black English is a separate language flies in the face of the evidence that it is a dialect. More problematic, perhaps, is the fact that the media heaped unrelenting scorn and ridicule on the policy statement and Ebonics, which undermined legitimate efforts to address the challenges Black English presents to students and teachers alike.

The rationale for the argument that underlies students' right to their own language (and ultimately that led to the statement on Ebonics) is similar to the argument underlying bilingualism: The home dialect defines who each student is; it is at the heart of important bonds between children and their families. When the schools require students to master and ultimately use Standard English, they are subverting students' sense of personal identity and are weakening the home bond. Arguments that Standard English is important for entry into the socioeconomic mainstream are dismissed as irrelevant and are countered with the suggestion that society must change to accommodate individual differences.

The biggest difficulty with the argument that students have the right to use their own language in school is that it oversimplifies a complex problem. Schools are obligated to provide students with the tools they need to realize their full potential, and they must do so within the framework of sociolinguistic realities. It is the case that people view certain dialects negatively; indeed, Wolfram et al. (1999) correctly noted that these negative views are held even by those who speak these dialects. Such views can hinder people's access to higher education and jobs. Students who in the late 1960s and early 1970s went through high school using texts written in Black English, for example, had an extremely difficult time when they enrolled in college. Many discovered that they could not read their college texts and dropped out. Any conscientious person must look at those experiences and question the cost in human terms of the political idealism that, ultimately, ended these students' dreams of a college education.

Equally important, there is no evidence to suggest that substituting Black English for Standard English has any effect whatsoever on academic performance in general or literacy in particular. Those who argue for students' right to their own language today have forgotten—or never learned—this lesson from the past. In addition, actions like those of the Oakland schools, even if we were to give them the benefit of the doubt, seem, below the surface, to be disturbingly racist. There is the undeniable—and unacceptable—hint that students who speak BEV are incapable of mastering Standard English. The suggestion that these students would learn Standard English in the way that English-speaking children currently learn, say, French in our schools cannot be taken seriously. Foreign-language instruction in the United States may be many things, but "effective" is not one of them.

The situation that speakers of Black English face may be unfair. It may even be unjust. But it reflects the reality of language prejudice. Language prejudice is extremely resistant to change because language is a central factor in how people identify themselves and others. Nonstandard dialects, because they are linked to SES and education levels, tend to be associated with negative traits. For this reason, many businesses may reject applicants for employment in certain positions if they speak nonstandard English. An African-American applicant for a receptionist position at a prestigious Chicago law firm may be rejected simply because he or she pronounces *ask* as *ax*.

Efforts to validate the use of nonstandard English in education do little to modify the status of students from disadvantaged backgrounds. They do not expand students' language skills in any way that will help them overcome the very real obstacle to socioeconomic mobility that nonstandard English presents. As Williams (1992) noted, these efforts keep "these students ghettoized" (p. 836).

Some people may complain that this perspective is predominantly socioeconomic and that there is much more to the concept of students' right to their own language than economic success. That is true. However, it is relatively easy for those who do not have to deal with closed socioeconomic doors to focus on political statements and abstract personal issues. In the name of ideology, they are always too ready to sacrifice the dreams others have for a better life. Most teachers understand that education is the key to opportunity and that mastery of Standard English is a key to education. Consequently, large numbers of educators believe that schools must adopt an *additive stance* with respect to dialects, and they view mastery and use of Standard English as complementing the home dialect, whatever it may be. This additive stance calls for legitimizing and valuing all dialects while simultaneously recognizing the appropriateness conditions that govern language use in specific situations. From this perspective, there are situations in which Black English is appropriate and Standard English is not; and there are situations in which Standard English is appropriate and Black English is not. The goals of schools, therefore, should include helping students recognize the different conditions and mastering the nuances of Standard English. Currently, the two camps—like those wrestling with bilingual education—are unable to reach agreement on basic principles, largely for the same reason. Bidialectalism is an intensely political issue.

JOURNAL ENTRY

What is your position on Ebonics? Is your position political or pedagogical?

Cultural Factors

Speakers of BEV bring more than their dialect to the educational setting—they also bring a distinct culture with values, standards of behavior, and belief systems that are different from the white mainstream. Delpit (1988) reported, for example, that in the black community authority is not automatically bestowed upon teachers or others in positions of power.[8] It must be extracted through authoritarian rather than authoritative means. For example, a teacher who uses a forceful, direct approach—"Fritz, read the next two paragraphs"—is more likely to get a positive response than one who uses an indirect approach—"Fritz, would you read the next two paragraphs, please?" White teachers in Delpit's account are more inclined to use the indirect approach, which commonly leads to conflict because black students do not respond.

---

[8]Whenever dealing with generalizations, it is important to remember that it is difficult (if not impossible) to generalize to particular instances. The fact that many individuals do not match the characteristics of the generalization does not invalidate the generalization.

Similarly, white culture stresses students' subordinate role. Students are not expected to talk out of turn, and when they do they are punished. The lesson is that a student should raise his or her hand when wishing to speak. Failure to do so is seen as a sign of disrespect for the teacher and other students. Black culture, however, does not stress turn taking of this sort but instead emphasizes a more active strategy, which leads black students to call out responses freely without waiting for permission to speak. Punishment imposes the white conventions on many African-American students but not all. Many continue to call out, but many more seem deflated to such a degree that they withdraw and turn silent. The results are twofold: White teachers often view those who continue to call out as being rude and disruptive, whereas they view those who fall silent as being slow and unmotivated. Teachers who decide to accept the classroom behavior of their black students in this regard face yet another challenge. Their white, Asian, and Hispanic students determine that the black children are receiving special treatment, and many become resentful because of it.

Labov (1964, 1970, 1972a) and Heath (1983) also have shown that the environment of language acquisition can have an effect on school performance. Their research suggested that different cultural-social groups learn to use language in different ways, as determined by variations in parent–child interaction. Heath, for example, noted that the ways lower-class black children learn to use language are fundamentally different from the ways upper-middle-class white children learn to use it. The determining factor is how parents interact with their children.

In the community she studied, Heath (1983) observed that among the black subjects adults rarely spoke to children and that little of the prelinguistic interaction between mothers and offspring described in the Trevarthen (1974) investigation took place. One result was that the black children appeared to place more reliance on contextual cues for comprehension than the white children. This factor proved to be extremely problematic for them in school, where the emphasis is on language use that has no immediate audience, feedback, intention, or purpose. Heath noted another important consequence:

[The black children] . . . never volunteer to list the attributes which are similar in two objects and add up to make one thing like another. They seem, instead, to have a gestalt, a highly contextualized view, of objects which they compare without sorting out the particular single features of the object itself. They seem to become sensitive to the shape of arrays of stimuli in a scene, but not to how individual discrete elements in the scene contribute to making two wholes alike. If asked why or how one thing is like another, they do not answer; similarly, they do not respond appropriately to tasks in which they are asked to distinguish one thing as different from another. (pp. 107–108)

The reliance on context inevitably leads to difficulties in composition, because writers must step outside the language event to avoid producing an essay that sounds like a conversation with the second party missing. They must create a context by explicitly providing some of the very factors that make conversations successful, such as audience, purpose, and intention. In addition, a holistic view of the world that is largely unconcerned with attributes and detail is at odds with the kinds of tasks children are asked to perform in school, where describing objects by listing their attributes is a common activity. It should be clear, however, that both the reliance on context and the holistic view are part of these children's linguistic processing. This is how they understand language and how they use it.

Michaels (1982) reported similar results after studying narrative patterns among black and white schoolchildren. The white children constructed narratives around a specific topic, developing a structure that included the topic at the beginning and that made reference to it throughout the paper. Black children, in contrast, mentioned a general topic at the beginning of their narratives, and what followed usually was only marginally related to that topic. For example, if the teacher assigned a narrative on the topic of "a shopping trip to the local mall," the white students might write a narrative about a specific trip that they took at some time. The black students, on the other hand, might identify "shopping" as the topic and might then develop a narrative about shopping for a Christmas tree, a new car, or even a new house. Michaels reported that the failure of the black students to meet the expectations their white teacher had for the assignment proved problematic: The teacher judged their narratives to be pointless and erratic. From the perspective of black culture, however, the point of a narrative is to tell an entertaining story, which may not be possible under the strict requirements of a writing assignment.

Cognitive Deficit

The notion that literacy increases intelligence and reasoning ability has enjoyed a certain cachet since the 1960s, in spite of a lack of reliable research findings to support this idea. In far too many instances, African-American children's difficulties with academic discourse has led to facile conclusions that they suffer, as a group, from cognitive deficits linked both to parenting and BEV. Therefore, it is important to state clearly that no evidence has been found to support the notion of linguistic or cognitive deficit among African Americans or any other group.[9] Labov (1972a), in fact, showed that Black English is just as rich as any other dialect and that children whose dominant dialect is BEV cannot be classified as "linguistically deprived."

Two of the strongest advocates of the claim that literacy increases intelligence, George Dillon (1981) and Walter Ong (1978), would perhaps claim that the problem is more accurately one of "literacy deprivation," which is no doubt accurate, but their conclusions about the interaction of literacy and mind are not. They argued that facility with the written word develops cognitive abilities related to abstract reasoning; literate people think better than illiterate people. On this account, blacks, who tend to score lower than whites on tests of reading ability (Coulson, 1996), would experience deficits in thinking ability. But such a conclusion is offset by the work of Scribner and Cole (1981), who, in the most detailed study published to date on the effect literacy has on cognitive abilities, found no significant correlation between literacy and cognition. They stated, for example, that "Our results are in direct conflict with persistent claims that 'deep psychological differences' divide literate and non-literate populations. . . . On no task— logic, abstraction, memory, communication—did we find all non-literates performing at lower levels than all literates" (p. 251).

In addition, Farr and Janda (1985) concluded that one of the more significant problems with their subject's writing was that it was not elaborated, with inexplicit and therefore ineffectual logical relations. But unelaborated content and weak logical relations are characteristic of poor writing generally (Williams, 1985), which again indicates that at issue is something other than the influence of Black English on cognition. The ability to elaborate content appears to be linked to reading and writing experience (Williams, 1987). Moreover, few oral-language situations call for extensive use of logic. Hence, the problem with logical relations that Farr and Janda reported could be symptomatic of students who do little reading and writing.

BLACK-ENGLISH GRAMMAR

Black English normally omits the *s* suffix on present-tense verbs ("He run pretty fast"), except in those instances where the speaker overcorrects in an effort to approximate standard patterns ("I goes to the market"). It drops the *g* from participles ("He goin' home"), and it

---

[9]Although there is no evidence of cognitive deficit, there is evidence that some groups, such as Asians, perform better than others on intelligence tests. Herrnstein and Murray (1994) noted that "East Asians have higher nonverbal intelligence than whites while being equal, or perhaps slightly lower, in verbal intelligence" (p. 269).

also uses four separate negators: *dit'n, not, don'*, and *ain'*. Consider the following sentences:

1. Vickie dit'n call yesterday.
2. She not comin'.
3. Fritz don' go.
4. Fritz don' be goin'.
5. She ain' call.
6. She ain' be callin'.

The last four sentences illustrate one of the more significant differences between Standard English and Black English, which is called *aspect*. Standard English marks verb tenses as past or present, but it provides the option of indicating the static or ongoing nature of an action through the use of progressive and perfect verb forms. Black English grammar, on the other hand, allows for optional tense marking but requires that the action be marked as momentary or continuous. Sentences 3 and 5 indicate a momentary action, whether or not it is in the past, whereas 4 and 6 indicate progressive action, whether or not it is in the past.

Another feature of aspect is the ability to stretch out the time of a verb, and BEV uses the verb form *be* to accomplish this. Sentences 7 and 8, for example, have quite different meanings:

7. Macarena lookin' for a job.
8. Macarena be lookin' for a job.

In 7, Macarena may be looking for a job today, at this moment, but she has not been looking long, and there is the suggestion that she has not been looking very hard. In 8, on the other hand, Macarena has been conscientiously looking for a job for a long time. We see similar examples in the following:

9. Jake studyin' right now.
10. Jake be studyin' every afternoon.

Studyin' agrees in aspect with *right now,* and *be studyin'* agrees in aspect with *every afternoon.* It therefore would be ungrammatical in BEV to say or write "Jake studyin' every afternoon" or "Jake be studyin' right now" (Baugh, 1983; Fasold, 1972; Wolfram, 1969).

Been, the participial form of *be,* is used in Black English as a past-perfect marker: It signals that an action occurred in the distant past or that it was completed totally (Rickford, 1975). In this sense it is similar to the past-perfect form *have + verb* and *have + been* in Standard English, as the following sentences illustrate:

11. They had told us to leave. (standard)
12. They been told us to leave. (black)
13. Kerri had eaten all the cake. (standard)
14. Kerri been eat all the cake. (black)
15. She had been hurt. (standard)
16. She been been hurt. (black)

Been is also used, however, to assert that an action initiated in the past is still in effect, as in the following:

17. I have known Vickie more than three months now. (standard)
18. I been been knowin' Vickie more than three month now. (black)

Many other grammatical features differentiate Black English from Standard English. A few of the more important are listed as follows:

- The present tense is used in narratives to indicate past action, as in *They goes to the market.*
- When cardinal adjectives precede nouns, the noun is not pluralized, as in *The candy cost one dollar and fifty cent.*
- Relative pronouns in the subject position of a relative clause can be dropped, as in *Fritz like the woman has red hair.*
- The possessive marker is dropped, as in *He found Macarena coat.*
- Double negatives are used instead of a negative and a positive, as in *He don' never goin' call.*[10]

BLACK ENGLISH AND WRITING

We can gain a better appreciation for the pedagogical issues speakers of BEV present by looking at writing samples that illustrate some characteristic patterns of error. The three samples that follow were

---

[10]Criticism of the double negative is made on the grounds that two negatives make a positive. On this account, "I ain' got no money" means that the speaker actually has a great deal of money. Although two negatives make a positive in mathematics, they often do not in language. No one ever, under any circumstances, would understand "I ain't got no money" to mean anything other than the fact that the speaker is broke. Furthermore, double negatives have a long history in English and are not peculiar to Black English. Consider the following: "It isn't unusual for teenagers to seek attention." Thus, we sometimes use the double negative for stylistic reasons and sometimes to emphasize the negative.

written by students who speak Black English. The first comes from a sixth-grade writer, Marcy; the second comes from a 10th grader, Tawanda; and the third comes from a 12th-grade writer, Bud. In each case the student attended a predominantly black school in an area at the lower end of the socioeconomic scale. Marcy and her class had visited the Aerospace Museum in Los Angeles several days before the writing assignment, which asked students to describe what they liked best about the field trip. Tawanda's teacher asked her class to write a paper describing their recent field trip to the Shedd Aquarium in Chicago. Bud, also from Chicago, was approaching graduation, and his English teacher asked him to write an essay describing his plans once he was out of high school.

1

My feel Trip

Lass weak we went to the natual histry museum. We seed the air Planes an they be big. If you be standin next to one of them Planes you be lookin real small. they could be goin real fast if they flyin. I think it be real nice to be flyin one of them planes. Maybe to hawae or someplace like that. When I grow up I think I be a pilot an fly one of them big planes.

2

I done been to the akwearium befor so I knows somethin about it already. They has lots of fish an some of them be bright colors. sometime my uncle go to the lake an ketch some fish but they not bright like dem in the akwarium. They be good to eat tho. sometime my momma come by granma's house when she infatween an we cook up some them fish that my uncle done catched. We have a real feast an my momma eat like they's no tomora. I do to. My uncle say he gon by him a boat one these days an when he do he take me out the lake. I laff when he do an tell him he kin take me all the way to Canada to git me out this ol city. Then he tell me that Canada even colder than Chicago an that make me kinda sad. Hard to imagin any place on earth colder than this place but I guess they is. Maybe we take that boat right to Jamaca, "mon." Be warm there all the time. Anyway, that's what I think about the akwariyum.

3

I know most good job needs a college education. I would like to go to college to git me a degree. but my grades isn't the best. It would be fun to be a docktor or a lawyer or something like that because then I have me a big fine car. May be a Benz. But like a says my grades isn't so good and I don't think I could be going to college. They is some good jobs in electonics that don't take that much training. And I think that I could maybe go into that. the important thing is to think positive. I know I can do good work. I can work hard when I wants to. My brother got him a job doing construction and it pays real good. The trouble is that it isn't all year long work. They git laid off alot. That might be good in a way though. Because then you could have more time to enjoy life. I know that no matter what kind of job I git after schools out I wants to be enjoying my self.

Oral-Language Interference

Some scholars have argued that the writing of BEV speakers like the students who produced the preceding passages is significantly handicapped by *oral-language interference*. Writing for these students becomes an act of transcribing their nonstandard speech (Dillon, 1981; Olson, 1977; Ong, 1978, 1982; Shaughnessy, 1977). In this view, failure to achieve mainstream standards can be accounted for on two levels. First, the writing displays the lexical and grammatical features characteristic of Black English. Second, the lack of organization and the paucity of content is the result of linguistic deprivation and its associated cognitive deficit.

Oral-language interference, however, is a description of the problem, not an explanation. Most of the problems in the aforementioned writing samples are not caused by oral language per se but rather by the students' lack of reading experience. Any student who lacks extensive reading experience has no alternative but to transcribe speech, which means that features of oral language find their way into student writing irrespective of race. White students who don't read commonly write "I could of made a good grade if I had studied" because they haven't seen the contraction "could've" in print often enough to have an internalized graphemic representation of it.

In the previous student examples, the surface problems speak for themselves. When Marcy writes "Lass weak" or when Tawanda writes "I laff," they are transcribing. Spelling instruction will have only a modest effect on these sorts of errors, yet spelling lists tend to be the approach of first resort. The difficulty with spelling lists is that they seldom are contextualized, so students rapidly forget how to spell the words after being tested on them. Students who manifest the sorts of surface problems shown in these examples need an intensive reading and writing program, not drills, exercises, and spelling lists.

More interesting than these surface errors, however, are Tawanda's and Bud's responses to their assignments. Tawanda was asked to describe the field trip she and her class took at the Shedd Aquarium, and the first two sentences suggest that she will respond appropriately.

But Sentence 3 takes Tawanda in a different direction. Certainly, her uncle's fishing in Lake Michigan has some marginal connection to the field trip, but it still is clearly off topic. Likewise, Bud started writing about his plans after graduation but then shifted focus to his brother. These responses are characteristic of the patterns Michaels (1982) identified, in which cultural differences related to how to use language often move black students down paths that have but a ghostly relationship to the assigned topic. Students who display this characteristic face a greater challenge than those who need more reading and writing experience because their concepts of what a narrative or a description is about are at odds with those held by mainstream teachers.

Although no studies have adequately controlled for reading experience, several studies have investigated the effects of speech on writing. Tannen (1982) found that speech and writing share each other's "typical characteristics," even though they differ in terms of level of abstraction, sentence length, sentence patterns, and vocabulary. Speech tends to have shorter sentences, to use less subordination and more coordination, and to use a simpler vocabulary than writing. Erickson (1984), studying the speech patterns of black teenagers, reported that the organizational pattern of Black English has its own structure, different from that of Standard English. He found, for example, that shifts from one topic to another were not explicitly stated but were implied through concrete anecdotes. Close analysis of Black-English speech patterns showed a "rigorous logic and a systematic coherence of the particular, whose internal system is organized not by literate style or linear sequentiality but by audience/speaker interaction" (p. 152).

Farr Whitemann (1981) correlated the speech of a group of Black-English-speaking students with their writing and found that oral-language patterns were present in the students' written language but that these patterns did not clearly reflect an attempt at transcribing speech. The most dominant characteristic of the subjects' compositions was the presence of Black-English grammatical patterns, specifically the omission of *s* suffixes and of past-tense *ed* suffixes.

Farr and Janda (1985) reported only modest oral-language interference in the writing of the black high school student they studied. They noted:

Although features of Vernacular Black English are part of . . . Joseph's linguistic repertoire, VBE features occur relatively infrequently in his writing, eliminating nonstandard dialect influence as a major cause of his difficulty in writing. Furthermore, Joseph's writing evidenced many "literate" characteristics, i.e., devices which have been found to be typical of written English. . . . What, then, is the problem with Joseph's writing? Why was he placed in a remedial writing class . . . ? His writing does not appear to be language that was generated by a human being in an attempt to express or create meaning. The form is there; the functional attempt to communicate does not seem to be. (pp. 80–81)

On the basis of this research, it is tempting to suggest that the missing factor in Joseph's writing, and perhaps in the writing of students like him, is motivation to succeed at school-related tasks. However, students who lack reading and writing experience will not be able to conceptualize writing tasks as communicative efforts. Texts represent a foreign medium that is almost as meaningless as calculus is to most English teachers.

The challenges presented by cultural differences will prove resistant to solution for many nonmainstream students, but it is important to stress that this is not the case for all. Children are adaptable, and large numbers of nonmainstream students adjust to the linguistic and cultural demands of school quite readily. Nevertheless, it often is useful for teachers to address cultural differences candidly with students, explaining how men and women and people reared in different cultures use language in different ways. Afterwards, teachers can move forward with activities that help students understand how writing assignments provide a focus for papers that students must follow to be successful. Efforts should include helping students recognize how their backgrounds and experiences affect their academic work and on showing them ways to broaden their experiences to accommodate standard conventions.

CHICANO ENGLISH

Chicano English (CE) is the term used to describe the nonstandard dialect spoken by many second- and third-generation Mexican-Americans, large numbers of whom do not speak Spanish, although they may understand it slightly (see Garcia, 1983). The term is also used to describe the dialect spoken by first-generation immigrants who have lived in the United States long enough to have acquired sufficient mastery of English to be able to carry on a conversation exclusively in it (see Baugh, 1984). *Chicano* itself emerged as a label during the 1960s as part of the growth in cultural awareness and identity among Mexican-Americans who began emphasizing their unique position between two heritages.

In many ways, Chicano English is more complex than Black English because it is influenced by monolingual Spanish speakers, monolingual English speakers, and bilingual Spanish-English speakers, all of whom are found in a single linguistic community. The number of influences appears to complicate children's acquisition of Standard English in ways that are discussed later in this section. One highly visible result of these multiple influences has been the rapid growth of *Spanglish* since the late 1970s. Spanglish is a blend of English and Spanish. Once ridiculed and derided as *pocho* English because of its long association with *pachucos,* young toughs prone to gang violence and criminal activity, Spanglish is now widely used throughout Mexican-American communities, even by radio announcers and television personalities.

For a variety of reasons, there has been far less research on CE than on BEV, so information about this dialect is sparse. Perhaps the more noticeable feature of CE is its incorporation of Spanish phonology (the sound of words) into English pronunciation. Spanish uses a *ch* pronunciation where English uses *sh*. Thus, CE speakers often pronounce a word like *shoes* as *choose,* which can affect how students spell English words. Students also will perceive the short *i* sound in the verb *live* to be a long *e* sound, producing sentences like the following:

- I used to leave in Burbank but now I leave in North Hollywood.
- Seens I been in L.A. I ain't found no job.

Other phonological differences produce additional difficulties, as the following student samples illustrate:

- I try to safe as much money as I can.
- When I'm a mother, I won't be as strick as my parents.

The Spanish influence is also evident on the grammatical level. Spanish, for example, uses the double negative, whereas English does not. As a result, students produce written statements such as "I didn't learn nothing in this class" and "I didn't do nothing." Spanish places adjectives after nouns, but this is rarely a problem when Spanish-speaking students use English. We don't find instances of students producing sentences like "The girl with the hair blonde lives on my block." Spanish also signifies possession through a prepositional phrase rather than possessive nouns. This pattern commonly influences CE constructions. Consider the following examples:

- El auto de mi hermana es un BMW. (The car of my sister is a BMW/ My sister's car is a BMW.)[11]

---

[11]In parentheses are the literal and then the figurative translations.

- Vivo en la casa de mi madre. (I live in the house of my mother/I live in my mother's house.)

Other syntactic influences on CE include topicalization, dropped inflections, inappropriate use of do-support, dropping *have* in perfect verb forms, and transformation of mass nouns into count nouns. Examples of these influences are shown in the following sentences:

- My brother, he lives in St. Louis. (topicalization)
- My parents were raise old-fashion. (dropped inflections)
- My father asked me where did I go. (inappropriate do-support)
- I been working every weekend for a month. (dropping *have*)
- When we went to the mountains, we saw deers and everything. (mass noun to count noun)

The paucity of research on CE is disheartening but understandable. The focus for decades has been on bilingual education for recent Spanish-speaking immigrants, not on bidialectalism. Only a few studies have examined the writing of CE speakers, and they are not particularly satisfying because they tend to focus on the sentence level rather than on the whole essay. Amastae (1981, 1984) evaluated writing samples collected from students at Pan American University in Texas over a 4-year period to determine the range of surface errors and the degree of sentence elaboration as measured by students' use of subordination. Amastae (1981) found that Spanish interference did not seem to be a major source of error in the compositions but that the students used very little subordination (also see Edelsky, 1986; Hoffer, 1975). Because subordination is generally viewed as a measure of writing maturity (K. Hunt, 1965), its absence in the essays of CE speakers could adversely affect how teachers judge their writing ability.

None of the available studies of CE examine rhetorical features such as topic, purpose, and audience. Without this research, it is impossible to determine best practices for students whose dialect is CE because we don't really know what the issues are. We can draw on the fictional, albeit realistic, work of Jose Antonio Villareal or the autobiography of Richard Rodriguez, but what we glean from these efforts probably is not generalizable. Carol Edelsky's (1986) study of bilingual, elementary-age Spanish-speaking students examined rhetorical features of writing, but it is not on point because her subjects were LEP Spanish speakers—not exactly the same as speakers of CE.

Nevertheless, Edelsky's (1986) work is suggestive. She found that when her subjects wrote in English, their compositions manifested rhetorical features similar to those found among weak writers whose first language is English; that is, the rhetorical problems were largely developmental. Her students appeared to be in the process of transferring their L_1 rhetorical competence to L_2. During the transfer period, the students' rhetorical skills in English, like their surface feature skills, contained identifiable gaps that continuing development of English proficiency was likely to eliminate. In addition, Edelsky found some oral influences on the students' writing, but concluded that they were not major and did not hinder a reader's comprehension. These results repudiate many of the notions commonly associated with bilinguals and literacy. For example, she found very little code switching between L_1 and L_2. Most of the switching she found was "like slips of the pen" that decreased significantly by the time children were in the third grade (p. 152). These findings suggest that writing instruction for nonmainstream students should focus on developing global skills rather than on surface errors.

Spanglish

Over the last couple of decades, as the native Spanish-speaking population has grown exponentially, Spanglish has become increasingly widespread. As the name suggests, Spanglish is a combination of Spanish and English. It is not quite the same thing as code-switching, which is discussed in the next section. Spanglish is a hybrid dialect of Spanish typically used by immigrants from Mexico who have resided in the United States for some time but who have acquired little if any English. Equivalent Spanish words are dropped from the lexicon and replaced by the hybrid terms, such as *wachar* for *watch, parquear* for *park,* and *pushar* for *push.* Thus, a native English speaker who does not know Spanish would have a hard time even recognizing Spanglish. By the same token, Spanglish presents significant comprehension problems for native speakers of Standard Spanish. Consider the following comparison of the sentence "I'm going to park my car":

- Voy a estacionar mi auto. (Standard Spanish)
- Voy a parquear mi caro. (Spanglish)

Neither *parquear* (*park*) nor *caro* (*car*) exist in Standard Spanish; the equivalent words are *estacionar* and *auto.*

Spanglish has little if any effect on students' writing in English, but it does exert an influence on students' efforts to become bilingual. As noted earlier, Mexican-American students face significant obstacles owing to the multiple sources of language input that they experience daily. With few exceptions, Standard Spanish speakers criticize Spanglish and those who use it for degrading the language. This criticism can have the effect of making students overly self-conscious and language adverse. The result is commonly marginal proficiency in both Spanish and English.

Code-Switching

Different dialects often have differences in grammar, as in the case of BEV and Standard English. They also have different usage conventions. Nevertheless, we often find that speakers of Standard English use nonstandard grammar and/or usage and that speakers of nonstandard English use Standard English grammar and/or usage. For example, people who otherwise use Standard English may say "It is me" rather than "It is I," even though "It is me" technically is "incorrect grammar." Other examples abound, such as the general confusion regarding *lay* and *lie* and the widespread disappearance of the relative pronoun *whom,* even in much formal, academic writing.

When people shift from one form of language to another, they are engaged in what is called code-switching. In its broadest sense, code-switching refers to the act of using different language varieties. Two factors account for code-switching. The first is simply that languages change, in spite of often vigorous efforts to prevent it, as in schoolteachers' prescriptive admonitions about what constitutes "correct" speech and writing. In this analysis, "It is me" may eventually become accepted as standard to reflect changes in usage. The second factor is that linguistic variation exists not only across dialects but within them. Sources of variation include age, occupation, location, economic status, and gender. Women, for example, tend to be more conscientious about language than men. As a result, in a family whose dialect is nonstandard, the woman's language will be closer to Standard English than the man's (Trudgill, 2001).

The phenomenon of linguistic variation led William Labov (1969) to suggest that every dialect is subject to "inherent variability." Speakers of a particular dialect fail to use all the features of that dialect all the time, and the constant state of flux causes some degree of variation. This principle accounts for the fact that Standard-English speakers periodically reduce sentences like "I've been working hard" to "I been working hard." More common, however, is variation of nonstandard features to standard features, nearly always as a result of sociolinguistic pressures to conform to the mainstream. Thus, people who speak nonstandard English typically will attempt to adopt Standard English features in any situation in which they are interacting with someone they perceive as socially superior. As a result, a student who uses a nonstandard dialect might write "I been working hard" but if asked to read his or her composition aloud is likely to read "I've been working hard." In the course of reading an entire essay, a student may change many of the nonstandard features, but not all of them.

This behavior raises an important question: Why do students produce a paper with nonstandard features when they so often know a great deal of Standard English? The answer is, in part, that most classroom writing assignments are decontextualized, which means that they do not conform to real language situations. Students know that the teacher will read and grade their papers. When writing tasks lack a meaningful context, students find it difficult to take them seriously enough to use standard features.

The inherent variability of language indicates that dialects are unstable and that the language people use at any given time can be located on a continuum that ranges in some cases from formal standard written English to informal nonstandard spoken English. People move back and forth on the continuum as context demands and as their linguistic skills allow. This movement can be with different dialects or with different languages. The following example was reported by Gumperz (1982) and reflects a temporal factor often associated with code-switching; the speaker uses Standard English when talking with his teacher, but then he shifts to Black English when talking to a classmate:

1 Following an informal graduate seminar at a major university, a black student approached the instructor, who was about to leave the room accompanied by several other black and white students, and said:

2 Could I talk to you for a minute? I'm gonna apply for a fellowship and I was wondering if I could get a recommendation?

3 The instructor replied:

4 O.K. Come along to the office and tell me what you want to do.

5 As the instructor and the rest of the group left the room, the black student said, turning his head ever so slightly to the other students:

6 Ahma git me a gig! (Rough gloss: "I'm going to get myself some support.") (p. 30)

Code-switching among bilinguals, however, seldom occurs at different times but occurs within a given language event. Labov (1971), for example, observed code-switching within single sentences or utterances when studying Puerto Rican English in New York, as the following passage shows. The brackets enclose the translation of the Spanish phrases:

> Por eso cada [therefore each . . .], you know it's nothing to be proud of, porque yo no estoy [because I'm not] proud of it, as a matter of fact I hate it, pero viene vierne y Sabado yo estoy, tu me ve hacia me, sola [but come (?) Friday and Saturday I am, you see me, you look at me, alone] with a, aqui solita, a veces que Frankie me deja [here alone sometimes Frankie leaves me], you know a stick or something. . . . (p. 450)

Observations like these offer evidence that bidialectal and bilingual speakers have proficiency with Standard English but choose not to apply it, leading some people to argue that code-switching is a reflection of "linguistic laziness" (N. Sanchez, 1987). Witnessing code-switching on a daily basis, many teachers have assumed that students who speak Black English are simply being perverse when they fail to modify their speech and writing to Standard English on a *permanent basis.* If these children can "correct" their nonstandard features to standard ones on some occasions, as when reading a composition aloud, then they must know Standard English and are simply too lazy to use it, or so the reasoning goes.

Most of the available research on code-switching suggests, however, that it is acquired behavior rather than learned (Baugh, 1983; Genishi, 1981; Labov, 1971, 1972a, 1972b; McClure, 1981; Peck, 1982; Wald, 1985). Wald, for example, examined the language of 46 bilingual (Spanish–English) fifth and sixth graders. The spontaneous speech of the students was sampled when they were interviewed in peer groups of four by a bilingual male investigator, when the peer groups were alone but observed surreptitiously by the investigator, and in individual sessions with a bilingual female investigator. The subjects not only switched from Spanish to English with ease, but, more important, preserved syntactic and semantic grammaticality in both cases, as in the following: "There's una silla asi, y como sillas de fierro . . . no, si, para de que se usan en de—para backyard" (There's a seat like this, and like metal seats . . . no, yes, that you use in the backyard). Given the spontaneity of the responses and the ambiguous results of grammar instruction, it seems unlikely that the subjects were applying learned grammatical rules through an internal monitor.

If code-switching is acquired, it is an unconscious process. The implication therefore would be that nonstandard speakers who change nonstandard forms to standard ones are unaware of the changes they make. Experience in the classroom tends to bear this point out. A student who speaks Black English and who writes "Rosie be workin' at

Ralph's" but reads "Rosie is working at Ralph's," is unlikely to change the sentence during essay revision or editing. As Farr and Daniels (1986) noted, "Many students do not know how to correct nonstandard features in their writing and, even when highly motivated to learn to write Standard English, are quite puzzled about which features in their writing to change" (p. 20).

Nevertheless, it is important to note that code-switching is a conscious process in many situations, although the process itself may not involve any deliberation on the structural properties of the dialects or languages in question. Those who speak English as a second language tend to code-switch under two conditions: (a) when speaking with an audience they know is bilingual and (b) when they need a word in L_2 that they don't have or can't remember.

The situation is different for nonstandard-English speakers. They generally do not code-switch when speaking with others who are bidialectal. Instead, they will use one dialect or the other, depending on the social relationship that exists among the group and on the setting. The dominant factor, however, is the social relationship: As it becomes more intimate, there is a greater tendency to use the home dialect, even in those situations in which other speakers do not share and have a hard time understanding that dialect. As the bidialectal speaker shifts further along the continuum toward nonstandard speech, the monodialectal participant may have to ask "What?" several times as a reminder that he or she is not understanding some of the nonstandard language. At such moments, the bidialectal speaker must make a conscious decision to shift in the other direction along the continuum.

TEACHING NONMAINSTREAM STUDENTS

Regardless of their subject area, all teachers are teachers of language. Consequently, they deal with universals of language, learning, and mind that transcend individual language differences. The universal factors that govern language and learning suggest that writing instruction for nonmainstream students will be very similar to writing instruction for mainstream students.

Much of what effective teaching involves was explained in earlier chapters, but it is important to emphasize that research over the last few years indicates that nonmainstream students work through writing tasks in about the same way that mainstream students do (Harrold, 1995; Zamel, 1983). They develop a pretext for the discourse that includes both rhetorical features and surface features. When they write, they engage in pausing episodes indicative of mental revisions of the pretext, just as mainstream students do. They revise recursively, modifying their discourse plans as they go along. And with nonnative speakers, planning and revising skills in L_1 transfer to L_2 (Jones & Tetroe, 1987).

Moreover, nonmainstream writers, like their mainstream counterparts, frequently use writing to clarify their thoughts on subjects. In other words, they use writing as a vehicle for learning. Their efforts require a high degree of interaction with the text, with their constructed audience, and with their intentions. To paraphrase Ann Raimes (1985, 1986), students "negotiate" with the text as they develop it; they engage in hypothesis testing.

If nonmainstream writers are to learn to negotiate with a text successfully, they need instruction that encourages risk taking. They need a methodology that promotes a high degree of interaction with the teacher and with peers, that allows them to write multiple drafts, to receive feedback as each draft is being developed, and to revise. The only environment that currently incorporates all these features is the classroom workshop.

Using a workshop approach with nonmainstream students initially may seem counterintuitive. Given the types of errors that appear in their writing, there is a strong temptation to resort to drills and exercises to reduce the level of home-language or home-dialect interference. In her much admired book *Errors and Expectations,* Mina Shaughnessy (1977) concluded that providing drills and exercises, along with a great deal of sensitivity to their difficulties, is about all one can do for nonmainstream students. The primary patterns they bring to school writing must be overcome, the common reasoning goes, and drill is the only way to accomplish the task. But in this case intuition, as well as Shaughnessy, is wrong.

Although anecdotal and therefore not truly generalizable, my own teaching experience has shown no benefits in drills and exercises. Over the years, I have taught large numbers of BEV and ESL students. My writing classes currently are about 80% ESL, mostly from Japan and Korea. Students' first papers indeed have numerous surface errors that are the result of second-language interference. Japanese lacks articles as well as inflections, so students have a very hard time using articles and inflections correctly. These errors, however, do not make their papers unreadable, just incongruent with standards for university writing. The biggest difficulties are related to the rhetorical features of aim, intention, and audience—and also to the need to reflect more deeply on the complexities of issues. Thus, these students manifest the same major problem that native English-speaking students do. Three quarters of the way through the term, students have learned the value of revision so thoroughly that their papers have few surface errors, but they are still developing their understanding of rhetoric. As for reflection, they have made significant steps forward but have much work ahead of them. None of these advances, however, would be possible outside of a workshop environment that stresses revision after revision after revision.

Neither my own experience nor the available research suggests that teachers should ignore the problems students have with surface features. Eliminating errors is an important goal for all writers. Yet errors seem best addressed on the spot, as students are working on drafts in their work groups. They can be dealt with as part of the composing process through individual conferences or through a presentation to the whole class, if several students are having similar difficulties. This approach keeps the emphasis on writing. Studies like Farr and Janda's and Edelsky's, set in the context of contemporary writing research, have prompted numerous teachers to reexamine composition pedagogy for nonmainstream students. The difficulties that such students have with writing appear to stem less from linguistic features of the second language or the second dialect than from the complexities and constraints of the act of composing itself (see L. White, 1977; Williams, 1993). From this perspective, an emphasis on error correction is neither reliable nor effective in helping students eliminate errors in their writing. Edelsky (1986) on this account explicitly called for a literacy methodology that links reading and writing as top-down, pragmatic activities.

8

The Psychology of Writing

MIND AND LANGUAGE

People use language, specifically writing, to interact with one another and the world around them. Part of this interaction is related to learning, for writing can be used in a general way to enhance knowledge. Language provides a kind of rehearsal that helps people remember things better. As a vehicle for analysis, it can reveal a subject's complexities, and it also can help organize thoughts. Given these factors, many teachers and scholars believe that a strong relation exists between mind and language.

The nature of this relation continues to be vigorously debated. Some believe that the nature of mind influences the nature of language. Based on the work of Jean Piaget, one of the foremost child psychologists, this view proposes that language is part of the capacity to represent ideas and objects mentally (Piaget & Inhelder, 1969). Hence cognition in general has structural parallels to language. Both, for example, are hierarchical as well as linear, and both are temporally ordered.

In Piaget's view, cognitive abilities developmentally precede linguistic abilities; thus, the development of linguistic structures depends on cognitive abilities. Trimbur (1987) suggested that this view finds expression in composition studies as an "inner/outer" dualism, in which "the writer's mind is a kind of box" that teachers try to pry open "in order to free what is stored inside" (p. 211). This view is implicit in those approaches to rhetoric and composition that stress writing as a discovery procedure. In these approaches, writers are deemed incapable of knowing what they want to say prior to writing.

In contrast to this view, Vygotsky (1962) and Whorf (1956) believed that language influences cognition. This view is the more popular in composition studies, and it serves to justify an emphasis on style and the notion that writing is inherently superior to speech. Its chief advocates, Dillon (1981), Hirsch (1977), Moffett (1985), and Ong (1978), have argued that writing promotes the ability to reason abstractly and that without the ability to read and write, people are limited to concrete, situational thinking.

COGNITION INFLUENCES LANGUAGE

The influence of cognition on language is inherent in Piaget's (1953, 1955, 1962, 1974) model of children's intellectual development. The goal of his model was to explain children's behavior so as to determine what is common to all people. According to Piaget (1955), children go through a continuum of three developmental periods that correspond to intellectual growth and reasoning ability. During the sensorimotor period, which starts at birth and ends at about 18 months, children are largely governed by reflexes and cannot really think in the sense that an older child or an adult can. They are extremely egocentric and initially have little or no awareness of the world beyond their own sensations of hunger, cold, warmth, and discomfort. Objects initially have no existential reality for them, as evidenced by the observation that children at this age will not reach out for a toy that is suddenly covered by a blanket. This phenomenon is interpreted as indicating that for the child the toy ceases to exist once it is out of sight. Intellectual ability during this period is viewed as very limited. Children seem able to deal with only one task at a time, in a serial fashion. In addition, they seem concerned only with functional success, with performance, and generally have no abstracting ability.

The concrete operational period is from 18 months to about 11 years. Piaget (1955) divided this period into two stages: the preoperational stage, which lasts until about age 7, and the concrete operational stage. This period is followed by the formal operational period, which begins in early adolescence and which marks the development of adult reasoning ability.

The preoperational stage is characterized by very limited thinking ability, by an inability to reason abstractly, by an inability to classify appropriately, and by a high degree of egocentricity that makes taking on the point of view or role of another difficult for children. They cannot, in the words of Piaget (1955), *decenter,* and as a result they are poor communicators. The concrete operational stage marks a shift in intellectual ability. When children's intellect becomes "operational," they become much better at identifying changes between states and understanding the relations between those different states. For example, a toy under a blanket is understood to be simply covered up, not to have disappeared.

The relation between these stages of development and language is clear in observations of infant behavior. Infants focus their attention on their immediate surroundings and the people and objects they interact with on a daily basis. Such observations led Piaget (1955) to characterize the first stage of children's cognitive development as being concerned with mental representations of reality. These interactions begin at birth, yet language typically does not appear until children are about 1 year old, when representations of reality are already well established. And as language does emerge, it is object related. Most of a child's first words are names of people and objects in the immediate environment (Bates, 1976; Bates, Camaioni, & Volterra, 1975; Macnamara, 1972; Nelson, 1973; Pinker, 1994). The order of development is essentially the following: Cognition related to people and things in the immediate environment leads to language use about those same people and things. This pattern of cognitive development/ language development appears to be fairly consistent from one culture to another (L. Bloom, 1970, 1973; Jackendoff, 2002; Schlesinger, 1971; Steinberg, 1993).

As infants develop, their object-centered language shifts to actions that they are engaged in. Piaget reported that children up to about age 7 commonly use language to describe their activities, such as "I'm dressing the dolly." Because children during this period are egocentric, Piaget (1955) referred to such language as *egocentric speech,* and he defined it as the thoughts that emerge in the minds of children: "Apart from thinking by images . . . , the child up to an age as yet undetermined, but probably somewhere about seven, is incapable of keeping to himself the thoughts which enter his mind" (p. 59). Children's egocentric speech, in other words, is thinking aloud. It is important to note, however, that for Piaget egocentric speech does not play any significant role in cognitive development; it simply marks a transition between the egocentric existence of children and the social existence of adults. After about 8 years of age, it disappears as a result of further cognitive development. Piaget's analysis of egocentric speech is a cornerstone of the view that cognition influences language: Changes in cognition that are the result of maturation and development have linguistic consequences.

In composition studies, the proposal that cognition influences language is embraced on two levels. On an applied level, it informs—

through Bloom's (1956) taxonomy of behavioral objectives, which are based on Piaget's insights into child development—assignment sequencing. Assignments move from the cognitively simple to the cognitively complex in keeping with Piaget's developmental taxonomy. On a theoretical level, the proposal can be seen as a reaction against Chomsky's (1965) argument that linguistic features are innate, which in its strongest form posits autonomous linguistic mechanisms outside the cognitive domain (Fodor, 1983). Along these lines, Fodor suggested that language processes, such as grammaticality judgments, parsing sentences into constituents, and comprehension, are essentially a *reflex*. Many people who study and teach reading and writing are understandably uncomfortable with this idea. If language is outside the cognitive domain, then school-related activities designed to develop critical thinking and other intellectual faculties are unlikely to have any measurable effect on language performance. The view that cognition influences language rescues the idea that teaching students how to think helps them become better readers and writers.[1]

Problems With Piaget

Although there is no denying the importance of Piaget's contributions to the understanding of child development, research into cognitive and linguistic development some years ago forced a reevaluation of his conclusions. Bates (1979), for example, engaged children in cause–effect tasks and symbolic play in order to measure cognitive development. She then compared their performance on these tasks with their performance on language tasks and found that cognitive knowledge did not always precede linguistic performance (also see Corrigan, 1978; J. Miller, Chapman, Branston, & Reichle, 1980). After reviewing several of these studies, Rice and Kemper (1984) concluded that there is no empirical support for the proposal that children's cognitive development has a significant effect on their language, other than what may be considered normal maturational changes. They also concluded that the relevance of Piagetian sensorimotor tasks to language performance is questionable.

---

[1]It is important to keep in mind, however, that Fodor's analysis focuses exclusively on oral discourse and is, in part, a response to two observations: that speakers rarely have to think about the language they produce and that when speaking people do not have cognitive access to the mechanisms associated with language production. Fodor was not concerned with, and thus did not consider, rhetorical features of language.

Part of the problem is that Piaget's analysis of children's intellectual abilities is flawed in numerous respects, which makes his formulation of the way cognition influences language highly problematic (Donaldson, 1978; P. Miller, 1989). The claim that children are poor communicators because they are egocentric provides an important example. The idea that preoperational children cannot decenter is based largely on investigations involving the *mountains task* (Piaget & Inhelder, 1969), on which children are seated at a table that has a model of three mountains on it. Each mountain is a different color, and each has a different summit: One is covered with "snow," one has a house, and the third has a red cross. The experimenter then introduces a doll, moving it to different positions around the table. The task becomes describing what the doll "sees" in each of the different positions.

This task can shed important light on the relation between cognition and language because effective language use involves the ability to take on the perspective of another. Role-taking ability is central to turn taking in conversations, and it also is central to comprehension. A speaker must be able to reason abstractly and judge from nonlinguistic cues that the listener is understanding. Children in Piaget's studies below the age of 8 years invariably failed at this task, leading Piaget to conclude that they cannot adopt the point of view of another. He further concluded that these children generally do not understand one another, and they understand only a small portion of adult speech, principally commands. A significant part of their failure to understand was deemed attributable to their egocentricity.

Hughes (1975), however, hypothesized that children's difficulty with the mountains task was related to its content rather than to undeveloped cognitive abilities. To test this hypothesis, he altered the task by intersecting two walls to form a cross; he then changed the dolls, introducing a policeman doll and a small boy doll. The policeman doll was situated so that it could "see" two areas of the intersection, as shown in Fig. 8.1.

The boy doll then was placed in the various sections made by the intersecting walls, and the subjects were asked whether the policeman doll could "see" him. Few subjects had any difficulty with this task, even those who were 3 years old. Next, subjects were told to hide the boy doll so that the policeman doll could not see him, and again they made few errors. At this point, Hughes increased the complexity of the task by introducing a second policeman doll and situating him at the top of the intersection, where he has a view of sections A and B, as shown in Fig. 8.2.

Subjects were told to hide the boy doll again, this time from both policemen, which requires coordination of two different points of view.

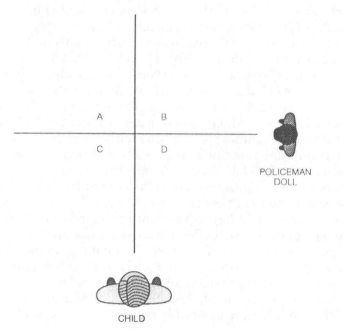

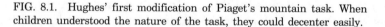

FIG. 8.1. Hughes' first modification of Piaget's mountain task. When children understood the nature of the task, they could decenter easily.

Ninety percent of the responses were correct. These findings suggest that children as young as 3 years of age are as able to reason abstractly as children 2 to 4 years older, as long as they understand the task. Commenting on Hughes' data, Donaldson (1978) suggested that the findings were congruent with "the generalization of experience: they [the children] know what it is to try to hide. Also they know what it is to be naughty and to want to evade the consequences. So they can easily conceive that a boy might want to hide from a policeman if he had been a bad boy" (p. 24) (also see Borke, 1975; Cairns, 1983; Carey, 1985; Case, 1985, 1991; DeLoache, K. Miller, & Pierroutsakos, 1998).

The general criticism of Piaget today is that his research failed to test children's cognitive abilities adequately.[2] The tasks he and his associates designed were removed from the world of children, and the young people they studied simply could not understand what they were being asked to do. Consequently, Piaget's interpretation of his re-

---

[2]Another major criticism is that his studies of young children involved only three subjects—his own children—which is insufficient for making generalizations.

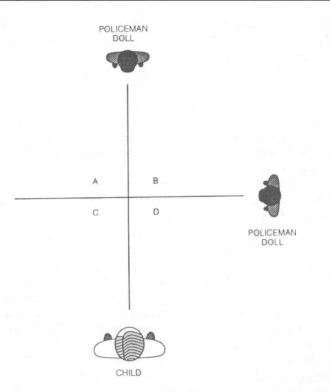

FIG. 8.2. Hughes' second modification of Piaget's mountain task. Even when the task was made more difficult through the addition of a second doll, children had no difficulty with decentering.

sults was significantly confounded. On this basis, many scholars have concluded that Piaget's view that cognition influences language is incorrect (Karmiloff-Smith, 1992). This conclusion is reinforced by the fact that modern studies, designed to ensure that the child subjects understand what is asked of them, consistently show the children are far more capable of abstract thought than Piaget determined.

LANGUAGE INFLUENCES COGNITION

The idea that language influences cognition is very appealing to composition specialists. Known as *linguistic relativism* among linguists and psychologists, this idea emerged around the turn of the century when French anthropologist Lévy-Bruhl published *Les fonctions mentales dans les sociétés inférierures* in 1910. The English translation, *How Natives Think,* was published in 1926.[3] Although successful as a sociologist early in his academic career, Lévy-Bruhl felt that his work was too theoretical, too removed from the realities of the everyday existence of mankind. He began anthropological investigations after questioning the widely accepted view that the human mind functions the same regardless of time or culture. He then set out to study mental operations in the remotest regions of Africa to determine what, if any, differences existed between the cognition of Europeans and tribal peoples.

In *How Natives Think,* Lévy-Bruhl (1926) argued that his field studies showed great differences between the cognitive operations of the two groups. The tribal subjects he studied proved to be *prelogical,* which did not mean that they were incapable of logical operations but that they were indifferent to logical contradictions that arose from their failure to identify myths and mystical experiences as unreal.[4] They were, however, incapable of abstract concept formation above a rudimentary type associated with mystical experiences. That is, the primitives in his research might look at a tree and recognize it as a tree without any consideration of the classification of that tree as a member of a broader group of living plants.

Lévy-Bruhl was attacked soundly by other scholars for these conclusions. English anthropologists were particularly forceful in their rejection of the idea that different cultures produced different mentalities. Nevertheless, Lévy-Bruhl's work attracted the attention of enough scholars to gain a certain degree of intellectual legitimacy. More significant, his ideas received coverage in the media and led to a popular folk psychology about cross-cultural differences in cognition.

This folk psychology was reinforced in the United States through the work of Whorf (1956), an anthropological linguist who did extensive work with American Indian tribal languages during the 1920s and 1930s and who was significantly influenced by the work of Lévy-Bruhl. Whorf proposed that linguistics was ideally suited to investigating cog-

---

[3]This title is not even an approximation of the original, and it's enlightening to consider that a literal translation of the original title is *Mental Functions in Inferior Societies.*

[4]Near the end of his life, Lévy-Bruhl abandoned the notion of prelogical thinking. In *The Notebooks on Primitive Mentality* (1975), he concluded that the logical incompatibilities he had observed were the result of mental juxtapositions of mythical reality and natural reality. As a result, positions that the European mind would find illogical the primitive mind found logical because of the "imperceptible passage from belief to experience" (p. 13). In other words, the primitive mind, according to Lévy-Bruhl, does not differentiate between mythical experiences and natural experiences.

nition, owing to his belief that all thought was verbal. Whorf noted that "the Hopi language is seen to contain no words, grammatical forms, constructions, or expressions that refer directly to what we call 'time,' or to past, present or future" (p. 57). On this basis, he proposed that the absence of time gave Hopi speakers a sense of reality far different from "classical Newtonian physics" (p. 58), and he linked this different reality to the sort of observations that Lévy-Bruhl had made earlier about the prelogical quality of tribal cognition. Thus Hopi, and by extrapolation all languages, creates not only a certain model of reality but also a certain way of thinking unique to that language. As Whorf stated:

> [Cognition] can only be determined by a penetrating study of the *language* spoken by the individual whose thinking process we are concerned with, and it will be found to be *fundamentally different* for individuals whose languages are of fundamentally different types. Just as cultural facts are only culturally determined, not biologically determined, so linguistic facts, which are likewise cultural, and include the linguistic element of thought, are only linguistically determined. (p. 67)

Although Whorf's work has always been well known among linguists, it never stirred much interest among those working in composition studies. This role fell to Lev Vygotsky, a Russian psychologist and contemporary of Piaget whose observations of child behavior during the late 1920s and early 1930s were unknown in America until the 1960s, when his books were translated into English. These works have provided composition specialists with a significant theoretical framework for the idea that language influences cognition. Especially influential has been *Thought and Language,* the last book Vygotsky wrote before his death in 1934.

The work of Piaget and Vygotsky has much in common. Both were constructivists who were strongly against nativism. Constructivism maintains that children lack any innate cognitive or linguistic structures or domain-specific knowledge. Nativism maintains that children have these structures, as the work of Chomsky most vividly illustrates. In Chomsky's account, language is innate. As Karmiloff-Smith (1992) noted, constructivism is similar to behaviorism because both see the child as a *"tabula rasa* with no built-in knowledge" (p. 7). Today, however, this view seems quaint. The notion that humans are born as blank slates and that we are little more than social constructs is difficult to maintain, given the advances in biology and cognitive science over the last couple of decades. After examining much of the research, Pinker (2002) argued convincingly that a number of fears prevent Western societies from endorsing publicly what is widely accepted privately—that IQ, preferences, personality, gender differences, taste in food, and a host of other characteristics of individuals are determined primarily by genes, not environment.

Both Piaget and Vygotsky (1962) noted that at about 3 years of age, children begin to talk to themselves when doing things, as though giving verbal expression to their actions. Such talk is inherently different from the conversations they have been having for some time with others, because it seems to lack a social function. When dressing a doll, for example, children will commonly utter such expressions as: "Now I'm going to put the dress on the dolly, and then I'm going to comb her hair." More often than not, children make these utterances as though no one else can hear them, so Vygotsky, like Piaget, referred to them as examples of egocentric speech.

Vygotsky (1962) also proposed that egocentric utterances mark the beginning of thought and that egocentric speech is thinking aloud. However, Vygotsky had a very different interpretation of the nature of egocentric speech. In his view, all language is social, including egocentric speech. One consequence of this view is fairly uncontroversial: Children develop the language of their community. Vygotsky took this perception to its logical conclusion and argued that the fundamental pattern of logical thought is evident in "social, collaborative forms of behavior" (p. 19). The emergence of egocentric speech signals the start of an internalization process in which those social patterns of behavior take the form of what Vygotsky termed "inner speech," or thought. On this account, not only thought but the very processes of thought are social.

As Vygotsky (1962) noted, there is "nothing to this effect in Piaget, who believed that egocentric speech simply dies off" (p. 18). Piaget proposed a developmental sequence that began with nonverbal thought, developed into egocentric thought and speech, and then developed into socialized speech and logical thought. Vygotsky, however, proposed a developmental sequence that began with social speech, then egocentric speech, then inner speech, and then fully developed thought. In his view, "the true direction of the development of thinking is not from the individual to the socialized, but from the social to the individual" (p. 20). Consequently:

> Verbal thought is not an innate, natural form of behavior but is determined by a historical-cultural process and has specific properties and laws. . . . Once we acknowledge the historical character of verbal thought, we must consider it subject to all the premises of historical materialism,[5] which are valid for any historical phenomenon in human so-

---

[5]Historical materialism, as defined in the writings of Marx, Engels, and Lenin, proposes that the prevailing economic system of any historical period determines the form of social organization and the political, ethical, and intellectual history of that period.

ciety. It is only to be expected that on this level the development of behavior will be governed essentially by the general laws of the historical
development of human society. (p. 51)

Vygotsky's influence on issues of literacy has been profound, and
the list of scholars attracted to his view of language is long, indeed. In
his thorough review of the language-influences-cognition question,
Walters (1990) identified Goody and Watt's 1968 essay, "The Consequences of Literacy," for example, as an important work that "influenced the discussion of literacy and its nature . . . more than any other
. . . because of the way . . . [the authors] chose to lay out the problems
associated with understanding the phenomenon" (p. 174). Goody and
Watt drew substantially on Vygotsky (as well as Lévy-Bruhl) but as
Walters explained, the focus in Goody and Watt was much more narrow than what is found in either:

> Stated in its strongest form, . . . [Goody and Watts's] theory claims that
> literacy and more particularly alphabetic literacy of the kind used for
> Western languages causes cognitive changes to the extent that literate
> people (that is, those literate in a language using alphabetic script) sim-
> ply think differently—that is, more logically—than those from cultures
> without alphabetic literacy—an idea that many Westerners find appeal-
> ing, no doubt because it "explains" what they perceive to be the superior-
> ity of Western culture. (p. 175)

In other words, Goody and Watt argued that Western culture is superior to others because it developed not just literacy but alphabetic literacy, which supposedly led to advances in cognition that other cultures
have been unable to match. This view, based on Vygotsky's work, became remarkably popular in composition studies.

Olson (1977), for example, used Vygotsky's theoretical framework
to explain the differences in academic achievement he observed among
students from diverse linguistic backgrounds. He argued that speech is
fundamentally different from writing in several important ways. In his
view, speech and writing do not use similar mechanisms for conveying
meaning: In speech, meaning is derived from the shared intentions
and context of speaker and hearer, whereas in writing, meaning re-
sides in the text itself at the sentence level and has to be extracted by
readers. Olson stated that writing has "no recourse to shared context
. . . [because] sentences have to be understood in contexts other than
those in which they were written" (p. 272). He went on to assert that
human history has reflected an evolution from utterance to text that
has profoundly affected cultural and psychological development.

These observations were consistent with folk theories about language as well as folk psychology. But more significant was Olson's (1977) additional argument that writing in general and the essay form in particular account for the development of abstract thought in human beings. Olson asserted that people in nonliterate cultures are incapable of abstract thought; he claimed that writing is the key to developing abstracting ability because it forces people to comprehend events outside their original context, which alters their perception of the world, in turn leading to cognitive growth. Walters (1990) noted in this regard that Olson "is among the most extreme of those who link the conventions of a particular literate form—in his case, the essay—with logical thought as represented in written language" (p. 177). Yet it is difficult to differentiate Olson's claims from those put forward by Goody and Watt. Following Olson's (1977) lead, Walter Ong (1978, 1982) took these ideas a step further and claimed that "without writing . . . the mind simply cannot engage in [abstract] . . . thinking. . . . Without writing, the mind cannot even generate concepts such as 'history' or analysis" (p. 39).

These are powerful claims, and many teachers and scholars in the field have embraced them enthusiastically (see, e.g., Dillon, 1981; Hirsch, 1977; Scinto, 1986; Shaughnessy, 1977) because they create an us–them dichotomy that can be used to explain why some students do not succeed in school. Followed to its logical end, this view suggests that children from backgrounds where written discourse is not stressed will have culture-specific cognitive deficiencies that make significant academic achievement essentially impossible. In addition, these claims validate the orientation of most writing teachers. If literacy affects the quality of thought in a positive way, it logically follows that the quality of literacy would bear directly on the quality of thought. Reading great works of literature therefore would have a more beneficial effect on thinking than reading a lab report or a book on history.

JOURNAL ENTRY

Reflect on your experiences with literacy and how it has affected you and those you know.

Problems With Linguistic Relativism

We know that society exerts a strong influence on language; language is, after all, a social action. We also know that society exerts a strong influence on cognition. The tragic cases of feral children and children whose abusive parents have kept them locked for years in attics and closets give graphic testimony of the importance of society on both language and mind: These children inevitably suffer irreparably and never fully develop language or cognitive skills. If they are not rescued at an early age, they tend to grow up semiretarded. On a more common level, Healy (1990) and Heath (1983) reported evidence of a strong social influence on language and cognitive development that affected school achievement. However, to propose that the quality of mind is affected by the quality of language, whether oral or written, is to make a much stronger claim. The educational implications are clear-cut: People who do not read and write, and also probably those who do not read and write very well, must be simpleminded.

It is difficult not to find an element of elitism in this position, and some people may even see it as being ethnocentric, especially when writers like Scinto (1986) argue that written language is a "culturally heritable trait" (p. 171). Although there is no doubt that literacy provides increased opportunities for social mobility in the United States and in most developed nations, there necessarily must be some question as to the specific culture in which written language appears as a heritable trait. In our pluralistic society, it is possible to speak of "American culture" in the abstract, but the United States simultaneously contains numerous subcultures—black, Hispanic, Asian, and American Indian, as well as the spectrum provided by SES and recent, massive immigration—that simply do not place the same weight on writing that mainstream, upper-middle-class, Anglo-European culture does. The task of teaching most likely would be far easier if, indeed, written language were a "culturally heritable trait." In truth, however, children from mainstream and nonmainstream backgrounds alike find much school-sponsored reading and writing to be complex and baffling puzzles.

The criticism of linguistic relativism does not rest on such social and educational concerns. It is important to understand that the notion that writing exerts a cultural and psychological influence grew out of anthropological studies that attempted to explain why some cultures have reached a modern stage of development and why some have not (see Finnegan, 1970; Goody, 1968, 1972, 1977; Greenfield, 1972; Levi-Strauss, 1966; Lévy-Bruhl, 1975; Luria, 1976). In these studies, researchers gave a group of nonliterate, usually non-Western, subjects a task designed to measure cognitive abilities, then gave the same task to a group of literate, usually Western, subjects and compared the results. Colby and Cole (1976), for example, found that on tests of memory, nonliterate subjects from the Kpelle tribe in Africa performed far below the level of test subjects in the United States who were on average almost 5 years younger.

Similarly, Luria (1976) (who was a student of Vygotsky) found that the nonliterate subjects in his study had more difficulty categorizing and sorting objects than the literate subjects. The nonliterates' method of cognitive processing tended to be more concrete and situation-bound than the literates'. For example, Luria presented his subjects with pictures of a hammer, a saw, an ax, and a piece of lumber, then asked which object did not belong with the others. The literate subjects quickly identified the piece of lumber, because it, unlike the other objects, is not a tool. The nonliterate subjects, on the other hand, seemed unable to understand the question. They insisted that all the objects went together, because there was little use for a hammer, saw, and an ax if there was no lumber to use in making something.

From Luria's point of view, that of a psychologist trained in the Western tradition, this functional response was wrong, and he concluded that the nonliterate subjects had difficulty formulating abstract categories. This conclusion is remarkably similar to those proposed by Lévy-Bruhl. However, it may well be that, as in the case of Piaget and Inhelder's (1969) mountains task, what was actually being tested had little to do with the ability to formulate abstract categories but had very much to do with understanding what the test was about. Lakoff (1987) and Rosch (1978) have explained in great detail that there are specific cultural characteristics related to accepting the attributes objects may have in common. The often noted differences between English and Eskimo regarding the number of words used to describe snow offer an interesting example. Even within a single culture there will be clusters of shared attributes that vary by gender, education, and SES. For many people in the United States, the term *car* embraces any vehicle that has four wheels and that is used principally for personal transportation. Included are pickup trucks, station wagons, Jeeps, limousines, and sport-utility vehicles. For many other people, *car* refers only to sedans and coupes. Luria's findings therefore simply could be an instance of the nonliterate group's refusal to accept the designated category attributes, not a demonstration of an inability to establish abstract categories.

Moreover, every recorded culture, whether literate or nonliterate, has (or had) some form of religious beliefs. Such beliefs tend to be highly abstract. Also, collective terms (which are inherently abstract) are used in every recorded language to designate groups of people and things. Although not all languages have discrete terms for *brother* and *sister,* it appears to be a universal that they have a term for *sibling* (Ullmann, 1963). A culture where it is possible to own more than one cow will have some term equivalent to *cattle* or *herd.* On this account, the inability of nonliterate people to perform certain tasks, such as categorization, may not be related at all to their ability to reason abstractly.

These rather obvious difficulties beset most of the existing studies of literacy's effects on cognition. Another factor, however, is even more problematic. As Scribner and Cole (1981) pointed out in *The Psychology of Literacy,* to date the most detailed evaluation of the link between literacy and cognition, earlier researchers consistently conflated *literacy* and *schooling.* Given that it is in the nature of schooling to strip situations of their context and to emphasize nonfunctional intellectual experiences, conflating literacy and schooling may jeopardize the methodological integrity of the investigations. Thus, it is impossible to look at studies like Luria's and determine any causal relations involved because there is no way to know whether the results were influenced by literacy or by schooling. Furthermore, as a consequence of this conflation, the research generally fails to compare similar groups of subjects. In the case of Luria, the groups he compared were not merely literates and nonliterates but literates with schooling and nonliterates without. These factors led Scribner and Cole to state that such studies "fail to support the specific claims made for literacy's effects. . . . No comparisons were ever made between children with and children without a written language" (pp. 11–12).

To address such difficulties, Scribner and Cole (1981) were very careful to design a study that would distinguish between the cognitive effects of schooling and the cognitive effects of literacy. Their research was conducted among the Vai, a group of people in West Africa who developed an independent writing system early in the 19th century. The Vai script is used regularly for notes and letters, but there is no body of literature written in the script. At the time of this study, only about half the people who were literate in the Vai script had some formal schooling. Consequently, there was a large group of literate but unschooled subjects to draw on.

Scribner and Cole (1981) evaluated more than 1,000 subjects over a 4-year period. The results showed that formal schooling had an effect on *some* cognitive abilities, but not on all. The schooled subjects were better at providing explanations, specifically explanations related to sorting, logic, grammatical rules, game instructions, and hypothetical questions. Outside the domain of verbal exposition, no other general patterns of cross-task superiority were found. Scribner and Cole suggested on the basis of these findings that schooling fosters abilities in expository talk in "contrived situations."

As for literacy itself, only four tasks showed any influence. Literates were better able to: (a) listen to uttered statements and repeat back their messages, (b) use graphic symbols to represent language, (c) use language as a means of instruction, and (d) talk about correct Vai speech. Given the nature of literacy, such differences would be expected. But the literates showed *no* superiority over nonliterate subjects with regard to classification, memory, deduction, and categorization. In other words, no evidence was found to suggest that literacy is linked to abstracting ability, cognitive growth, or the quality of thought. Summarizing their work, Scribner and Cole (1981) noted: "Our results are in direct conflict with persistent claims that 'deep psychological differences' divide literate and nonliterate populations. . . . On no task—logic, abstraction, memory, communication—did we find all nonliterates performing at lower levels than all literates" (p. 251).

Further evidence against the idea that language influences cognition comes from studies of deaf children who have learned neither speech nor sign language. According to this view, such children either should have no thought at all or should have thought that is profoundly different from what is found in hearing children. Because it is difficult to evaluate cognitive processes without using language in some form, studies of deaf children's intellectual abilities are often less than definitive. Nevertheless, certain conclusions have been widely accepted. After conducting a series of studies into cognitive development, Furth (1966) reported that "language does not influence development [among deaf children] in any direct, general way" (p. 160). Similarly, Rice and Kemper (1984) reported that "deaf children's progress through the early Piagetian stages and structures is roughly parallel to that of hearing children" (p. 37). Clearly, then, cognitive development can proceed without language.

The weight of the evidence against the idea that language influences cognition—at least the strong version—is so compelling that its most ardent contemporary advocates have quietly retreated somewhat from their earlier positions. Goody (1987), for example, criticized his paper with Watt for placing too much importance on the alphabet as a tool for elevating culture. Olson (1987) suggested that his claim regarding the salutary effects of the essay on cognition may have overstated the case. If both the Piagetian and the Vygostkian views are discredited among psychologists, what remains?

JOURNAL ENTRY

Although the work of both Piaget and Vygotsky is suspect, they remain immensely popular—Piaget among educators, Vygotsky among composition specialists. Consider some of the factors that account for their popularity.

A PHASE MODEL OF COGNITION
AND LANGUAGE

Both Piaget and Vygotsky proposed models of development that involve stages. In Piaget, children move from the sensorimotor stage,
for example, to the concrete operational stage. In Vygotsky, children
move from the egocentric-speech stage to the inner-speech stage. Neither of these models accurately reflects actual language development.
As children mature, their accomplishments with language and cognition are largely incremental, and they often reach behavioral milestones and then retreat from them in a recurrent ebb-and-flow movement. The same may be said of older children and even adults with
respect to a range of different behaviors, particularly language. Moreover, the recurrent characteristics of development are mirrored in
changes in neural structures associated with learning, where dendrites demonstrate recurrent growth and reduction over time in response to external stimuli.

The stage models of Piaget and Vygotsky do not recognize these features of development. Instead, they posit discrete transitions from one
kind of behavior and form of existence to another. As an alternative to
the stage model, Karmiloff-Smith (1992) proposed a phase model that
she referred to as *representational redescription*. In describing the different stages and phases, Karmiloff-Smith noted:

> Stage models such as Piaget's are age-related and involve fundamental
> changes across the entire cognitive system. Representational redescrip-
> tion, by contrast, is hypothesized to occur recurrently within micro-
> domains throughout development, as well as in adulthood and for some
> kinds of new learning. (p. 18)

In Karmiloff-Smith's (1992) model, development involves three
phases. For the purposes of this discussion, these phases may be
thought of as: (a) data collection, (b) reflection, and (c) reconciliation.
Data collection encompasses gathering information from the environment so as to develop internal representations of reality. During reflection, these internal representations are the focus of attention to
the extent that they dominate external data and thereby may result in
performance errors. Reconciliation involves more closely matching internal representations with external data. These phases seem congruent with the connectionist model of language acquisition that is widely
accepted in psychology.

Phase models have several advantages over stage models, but one of
the more important is that they propose that cognition and language

interact in a reciprocal process. Evidence to support this idea comes from a variety of sources (see Jackendoff, 2002; Rice & Kemper, 1984), but one of the more elegant arises out of work with terms that indicate location. It is generally accepted that children's understanding of spatial relations follows a set pattern. First to develop are notions of *on* and *in,* followed quickly by notions of *top* and *bottom.* Other spatial concepts, such as *between, behind,* and *across,* develop much later (E. Clark, 1980). The development of spatial concepts is reflected in children's acquisition of the terms to identify them. Dan Slobin, however, hypothesized that linguistic variables can influence the pattern of development: The pattern may not be uniform across cultures and languages, because some languages use complex grammatical features to indicate spatial relationships. This complexity might make it harder for children in those cultures to formulate notions of location.

To test his hypothesis, Slobin (1973) first studied a group of toddlers who were learning both Hungarian and Serbo-Croatian. He discovered that the children learned how to express location in Hungarian before they could do so in Serbo-Croatian. Of the two languages, location is easier to express in Hungarian. His follow-up study compared acquisition of location terms in four languages: English, Italian, Turkish, and Serbo-Croatian (Slobin, 1982). Again, linguistic variables appeared to influence the development of spatial understanding. In this case, English and Serbo-Croatian proved more difficult than Turkish and Italian. As Slobin pointed out, Turkish and Italian use single words for the various spatial relations, whereas English and Serbo-Croatian have multiple terms, such as *on top of, next to,* and *in front of.*

The proposal that cognition and language exert reciprocal influences strikes many teachers as commonsensical, but it has two disadvantages for composition theorists. First, it fails to validate the study of literature as a causal factor in the improvement of mind. The argument that language arts curricula should include a heavy emphasis on literature is thereby diminished. Students of low intelligence and students with a variety of problems that make them less than ideal learners will not be transformed through a Great Books program. Second, it fails to provide the sort of intellectual controversy that attracts readers. In comparison to claims that anyone without literacy cannot have a sense of history, the proposal of reciprocal influences is a bit dull.

Nevertheless, the phase model that supports the notion of reciprocity is congruent with the work in cognitive science pertaining to association and neural networks, which was summarized in chapter 6. In both, language acquisition is intimately allied with experiences and internal representations of reality. The interaction of reality and internal representations of reality, when examined via a phase model, suggests that writing performance is influenced by both cognitive and social domains, which include published texts. Reading and immersion in a given discourse community will develop internal representations of audience, rhetorical aims, argumentative structure, and so forth; instruction, likewise, will develop internal representations of prewriting techniques, drafting, planning, sentence and paragraph structure, topic sentences, and theses. However, the existing stage model of composing does not explain why reading, immersion, and instruction fail to result in significant improvement in writing skill. A phase model, on the other hand, maintains that the internal representations are in a steady state of flux. They always are in the process of becoming as each person strives to achieve a perfect match between those representations and external reality. Because a perfect match remains always elusive, Williams (1993) argued that:

> There is a sense in which writers, even experienced ones, must approach every writing task as though it were their first. They are faced with individual acts of creation each time they attempt to match a mental model of the discourse with the premises, paragraphs, examples, proofs, sentences, and words that comprise it. (p. 564)

When we apply the stage model to writing, there is the clear implication that students achieve developmental milestones that allow them to pass on to higher levels of achievement. This implication is valid only insofar as we recognize a general pattern of maturation in all areas of behavior. For example, a student in graduate school will be better able to find materials in a library than a student in elementary school because he or she has more experience with libraries and research. Nonetheless, both will have to use the same procedures and resources to locate those materials. The number of shortcuts are limited, and the procedures never become automated—they never become unconscious—to the extent that one can concentrate all energies on reaching the next stage, whatever that might be; they simply become more efficient. The early stages are always as important as the latter stages and are always omnipresent in the process.

The phase model of composing acknowledges this omnipresence without focusing on chronology. Students learn to spell before they learn to revise, and both are important in successful writing, but attention to spelling does not necessarily come before attention to revision, even though spelling was learned first. By the same token, attention to revision does not supersede attention to spelling, even though revision may be more important to the overall success of the writing. The stage model proposes a hierarchy based on importance. The phase model does not. Instead, it proposes that attention to spelling and attention to revision co-occur in the act of writing and that the co-occurrence cannot be differentiated on the basis of whether the writer is experienced or inexperienced.

If we extend the phase model along the lines suggested by Rumelhart and McClelland's (1986a, 1986b) work in neural networks, we see that the various phases, existing as they do simultaneously, place competing demands on writers. Audience competes with message, which in turn competes with structure, which in turn competes with punctuation, and so on. This competition may serve to explain why good writing is and always has been such a premium and why education per se does not ensure that people become good writers. Instruction adds information and levels of expertise to the phases, but it does not reduce the level of competition or make writing any easier. Only years of practice and reflection will do that.

PAUSES, PLANS, MENTAL MODELS, AND SOCIAL ACTIONS

With good cause, most teachers are concerned that their students treat topics superficially. They note that their students seldom venture beyond the most obvious analyses. In classes from history to science, the badly written essay is the one produced by the student who not only hasn't mastered the material but also hasn't thought about it deeply.

Investigations into pausing and planning have shown that good writers spend more time thinking about what they write, perhaps developing and working from more elaborate mental models of the proposed text. Flower and Hayes (1981) concluded from their research on pausing episodes that good writers and poor writers use pauses in different ways. Good writers engage in global planning that incorporates rhetorical concerns such as audience, purpose, and intention. Poor writers, on the other hand, engage in local planning that focuses on surface features.

Steve Witte (1985) suggested that when writers decide to compose, whether on their own or because of a teacher's assignment, they conceive an internal "pretext" that has both global and local discourse features. Planning would therefore involve a complex process of formulation, monitoring, and revision of the pretext. The physical act of writing would be largely the transcription of an already revised pretext, which would account for the observation that experienced writers frequently do less revising on drafts but still produce writing superior in quality to that of their less-skilled counterparts. Quite simply, they have performed more revision during planning. If this is the case, teaching probably should be directed toward getting students to focus more attention on planning at the global level and less at the sentence level. They need to think more during writing activities.

Empirical support for the notion that good writing is linked to the amount of thinking students do during the composing process is difficult to obtain because of the very nature of the problem. How does one measure the mind at work? The answer may lie in minute physical responses in certain muscles, such as those around the mouth and larynx, that appear to correspond with mental activity. These responses, usually called *covert,* or *subvocal, linguistic behavior,* can be measured only with the aid of special equipment, but they nevertheless have been studied extensively. A large body of research now indicates that when people listen, read silently, solve math problems, remember, and write—that is, when they engage in almost any mental task—there is evidence of covert linguistic behavior. The more difficult the mental task, the greater the muscular response (see Conrad, 1972; Edfelt, 1960; Hardyck & Petrinovich, 1967; McGuigan, 1966, 1978; Sokolov, 1972; Williams, 1983, 1987). The link is so strong that many researchers are convinced covert linguistic behavior is a measurable manifestation of thought.

Williams (1987) found that the below-average writers in his investigation demonstrated much less covert linguistic behavior during pauses than the above-average writers. This finding suggested that the poor writers were doing less work on their internal pretext than the good writers. The models proposed by Flower and Hayes (1981) and Witte (1985) make it reasonable to conclude that it was the global, rhetorical aspects of the pretext that were being neglected. If poor writers are thinking about surface features rather than rhetorical ones, as seems indicated, it is easier to understand why they so often produce essays that lack depth, essays deficient in identification of topic, articulation of intention, and specification of audience, even when these features are delineated by their teacher (see Bamberg, 1983; Williams, 1985; Witte & Faigley, 1981).

Why poor writers fail to spend much time planning their essays and thinking about their topics is unclear, but at least part of the problem is experiential and educational. Such students have not had much practice reflecting deeply on events and ideas, and they have been educated in an environment that does not consistently call for reflection. Much schooling, after all, relies on rote memorization.

Viewing the relation between mind and language as reciprocal is useful in this regard. The mind-as-a-box metaphor (Trimbur, 1987) won't work if the box isn't very full, which will be the case with students who generally have been treated as empty vessels waiting to be filled. They have not had much help in loading the box with ideas of their own. By the same token, reading and writing per se are not likely to lead to more thought. Such activities have to be part of a social context that acts on each student—through questions, differences in perspective and opinion, demands for more detail—as the student attempts to act on the social context through writing and sharing that writing. Writing as busywork, therefore, has absolutely no value.

The idea of building new skills on old ones is implicit in this account, but writing assignments nonetheless should be challenging if they are going to lead to cognitive growth. If children are already very familiar with object-related cognition and language, teachers should not bore them with endless object-related tasks. Because narratives and descriptions are inherently object related, students may not be challenged by such activities after one or two essays. Challenging tasks will be those that ask students to think, to formulate hypotheses concerning the way things are, and to find support for their hypotheses. The implications for writing assignments should be obvious.

In addition, it seems clear that writing assignments should be sufficiently related to the world of students as to be understandable. A teacher who asks students to examine Marx's theory of the alienation of labor may be disappointed with the resulting essays, whereas one who asks students to examine why they attend a closed campus may not. This isn't to say that our students should be ignorant of philosophy, history, and literature. But "big topics" often force beginning writers on themselves, effectively isolating them from any recognizable social factors that could help make their writing meaningful, largely because they lack sufficient subject expertise to explore such topics in meaningful ways. These topics are hard for students who do not yet see a connection between their world and the one reflected in the topic. They become like the children in Piaget and Inhelder's (1969) mountains task: They want to cooperate, they want to do well, but they just can't understand what they are being asked to do or why they are being asked to do it.

What does this mean for teachers? They need to link writing assignments to content knowledge in ways that enhance expertise and that make the writing tasks meaningful. Writing just for the sake of writing does not appear to provide any benefits. Linking writing tasks to content may be contrary to the prevalent orientation in our language arts classes that strives to avoid writing about content, but what we understand about how mind and language interact indicates that this orientation is taking students and teachers alike down a dead-end street.

9

Writing Assignments

MAKING GOOD WRITING ASSIGNMENTS

When students turn in essays that have little to say and that are boring to read, teachers often blame the students for not trying. Actually, the problem may be in the assignment. There is no such thing as "the perfect assignment," but some are definitely better than others and lead to more thoughtful responses from students. Too often, problems in students' writing can be traced back to poorly constructed assignments. Fortunately, assignments can be improved significantly through following a few simple steps.

Planning and Outcome Objectives

Good assignments take time and planning. They have measurable outcome objectives that are linked to broader goals and objectives defined by the course and by the series of courses in which writing instruction occurs. Educators generally differentiate goals and objects on the basis of specificity. Goals tend to be expressed in terms of mastery, whereas outcome objectives tend to be expressed in terms of performance or demonstrable skill. (Years ago, outcome objectives were expressed largely in terms of *behaviors,* reflecting the influence of behavioral psychology.) In a language arts class, for example, we might find statements similar to the following:

- *Goals:* Students will study and understand various forms of expository writing, including reports of events and information, interpretation, argumentation, and evaluation.

- *Objectives:* At the end of the course, students will be able to write effective, error-free reports of events and information, interpretations of events and information, arguments, and evaluations.

At the public school level, goals must include preparing students to write at the college level, which means that objectives must reference students' ability to produce the kind of writing required at university. At the college level, goals must include preparing students to write for a variety of audiences, such as faculty in other departments, the general public, and workplace professionals. Objectives must reference students' ability to write in several genres and for difference audiences.

The importance of setting realizable goals and objectives cannot be overemphasized, yet, sadly, it is the case that large numbers of teachers do not understand the importance of planning and specifying outcome objectives. Few teachers develop their language arts or composition courses around the idea of goals, and fewer still reflect on appropriate learning outcomes for their classes. At every level, the idea that students who finish these courses should be able to *do* something that demonstrates what they learned seems totally foreign to the majority of teachers I have worked with over the years. More often than not, teachers put together a writing assignment the night before they give it to students, and it is commonly unrelated to any instruction that preceded it.

A knowledge of district or state guidelines across grade levels is important to proper planning because they specify the particular skills students are expected to master from grade to grade. These guidelines, however, commonly repeat the same outcome objectives for every grade level. As a result, we see students asked to perform the same type of writing tasks from year to year. Equally problematic is the fact that writing assignments in high school rarely call for the kind of writing students are expected to produce in college. Personal-experience essays and plot summaries of literary works do not lead to mastery of the skills students need to succeed as college students.

High school teachers therefore can benefit greatly from having a clear understanding of what college composition programs expect students to be able to do after taking composition during their first year. They can tailor their own writing instruction and learning outcomes to be more congruent with the demands their students will face after graduation. Although state curriculum standards and guides provide the framework for what teachers do in language arts classes, they commonly ignore writing requirements at university.

Most college writing programs differ in numerous ways, but they have many goals in common. These goals were described by the Council of Writing Program Administrators (WPA), a national organization for those in charge of college programs, and published as an outcomes statement in 1999. At the time of this writing, the president of the WPA, Kathleen Yancey, was such an important person that she was far too busy to write a one-page permission letter allowing us to reproduce the outcomes statement here (usually deemed a simple matter of professional courtesy), so instead of reproducing the statement, I have summarized its key features:

Outcomes Statement

Rhetorical Knowledge

The first-year composition course should help students demonstrate a range of rhetorical skills. They should be able to:

- Have a purpose when writing.
- Recognize that different audiences have different needs.
- Use writing conventions that are appropriate to a given situation and/or audience.
- Use a level of formality that is appropriate to the task.
- Recognize and use different genres.

Critical Thinking

Critical thinking is crucial for effective writing. The first-year composition course should help students:

- Use critical thinking to understand texts and to produce writing that addresses complex topics.
- Understand that writing assignments require a variety of tasks, including but not limited to collecting information using primary and secondary sources, analyzing those sources and determining whether they are appropriate to the assignment, and using the sources to support the claims of the paper.
- Use sources to support their own ideas and claims.

Writing as Process

The first-year composition course should help students:

- Understand that revision is a central factor in effective writing.
- Develop strategies for writing, revising, and editing texts that are based on audience and purpose.
- Recognize that writing is a social action that usually involves collaboration.

- Develop the ability to analyze their writing critically and to implement effective strategies for revision.
- Work collaboratively with others on writing tasks.

Writing Conventions

The first-year composition course should help students:

- Master the formats for writing in science, social science, and humanities.
- Master the most widely used documentation styles (APA, MLA, and
  scientific method).
- Have ample practice in using documentation in their writing.
- Master academic conventions related to surface features, including
  usage, punctuation, paragraphing, and organization.

SEQUENCING ASSIGNMENTS

The goal of sequencing is to guarantee successful learning. In the mid-1950s, educational psychologist Benjamin Bloom (1956) developed a taxonomy of behavioral objectives to serve as a guide for sequencing, and it has been a cornerstone of composition studies ever since. Bloom proposed that effective teaching moves from the cognitively concrete to the cognitively abstract and that learning activities should be sequenced accordingly. In many respects, this idea is congruent not only with common sense but also with how teachers always have operated—children learn addition and subtraction of whole numbers before they go on to work with fractions.

Writing, however, has never really fit the taxonomy. One reason is that the taxonomy encourages a bottom-up methodology that is not congruent with how people learn to write. Focusing on punctuation, sentence types, and how phonemes make words and how words make sentences does not teach writing. It merely teaches punctuation, that phonemes make words, that words make sentences, and so on.

Another reason is that Bloom's taxonomy has led to some flawed assumptions about students and writing. For example, the idea of moving from the concrete to the abstract has led to the assumption that students perform best when they write about what they already know really well. And what do students presumably know better than anything else? If we ignore the last 2,500 years of philosophy and forget the dictum "Know thyself," which Socrates held to be one of life's greater challenges, the answer is obvious—themselves. Consequently, the easiest, most concrete form of writing is assumed to be self-expressive, consisting of autobiographical sketches that narrate real events in the writer's life. Out of these assumptions emerged a pedagogical sequence based on Bloom's taxonomy that begins with narrative–descriptive writing, usually of the autobiographical sort, that shifts to exposition, and that ends with argumentation. Few classes, apparently, ever reach argumentation. Most never get beyond narration, description, and exposition. Influenced by bottom-up pedagogy, the sequence never deals with exposition as a whole unit of discourse. Instead, it is broken up into expository modes: definition, comparison–contrast, process analysis.

A moment's reflection reveals some serious problems. Without discounting the value of subject-matter knowledge in composing, we must recognize that the idea that students perform best when they write about what they already know is extremely restrictive. It immediately limits the role writing can play as a vehicle for learning. Yet this role can be one of the more important factors in writing instruction.[1] Some of the best writing students produce is linked to mastering new information and exploring new ideas. Furthermore, focusing on expository modes rather than whole essays interferes with students' growth as writers and stunts their perception of writing as a meaningful act. Also, the assumption that students perform best when they write about themselves confuses the content of a writing task with the rhetorical skills required to communicate that content effectively. The proposition that narrative–descriptive autobiographical writing is "easy" flies in the face of everything we know about narration in general and autobiography in particular. Rhetorically, this is an extremely difficult—arguably the *most* difficult—form of writing. The genre of autobiography is very similar to fiction in that both involve the interaction of characters to convey a message. Unlike argumentation, which has an easily identifiable thesis supported through examples, analysis, and references, narrative–descriptive writing (even autobiography) conveys messages much more subtly through dialogue, descriptions of characters, setting, tone, atmosphere, and so on. In the hands of talented and experienced writers, these various elements come to-

---

[1]There is another role for autobiographical writing, of course, an important one—learning about oneself. I would argue, however, that a journal or a diary is the appropriate place for such writing. My argument is predicated on the view that the primary goal of formal schooling is to help students acquire content knowledge and to master a variety of skills. In the process, they learn quite a bit about themselves. Yet many educators hold the view that the primary goal of formal schooling is to help students learn more about themselves; content knowledge and skill mastery are secondary.

gether to edify and entertain. In the hands of inexperienced writers, the elements rarely come together, and the task is more frustrating than edifying, as anyone who has tried to write believable dialogue knows. Especially problematic is the fact that talented and experienced writers also have interesting stories to tell; typically, students do not because they have not lived long enough. It is not surprising, therefore, that we find students simply tacking a moral onto the end of their stories. They are astute enough to know their limitations as well as at least one convention of the genre.

On the *cognitive* level, which governs content and overall structure, we can say that narrative–descriptive writing *is* easier than argumentation. The reason is that organization in the former is based on chronology, whereas in the latter it is based on claims, support, and examples. All students, even very young ones, understand chronological sequencing fairly well, which helps them with organization. But on the *rhetorical* level, narrative–descriptive writing is much more difficult. The most widely used sequence for the forms of writing is therefore incongruent with what we know about rhetorical complexity and writing. It moves from the rhetorically abstract to the rhetorically concrete, thereby creating conflict between the rhetorical demands and the cognitive demands of writing and also rendering the sequence largely useless when it comes to effective pedagogy.

Moreover, it is worth considering Giroux's (1987) suggestion that the goal of improving student literacy is to enable young people to "locate themselves in their own histories and in doing so make themselves present as agents in the struggle to expand the possibilities of human life and freedom" (pp. 10–11). Freire and Macedo (1987), in a similar vein, suggested that realizing this goal requires students to immerse themselves in "interrogation and analysis." In other words, literacy must focus on critical thinking, formulation of hypotheses, reasoning, and reflection, which are more explicitly realized in exposition than in narration.

Currently, there is no evidence that the traditional sequence accomplishes this goal. In fact, the repetitive nature of the modes approach and the unavoidably arhetorical practice of presenting modes in isolation actually have a negative effect on student perceptions of writing. The endless round of personal narratives, definitions, and comparison–contrasts fails to offer intellectual challenges to students who understand that there are few demands for autobiography outside the walls of the English class. In school and out, students are called on to analyze and to reach conclusions on the basis of their analytical ability. They are called on to defend their positions. A viable sequence of writing assignments will help students practice these tasks; it will prepare them for the kinds of writing they actually are asked to do in other courses and in life, where analysis and argumentation are the most frequent writing activities outside of composition classes.

Some scholars have argued that the frequency of analysis and argumentation in subjects other than English offers a rationale for the existing focus on narration and description in writing classes. Britton, Burgess, Martin, McLeod, and Rosen (1975), for example, suggested that language learning takes place in the intimate environment of the family and that "expressive" discourse, which includes personal narratives and autobiography, should be encouraged as a means of continuing language development. The problem with this argument is fairly obvious: By the time students are old enough to write, usually around third grade, they have moved outside the narrow sphere of home language and are interacting with a variety of people and situations that call for more extensive language skills. These skills are linked to interpreting, analyzing, and arguing. If students don't practice these skills in school, where will they?

Given these issues, a key question for producing good writing assignments is this: How do we produce a sequence that is sound in terms of both cognitive and rhetorical difficulty and that helps students develop a range of rhetorical skills?

Answering this question requires a willingness to step away from the familiar and the ability to reconsider established practices. A pedagogically sound sequence for teaching the forms of writing would indeed begin with what students already know well, but in terms of rhetorical skill, not content. This immediately rules out autobiography on the grounds that few people, particularly children, truly know themselves well. Yet even first graders have internalized models of narration, a series of events temporally connected events, and they are capable of closely observing events. A viable assignment sequence therefore would begin with a simple **report of observed events** that does not attempt to present an argument or a message.[2] The next step in the sequence would move students to a slightly higher level of abstraction, asking them to read and comprehend texts and report what they have read to others. These **reports of information** would consist of summary and would not present an argument or a message. Such assignments have the added benefit of improving students' reading and comprehension skills.

---

[2]See Williams (2001) for a full elaboration of this sequence in a rhetoric text.

Interpretation is a fundamental act of human cognition. We experience the world, and we try to understand what it all means. There are different levels of interpretation, and the most concrete involves **interpretation of observed events.** Asking students to observe an event and then explain what it means is significantly more challenging rhetorically and cognitively than simply reporting an event. Interpretation, of course, is a form of argument, but interpretations of events do not require the formal apparatus of a written argument; rather, students can draw on their own experiences and knowledge to support their explanations. And herein is the bridge between the interstice that separates personal experience and academic content. Learning is made meaningful by the knowledge and experiences students bring to their studies. This axiom applies particularly to the next step in the sequence, **interpretation of information.** The information that gets interpreted is mostly in books or some other medium, but it also is in lectures and presentations. Being able to interpret the information in texts is a fundamental requirement for most academic work, especially in college.

When the sequence shifts to interpretation of information, students are engaged in argumentation, which takes many forms. Most of the argumentative papers students produce for school advocate a particular interpretation or perspective. A few make a call to action. Somewhat more challenging are **evaluation of events** and **evaluation of information.** These forms are more difficult rhetorically and cognitively because they require not only an explanation of what something means but also an assessment of its value. Finally, at the end of the sequence and the most demanding of all types of writing, we have **fiction and autobiography,** which require a good story as well as the ability to employ all the various features of setting, plot, characters, dialogue, and theme to convey a message.

For ease of reference, the sequence is illustrated in Table 9.1.

It is important to recognize that this sequence is best developed over a period of years, not weeks. Developmentally, children in second or third grade will have a hard time with evaluation. Nevertheless, this sequence provides a framework for instruction at each grade level, allowing teachers to develop outcome objectives that are realistic and realizable.

Keeping a sequence organized and coherent can be difficult if one develops each assignment separately as the term progresses, so it is very helpful to put together all assignments for a course before classes start. Outlining the work in advance can help a great deal, especially when the outline includes activities for each term, with due dates for all papers. Students appreciate receiving a copy of the outline on the

TABLE 9.1
Assignment Sequencing Based on Rhetorical Difficulty

Task	Description	Common Examples
Report of Events	Provides a simple report of an observed event, without interpretation or message.	lab report, news article, letter of complaint, letter of compliment
Report of Information	Provides a report or summary of information, without interpretation or message.	elementary book or film report, précis, summary, examination
Interpretation of Events	Explains what an event means and thus is a form of argumentation.	lab report, news article
Interpretation of Information	Explains what information means and thus is a form of argumentation.	research paper, book report, examination, critical essay
Evaluation of Events	Explains what an event means and then evaluates its significance and its role in the larger scheme of things.	lab report, research paper, examination, news article, letter of complaint, letter of compliment
Evaluation of Information	Explains what information means and then evaluates its significance and/or quality.	research paper, book or film review, critical essay, examination
Fiction	Provides a fiction-based representation of reality that builds on a theme or themes and that conveys a message or messages through the interaction of characters, plot, setting, point of view, dialogue, etc.	novels, short stories
Autobiography	Provides a fact-based representation of reality that builds on a theme or themes and that conveys a message or messages through the interaction of events, characters, setting, dialogue, etc.	

first day of class; they then have a better understanding of what is expected of them and can begin planning their writing early. Giving a writing assignment orally or on the board is never a good idea. At least half of the class will not hear an oral assignment, and the majority of the other half will misunderstand it or forget it an hour later.

Good writing assignments also are relatively brief, although they generally provide enough information to put the task in a context and to help students discover a purpose for the writing. Some teachers mistakenly assume that the more detailed they make the assignment, the better students will respond, but this just is *not* the case. Overly detailed assignments lead to "cognitive overload" that inhibits writing performance. An assignment that consists of a single directive, however, is too brief because it fails to offer a context.

FEATURES EVERY ASSIGNMENT SHOULD HAVE

To write a good assignment, teachers must consider the rhetorical nature of the tasks they are setting. As Erika Lindemann (1993b) noted, teachers must decide what they want students to do in an assignment, how they want them to do it, who the students are writing for, and what constitutes a successful response to the assignment. Perhaps the most important of these factors is the need to let students know clearly what they are expected to do. When assignments ask students to "discuss," "examine," or "explore," they may express a teacher's understanding of what is expected, but this understanding is based on years of education and experience. Students seldom know what they are supposed to do when asked to "discuss." Consequently, good assignments state the task in rhetorical terms; they ask students to report or describe or narrate or analyze or interpret or evaluate. In addition, they rarely include more than one rhetorical task.

Many teachers expect to use class lectures to instruct students in what terms such as *discuss* actually mean in the context of writing. Although well intentioned, this approach falls short. In every class, some students will not listen to the lecture; others will take inaccurate notes or no notes at all and will then rely on their memory when they start writing the assignment hours or even days later. On the other hand, class discussions of assignments are more effective than lectures because students have an active rather than a passive role. They are excellent opportunities to start students talking about their writing, articulating not only their understanding of the assignment but their initial conceptualization of how they plan to proceed. (Such discussions are best begun in work groups, where the give-and-take of ideas can be more rapid owing to the relatively small size of the group.) But discussions should not be used to convey information crucial to the satisfactory completion of the task.

To summarize, good assignments generally will:

- Be part of a sequence designed to develop specific discourse skills.
- Tell students exactly what they are expected to do. The mode of the response should be clear.

- Tell students exactly how they are expected to write the assignment. If students are expected to use a formal tone, this expectation should be stated; if students are expected to use outside sources to support a claim, this expectation should be stated. The assignment should include practical specifics such as whether the paper should be typed, due date, length, and documentation format (see Tarvers, 1988).

- Tell students something about the purpose and the audience for the paper. What is the paper supposed to do? Who other than the teacher should the writer be addressing?

- Tell students what constitutes success, including some statement regarding the criteria the teacher will use to assess the quality of the response.

JOURNAL ENTRY

Evaluate some of the assignments you've had for classes in the past. Are they part of a sequence? Do the assignments reflect a clear pedagogical purpose that can be described in terms of cognitive or rhetorical growth? If the assignments have some other pedagogical purpose, what is it? Finally, what can you learn from assignments you've worked on that will help you produce better assignments for your students?

SAMPLE ASSIGNMENTS

The sample assignments that follow can make these features more concrete. They were collected from teachers at various grade levels. They are presented out of the sequences they belong to simply to make the analysis a bit easier at this point. Some sequenced samples are presented later in the chapter.

Sample Assignment 1. For a group of third-grade students studying poems; the teacher was linking reading with writing:

> We have been studying poems for two weeks. Last week we wrote our own version of "Over in the Meadow." We took Olive Wadsworth's poem and put in our own words to tell a story. Now I want you to write another poem. I want this poem to be all your own. Tell your own story in rhyme. The story can be about your dog or cat. It can be about your favorite toy, or even your best friend. Just make it your own special poem. When all the poems are finished, we will put them together in a book. Then we will make copies so everyone will be able to read your poem. We will even make enough copies so you can give one to a friend.

Sample Assignment 2.   For a group of ninth-grade students study-ing poetry; the teacher was linking reading with writing, focusing on an-alytical skills:

> On your last assignment, you analyzed three of Charles Webb's prose po-ems to get ready for his visit to class. For this next assignment, I want you to begin with your earlier analysis and then to add to it an evaluation that explains which poem you like best and why. Successful analyses will support the explanation with good reasons and illustrations from the text. We will then mail our essays to Mr. Webb, who has promised to re-spond to several of them.

Sample Assignment 3.   For a group of 12th-grade students study-ing analysis; the teacher was focusing on relating writing tasks to situa-tions students might encounter outside school:

> Last week we studied the brochures we received from the travel agency to decide where we would like to spend our ideal vacation. Suppose that the agency were to sponsor a contest that would send the winner wher-ever he or she wanted to go, all expenses paid. All you have to do to win is write an essay *explaining why* you want to vacation in the spot you se-lected; and write the best essay. That is your task for this assignment. Each peer group will choose its best essay to enter into the finals, and then the whole class will choose from the final four which one is the win-ner. Our judging criteria should include knowledge about the vacation spot and the reasons the writer wants to vacation there.

In each of these samples, the teacher provided a background for the task, told students what they are supposed to do, how they are sup-posed to do it, and what she would be looking for as she evaluated re-sponses. In Sample 2, for example, students can see that the reasons they supply to support their analyses will be a significant factor in the teacher's evaluation. The assignments are not overspecified; the teachers did not overwhelm students by providing too much detail in regard to audience, purpose, assessment criteria, and so forth.

The next set of sample assignments offer a point of comparison for the first set. They also were collected from various public school teach-ers, and they were not part of any identifiable sequence.

Sample Assignment 4.   For a group of 10th-grade students study-ing exposition; students had previously discussed film plots and had spent some time analyzing the movie *Harry Potter and the Sorcerer's Stone:*

Pretend you are Harry Potter. How would you describe your school to the folks back home, who know almost nothing about magic?

Sample Assignment 5. For a group of seventh-grade students studying exposition; students had recently read an essay about how to build a kite:

Describe the process of making a peanut butter and jelly sandwich to someone who doesn't know how to make one.

Sample Assignment 6. For a group of 10th-grade students studying exposition; students had just finished a unit on poetry:

Everyone has done something they felt ashamed about later. Describe an event in which you did something that made you feel ashamed.

Sample Assignment 7. For a group of 10th-grade students studying exposition; students had previously read a short story in which the main character enjoyed reading:

For this assignment you will write a comparison and contrast paper. Be certain to describe each of your topics in detail. Select one from the following choices: (a) compare and contrast two types of music such that readers will understand why you prefer one to the other; (b) compare and contrast the sort of books you enjoy reading today with the sort of books you enjoyed reading five years ago, and describe how your taste has changed; (c) compare and contrast a place, such as a neighborhood, you knew as a child with how it is today.

Sample Assignments 4–7 are problematic for several reasons. One immediate difficulty is that the teachers who wrote them seemed to mistake what students find interesting with what is personal. In Sample 6, narration and description are confused; the narrative is stated in terms of describing an event. More troubling still is the way it asks students to reveal their personal shame. Teachers simply should not use their implicit authority to get students to divulge intimate details of their personal lives.

In addition, there is a serious question as to the significance of some of the assignments. Under what circumstances would anyone ever be expected to explain rather than show how to make a peanut butter and jelly sandwich? The Harry Potter assignment is cute, if one likes Harry Potter, and there is something to be said for role playing. But why that role when there many others that ultimately are more immediate, more challenging, and more educational?

Sample 7 is especially interesting because it gives students choices regarding the exact nature of their responses. Initially, this technique may seem very appealing, but closer consideration shows that the teacher isn't doing students a favor here. As is often the case when students have several choices for their responses, the question of validity arises because students will be performing quite different tasks on this assignment, depending on the topic they select. Although there are several different kinds of "validity," in this case the term refers to the idea that assessment criteria must match what is being measured. In most instances, and clearly in Sample 7, what is being measured is not simply a broad construct like "writing ability" but is much more specific. For example, topics (a) and (b) call for analyses that substantiate conclusions—a weak form of argumentation—whereas topic (c) calls for simple analysis. Any subsequent assessment of responses will be invalid if even one student makes a selection different from the rest of the class, because the assessment criteria must be different. And if this problem is not serious enough, there is also the fact that students may be confused when they perceive that they are told they can perform significantly different tasks and still meet the requirements of the assignment.

The three assignments that follow, taken from a series of six, reflect how one teacher actually organized a sequence. They were written for a class of 10th graders:

Sample Assignment 8.

Last summer the school board met to discuss potential health hazards to students resulting from the growing number of reported AIDS cases. The question before the board was whether or not school nurses in the district should be allowed to distribute condoms to sexually active students who ask for them. Before making a decision this fall, the board wants to hear from the community to weigh the arguments for and against this proposed policy. As a student at this school, you will be directly affected by the board's decision. Based on what you know about the needs of students on this campus, write a persuasive essay that will influence the board members to support your position on the proposed policy. Successful papers will be free of surface errors, will have a clear call to action, will provide detailed reasons for your position, and will recognize an alternative point of view. (After we evaluate the final drafts, we will mail the essays to the board.)

Sample Assignment 9.

In the last assignment, you drew on your own knowledge to support your claim. This assignment asks you to draw on the knowledge of others.

Last year three students at this school were suspended for drunkenness on campus. Our principal is very concerned that many students may be doing poorly in their classes because they are often under the influence. In the superintendent's office there has been talk of random locker searches to cut down on the amount of drinking on campus. Many parents believe the superintendent is overreacting and are reluctant to support searches. Our principal must consider both sides of the issue before making a decision. Your task on this assignment is to advise the principal. Your advice, however, may not be very influential if you speak solely for yourself. You will therefore want to interview at least ten other students (and perhaps some teachers) to find out their views on the matter. Use their reasons for or against the searches to make your advice more informed and more significant. Successful papers will present findings clearly and objectively; they will include some background information for the reader. (After we evaluate final drafts, we will forward them to the principal for consideration.)

Sample Assignment 10.

Your last assignment asked you to use other people's views, rather than just your own, to support your position. This assignment will take you one step further in that direction by asking you to go to the library to find books, magazines, or newspaper articles that have information you can use to support your position on the following claim: *American public education is failing to prepare students for the demands of the workplace and of higher education.* You must take a position either in support of or against this claim. Keep in mind that written arguments, unlike oral ones, are not so much concerned with "winning" as they are with getting readers to accept your view. Successful papers will be clearly documented using either the MLA or the APA documentation format; they will use library sources to support your view such that the tone is objective.

The first two assignments are specific to this teacher's school; they are not generic. Such specificity will be characteristic of assignments designed to evoke functional responses. They engage students in the world around them as much as possible to allow writers to consider immediate experiences. Also, such assignments take advantage of the fact that much argumentation reflects a need to make a decision about some course of action. The third assignment is far less functional, being essentially the sort of task students are often asked to do in a research paper. It is important to understand, however, how this assignment follows naturally from the other two. The distance between writer and content increases progressively from the first assignment to the last. In addition, the third assignment makes it clear that students are using research to support a personal belief, just as they were in the first assignment. This idea is usually absent in most research tasks, even though a majority of the research that people do when writing is conducted with the aim of supporting a personal view or representation of reality.

COLLABORATIVE ASSIGNMENTS

An important advantage to setting up work groups is that they increase the opportunities for meaningful collaboration among students. Collaboration is a natural part of the writing process. Thus, collaborative assignments move students closer to realistic contexts for composing and are likely to motivate students to do well.

A goal of such assignments is to get students to work together on a group project, and often groups will be in competition because they may be working with the same material. Consider, for example, the following two assignments. The first was written for a class of 5th graders, the second for a class of 12th graders.

Sample Assignment 11.

Surveys of young people show that just about everyone would like to be on television reading the evening news. Few will ever get the chance, but it is fun to dream of gathering the news and reporting it. For this paper, you will have the chance to be a reporter. Each group will find a topic or event related to our school or our neighborhood and report on it. Each group member will work on one part of the report, and then the whole group will put the parts together to make a complete paper. After the reports are finished, groups will read them to the class so we can have our own evening news! Remember to supply details for every story and to avoid making your report sound like a conversation.

Sample Assignment 12.

In the minds of most people, an expert is someone who knows all the answers in a given field. This is a common and somewhat misconceived view. But there is another way of looking at things. In this alternative view, a knowledgeable person, an expert, isn't one who knows what the answers are but rather one who knows what the questions are in a given field. On this assignment, each group will be responsible for explaining what the significant questions are in a given field, whether it be criminal law, local government, American history, film, computer technology, or whatever. Divide the work among group members such that everyone has a task and everyone writes part of the report. Give your papers a professional tone. Keep them free of spelling and punctuation mistakes. Be sure to explain the questions in detail, and discuss why they are relevant to all of us.

These examples illustrate how collaborative assignments can be structured, although it is important to note that Sample 12 is not as strong as it could be because it fails to inform students what function the task will serve. Generally, the only conceptual problem with collaborative assignments is finding tasks that lend themselves to group work. Monitoring collaborations is a bit more difficult, because teachers have to guard against any effort in each work group to make one or two members responsible for the whole project. Although it is often a good idea to have one member act as a "chief editor" to delegate the work and to oversee combining the several parts into a coherent essay, each member must be productive. Perhaps the most effective way to monitor collaborative assignments is to pay careful attention to workshop activities. When students are idle or are not writing, teachers should ask them to show the draft they are working on. If they have little or no work to show, they may be shirking their responsibility.

Experience shows that students not only enjoy group projects enormously but also learn a great deal about the writing process from them. They gain a new appreciation of audience, for example, when their ideas, style, and tone have to be compatible with those of the rest of the group.

JOURNAL ENTRY

If you could give your students your ideal writing assignment, what would be its major characteristics?

RELATING WRITING TO THE REAL WORLD

If students were performing a "real" writing task, one arising in the natural context outside school, their writing would be directed by the social conventions of the stimulus. Writing a love letter or making a diary entry, they would automatically take into account such factors as audience, purpose, intention, and tone. Most school-sponsored writing assignments, however, provide little in the way of context, so student responses often seem pointless, vague, and rambling. Developing a context for each writing assignment therefore is important. This does not involve simply describing a supposed audience or asking students to role-play. Rather it involves setting tasks that allow students to do something with their writing other than simply turning it in for a grade.

A personal computer and the appropriate software now make it possible to produce, quickly and easily, high-quality copy in either a newspaper or magazine format. Teachers with access to such equipment can organize a publishing program for their writing classes, where student writing is printed for everyone to read. Such programs seem to be particularly successful with elementary students, who are eager to enhance their writing with artwork (some of which can be done on the computer).

Students in junior and senior high can benefit greatly from contact with local businesses, either through field trips or classroom visits by business people, which introduces them to the demands of writing in the workplace. This introduction can be followed by a unit on business writing, where students establish their own company, with the work groups taking on the roles of its various divisions. Assignments can simulate the wide range of written discourse we find in business. In addition, assignments dealing with reports and proposals lend themselves nicely to oral presentations, so teachers can draw on the advantages inherent in a whole-language approach to activities.

Students of all ages can benefit from visits by working writers in the community. Some communities are fortunate to have published poets, essayists, or even novelists as residents, and many times these writers are pleased by invitations to visit schools. Most communities are served by newspapers and radio stations, and it is possible to have journalists, copywriters, or disc jockeys come to talk about their work. Radio disc jockeys are especially popular, because their music and on-air chatter make them local celebrities. Yet few students are aware of the fact that DJs are often reading a script when broadcasting. This discovery can have a lasting effect on their perception of writing. Local colleges and universities are virtually untapped resources. Professors publish regularly, yet public schools never invite them to campuses to talk to students about their writing. Doing so would offer an additional benefit to students, allowing them to ask questions about academic expectations of college teachers.

10

Assessing and Evaluating Writing

WHAT IS ASSESSMENT?

Although assessment and evaluation often are used synonymously, they are not exactly the same. *Assessment* designates four related processes: deciding what to measure, selecting or constructing appropriate measurement instruments, administering the instruments, and collecting information. *Evaluation,* on the other hand, designates the judgments we make about students and their progress toward achieving learning outcomes on the basis of assessment information.

Writing teachers have a much harder job than many of their colleagues when it comes to assessment and evaluation. Not only does it take them more time than, say, their counterparts in math, but it also is more difficult. With a math problem, or even a social studies question, collecting information related to student mastery of the material is fairly straightforward, as is evaluation. Answers on any test are right or wrong. Writing assessment, however, requires teachers to consider a complex array of variables, some of which are unrelated to specific mastery of a given writing lesson.

At its most basic level, evaluation is a comparison. The comparison in many subjects is an objective standard of correctness. For example, students' answers to math problems on a test are compared to the objective standard that governs correct addition, multiplication, subtraction, and division. Any deviation from the standard constitutes error. With writing, the situation is significantly different because evaluation involves comparison on two levels: the standard set by other students in the class and by some preestablished standard of good writing. This preestablished standard may be provided by the school district, in which case it often is linked to districtwide or even statewide testing. It may be provided by teachers—usually those in language arts—at a given school, in which case the standard will arise out of discussions and finally a consensus regarding the features of good writing. Or the standard may be one that individual teachers bring to their classrooms, formed initially on the basis of experiences at university during a degree and then a credential program. The individual standard is not only the most common but also the most problematic because it naturally varies from teacher to teacher, creating uneven evaluation of students engaged in similar activities. Uneven evaluation is unfair and is contrary to the one of the more important factors in assessment—reliability.

The existence of a preestablished standard raises important questions that educators have to wrestle with daily: What is the basis of the standard? Is the standard appropriate for a given group of students? Is the standard fair? What does a grade on a student's paper mean? These are hard questions for many reasons. As Pellegrino, Chudowsky, and Glaser (2001) noted:

> Every educational assessment . . . is based on a set of scientific principles and philosophical assumptions. . . . First, every assessment is grounded in the conception or theory about how people learn, what they know, and how knowledge and understanding progress over time. Second, each assessment embodies certain assumptions about which kinds of observations, or tasks, are most likely to elicit demonstrations of important knowledge and skills from students. Third, every assessment is premised on certain assumptions about how best to interpret the evidence from the observations to draw meaningful inferences about what students know and can do. . . . These foundations influence all aspects of an assessment's design and use, including content, format, scoring, reporting, and the use of the results. (p. 20)

Determining the basis of a standard requires exploring notions of excellence as well as the assumptions underlying comparisons among students. Determining whether a standard is appropriate involves analysis of student abilities in a given school and consideration of how those abilities rank compared to students at similar grade levels but from different circumstances. Questions of fairness are likely to require jettisoning appealing ideas of equality in favor of equitable treatment and opportunity. Contrary to popular opinion, a low grade on a paper does not necessarily mean that the assessment and evaluation were unfair. Fairness in evaluation is related to consistent application of the standard regardless of who any given student is—this is equity. It is not related to equal outcomes.

Scholars who study evaluation have found widespread confusion among teachers regarding writing assessment. More troubling is Ed White's (1986) suggestion that many teachers know almost nothing about writing assessment and that large numbers of them are arrogant about their ignorance. The tendency is to give little thought to what is being measured when putting grades on papers. Are teachers measuring the content of papers? Are they measuring "writing ability"? Or are they measuring students' performance on a given task at a particular time? Some might argue that they are measuring all of these factors and more, but this argument is fraught with difficulties.

Many people, both in and out of education, assume that when teachers assess writing they are measuring writing ability, but careful consideration indicates that this assumption may be wrong, or at least simplistic. The patterns of students' writing growth shed light on the problem. Any given class will have good, average, and poor writers. At the end of the term, all the students will show growth; all will have improved their language skills to some degree. Generally, however, the patterns remain the same: Those who were good writers at the beginning of the term may at the end be excellent writers, those who were average writers may be good writers, and those who were poor writers may be average writers. With respect to overall writing ability, it is uncommon for students to skip ability levels; it can happen, but only when a student invests totally in improving. Few students who start a term as poor writers end it as excellent writers, perhaps because growth in writing is such a slow, incremental process. Nevertheless, students of all ability levels may display performance that differs from assignment to assignment or from task to task. Students who have been writing C papers for weeks will get excited about an idea or a project, will work away at it for days, and will produce B work or better. Then the next assignment finds them really struggling to put together something meaningful. By the same token, students who generally are very good writers occasionally will stumble, producing a paper that is barely passing. In both cases, it is hard to say that the grades on these uncommon papers truly reflect overall writing ability, but they do appear to reflect a degree of success on a particular task.

It may be that adding up all of a student's grades at the end of the term offers some indication of overall writing ability, but because evaluation is a comparison, the question of the standard emerges again. Will the good writer who shows little improvement receive the same grade as the poor writer who shows much improvement but who nevertheless still writes worse than the good writer? Will these students receive different grades? University writing teachers experience the reality of a comparative standard every fall, when tens of thousands of freshmen enter college having received nothing but A's on all their high school essays. By the tens of thousands, these students discover that they cannot earn anything higher than a C in freshman composition. The skills that served them well in high school will not enable them to excel at university.

This analysis suggests that the terms *good, average,* and *poor writers* are constrained by context. They apply with a degree of accuracy only when the group that forms the basis of individual comparisons is fairly limited and well defined. But if this is the case, then even cumulative or averaged grades may not be true indications of writing ability, at least not in any absolute sense. On this account, the grades teachers put on papers are related to performance on a specific task at a given time, not to the broader concept of ability. Indeed, many composition scholars now view successful writing as being the application of quite specific rhetorical skills to equally specific rhetorical situations. In other words, one does not simply learn how to write but rather learns how to write very particular texts for particular audiences (Bizzell, 1987; Faigley, Cherry, Jolliffe, & A. Skinner, 1985).

It is possible to measure writing ability, but any straightforward effort to do so in a composition class is likely to have undesirable pedagogical consequences: Large numbers of students will receive low grades. In most situations, what a teacher is evaluating is reflected in the way he or she teaches, because what one intends to measure affects methodology (see Faigley et al., 1985; Greenberg, Wiener, & Donovan, 1986). For example, teachers who want to evaluate how successfully students use writing in a social context, how they respond to specific writing situations, and how they revise are likely to use a method that stresses making students feel good about themselves as writers, providing realistic writing situations, and offering ample opportunities for revision. They probably will search for relevant, interesting topics, and they probably will make much use of workshops and conferences, where instruction is as individualized as possible. Grades in this case will reflect a complex array of abilities, such as cooperation with others during group activities, not just writing ability.

Evaluation also can serve a pedagogical function, as when teachers assign average grades to papers that are barely passing in order to build poor writers' self-confidence and sense of accomplishment. Evaluation in this case is not a measure of writing ability at all but is, if anything, a pedagogical tool used to manipulate student behavior and attitudes. If a teacher were concerned strictly with measuring writing ability, there would be no need to consider the relevance of writing assignments, and certainly the use of grades to manipulate behavior would not be an issue. The sole interest would be in making certain that the assignments were valid tests of writing ability. *Each assignment would be structured so that the good writers would consistently receive high grades on their responses and the poor writers would consistently receive low grades.* The issue would be how accurately the task and the subsequent assessment measured students' abilities.

KEY FACTORS IN ASSESSMENT
AND EVALUATION

The temptation to simplify assessment is strong and understandable. Grading has become a high-stakes endeavor in an increasingly competitive society. The lives of teachers probably would be less complicated if assessment and evaluation were a simple response to students' work. But it isn't. If anything, the situation is more complicated than ever owing to shifting demographics that raise questions related to English as a second language and to state-mandated testing in public schools. In addition, a great deal of assessment and evaluation is not about individual student performance but rather is about the performance of all students in a given school, district, or state. "Accountability"—the effort through mandated testing to hold teachers and schools responsible for meeting established standards of performance—is a reality that influences what teachers do on a daily basis. Effective writing assessment and evaluation therefore require understanding what underlies assessment in general. The key factors are:

- Validity.
- Reliability.
- Predictability.
- Cost.
- Fairness.
- Politics.

Validity

The question of what teachers are measuring when they assess writing is at the heart of assessment validity, which may be thought of as the match between what is being taught and what is being measured. If a lesson includes thesis statements, supporting evidence, and conclusions, and if the writing assignment calls for these features, then the assessment should consider how well students demonstrated mastery. In other words, writing assessment—like all other forms of assessment—*should measure what was taught.* Valid assessment *will not* measure anything that was not taught. Quite simply, teachers need to be certain that they are *measuring what they are teaching* (E. White, 1986).

Although this injunction appears commonsensical, observations of classroom practices indicate that it rarely is honored where writing is concerned. In the typical language arts class, "writing instruction" focuses almost exclusively on surface features such as punctuation, subject–verb agreement, the three types of sentences (declarative, exclamatory, interrogative), and the parts of speech (nouns, verbs, adjectives, etc.). These features are taught through exercises that provide students with lists of error-filled sentences that they must correct and with fill-in-the-blank worksheets asking them to identify terms such as *thesis statement, topic sentence,* and *timed writing*—as though such knowledge somehow is related to effective writing. Students add a comma here, an inflection there, and most do fairly well after a little practice. This instruction usually is embedded in a literary context; that is, the lessons on surface features occur in conjunction with reading works of literature, from which most writing assignments emerge. Junior high school students, for example, read *Romeo and Juliet* over a 2- or 3-week period, and during this period they also work on their exercises dealing with sentence structure. At the end of the unit on *Romeo and Juliet,* students are asked to write a paper on the play, and each paper is assessed and evaluated on the basis of the student's expressed understanding of the play and on his or her ability to write error-free prose.

However, the grades teachers put on these papers do not reflect anything that students have learned about writing because the task is unrelated to anything that was taught. The instruction involved discussions related to *Romeo and Juliet* and teaching students how to find and correct errors in punctuation. Valid assessment of what they learned necessarily would require some measure of students' knowledge of the play and a list of error-filled sentences that students are to correct. Clearly, it is silly to suggest that the study of the play is somehow related to learning how to write a piece of literary analysis. Likewise, it is incorrect to suggest that students can transfer what they learned from the punctuation exercises to their own writing. This is faulty bottom-up assumptions about language learning at their worst and a failure to recognize that knowledge does not always lead to successful application.

The first step toward validity in writing assessment is to teach writing. The second step is to assess what is taught. The concept of assessing what is taught is so basic that it lies at the heart of the debate over the use of standardized tests of writing such as the Test of Standard Written English (TSWE). Such tests do not require writing, just the ability to recognize sentence errors.

On this account, we can understand that if revision is an important part of a teacher's instruction on every project, he or she needs some way to account for this skill when assessing and evaluating students' written work. Some teachers address this particular issue by assigning grades or scores to rough drafts, as well as to participation in work groups. This approach has at least two drawbacks, however. First, it reflects an attempt to grade process, even though composing processes appear to differ from person to person and from task to task. There really is no such thing as *the* composing process, and evaluation is valid only when teachers measure similar student behavior against a preestablished standard. Second, this approach defeats the purpose of formative evaluations by adding a summative component that too easily results in a shift in focus from, say, having a rough draft to having a *good* rough draft.[1] Such a shift is significant and counterproductive because it reinforces the erroneous perception students have that the only difference between a first draft and a final draft is neatness.

A more effective means of assessing and evaluating something like revision skill therefore would involve having students submit their rough drafts along with final drafts to allow for comparisons between the revisions and the finished product. By comparing the initial drafts and then matching them against the final draft, one can more clearly evaluate how successfully any given student is grasping the skill being taught. The grade on the final draft, the summative evaluation, would reflect the quality of the finished paper as well as revision skill, because the two are inseparable. In other words, one grade would indicate an overall evaluation. Another method that yields similar results involves conferring with each student frequently through the entire drafting phase. This approach has the advantage of allowing the teacher to provide advice when it is needed most. The difficulty is that most teachers in public schools have so many students in their classes that they lack the necessary time for conducting numerous conferences.

---

[1]Two terms that appear regularly in discussions of assessment are *formative* and *summative evaluation*. Formative evaluation occurs when a work is in progress. For example, when a teacher reads a draft of a paper and offers comments on strengths and weaknesses, she is engaged in formative evaluation. When reading a final draft and assigning a grade, she is involved in summative evaluation. These concepts are important not only because they provide a better understanding of assessment but also because they can shape pedagogy. Composition scholars widely advocate that the bulk of a teacher's comments about a paper should appear as formative rather than summative evaluation.

Assessment validity can be affected by the structure of assignments. One of the more frequent instances of this problem occurs when teachers give students a list of optional topics for a given paper. The difficulty is this: Typically, the list encourages different rhetorical tasks, and the teacher has no principled way to evaluate responses that are essentially different. If one student writes a narrative report and another an argument in response to the same assignment, which may ask for description, the criteria for what constitutes a successful response will vary from essay to essay, seriously compromising evaluation. Often students who attempt the more difficult task, the argument, will receive a lower grade on the assignment than they would have received had they performed the easier task and written a narrative report. Under these circumstances, teachers have almost no way of knowing what they are measuring.

Reliability

Reliability in assessment is related to the consistency of the comparison to the preestablished standard. In a paper that illustrated clearly the importance of reliability in composition studies, Diederich, French, and Carlton (1961) distributed 300 student papers to 53 professors from six different disciplines. The professors were asked to read and grade the papers. About 90% of the papers received seven different scores on a 9-point scale, indicating that the professors demonstrated no consistency at all with respect to assessment and evaluation. Reliable assessment and evaluation will be consistent across evaluators and across time. It is *generalizable*. When dealing with a subject like math, it is easy to conceptualize the reasonableness of what this means: If a student gets a score of 85 on a math test from one teacher, he or she should get the same score if the test were graded by yet another teacher. Unfortunately, reliability just doesn't occur spontaneously with respect to writing but must be built into the assessment process through adherence to standardized procedures that reduce (if not eliminate) capriciousness and subjectivity. Standardized multiple-choice tests like the SAT (Scholastic Aptitude Test) are reliable, in part, because they have been piloted and normed against representative populations and because test administrators follow a specific protocol for administration and scoring.

There are several reasons why it is important that writing assessment and evaluation be reliable. Students deserve to know that the procedure is consistent and objective, not capricious and subjective. Just as important, reliable evaluations throughout schools will avoid unacceptable (but recurrent) situations in which a student receives

D's on written tasks in one class and A's in another. Unless teachers in a school work together to make their assessments and evaluations reliable, some students will indeed get high grades on papers in one class and low grades in another, even though their writing remains pretty much the same from teacher to teacher. Part of the problem is that different teachers look for different things in a well-written assignment—hence the inconsistency in evaluation—but another part lies in the fact that teachers do not talk with one another sufficiently about grading to make their efforts more reliable. In such circumstances, students are forced to conclude, quite correctly, that writing evaluation is largely subjective, which has the effect of motivating them to write only to please the teacher while simultaneously making them frustrated. Writing for an audience of one is an arhetorical exercise that does little to improve writing skills.

The only way to make assessment and evaluation more reliable is to reach agreement on what constitutes good writing and what does not. In other words, teachers who are responsible for writing instruction must reach a consensus on the standard that will form the basis of their evaluations. This consensus is formed through discussions and workshops related to effective writing and grading in which teachers share and talk about papers that range from outstanding to unacceptable. With the proper guidance, even teachers from different disciplines can reach agreement fairly quickly on what constitutes good writing. Periodic follow-up meetings ensure that the standard remains stable and in place.

Predictability

Many assessments are intended to predict student performance. The SAT, for example, is intended to predict how well students will perform in college. Given the nature of the test, the large database, and the norming procedures that underlie the SAT, its level of accuracy is fairly good. The verbal portion of the test predicts that students will be good readers and writers in college, and this prediction is borne out when we compare SAT verbal scores with grades in first-year composition. AP scores are also used by many colleges as predictors. Students with high scores may be exempted from first-year composition entirely or exempted from the first term and placed in the second. But AP scores are not very good predictors of students' writing skills and should be used very cautiously.[2]

---

[2]When I was director of the writing program at the University of North Carolina, Chapel Hill, AP scores were used to place students in the University Writ-

All categories of placement tests also have a predictive component. Writing placement tests predict that students will or will not succeed in first-year composition. Public schools generally do not employ placement tests, but many colleges and universities do, especially when they have high enrollments of under-prepared students. A low score on such a test places a student in a developmental or basic-writing class, provided the school has the resources to fund these courses, which inevitably are quite expensive to staff because of smaller class size.

Writing placement tests commonly are developed in house by the director of the writing program and his or her staff. This process is not easy if the goal is to develop a valid test. Each writing prompt needs to be piloted, scored, and analyzed to ensure that it is valid and yields usable data. Because many schools lack the necessary resources to implement standard development and scoring procedures, they ignore them. In other cases, the writing program director may believe that the standard testing protocols are irrelevant to placement and will alter them without realizing that doing so is likely to affect validity or reliability or both. Standardized instruments, such as the Test of Standard Writing English (TSWE), allow schools to circumvent the difficulties associated with in-house tests, but they are multiple-choice exams and raise the specter of invalid assessment owing to the fact that students produce no writing. Most universities still require SAT scores for all applicants, and the verbal portion of this test is a fairly good predictor of writing success, but few administrators are willing to use these scores owing to the political issues surrounding the SAT as a result of allegations that the test is racially biased.[3]

Unlike standardized instruments such as the SAT verbal, in-house writing placement exams commonly lack a large database, and they rarely are normed. The writing program director at a school should construct an exam for each administration; the exam normally consists of a reading passage designed to give students a general introduction to the topic to be discussed and a writing prompt that requires students to write an argumentative essay that takes a clear stand on the issues associated with the topic. Two decades ago, it was fairly common

---

ing Program. I examined students' AP English scores and their grades in first-year composition over a 5-year period and found no significant correlation, indicating that the AP scores were not valid predictors of success in writing for students admitted to the university during that period.

[3]The issue of racial bias in testing is complex and somewhat beyond the scope of this text. I can say here, however, that these allegations are generally lacking supporting evidence. The fact that whites and Asians perform better on the SAT than their black and Hispanic counterparts is not dispositive. We also find that high SES test-takers outperform low SES test-takers, which suggests that the grouping variable may be SES, not ethnicity.

to find two separate prompts on in-house placement exams: one requiring argumentation, the other autobiography. Most schools dropped this structure by the mid-1980s, however, because it became evident that writing performance, as well as evaluation, varies significantly by topic and genre. Students would receive high scores on their autobiographies and low scores on their argumentative essays, thereby confounding the evaluation. Because writing placement exams have topics that vary from year to year and because even the most rigorous training cannot result in completely uniform assessments, norming in-house exams is extremely difficult. Consequently, we must be very cautious in how we use writing placement exams. They may not provide a very clear picture of the skills of individual students.

The same caution must be applied to so-called "diagnostic" essays that many teachers ask students to write at the beginning of a writing class, especially in college composition courses. These essays are believed to provide insight into students' writing skills and are used predictively to place students in work groups. Their level of accuracy, however, is remarkably low.

With regard to all writing exams used for placement, it is important to recognize that producing an essay is a complex task quite unlike solving a problem in algebra or remembering the date of the Norman invasion of England. Success depends on several factors—knowledge related to the topic, familiarity with the genre, ability to organize and structure ideas quickly, and so forth. In addition, an impromptu writing task may not be a valid method of assessment, given that writing classes focus on soliciting and receiving input and advice on multiple drafts of every assignment, not on impromptu compositions.

Cost of Assessment

Every assessment involves cost of one form or another. For individual teachers, the cost is normally measured in terms of time—the time required to put together a method or instrument of assessment and the time required to conduct the assessment. For program, school, district, and state assessments, the costs are primarily monetary, and they rise significantly as the number of students increases, which is why standardized tests have great appeal: They are cost effective. Large-scale assessments also involve another cost that should be considered—the psychological strain placed on students by high-stakes testing and the time taken away from the curriculum when teachers inevitably teach to the test.

The cost effectiveness of standardized tests must be weighed against validity. Currently, the only way to ensure some measure of validity for large-scale assessment is through holistic or portfolio programs, which are discussed later in this chapter. But both of these forms of assessment are labor intensive and costly. Many schools therefore opt to sacrifice validity to save money. It is important, therefore, to recognize that not all standardized tests are equal. Tests that focus on vocabulary, like the SAT verbal, seem to be more effective at predicting writing performance than tests that focus on sentence errors, like the TSWE. The reason is that vocabulary, reading, and writing are connected in several ways, such that students who have read extensively have superior vocabularies and also have internalized many of the features of effective writing. Thus, when cost requires use of a standardized test to assess writing, an instrument that assesses vocabulary may be the best investment.

Fairness of Assessment

All assessment should be fair. We demean ourselves and the profession when it is not. But what does it mean to have a fair assessment? Many people mistakenly assume that fairness is somehow related to equal outcomes. Intelligence tests and the SAT, for example, are popularly viewed as being unfair because outcomes are consistently unequal for different segments of the population.

There are several factors that make an assessment fair. It must be valid, measuring what actually was taught, and it also must produce comparably valid inferences about knowledge and skill mastery from person to person and group to group (Pellegrino et al., 2001). In addition, an assessment must be administered appropriately, so that no student has an advantage as a result of being given additional information about the assessment or of having more time[4]; and it must be evaluated properly and accurately, without the influence of subjective factors that may advantage some students while disadvantaging others.

The Politics of Assessment

Over the last decade, assessment increasingly has become a political issue. The most obvious examples of the political dimension are state-mandated testing and performance funding, which were implemented, ostensibly, as a response to parental pressure for greater accountability in public schools. If we accept Moffett's (1992) report that most par-

---

[4]In many schools, students with disabilities are given more time on class assignments and tests so as to accommodate their special needs. There is little evidence available at this point to suggest that such accommodations lead to unfair assessment (see, e.g., Abedi, Hofstetter, & Baker, 2001).

ents are happy with their children's schools and believe that the schools are doing a good job of educating their children, even when test scores show the contrary, the claim that state-mandated testing and performance funding are parent driven seems highly suspect. Indeed, both may be viewed more accurately as efforts to shift control of schools from local communities to state legislators and governors— and eventually to the federal government.

Centralizing control of public schools is often perceived as the most effective means of improving overall academic performance and reducing growing differences in performance between whites and Asians on the one hand and blacks and Hispanics on the other. Supporters of centralized control argue that it is necessary to establish uniform standards and to hold under-performing schools accountable.

This argument is based on three premises: a) teachers in these schools are slackers, b) these schools are under-funded, and c) higher expenditures per pupil result in higher academic performance. The first of these premises is powerful because it is congruent with popular perceptions of public education; the remaining two are popular because educators and politicians have, for the last 40 years, made excuses for the failure of our public schools, particularly those with high black and Hispanic populations, almost entirely in terms of money. On the surface, the funding argument seems quite simple: Schools that serve black and Hispanic students are located in poor communities with a minimal tax base (local property taxes provide most of the funding for public schools); consequently, these schools lack the money necessary to provide the books, supplies, and even desks and teachers necessary for education. And urban legends abound to demonstrate supposed funding inequities—reports circulate freely among teachers of how district X spends $14,000 per pupil, whereas district Y (usually their own) spends only $6,000 per pupil. Politicians therefore push state-mandated testing as an investigative tool to uncover the extent to which teachers at poor-performing schools are failing to do their jobs. Performance funding is labeled an incentive to get teachers to work (harder) and as a means of providing additional funding to needy schools.

As one might expect, the situation is far more complex than supporters of testing and centralized control admit. Some critics argue that centralized control is nothing but thinly disguised socialism, allowing for the redistribution of education funds from districts with a solid tax base to districts without. They also note that numerous studies have shown little if any correlation between high academic performance and funding. For example, in his analysis of the Ohio Proficiency Test, a state-mandated test used for accountability and performance-based funding initiatives, R. L. Harris (1997) found an in-

verse relation between the amount of federal funding and performance. That is, under-performing schools in Ohio received significantly
more federal dollars than schools with average or above average performance. Under-performing schools also received more state funding
than average and above-average schools. As R. L. Harris stated, "In
general, under Ohio's current funding formula, economically disadvantaged districts do receive greater state subsidies than do economically advantaged districts" (np). Even more revealing is the analysis of
performance and local funding: "Though there is a slight positive correlation between local revenue and actual district performance, it is
not statistically significant" (np).

Stiefel, Schwartz, Iatarola, and Fruchter (2000) provided a more
detailed analysis of funding and academic performance for schools in
New York City, and they also found that increased funding for schools
was not correlated with higher academic performance. Stiefel et al.
reported:

> Low performing schools receive significantly more funding than high
> performing schools overall. . . . Spending in low performing elementary
> schools averages $9,136 while spending in the high performing schools is
> $1,330 per pupil lower at $7,916. The divergence is more profound in
> middle schools—spending in low performing middle schools is $10,305
> while high performing middle schools receive only $7,622. . . . Note . . .
> that low performing schools also spend more on almost everything—edu-
> cation paraprofessionals, textbooks, librarians and library books, and
> professional development. (p. 22)

In addition, Stiefel et al. found a significant difference in pupil–teacher
ratios. Low performing elementary schools in their study had a ratio
of "approximately 14.2 compared to almost 17.5 for high performing
schools. The disparity is greater in middle schools (12.7 versus 17)"
(p. 21).

If funding is not a significant factor in student performance, what
is? One of the more thorough efforts at answering this question is *The
Black–White Test Score Gap,* by Jencks and Phillips (1998). They concluded that the most significant factors in academic performance are:
a) the ways in which parents prepare their children for schooling, b)
the quality of children's preschool experience, and c) the quality of
children's teachers. This last factor is particularly important because,
as Stiefel et al. (2000) reported, low performing schools typically have
more teachers without credentials than average and high performing
schools, and they also have more teacher absences. State-mandated
testing, of course, cannot have any effect whatsoever on either teacher
credentialing or absenteeism.

Nevertheless, politics have pushed most states to implement testing at all levels. Many different instruments exist, and it is impossible to describe all of them here, so I will mention just a few. The Ohio Proficiency Test, mentioned earlier, is given to students in grades 4, 6, 9, and 12. The test includes citizenship, math, science, reading, and writing. Students cannot graduate from high school without the ability to pass at least the ninth-grade test. An instrument used by many states at the elementary level is the Standardized Test for Assessment of Reading (STAR), a normed test of reading ability. Another widely used instrument is the Stanford Achievement Test, version 9 (SAT 9), which consists of a series of normed tests, administered in grades 1–11. The individual tests measure performance in reading, spelling, language, mathematics, reference skills, science, and social studies. Although sampling procedures were designed to provide fall and spring norms based on a representative national school-age population, a majority of states conduct testing in the spring so that they can publish results toward the end of the summer. The SAT 9 has been used for several years and has been shown to be both valid and reliable in all test areas.

In many states, schools that show improvement in test scores are rewarded financially, whereas schools that fail to show improvement are "sanctioned." Regardless of whether a school is rewarded or punished on the basis of test results, teachers understand that they are involved, willy-nilly, in a high-stakes activity, so it is common for them to teach to the test, with the encouragement of principals. In some instances, this practice takes the form of modifying the curriculum to ensure that instruction targets those skills and knowledge areas that will be on the mandated test. In other instances, schools adhere to the standard curriculum but set aside two or three weeks prior to the testing period for test preparation. Many of these mandated tests, such as the SAT 9, take two weeks to administer, which means that a minimum of four to five weeks of the spring term are dedicated to testing. This represents a significant investment of time, especially considering that American schools have the shortest academic year in the developed world.

Blaming teachers for the failures of America's schools is a simplistic response to an extremely complex problem. News reports frequently circulate horror stories of teachers who send home notes that are so poorly spelled as to be nearly unreadable, and there is no question that many teachers have egregious gaps in their subject-area knowledge. However, these stories are not representative of the vast majority of teachers, who are hard working, dedicated, and caring people. As Fukuyama (1999) and Jencks and Phillips (1998) indicated, the real issues are social, involving the largest wave of immigration in the nation's history, the breakdown of the family, a stratospheric rise in illegitimate births, and disdain for institutions and authority. Our schools and our teachers cannot even begin to address the medley of problems that emerge from these social issues.

Furthermore, there is little evidence that mandatory testing has any influence on how teachers teach. Ketter and Pool (2001) reported that the only measurable effect of such testing was a decrease in reflective practices associated with individualized instruction. Cimbricz (2002) found that state-mandated testing did not have a substantial effect on teachers' practices, with the obvious exception of motivating them to teach to the test. Nevertheless, the move toward requiring even more testing has picked up momentum. In 2002, President Bush signed into law the new Elementary and Secondary Education Act (also known as the Leave No Child Behind Act) that governs state assessment programs under Title I. Section 1111 of the Act requires all states to present an assessment plan with the aim of establishing uniform standards for academic achievement and for holding schools accountable for reaching those standards. From any perspective, the Act is historic because it takes a significant step toward changing the pattern of local control over schools that has been in place since the founding of the nation. Assessment is, indeed, a powerful political force.

Not all educators have recognized this force, however. Among postmodern rhetoricians, discussions of assessment and evaluation have moved in the opposite direction, rejecting even such basic notions as validity and reliability. As Hout (1996) noted: "Instead of generalizability, technical rigor, and large scale measures that minimize context and aim for standardization of writing quality, these new procedures emphasize the context of the texts being read, the position of the readers, and the local, practical standards teachers and other stakeholders establish for written communication" (p. 561). Broad (2000) likewise described how the postmodern position discounts standardization and reliability in assessment while limiting validity to a writing task that produces an "authentic voice." This view is related in some ways to the sociocultural perspective on assessment, which Pellegrino, Chudowsky, and Glaser (2001) described as learning "to participate in the practices, goals, and habits of mind of a particular community" (p. 63). Performance is deemed to be mediated by both context and community. On this account, assessment should take into consideration the experiences and histories students bring to the task. Whereas traditional assessment presents decontextualized, abstract situations—such as the writing prompt that asks students to take a position on a topic like gun control—sociocultural assessment locates the task in real contexts that call for real responses. It then measures how students use their skills to participate as a member of that community. Student teaching represents a concrete example of this sort of assessment.

In other respects, however, sociocultural assessment is quite different from the postmodern perspective. The former does not reject concepts such as validity, reliability, and generalizability, for example. Rejecting generalizability is important in the postmodern position (see Englehard, Gordon, & Gabrielson, 1992; Michael, 1995). One reason is that generalizability is based on a pre-established standard. The very nature of a standard entails absolute criteria for "good writing," and traditional notions of teaching and learning maintain that it is the responsibility of teachers and students to strive to meet those criteria. The postmodern position rejects absolute criteria and traditional notions of teaching and learning. Absolute criteria are considered to be antithetical to diversity, imposing not only a uniform level of achievement but also levels and types of performance that not all students can meet.

Rejecting generalizability has the immediate effect of eliminating concern for reliability. If evaluators believe that it doesn't matter whether their assessment of student writing is congruent with the assessment that evaluators at another school might make of those same pieces of writing, the imperative to provide reliable assessment disappears, leading to a celebration of inconsistency and the insupportable claim that it is impossible to assess writing objectively and that evaluation must recognize the inherent subjectivity of the process. Local criteria and an individual standard, rather than absolute criteria and a generalizable standard, govern the assessment.

Perhaps the biggest problem with the postmodern position is that it makes it even more difficult to determine what an assessment means. If an assessment is dependent on context and the associated local criteria for success and if it lacks standards associated with general writing quality, then it is remarkably difficult to compare one response to another. All responses to a given assignment must be deemed equally acceptable and equally successful because *any* standard (or *no* standard) is a viable measure of success. Attempts to differentiate good writing from poor writing are rendered meaningless because what matters is not the writing but the evaluator's personal judgment and the act or performance that put words on the page. The effect is to return to the situation that Diederich, French and Carlton (1961) described, in which there is no consistency in the assessment of a given paper.

Many teachers find this position unacceptable because they see it as inherently unfair to students. Any given assessment will vary on the basis of those who happen to be evaluating the writing at any given time, leaving students exposed to the random subjectivity of their evaluators. One group of evaluators will apply their local standards to one assessment whereas another group will apply different standards. Students with identical writing skills will experience completely different evaluative decisions.

JOURNAL ENTRY

Have you ever felt that a teacher graded your writing subjectively or capriciously? If so, what prompted those feelings? What lesson is there in your experience that you can apply to your teaching?

REDUCING THE PAPER LOAD

All writing teachers know how difficult it is to grade numerous student papers. It is a time-consuming, tedious task. The problem is especially acute at the junior and senior high school levels, where teachers often have as many as four writing classes each term, with 30 or more students per class. Four classes with an assignment a week creates a crushing paper load. If teachers spend 15 minutes evaluating and commenting on each paper, they will need at least 30 hours a week to assess them all. Faced with such a paper load, most instructors do not give an assignment each week. But reducing students' writing assignments is not really an acceptable way to reduce the paper load, because students have to write frequently if they are going to improve.

The crux of the problem is the way teachers assess student writing. Most teachers, even those who have adopted a process approach to instruction, use a very traditional grading method. They read each finished paper, writing comments in the margins as they go along, concluding with a summary comment at the end of the essay, then affixing a grade. This process is extremely time consuming, taking anywhere from 15 to 40 minutes a paper. In addition, research suggests that it is largely ineffectual, offering little that improves students' writing performance.

Teacher Comments on Papers

Given the labor-intensive nature of writing comments, teachers have only two choices when deciding on a method. They can assign little writing but try to provide copious written comments, or they can assign much writing but make few, if any, written comments. Most teachers opt for the first choice.

The rationale for this choice is that comments are an effective pedagogical tool. In theory, the teacher uses them to engage in a kind of discussion with writers, pointing to those things done well, those things done not so well, then offering suggestions and advice not only on how to fix the weak parts of the current paper but on how to improve the next one. Students are expected to study the comments, learn from them, and transfer this learning to other assignments.

Several studies have examined teacher comments on papers, examining not only the types of comments teachers provide but also their usefulness. Much of the research indicated that participating students did not use written comments to improve their performance from one paper to the next (Gee, 1972; Hausner, 1976; T. Schroeder, 1973; Sommers, 1982). One reason may be that the comments were not particularly clear or useful. Sommers, for example, found that "most teachers' comments are not text-specific and could be interchanged, rubber-stamped, from text to text" (p. 152) and therefore are not helpful to students. She concluded that "teachers do not respond to student writing with the kind of thoughtful commentary which will help students to engage with the issues they are writing about or which will help them think about their purposes and goals in writing a specific text" (p. 154).

Connors and Lunsford (1993) provided a slightly different view. They examined 3,000 student papers with the aim of analyzing the nature of the global comments on papers. These comments were defined as "general evaluative comments found at the end or the beginning of papers" (p. 206). They found that most global comments appeared at the end of papers and that 42% of these started out with positive evaluations but then shifted to negative ones. Only 9% of the comments were purely positive, and these were found only on A papers. The most frequent type of global comment addressed details and supporting evidence, whereas the most frequent type of surface comment addressed sentence structure.

More recently, Straub (1997) looked at teacher comments and found that students view as cryptic the abbreviations so many teachers use, such as AWK (for *awkward*), AMB (for *ambiguous*), and MM (for *misplaced modifier*). In addition, students in Sraub's study reported that comments were most helpful when they suggested ways to improve a paper and when they explained clearly what was good and bad about a paper. This meant that the most useful comments were in the margins of the paper where they targeted the text directly. Yet most of the time, when teachers make comments on final drafts, they put their detailed comments at the end of the paper and use them to justify their grades, especially when the grades are low (Lindemann, 1993b). Students quickly learn how this works, so they tend to look at the grade and ignore the comments (see Sommers, 1982).

Even so, some question remains as to how effective all comments are pedagogically. Telling students they have misplaced a modifier doesn't really help them understand its proper placement. Furthermore, the assumption that comments on one paper lead to better writing on a subsequent paper is highly questionable. Indeed, there is no evidence whatsoever to support it. Everything we know about how students learn indicates that improvement comes when comments are made on a draft that students will revise; otherwise they have no chance to incorporate comments into their texts, and they have no chance to practice the immediate skills they are supposed to learn. Consequently, some educators recommend marking rough drafts, but to do so increases a teacher's work load exponentially, especially in light of the fact that good papers commonly require three or more drafts.

Regardless of research and theory, the pressures to apply comments must be acknowledged. Written comments on student essays are so thoroughly institutionalized that parents, administrators, fellow teachers, and certainly students expect them as a matter of course. To forgo them completely takes a bit of daring, even though everyone concerned might be better for it. After all, oral comments provided as students are working on their drafts are more immediate, more personal, more detailed, and more effective. Yet the following suggestions may help make written comments during summative evaluation more useful:

- The teacher should read papers twice rather than once. The first reading should be completed very quickly, almost skimming, without a pen or pencil in hand. The goal is to get a sense of the strengths and weaknesses of the papers, to grade them mentally, without making any marks.

- After finishing the first paper, the teacher should compare it with his or her internalized standard for an excellent response and then set it aside.

- When starting on the rest of the essays, the teacher should compare them not only to his or her internalized standard of an excellent response but also to one another.

- Upon finishing each paper, the teacher should put it with other papers of similar strength, setting up three stacks, one for excellent, one for adequate, and one for unsatisfactory.

- The teacher then should read the unmarked papers a second time, more slowly, making comments in the margins. If the teacher has conducted successful workshops, he or she already will have seen each paper at least once and will have established a dialogue concerning content and form. Comments should be continuations of each dialogue and should be the sort of things the teacher would tell the writers if they were there in a conference.

- Typical comments will focus on changes students made or failed to make during revisions, what the teacher liked about the paper and why, and what effect the content had. *They also (and quite effectively) may take the form of questions.* In any event, it is extremely important that the teacher respond as a real, interested reader during such evaluations, not as a teacher. Remember, the grade is already fixed mentally, so there is no need to use the comments as a justification for the grade.

- Comments should be brief, and the teacher should avoid entirely the temptation to rewrite any sentences and to engage in any editing by correcting spelling, usage, or punctuation errors; these problems should have been corrected during writing workshops.

- The teacher should remember that once a final draft is turned in, instruction is over for that assignment. Any weaknesses are better addressed on the first draft of the next task.

- *Severe* mechanical problems in final drafts indicate the need to monitor groups more closely.

- If the teacher provides a final comment at the end of the paper, it should not be next to the grade.

- As a reasonable goal, the teacher should try to limit commenting to about 5 minutes per paper.

- Finally, use a pencil rather than a pen. Students tend to find penciled comments more friendly than those in ink, especially red ink.

JOURNAL ENTRY

Many teachers are reluctant to talk about how they evaluate student papers and how they arrive at grades. Reflect on how you might be able to stimulate more discussion when you're a teacher, discussion that may lead to more reliable assessments.

HOLISTIC SCORING

Until the 1960s, assessment of large numbers of students was performed using multiple-choice exams. Some teachers and researchers, however, were concerned that such exams were not very effective. Lack of reliability was deemed the biggest problem with classroom assessment, and lack of validity was deemed the biggest problem with large-group assessment. In the latter case, people argued that the only way to measure writing was to ask students to write and that multiple-choice tests were invalid.

Largely in response to this criticism, Educational Testing Service (ETS), the group that sponsors the National Teachers Examination and the AP tests, decided to explore the possibility of developing a valid and reliable way to evaluate writing. After several years of effort, ETS came up with the method known as holistic scoring (E. White, 1986). It quickly became popular as an effective means of testing large numbers of students, especially at the university level, because it is valid, highly reliable, and doesn't take much time. In the early 1980s, individual teachers started using holistic scoring in their own class-rooms as a means of reducing their paper load while simultaneously increasing the reliability of assessment. This procedure requires training students to evaluate one another's writing, and it also requires teachers to give students more responsibility for their own success or failure on tasks. What follows is a description of how to conduct holistic scoring. This description of procedures, or protocol, applies generally to any holistic scoring and, with minor modifications, can be used for an entire program as well as for an individual class.[5]

The rewards of holistic assessment are significant for everyone involved. An entire batch of essays can be scored in a 50-minute class session, freeing evenings and weekends that otherwise would be devoted to marking papers. Because they are assessing their own writing, students gain an increased sense of control over their learning, especially if, as recommended, holistic scoring is used in conjunction with writing workshops. Also, the teacher–student relationship changes. Because the teacher is no longer assigning grades to papers, he or she can be accepted more readily as a resource person, or coach, who can help improve skills.

As the name suggests, holistic scoring involves looking at the whole essay, not just parts of it. The procedure is based on the notion that evaluating writing skill does not consist of measuring a set of subskills, such as knowledge of punctuation conventions, but rather of measuring what Ed White (1986) called "a unit of expression" (p. 18). Clearly,

---

[5]One significant difference between the two is that the protocol for programwide assessment requires piloting the writing prompt to ensure that students respond as expected. In programwide assessment, students get only one chance to demonstrate their skill, so it is important that the prompt measures what it is intended to measure. Piloting is not crucial for in-class assessment for a simple reason: Students have additional chances if one writing assignment fails. The teacher then can revise the poor assignment for another term. Another significant and obvious difference is that students are not involved in developing rubrics for programwide assessment.

some things are more important than others when it comes to a successful response. For example, quality is more important than quantity, and content and organization are more important than spelling and punctuation. The goal therefore is to make an overall assessment of the quality of the writing as a whole. Readers make this assessment more reliably when they read a paper very quickly. Skilled holistic readers will take only about a minute or two to go through a two-page paper. The more time readers take to get through a paper, the more inclined they are to begin mentally editing, focusing on the surface errors. A typical two- to three-page paper should take student readers no more than 4 minutes to complete.

Scoring Rubrics

The earlier discussion of reliability noted that even good writers may receive different assessments from different people because each evaluator is likely to look for different qualities in a given paper. Unless evaluators agree in advance to look for the same qualities during an assessment, unless they reach consensus regarding the standard they will apply during assessment, there is little chance that their reliability will be high. Holistic scoring solves this problem through a process of "socialization," during which evaluators agree to reach a consensus on a specific set of criteria, called a *rubric*. Sample rubrics appear later in this chapter.

Rubrics for older students usually use a 6-point descending scale to gauge the quality of each response. A paper that scores a 6 is very good; one that scores a 2 is not very good at all. In addition, a rubric is divided into lower half and upper half to specify the general quality of a response. Upper-half papers (6, 5, 4) are well written, whereas lower-half papers (3, 2, 1) are not. No direct correspondence exists between numeric scores and letter grades. Translating scores into grades is a separate procedure and should not even be discussed as part of a round of holistic scoring.

Implementing Holistic Scoring in the Classroom

A workshop approach to writing instruction makes implementing holistic scoring easier because students already will have been working together in teams before their first scoring session. However, holistic scoring does not require a workshop approach to be successful.

Evaluators have to agree on the characteristics of good writing before any scoring can begin, so the first task is to analyze some writing samples that show a range of skill, from good to bad. The goal is to help students develop a standard for good writing, which requires that students become more critical readers.[6] The first socialization is critical to the success of the entire procedure, and it requires about a dozen sample papers, which the teacher must evaluate carefully in advance and assign a score on the basis of a preestablished rubric that he or she has created for the assignment. The samples must all be on the same topic for valid assessment.[7]

The first step in socialization is to examine a *general rubric*. This rubric articulates the general standard of good writing that the teacher will bring to every assessment. As noted earlier, this standard may be one that a given teacher bases on prior experiences, it may be one developed in conjunction with fellow teachers at a given school, or it may be one provided by the school district. (The standard based on consensus is recommended whenever feasible.) In any event, the general rubric should be produced before classes begin. It will serve as the basis for the *specific rubrics* that the class will develop for each writing assignment. The two sample rubrics that follow provide helpful examples. The first was developed for an elementary class, the second for a high school class focusing on argumentation.

General Rubric 1: Elementary

A Very Good Composition:
has a beginning that lets readers know clearly what the composition is about; gives readers much information; is interesting; has fewer than three errors in capitalization and spelling.

A Good Composition:
has a beginning that lets readers know what the composition is about; gives readers some information; has at least one interesting point; has fewer than five errors in capitalization and spelling.

---

[6]New teachers may have to borrow sample papers from more experienced colleagues.

[7]Photocopying enough samples for all students is expensive. Some teachers try to get around the problem by making transparencies of the samples for use on an overhead projector. Unfortunately, handwriting does not transfer very well, so some papers may require typing. In large classes, students at the back may not be able to see very well, which many will take as an excuse to disengage.

A Composition That Needs More Work:
does not let readers know what the composition is about; does not give readers much information; has no interesting points; has more than five errors in capitalization and spelling.

General Rubric 2: Middle and Secondary

In general, thoughtful, critical responses to the assignment will be placed in the upper half; in addition, those that demonstrate global organizational and argumentative skills usually will be rewarded over those that merely demonstrate sentence-level competence.

Upper Half

6-point essays will:
have a clear aim, a strong introduction that clearly states the thesis to be defended, and a thoughtful conclusion; effectively recognize the complexities of the topic, thoughtfully addressing more than one of them; contain strong supporting details and a judicious sense of evidence; be logically developed and very well organized; use a tone appropriate to the aim of the response; show stylistic maturity through sentence variety and paragraph development; be virtually free of surface and usage errors.

5-point essays will:
have a clear aim and a strong introduction and conclusion; effectively recognize the complexities of the topic, addressing more than one of them; contain supporting details and a good sense of evidence; be logically developed and well organized; use a tone appropriate to the aim of the response; have adequate sentence variety and paragraph development; lack the verbal felicity or organizational strength of a 6-point essay; be largely free of surface and usage errors.

4-point essays will:
have a clear aim and a strong introduction and conclusion; recognize the complexities of the topic; contain supporting details and a sense of evidence; display competence in logical development and organization, although it may exhibit occasional organizational and argumentative weaknesses; use a tone appropriate to the aim of the response; display basic competence in sentence variety, paragraph development, and usage.

Lower Half

3-point essays will:
acknowledge the complexities of the topic and attempt to address it, but the response will be weakened by one or more of the following: lack of a clear aim, thesis, or conclusion; lack of sufficient support or evidence; supporting details may be trivial, inappropriate, logically flawed; flaws in organization/development; inappropriate tone; stylistic flaws characterized by lack of sentence variety and/or paragraph development; frequent usage and/or surface errors.

2-point essays will:
address the topic, but will be weakened by one or more of the following: thesis may be too general or too specific; makes a vacuous or trivial argument; lack of support or evidence; lack of organization; inappropriate tone; serious stylistic flaws; serious usage and/or surface errors.

1-point essays will:
be seriously flawed in terms of argument, organization, style, or usage/surface errors.

Before examining the sample papers, the class should study the general rubric and talk about what it means. The teacher then should hand out a *specific rubric* for the sample papers. This rubric, again written in advance by the teacher, describes the features of a range of possible responses, just as the general rubric does. However, the description will be particular to this prompt and these responses. It is very important to understand that teacher and students must generate a new specific rubric for each writing assignment and that they cannot rely solely on the general rubric.

The teacher's role in the assessment is that of "chief reader." The chief reader uses his or her greater experience with writing to help students understand the rubric and see why one paper is better than another. This role is vital to the socialization process because students commonly disagree over the merits of a particular paper. Many will reward poorly written papers merely because they like the topic. Students need the chief reader to resolve disagreements and to help them understand that liking a topic is not a viable criterion for evaluation. Also, the teacher must guide students to ensure that their evaluations eventually agree with those articulated in the rubric. In other words, an important part of socialization is to get students to accept and then apply the teacher's standard for what constitutes good writing. This means that the teacher must allow enough time to discuss various features of the writing prompt, the characteristics of the samples, and the standard expressed in the rubric. Thus, as chief reader *the teacher models critical reading.* Guidance in all cases must be persuasive rather than coercive. A rubric is invaluable in this regard because it objectifies evaluations: A paper is poorly written because it has lower-half characteristics, not because readers don't like it (or vice versa).

The class should read three samples quickly, first ranking them informally as upper half and lower half and then applying scores.[8] Papers used in each socialization are read once. (Papers in an actual scoring session, however, are read twice, by two different students, so that each paper receives *two scores.*) If socialization was successful, these scores will agree with a high level of reliability. The teacher then should ask students how they scored each sample response in the set. There will be a spread of scores, and on the first set of three papers the spread may be fairly wide. A paper that the teacher scored as an *anchor 5,*[9] for example, is likely to receive several scores of 6, several of 4, and some of 3 and 2. The teacher must guide students through these scores by asking those who were very wide of the target score to identify features in the response that correspond to characteristics in the rubric. When asked to make this connection, students begin to recognize that they misread the paper because it will not have the features they thought it had. Students who do not see this right away can be helped along, normally with comments and suggestions from the teacher as well as from classmates. It is entirely appropriate for the teacher to tell individual students that their scoring is too harsh or too lenient and that they should adjust their scoring on the next set.

After the class has analyzed the first set of papers in this way, they go on to the second set, then the third, then the forth, until they have scored each paper and discussed it with respect to the rubric. As they proceed through the sets, their reading becomes more consistent, more reliable, and the spread of scores decreases. This is a sign that socialization is succeeding.

This first socialization may take four class sessions and should use all 12 samples. With some classes, socializing may take even longer. It is important that students reach agreement, so effective teachers do not rush them. Subsequent socializations proceed more quickly, even-

---

[8]It is a good idea to identify each sample paper without using names. Because the score is a number, many teachers follow an alpha format: paper GG, paper HH, paper ZZ, and so on.

[9]Meaning that it is a representative 5-point response and should serve as a standard for other 5-point responses.

tually taking about one class session. The time certainly is not wasted, because students are practicing critical-reading skills every time they evaluate samples. After completing this socialization, students will be ready to score their own papers.

Again, each time the class scores an assignment they must have a rubric designed specifically for that assignment. For older students, the class itself should generate these rubrics, with guidance from the teacher. The most effective approach is to spend some time talking with students about the assignment and then to ask them to offer suggestions for what a 6-point response to that assignment might look like. One student serves as secretary, taking notes that the teacher then types up after class with the understanding that he or she will devolve the 6-point response so as to provide descriptions for the other scores on the rubric. When the rubric is typed, the teacher should share it with the class and ask students whether they want to make any changes. If they do, the teacher then produces a revision for the next class. This procedure helps students to feel that the rubric is theirs, that it reflects their views on what successful responses will look like. The empowerment that comes from this procedure is highly beneficial to students and their progress as writers.

Split Scores. Perfect agreement on every paper scored by 25 to 30 people is very difficult to achieve. Some variation in the scores assigned to papers should be expected. For example, a given paper might receive a score of 3 from the first reader and a score of 4 from the second. This variation is *acceptable* because it does not exceed one point. A 3/4 score is viewed as a single score. A 2-point difference, however, is *not* acceptable. In situations where the first readers gives a paper a 5, for example, and the second reader gives it a 3, the paper has what is called a *split score.* Papers with split scores go to the chief reader for another assessment. In other words, the teacher gives it a third reading. The chief reader is the final arbiter. The scores are not simply averaged; the teacher must carefully evaluate the paper and assign an appropriate score. Usually, this score will agree with one of the student scores, but not always.

Scoring Student Papers

To reduce subjective factors during scoring, students' names should not appear on their papers. The teacher should assign each student a code number at the beginning of the term, recording the number in his or her record book next to each name. Teachers who use work groups should number them as well. If there are five students in Group 1, their code numbers would be 1–2, 1–3, 1–4, and 1–5. Students use the code number rather than their names whenever they turn in a composition.

Students should have copies of their general and specific rubrics before they begin writing their papers so that they function as concrete guides as they are working on drafts. With the exception of the general rubric and the rubric for the first socialization, students should have primary responsibility for generating each rubric; their participation will give them a greater sense of control over their achievement. Developing a rubric involves carefully examining the assignment and reaching a consensus regarding the characteristics of good, average, and weak responses. The best way to structure the activity is to have on hand at least three sample papers written in response to the assignment. Students can then analyze the papers and work through the rubric on the basis of their analysis of how other students responded to the assignment.

New teachers may find this approach difficult unless they have established a file of writing samples. Colleagues can serve as a valuable resource for sample papers, but this approach entails being willing to use their assignments. If it isn't possible to obtain enough samples for both the initial socialization and the first round of assignments, teachers may want to analyze a professional model that approximates the type of task assigned. This approach has some drawbacks, however. Students are likely to have some difficulty relating the model, and therefore the rubric, to their own writing. In addition, they will have only one sample essay rather than several, which will limit their understanding of the range of possible responses. The only other alternative is for the teacher to focus on the assignment and to use his or her experience with varieties of discourse to help students identify the characteristics they should strive for in their papers. In effect, the teacher helps them discover what will characterize an upper-half response and what will characterize a lower-half response.

Teaming With Another Teacher. Although students are perfectly capable of scoring one another's papers, they usually aren't happy about it. Most complain about the responsibility, and the loudest complaints normally come from the better students. An effective way to help students feel more comfortable with holistic scoring is to team with another teacher and to trade papers at the time of each scoring session. This approach requires some minimal cooperation. For example, the teachers must coordinate their writing assignments so that students are writing on the same topics at the same time. They also must coordinate their lessons to ensure that their units on writing instruction match. And they must coordinate due dates for papers and scoring sessions.

This sort of cooperation does not take much time, and it provides numerous benefits for teachers and students alike. When teachers work together and communicate their ideas and approaches, their teaching improves as does the collegial spirit at the school. Students feel as though they have a real audience for their papers and will be more motivated to succeed. And, as noted, exchanging papers with another class makes the scoring experience more positive.

Setting Anchor Scores. After collecting students' papers on a given assignment, the teacher will have to resocialize the class. This requires a set of sample papers on the topic for students to evaluate. In this instance, however, the set need not be as large as the one used for the initial socialization because much of what constitutes good writing will already be partially internalized. Three or four samples usually are sufficient. The aim is to provide samples that illustrate a range of responses, so the papers should reflect at least one very good response, an average one, and a weak one. Unless the teacher has sample papers from another class, he or she will have to pull anchors from those the class is preparing to score.

Selecting samples from the papers students submit means that the teacher must read all the papers in advance of the scoring. Reading them holistically does not take very long; most teachers will be able to read a set of 30 in about an hour. The procedure is identical to the one described earlier in the section Reducing the Paper Load. The teacher should read the first paper and mentally evaluate it according to the rubric. The second paper should be compared to the first one. If the papers are of about the same quality, they go together in a pile, but if they differ, they go in separate piles. As the teacher completes each paper, he or she puts it in a stack of similar papers, so that when finished there are three stacks of papers grouped on the basis of similar quality. After this grouping, the teacher should pull a sample paper from each stack, read it holistically a second time, and assign a score from the rubric. These papers are the scoring anchors that will be the basis for the socialization session prior to scoring all the other papers.[10]

Conducting the Reading. After analyzing the anchors and reaching a consensus on scores, the class is ready for the actual reading. Teachers who use work groups should separate the papers by group, giving Group 1 the papers of Group 2, and so forth. With each assignment,

---

[10]It isn't fair to use the same students more than once for anchor papers, so teachers should note in their record book the names of those whose papers were selected as samples.

the teacher should alternate the arrangement to avoid any regularity of grouping. Reliability and validity will be seriously compromised if readers are able to see one another's scores, so the teacher needs some self-adhesive patches—round labels available in any store that sells office supplies—to cover the first score. When the first reader finishes a paper, he or she must affix a patch over the score before passing the paper on for the second reading. The second reader does not need to put a patch over his or her score.

After all the papers have been scored, students remove the patches, check the scores, and then circulate the papers back to their owners. Students should have a minute or two to look at their scores; then they should pass the papers back to the teacher. The teacher's task at this point is twofold. First, he or she must check for split scores. These papers must be given a third reading. Second, the teacher needs to read through all the papers another time to compare the scores the students gave with those he or she would give. This procedure acts as a support for students, most of whom will doubt their ability to score accurately. They need to know that the teacher checks all scores to ensure that they are fair and accurate. In some cases the teacher may find that a paper has been evaluated incorrectly, which requires changing the score.

Converting Numeric Scores to Letter Grades

At some point, numeric scores must be converted to letter grades. Although some teachers do this early in the term, most delay conversion until the end of the term. The rationale is that they do not want students to be applying letter-grade criteria to papers during scoring sessions. This rationale is sensible, although teachers who apply it sometimes have problems with students who become anxious when they do not know what their grade is in writing.

There are no definite guidelines for converting numeric scores to letter grades, because teachers differ in how they perceive grades. Some teachers, for example, may want a simple assignment: 6 = A, 5 = B, 4/3 = C, 2 = D, and 1 = F. This sort of distribution seems entirely appropriate for most grading situations, but it may make students unhappy, considering that grade inflation has boosted the average grade in most schools to a B or B+. Generally, it is a good idea to put the score distribution on the board for students because it gives everyone a chance to see how he or she did in comparison with everybody else. If no papers scored a 6, students will be inclined to argue that A grades should begin with the highest score, even if it is a 3. The teacher should explain that it is not unusual for a class to have no A's on a given assignment and to resist grade inflation as much as possible. More often than not, establishing letter grades is a matter of compromise, with the teacher trying to reduce inflation and students trying to increase it.

After going through the process of compromise many times with many different groups of students, it seems that the following grade equivalencies arise again and again. It gives some idea of the direction the compromise is likely to take:

6 = A	4/5 = B	3 = C
5/6 = A–	4 = C+	2 = D
5 = B+	4/3 = C	1 = F

JOURNAL ENTRY

The biggest obstacle to using holistic scoring in the classroom is student resistance. Consider ways you might reduce this resistance.

Following the Protocol

The steps outlined in the preceding sections constitute the complete protocol for holistic scoring. Programwide assessment requires making certain adjustments to the protocol, but these are relatively minor. Failure to adhere to the protocol seriously compromises the reliability of the holistic procedure. Therefore, I highly recommend that teachers consult with someone who has been properly trained before they implement holistic scoring in their schools or classrooms. Because holistic scoring is frequently used for placement and exit-proficiency assessment, the stakes for students are high. They deserve to have the assessment administered properly.

In my experience, however, the biggest problem with holistic scoring is the tendency among test administrators to modify the protocol. They may forgo piloting; they may begin focusing on surface features; they may reduce the amount of time devoted to socializing readers; and so forth. The results of such modifications are obvious to anyone trained in writing assessment but may be invisible to those who are not. The assessment may give the *appearance* of conforming to established standards and of providing placement, but the lack of reliability means that the assessment has little if any value.

PORTFOLIO GRADING

Some teachers object to holistic scoring on several grounds. Many believe that putting grading in the hands of students will aggravate the already bad state of grade inflation. (There is no evidence to support this belief, however.) Others believe that no matter how carefully one socializes students they will never be as accurate in their assessments as teachers, owing to the disparity in maturity and reading experience. Still others are convinced that it is a mistake to grade every composition students produce because students will be inclined to focus on grades rather than process. And finally, some believe that student writing performance can be assessed accurately only by an outsider, not by the students' teacher or by the students themselves.

Many of these objections have some measure of truth, and portfolio assessment emerged largely as an alternative to holistic assessment. It gained popularity quickly, in part owing to the perception that writing performance is uneven: Students have different strengths that allow them to excel on some assignments but not on others. Consequently, instead of evaluating every paper students produce, a more realistic approach to assessing writing skill would allow students to select their best work for evaluation. Students would save all their work and, periodically throughout the term, would select two or three of their best papers and put them in a folder, or portfolio, to be evaluated.

Like holistic scoring, the portfolio approach initially was used for programwide assessment, and the protocol for administration was based on holistic scoring procedures, involving rubrics, socialization of readers, and rapid reading of compositions. Like holistic scoring, it also was adopted for classroom use fairly quickly. When this occurred, the assessment protocol was almost universally dropped. The focus shifted from validity and reliability to the portfolios themselves. Somehow, allowing students to submit papers in a folder became the most important factor in the assessment, even though there is nothing whatsoever in the mere act of submission that is relevant to the assessment procedure.

The protocols for portfolio assessment and holistic scoring differ in several respects, and here we consider only the procedure for using portfolios in the classroom, with the understanding that it is very similar to what is used in programwide assessment. First, portfolios require the participation of at least three faculty members. In a typical grading situation, these three instructors will evaluate student papers for one another, alternating with each scoring session. Second, to reduce the paper load, students' papers are not assessed as each one is completed, nor is every paper evaluated. Instead, students keep their work in individual files that are stored in the classroom. After several papers are finished, students select the best three or four, depending on the teacher's directions, for assessment.

In a hypothetical high school situation, a teacher would have students write a paper each week, for a total of 14 or 15 papers each semester. Five weeks into the term, the teacher would announce the first grading session and would ask students to select the best three of their first five papers. (Additional grading sessions would occur during the 10th week and at the end of the term.) These three papers go into a folder along with each assignment and the rubrics the class worked out for each task. The participating teachers then meet with their students' folders. Together the teachers discuss the various rubrics and some sample papers until they reach a consensus on scoring standards. They then exchange folders and begin scoring, using the 6-point scale (or 3-point for elementary students) described previously. After each portfolio has been read twice, the scores on the individual papers are averaged into a single score for the entire portfolio. Thus, if a student received 5's on one composition, a 5/4 on the second, and two 4's on the third, his average score would be 4.5. This score would then be converted to a letter grade.

This approach has some clear advantages. It forces students to consider readers other than their teacher and their peers as part of their audience. It may make the paper load slightly smaller than holistic scoring because there is no need to read papers to check student scoring. It also creates a sense of collegiality often missing among faculty members. Recognizing the value of portfolio assessment, some states, such as Kentucky, mandated this approach in the mid-1990s for all writing assessment in public schools statewide. To avoid the problems that arise from failure to adhere to the standard protocol, these states have provided training for all teachers, but the results have been uneven.

Examining portfolio assessment in three states, Williams (2000) reported several difficulties in how the procedure is administered. The goal of the investigation was threefold: to evaluate portfolio implementation and administration; to determine whether demographic features, such as SES and ethnicity, appear regularly in student writing; and to determine whether these features influence teachers' evaluations. A variety of data was collected from 100 teachers and their students in Grades 5–12. From this group, 50 teachers were selected at random for the analysis portion of the study. All the teachers were experienced and had been trained in portfolio assessment. One of the aims of the investigation was to examine the degree to which student portfolios reflected identifiable demographic features related to ethnicity, gender, and SES. The 1824 students who were part of the data analysis represented a range of ethnic and socioeconomic groups. Portfolios were selected at random from this group, and a total of 600 were evaluated by a group of independent readers.

The results showed that 42 of the 50 teachers failed to follow the standard protocol for portfolio assessment. Rather than team with other instructors for evaluation, they graded students' papers themselves. They did not develop rubrics for each assignment, nor did they read individual portfolios holistically; instead, they used the traditional method of marking student errors and providing marginal and terminal comments. Follow-up interviews with the teachers revealed that the primary reason they failed to follow their training and adhere to the standard protocol was that they did not believe that it was important in assessing student writing. Many stated that they could "recognize good writing when they saw it" and that the training in portfolio assessment did not add anything to their existing ability.

More troubling were the findings related to demographic features, which appeared regularly in the student papers in the form of linguistic structures, references related to SES, and handwriting. These features significantly influenced the teachers' evaluations. The most salient factors were SES, ethnicity, and gender. High SES correlated with higher grades from the teachers, whereas low SES correlated with lower grades. With regard to ethnicity, the two most frequent features were related to BEV and CE, and the more often these features appeared in a portfolio, the lower the teachers' grade. Finally, teachers graded the portfolios of boys significantly lower than the portfolios for girls. These findings are congruent with those reported by Supovitz and Brennan (1997), who compared standardized test results and portfolio assessment among first and second graders and found that gender, socioeconomic, and racial inequalities persisted with the portfolio assessment. The gap between girls and boys was significantly greater in favor of the girls with portfolios.

In his conclusion, Williams (2000) noted that part of the problem for these teachers was that they were not properly monitored after their training, which left them free to ignore what they had learned about portfolio assessment. It seems reasonable to propose that adherence to the standard protocol would have ameliorated the negative influence of demographic features. If this is the case, the need to follow the protocol is great, indeed, for any deviation appears to result in egregiously unfair evaluations of students' writing.

SAMPLE RUBRICS AND SAMPLE PAPERS

The following sample rubrics and papers are offered to illustrate further how rubrics are used to assess writing. The score—or in the case of the elementary samples, the evaluation—each paper received in holistic assessment is shown at the end of the response.

Assignment 1 (Grade 6)

Two years ago, the school board of Ocean View School District voted to ban gum chewing in all schools. At next month's meeting, the board members will evaluate the ban and decide whether or not to make it permanent. Write a composition either for or against gum chewing. Take a position and then support it with good reasons and examples. We will send the finished papers to the district office so the school board will know how students feel about the ban.

Rubric: Assignment 1

A Very Good Composition:
has a beginning that lets readers know clearly what the composition is about and what the writer's position is; gives several good reasons for that position; is interesting; has fewer than three errors in capitalization and spelling.

A Good Composition:
has a beginning that lets readers know what the composition is about and what the writer's position is; gives some good reasons for that position; has at least one interesting point; has fewer than five errors in capitalization and spelling.

A Composition That Needs More Work:
does not let readers know what the composition is about; does not state the writer's position clearly; does not give good reasons for why the writer takes that position; has no interesting points; has more than five errors in capitalization and spelling.

Sample 1

The Right to Chew Gum

[1] The school board banned gum at school two years ago, probably because gum can be pretty messy if kids spit it on the ground or put it under desks. It banned gum because it believed that students can't be responsible enough to handle gum chewing. I not only disagree with the ban but I disagree with the idea that we aren't responsible.

[2] We know the board has the power to ban gum, but it isn't so clear that it has the right. As long as students act responsible and don't spit their gum on the ground or pop it in class, gum chewing doesn't hurt anyone. It is a private act. We may be kids, but that doesn't mean that we don't have the right to eat what we want or say what we want or chew

what we want, as long as it doesn't bother others. The problem is that the board never gave us the chance to act responsible. If there was a problem with kids abusing the right to chew gum, the board should have explained the situation to us. It should have told us what would happen if we didn't stop abusing the right. But it didn't do that. Instead it just banned gum chewing without ever talking to us. That isn't fair.

(A very good composition)

Sample 2

No gum On Campus!

[1]   I agree with the school board's decision to ban gum chewing in Ocean View School District. Chewing gum is real messy. If you spit it on the ground it gets stuck to your feet and you can't get it off your shoes. If you chew it in class it can be real loud so that you can't hear what the teacher is saying. And maybe if you blow bubbles the other kids won't be able to hear either, especially if the bubble pops and makes a loud noise.

[2]   If teachers step in the gum that you've spit on the ground they can get mad. That means that everybody gets into trouble because one person spit his gum on the ground. That isn't right. Only the one who spit the gum should get into trouble. But if you don't know who spit it in the first place, then I guess it's right that everybody gets punished.

[3]   We're here to learn things and I think that chewing gum in class can keep us from learning. We can get so involved with chewing that gum that we don't pay attention to what the teacher is saying. The next thing you know we end up dumb and we can't find jobs when we grow up and we have to go on welfare.

[4]   Chewing gum is just a bad idea. I support the ban.

(A good composition)

Sample 3

Chewing Gum

[1]   I think the ban on chewing gum is stupid. I have friends in Sunny-side school district and they can chew gum. If they can chew gum we should be able to chew gum to. It doesn't hurt anything and it's relaxing. Also it keep us from talking in class. It's hard to talk and chew at the same time. So I think the school board should forget about the ban and let us chew gum like my friends in the sunnyside district.

(A composition that needs more work)

Assignment 2 (Grade 8)

The United States is a country of immigrants. Essentially we all have roots extending somewhere else. Over the last few years, more and more people have become interested in tracing their roots, turning into amateur genealogists. Using all the resources available to you, including interviews with family members, trace your family history as far back as you can and write a report of your investigation, telling readers what you discovered.

Rubric: Assignment 2

6—A 6-point essay will be characterized by all of the following features: establishes a context for the essay by providing background and purpose; purpose will be easily identifiable, although not stated directly; addresses the complexities of human behavior; operates on a very high level of significance; is rich in detail; is well organized, easy to follow, easy to read; tone is entirely appropriate to the task and the audience; has variation in sentence and paragraph structure; is virtually free of spelling, punctuation, sentence/paragraph errors.

5—A 5-point essay will be characterized by all of the following features: establishes a context for the essay by providing background and purpose; purpose will be identifiable, although not stated directly; addresses most of the complexities of human behavior; addresses significant points; has many details; is generally well organized, easy to follow, easy to read; tone is generally appropriate to the task and the audience; is generally free of spelling, punctuation, sentence/paragraph errors.

4—A 4-point essay will be characterized by the following features: establishes a context for the essay by providing background and purpose, but the context will not be as detailed as the 5-point response; purpose may not be easily identifiable; addresses some of the complexities of human behavior; addresses a few significant points; has some details; is organized, although may not be as easy to follow as the 5-point response; tone may occasionally be inappropriate; may have occasional spelling, punctuation, or sentence/paragraph errors.

3—A 3-point essay may be characterized as having some combination of the following features: attempts to establish a context for the essay by providing a background; attempts to provide an identifiable purpose; addresses few of the complexities of human behavior; attempts to address at least one significant point, but overall the composition tends to be trivial; is not very detailed; is not well organized; frequent errors in punctuation, spelling, and paragraph structure.

2—A 2-point essay will significantly compound the problems of the 3-point essay.

1—A 1-point essay may be characterized as having some combination of the following features: lacks background; the purpose may be unidentifiable or may be stated explicitly; lacks details; may be off topic; fails to address the complexities of human behavior; composition is trivial; is unorganized and hard to follow; uses inappropriate or inconsistent tone; serious surface errors in spelling, punctuation, or sentence/paragraph structure.

Sample 4

Realizing the American Dream

[1]   I feel very unfortunate not to have known my great grandfather on my father's side of the family. He passed away in 1972, the year I was born.

[2]   His name was Anton, but my mother says everyone called him Poppi. Poppi was born in 1880 in Norway, where he learned to be a tailor by apprenticing himself when he was only 13. At nineteen he was so well trained that he decided to open his own small shop, and during his first year of business he was successful enough to take on two apprentices. But at the end of that year he was ordered to fulfill his military service. Being against war and weapons, he preferred to leave his country rather than serve in the army. In the summer of 1900, he set sail for America.

[3]   When he arrived on Ellis Island, he immediately arranged to travel to Minnesota, which at that time had several large Norwegian communities. Knowing almost no English, Poppi felt he would have an easier time surviving among people from a similar background, people who spoke his language. With the small sum of money he had brought with him, he opened another tailor shop. He owned the shop until 1940, making a modest living for himself and his wife and children. In 1940 he had to sell the shop because more and more people were buying ready-made clothes rather than having them tailored. Without a shop of his own, he had to find work where he could, so he and his family moved to St. Paul, where he worked in several department stores, altering the ready-made suits and pants customers bought off the rack.

[4]   Poppi's only daughter married Paul Alphaus, who was my grandfather and who I always called Grandpa Alphi. He was born on a farm in Iowa. Even when he was a young boy he was determined not to become a farmer like his father, because there was no way to make a good living on the farm. So while many of the other farm boys quit school to go to work in the fields, Grandpa Alphi studied hard and finished high school. After he finished, he enrolled in a small Lutheran college not far from his home. He got good grades and enjoyed the work, but he had to drop out

at the end of his first semester because he ran out of money—his family couldn't help him, either.

[5]   Grandpa Alphi was good with numbers, which may be a reason why he was offered a job as bookkeeper at a local insurance company. He worked hard in those early years. He took classes evenings and on weekends that were offered through the insurance company, and he studied banking and investments. Five years latter, after his studies were finished, he was given an award for his high grades. He worked at the insurance company for forty-six years, until the company went out of business. He then went to work at the local bank as a senior trust officer, a job he kept until 1986, when he finally retired at age 79. Living in a small town made job opportunities scarce, but Grandpa Alphi managed to succeed through determination.

[6]   My grandfather on my mother's side was John Walter, who I knew as Pop Pop. He was born in 1915 in Pennsylvania. Pop Pop had to drop out of school after the ninth grade because of the Depression—his family needed him to work and to bring in extra money. Jobs were scarce, but he found work in a lumberyard, where he worked stacking lumber until the war started. Then he began working at a local arsenal making bullets. After a year, he went on to the shipyards in Philadelphia, where he worked as a welder.

[7]   After the war, Pop Pop sold jewelry, while in his spare time he made lawn furniture out of scraps of metal, using the welding skill he had picked up during the war. He liked the furniture work so much that he borrowed money to open his own shop, where he made wrought iron railings, furniture, and interior rails. He never seemed to make much money, but somehow he managed to put his two daughters through college. After thirty years of welding, Pop Pop retired, only to die a year later of cancer. On his deathbed he told us not to feel sad, because he had lived a good life and had done just about everything a man could hope for.

(Holistic score = 5)

Sample 5

Mother's Love

[1]   During World War II, with all its abandonment and loneliness, Harrison Richards met Mary Rogers. Harrison was from Port Orchard Washington, where, at age 18, he was drafted and sent to Southern California, where he was stationed. Mary was living in San Diego.

[2]   They began seeing each other and before long Mary became pregnant at the age of 16. Harrison and Mary got married before the baby was born because the war was still going on and they wanted to be mar-

ried in case Harrison had to leave for combat. Mary's parents accepted her pregnancy and the marriage because she was one of their favorite children. In the hot, dry month of July, 1942, Mary gave birth to a little baby girl she named Hilda LaVerne and she became a mother for the first time. Needless to say, at the age of 16 she was still a child herself and not responsible enough to handle a child. After the baby was born Harrison left for the war and was never heard from again. It had just been a wartime romance for him and he knew that it was too great a responsibility for him to handle. Mary didn't even acknowledge that she had a child, she didn't even want to give the child Harrison's last name.

[3]   Mary would leave the baby with her brother and his wife to take while she went out on dates and late night parties. Mary's sister-in-law showed more love and attention to the baby than Mary did. In 1947 Mary decided to give the baby up for adoption, and her brother and sister-in-law decided to adopt the baby because they were unable to have children because she had Scarlet fever as child which caused her to get a hysterectomy. They changed the baby's name to Tonya LaVerne, and after that Mary never made any attempt to see her. Mary got remarried in 1955 to Bud Hevert who owned his own floor covering business. Mary owned her own beauty shop and was doing good for herself now that she had given up Hilda. When Bud and her would come to family get togethers she wouldn't even act like Hilda, who was now Tonya, was her real daughter. Even Mary's grandmother, Myrtle Lola Chrissy Moore, treated her like she wasn't part of the family.

[4]   Mary met a construction worker and began to see him behind Bud's back. Bud became suspicious of her because she would work late hours to see this man and she was always acting tired. One night, in 1966, Bud followed her and waited in the parking lot to see what was going on. He saw the man enter the shop with a six pack so he decided to go in. He found them together in the back room and shot them both dead, then he turned the gun on himself. Tonya was 13 when she found out about being adopted and she has never acknowledged Mary as her mother. She is not ashamed of her and she doesn't hate her for giving her up because she got a mother who would show her the love she needed. Tonya married Wayne my father in 1966 and they had a daughter that they named Trisha in 1972. Tonya gives her daughter the love and attention that a natural mother should give a child but that she received from an adopted mother.

(Holistic score = 3)

Sample 6

Brothers

[1]   The year was 1865 and it was the beginning of the Civil War. Samuel Lloyd was 17 years old. He had never fought in a war before. Now here he was assigned to General Rosser's troop and he was expected to

fight and to kill. He had been called in for duty from his West Virginia home and had expected to be in battle within days. However, he and the other troops found themselves marching South for weeks only to see the abandoned burned down plantations and homes of Southern Virginia farmers. They continued this monotony until they reached the border. He found there the action that he had anticipated in the previous weeks.

[2]   The North fought a long and hard battle. The casualties number almost 600 for the South. As they set out the next morning to head North and take their prisoners to a camp, Sammy Lloyd was called to the back of the line to help a dying prisoner. While he was approaching the man, he could hear him coughing with all his might in his body. Sammy reached over to roll the man on his back to ease the coughing. As he did so he saw that it was the face of his only brother staring up at him. Sam Lloyd never forgave himself for having been a part of the killing of his own flesh and blood. The war that he so anxiously awaited had brought him nothing but hardship and sorrow and it left him cold and bitter.

(Holistic score = 2)

Assignment 3 (Grade 12)

In the minds of most people, an expert is someone who knows all the answers in a given field. This is a common and somewhat misconceived view. But there is another way of looking at things. In this alternative view, an expert isn't one who knows what the answers are, but one who knows what the questions are in a given field. Your task for this assignment is to find out what the questions are in a given field, whether it be math, chemistry, history, or business. Begin by interviewing one of your teachers, asking him or her about the significant questions in the field. Then use the library to get additional information. Your paper should be about five pages. It should not only identify the questions but explain why they are significant, how they are being investigated, and why they are relevant to readers.

Rubric: Assignment 3

6—A 6-point essay will be characterized by all of the following features: It will be well organized: (a) it will clearly introduce the topic and provide an interesting and detailed background for the essay; (b) it will then move to the body of the paper, where it will identify the significant questions, explain in depth why they are significant, how the questions affect the field, how the questions are being investigated, and why the questions are relevant to readers; in each case the author will provide abundant details and examples to illustrate his or her points; (c) it will have a conclusion or summation that offers a more explicit statement of relevance; it will be factual and highly informative, providing readers with new information; it will be coherent; each of the several parts will flow together smoothly; the tone will be objective and appropriate to the task; stylistically, the essay will demonstrate variety in sentence structure and paragraph development; the essay will be virtually free of surface errors.

5—A 5-point essay will be characterized by all of the following features: It will be well organized: (a) it will introduce the topic and provide an interesting background for the essay; (b) it will then move to the body of the paper, where it will identify the significant questions, explain why they are significant, how the questions affect the field, how the questions are being investigated, and why the questions are relevant to readers; in each case, the author will offer details and examples to illustrate his or her points; (c) it will have a conclusion or summation that offers a more explicit statement of relevance; it will be factual and informative, providing readers with new information; it will be coherent, although the various parts will not flow together as smoothly as in the 6-point essay; the tone will be objective and appropriate to the task; stylistically, the essay will demonstrate variety in sentence structure and paragraph development; the essay will be largely free of surface errors.

4—A 4-point essay will be characterized by all of the following features: It will be organized: (a) it will introduce the topic and provide a background for the essay; (b) it will then move to the body of the paper, where it will identify the significant questions, explain why they are significant, how the questions affect the field, how the questions are being investigated, and why the questions are relevant to readers; the author will offer some details and examples to illustrate his or her points, but they may not always be effective or appropriate; (c) it will have a conclusion or summation that offers a more explicit statement of relevance; it will be factual; there may be occasional transitional flaws that prevent the various parts from flowing together as smoothly as they should; the tone will be objective; stylistically, the essay will demonstrate some variety in sentence structure and paragraph development; the essay may have occasional surface errors.

3—A 3-point essay may be characterized as having one or more of the following features: It will not be well organized, as characterized by one or more of the following: (a) it will introduce the topic but will not provide an adequate background for the essay; (b) it will move to the body of the paper, where it will identify the significant questions, but it will fail to explain in much detail why they are significant, how the questions affect the field, how the questions are being investigated, and why the questions are relevant to readers; the author may attempt to offer some examples to illustrate his or her points, but they will generally be ineffective; (c) it will have a conclusion or summation that attempts to offer a more explicit statement of relevance, but the conclusion may be confused or may be merely a repetition of what has already been said; it will be factual but uninformative, telling readers things they already know; it will have significant transitional flaws that prevent the various parts from flowing together smoothly; the tone will be inconsistently objective or inappropriate to the task; stylistically, the essay will lack variety in sentence structure and paragraph development; the essay may have frequent surface errors.

2—A 2-point essay may be characterized by one or more of the following features: Organization will be seriously flawed in that the writer fails to offer adequate background information; there will be insufficient details in the body of the paper, and the summation may not be relevant to the topic; the tone may be inconsistent; the frequency of mechanical errors increases.

1—A 1-point essay may be characterized by one or more of the following features: It will be unorganized, lacking background and context, details of fact, and a summation; the tone will be subjective and inappropriate; the essay will have serious mechanical errors.

Sample 7

Math

[1]   When most of us think of mathematics, we think of practical applications, such as using math to balance a checkbook. Such applications of math are used everyday by many different types of people. For example, economists use differential calculus to determine the maximum and minimum points on supply and demand curves. Civil engineers use principles of trigonometry to calculate the tensions on certain beams on truss bridges. Even school teachers use algebra to set bell curves for exams.

[2]   But the field of mathematics is actually much more complex. Another aspect of math is theory, which deals with explanations of why mathematical equations and theorums, such as the quadratic equation, work. This side of math is also called pure mathematics. If this pure math cannot be applied, it is virtually useless. Therefore, a very significant question in the field is brought forth: How can pure math be related to applied math?

[3]   This important question has had a great effect on the field of math. The field has been split into two parts: pure math and applied math. Researchers in pure math deal with theoretical principles and come up with abstract theorums. Although pure math by itself is not practically used, research is very important because it broadens the field of math. A broader field in turn gives applied mathematicians more to work with. Greater importance is being given to applied mathematicians, because they make math useful, by applying it to practical matters. They include researchers in many fields, some of which are in the natural sciences, engineering, and business. They in turn broaden many other fields, such as chemistry, economics, and electrical engineering.

[4]   Many different approaches have been tried to find a sure method to apply pure math to answer all the questions in a given field. In one technique, trial and error is used to try to apply mathematical principles to a certain case. If a mathematical principle works, it is attempted with many other similar situations. If this approach can be repeated over and over in every case, a formula or equation is derived, which can be applied in practical situations. Unfortunately, this technique does not always work, because the same repetitive steps can rarely be used for all cases. Also, numerous complexities frequently come up, which in turn bring up more questions to be answered.

[5]   In another technique, abstract mathematical principles are converted into physical models. These models link the pure math to certain applications. A good example of this method is the differential analyzer. Most problems in physics and engineering involve differential equations. The problem was that in theory the solutions of this type of equation are rarely expressed in term of a finite number and therefore cannot be practically used. But in 1928, an engineer named Vannevan Bush, along with his staff at MIT discovered that when differential equations are applied to physical situations, a finite answer is not necessary if a graphic solution is obtainable. Using this fact, they designed and constructed the first differential analyzer. Today these analyzers are used throughout industry.

[6]   In conclusion, how we can relate pure math to applied math is a very significant question, not only in the field of mathematics itself, but also in many other fields. A universal answer to this important question would make many aspects of mathematics more useful. For normal people like you and me, the answer would greatly speed up technology. Many more practical applications would lead to many new inventions and break throughs that would have a great impact on the way we live.

(Holistic score = 5/6)

Sample 8

The World of Economics

[1]   Most people do not notice that the movies shown during the summer are either comedies, adventures, or teen related, while those played in the winter are dramas and adult comedies. We might wonder why this is. During the summer months, what type of audience can a film bring it? Young people. Also for us, the summer means good times and lots of adventure. Most of us want to keep those good times rolling and do not wish to take on a serious film. This interesting observation has to do with economics, because economics has to do with each and very one of us.

[2]   The people who create and produce films we watch need to answer three questions before they can get the film rolling. In fact these are the same questions that every nation, economist, businessman, and individual needs to be able to answer, because without them products would not be created and an economy would not exist. We need to know what to produce, how much to produce, and whom to produce it for.

[3]   The question what to produce is significant because if we do not know what to produce then we won't have certain goods or services. An economy cannot exist without production, and the more products available the stronger the economy and the cheaper the product. The cheaper the product the greater the demand for the product. The more demand means more product sold, which creates a healthier economy. Therefore if we can answer what to produce, more of our wants will be satisfied, the goods and services will be cheaper, and the economy will be growing. This makes us happier and our nation stronger.

[4]   However before the good or service can be produced, it must be known for whom you are producing it for. We need to know if there is a market for the product. If there is not a market for the product, there is no reason to produce it. Music groups are a good example. Music groups provide a service however if there is not a demand for their type of music they will not be able to sell albums. If they do not produce a product that is desired, it does not help economy. In fact groups in demand could increase the cost of their material, because they now hold a monopoly on the music that is in demand. This means higher prices for you and me. This question is investigated through market research. These individuals study the market system and predict what is and what will be in demand. This helps companies create future products, which help satisfy our wants and desires.

[5]   Although what and for whom to produce it for isn't known, how much to supply or produce is still unanswered. The less product that is produce the cheaper it is to produce it. For example, it is cheaper to buy the materials to wall paper one room then it is for a whole apartment complex. More materials, supplies, and hired help need to be bought and it takes more time. However, items with little demand are not heavily produced and cost more. For example, there is little demand for dialysis machines, so few are produced. There is a monopoly on these machines because they are needed. So manufacturers can charge as much as they see fit because, although it is small, there is always a demand for it. Therefore, how much product is produce affects the price that you and I have to pay. However, we decide how much demand there is for the product by deciding whether to purchase it or not.

[6]   As it can be determined, these questions are always being asked and answered. They affect everyone because the products are produce for us and bought by us. They are investigated through market systems and

market research. These questions affect the field of economics, because they are economics. Without these questions, there would be no products and therefore no economy. Economics is the study of how goods and services get produced and how they are distributed. Consequently the study of what, for whom, and how much to produce, is economics. The attempt to answer them gives us the field of economics.

(Holistic score = 3)

Sample 9

Questions in french

[1] At one time, people concentrated on learning as much as possible about their native language. This was sufficient until society became more complex and knowing more than one language was almost essential. As one strolls the isles of a local grocery store, one notices products with names derived from the french language. Some examples are Lean Cuisine, Au Gratin and Le Jardin, all three of this parents have french words in their title. The television companies even broadcast a Perma Soft commercial spoken in french. These are just two subtle examples used to show the need to have a knowledge of the french language is increasing. This has caused many people to seriously consider or go forth with the learning of french. One can not simply learn a language overnight. It requires determination along with an effective method. This has raised a very significant question in learning the french language. Despite research, the question still remains of what is the most effective method to adopt in learning the french language.

[2] One of the methods of teaching concentrates on grammar translation. This method involves translating from french to english as well as from english to french. Students translate sentences, paragraphs, and even complete sentences. The translations are checked for accuracy in grammar usage, proper word placement in sentences, accent marks, and consistency of the choice of words. This method has advantages but is not free of disadvantages. Since there is little oral work, the students are not familiar with correct pronunciation, the ability to perform well on dictation and communicate with other french speakers. Researchers have found this is an effective method in learning how to read and write the language but feel more oral activities. They also have found through grammar translation, students appear to be able to retain their knowledge of french over a long period of time.

[3] A second method of teaching French involves audiolinguism. This method is based on listening to cassettes of French conversation and students will learn by repetition. There is some written work involved since students are asked to write what is heard on the cassette. The information heard ranges from daily conversation to sentences with specific ex-

ceptions in french. Researchers have found this method to be less practical since one is confined to listening to the french spoken and many are bored with this. Since many people learn through repetition, it quite effective.

[4]   The final method is communative competence. Their is a great amount of concentration on distinguish this "method" the ability to understand french in day today situation and the culture. The majority of this would include oral work. Students learn greetings, answering and asking questions, interests and information concerning the french culture. There is more emphasis on the ability to be able to say a sentence correctly than the ability to write one. Researchers have found students in this type of class were able to communicate but their writing and grammar skills were not quite strong. They felt a student had a liberal education in french but more precision was needed to help the student have a better grasp of the language.

[5]   Deciding on which method to adopt in teaching french is an unanswerable task. Choosing one method would satisfy all french students. Researchers have found a certain amount of certains performed will in each method of teaching. Experts in the field of foreign language study feel they are not at liberty to pick a single method because, as mentioned earlier, who is to say which is the best method. Research on the french language continues. There have been many cons found since many feel the purpose of learning a foreign language is the ability to communicate. Researchers have stated there should always be a purpose behind taking the foreign language. The question remains unanswered concerning the most effective method to adopt in teaching a foreign language.

(Holistic score = 1/2)

Writing Myths

All writers are concerned with form to one degree or another. At the elementary and secondary levels, the focus of writing instruction often is on simply producing complete sentences, correct spelling, and correct punctuation. More complex matters related to organization, content, and purpose are ignored or treated inadequately. A focus on form generally involves a reliance on *rules* to explain to students what writing is about. These rules can come to regulate every aspect of writing, such as spelling, the number of paragraphs that make an essay, sentence length, and so on. In some classes, the consequences for violating these rules are dire. A misplaced comma or a misspelled word has been enough to earn more than a few students an F on a given assignment.

Accuracy and correctness in form are important. Also, classroom experiences can be trying, as when a student asks for the 20th time why commas and periods go inside quotation marks rather than outside. It is just easier to tell them, "Because that's the rule!" Nevertheless, we need to keep in mind that a large part of what people do with writing is governed by conventions—conventions of spelling, genre, and punctuation. Rules too commonly are understood as *laws,* which they are not. Conventions are quite arbitrary and therefore changeable. At any point it would be possible to hold a punctuation conference of teachers, writers, and publishers to adopt some alternative to what writers currently use.

Several rules are not matters of convention but rather are outright myths. They seem to get passed on from teacher to student year after year. This appendix is intended to summarize and discuss a few of the more egregious writing myths that nearly everyone has received as absolute truth.

SENTENCE OPENERS

Every year thousands of students are told that they never should begin a sentence with a coordinating conjunction, such as *and, but,* and *for.* They also are told that they never should begin a sentence with the subordinating conjunctions *because* and *since.* The origin of this prohibition probably lies in the fact that many students transfer some speech patterns to writing. Most conversations have a strong narrative element, which means that they consist of strings of actions and events linked chronologically. The most common way to connect these events is through the coordinating conjunction *and.* When students apply conversational patterns to their writing, *and* appears with great frequency. Yet most sentences in written English begin with the subject, not with a coordinator, and teachers may unconsciously be attempting to reduce conversational patterns through the injunction against starting sentences with the conjunction. Although well intentioned, this injunction is wrong because it is incorrect.

With respect to subordination, information supplied by the context of a conversation allows us to use sentences in speech that are shorter than those we characteristically use in writing. Moreover, we often express utterances that are not sentences at all, in the strict sense, but are simply parts of sentences, which in composition we usually term fragments. If, for example, a man were to tell his roommate that he is going to the market in the afternoon, and the roommate were to ask why, most likely the man would respond with: "Because we're out of milk." This response is not a sentence; it is a subordinate clause. It has a subject and a predicate, making it a clause, but the subordinating conjunction *because* makes it a modifier, in this case supplying information related to the reason for going to the market. Because modifiers must modify something, they are dependent, and by definition dependent clauses are not sentences. If the speaker had not taken advantage of context in this exchange, the response to the roommate's question would have been: "I am going to the store because we're out of milk." Here the dependent clause is attached to its independent clause, "I am going to the store." But having already declared the intention to go to the store, the speaker could limit his response to the subordinate clause.

This rather long explanation is designed merely to suggest how prohibitions against certain sentence openers may have originated. The goal may have been to reduce the number of fragments that potentially could be produced when students transfer a pattern very common in speech, like "Because we're out of milk," to writing. Yet the answer to sentence fragments lies in students understanding the nature of sentences, not in arbitrary prohibitions that have no basis in fact. *There simply are no rules, conventions, or laws that decree sentences cannot begin with conjunctions.*

Actually, sentences in English can begin just about any way one chooses, which is apparent to anyone who looks closely at published writing. Authors will open sentences with *and* or *for* or *because* quite regularly. In an unpublished study of sentence openers that I conducted some years ago on 100 well-known authors of fiction and nonfiction, using 500-word excerpted passages, 9% of the sentences began with a coordinating conjunction.

SENTENCE CLOSERS

Teachers also tell students that they never should end a sentence with a preposition—another myth. There is evidence that this myth has circulated for many years; Winston Churchill is reported to have mockingly responded to the injunction against prepositions by saying: "This is the sort of English up with which I will not put." In certain types of constructions, such as questions, English grammar allows for movement of prepositions. The following two sentences, for example, mean the same thing, and both are grammatical:

1. In what did you put the flowers?
2. What did you put the flowers in?

One might argue that Sentence 1 is more formal than Sentence 2, but one cannot argue that it is more correct. Issues of formality have nothing at all to do with correctness; they are related to appropriateness, much like questions of dress. Sentence 1 probably sounds a bit awkward to most readers, and it would sound awkward, and probably incorrect, to elementary and high school students.

The most common situation that might leave a preposition at the end of a sentence occurs when using a relative clause. Relative clauses begin as sentences, and then they are joined to an independent clause. Consider Sentences 3 and 4:

3. Fritz waited for the boat.
4. Macarena arrived on the boat.

These sentences can be combined to provide Sentences 5 or 6:

5. Fritz waited for the boat on which Macarena arrived.
6. Fritz waited for the boat which Macarena arrived on.

The details of relativization can be a bit complex, but essentially the process involves taking a duplicate noun phrase—in this case "the boat"—and replacing it with a relative pronoun. In Sentence 4 "the boat" becomes "which." Notice, however, that the preposition *on* remains. When relativization involves noun phrases at the end of constructions, as in Sentences 3 and 4, English grammar provides the option of shifting the whole prepositional phrase ("on which") to the front of the relative clause *or shifting just the relative pronoun.* The second option produces Sentence 6, which is perfectly grammatical and correct, even though it ends with a preposition.

For inexplicable reasons, people with an overconcern for matters of structure actually spend time thinking up truly ungrammatical constructions that occur when a sentence ends with a preposition. Consider the examples that follow, which are from a popular handbook on writing:

7. It was really funny, the way which he ate in.
8. We gave money for fame and fame for love up.

These sentences are variations of:

7a. It was really funny, the way in which he ate.
8a. We gave up money for fame and fame for love.

The problems here are interesting. The writer of Sentences 7 and 8 actually violated English grammar to produce examples of ungrammatical sentences ending with prepositions. Sentence 7a is understood to begin as two sentences:

7b. The way was really funny.
7c. He ate in a way.

When these are combined through relativization, the result is:

7d. The way in which he ate was really funny.

addition, Sentence 7a has undergone a process known as *topicali-* which increases the focus of the sentence on the funniness of ect's eating. The process involves taking the predicate "was really funny," putting "It" in place as a pseudo subject, and fronting the new construction, "*It* was really funny":

7e. It was really funny/the way in which he ate.

This construction, however, is fundamentally different from the result of combining Sentences 3 and 4 because the noun phrase "the way" was not at the end of both. It was at the beginning of Sentence 7b and at the end of Sentence 7c. Consequently, the preposition cannot be moved—movement simply is not an option here. Thus, Sentence 7 is ungrammatical because the writer made it so, not because it ends with a preposition.

In Sentence 8 the problematic *up* is not even a preposition. It is called a *particle* and is part of the verb *gave*. Although English grammar does allow particles to move, they can do so only under certain conditions, as in the following sentences:

9. Fred looked up the number.
9a. Fred looked the number up.

That is, particles can move *only* to the right of the noun that immediately follows the verb + particle phrase.

Students do have problems with prepositions, especially nonnative speakers. Producing ungrammatical constructions by putting prepositions at the end of sentences, however, is not one of these problems. Because so many English sentences can and do end with a preposition, passing on the myth that they cannot confuses students.

TO BE OR NOT TO BE:
WEAK VERBS/STRONG VERBS

This myth maintains that writers should avoid using forms of *to be*. Very often forms of *to be* are classified as "weak verbs," and all other verb forms are classified as "strong verbs." The idea that some words are better than others lies at the heart of the weak verb–strong verb myth. A kernel of truth exists here, but it is a truth that must be qualified. Words themselves have no value. They only assume value when they are put together with identifiable intentions in specifiable contexts, thereby achieving specifiable effects. The origin of this myth lies, in part, in the tendency of many young writers to focus on two aspects of their individual realities: first, the existence of things, and second, the classification of things. The short essay that follows, written by a sixth grader and presented essentially unedited, illustrates this focus in a typical manner. The assignment asked students to describe an important experience in their lives:

> The Olympics at my school **were** on June 6, 7, 2003. There **was** a lot of different events and I was in a 400 meter relay with three other people. We **were** from South America. we had very fast runers. They **were** Erica, Peter, Jack, and myself and my name is Jason. Peter **was** first to run 100 meters then Erica then Jack, and I **was** anchor. I came in 1st place. It changed the way people felt about me in a positive way. Now I have races againest more people.

The boldface type highlights the various uses of *to be;* we see how this verb form establishes existential relations ("The Olympics at my school were on June 6, 7, 2003") and classifications ("We were from South America"). The difficulty the student faces in focusing on existence and class is that he captures none of the excitement that he assuredly felt when he won his race. His tone is that of a police report or an insurance policy (typical narrative reporting). It is inappropriate for this particular assignment. In this case, the various forms of *to be* simply reflect a much larger problem, one related to the purpose of the writing task. The writer doesn't appear to have a solid grasp of what exactly a description of a memorable event is supposed to do.

A more likely source of the injunction against forms of *to be* is the tradition of the belle lettres essay, which is a literary genre that stands in stark contrast to the utilitarian prose of reports, proposals, and journal articles. From this perspective, the injunction is intended to make student writing more literary. Such a goal would be appropriate if the belletristic genre were not moribund or if the existing need for competent writers of utilitarian prose were not so great. The reality is that most of the writing that people produce is related to business and government, and it relies heavily on forms of *to be* out of sheer necessity. When teachers make artificial distinctions between verb forms based on humanistic preferences, they run the risk of hindering students who need to master a variety of prose forms.

THE POOR PASSIVE

Passive constructions are interesting for several reasons. They allow us, for example, to reverse the most common order of subject–object positions in sentences, as in:

10. Betty kicked the ball.

10a. The ball was kicked by Betty.

Sentence 10 is a simple active sentence, where *Betty* is the subject, *kicked* is the verb, and *the ball* is the object or the recipient of the action conveyed by the verb. *Betty* also is the topic of the sentence. In Sentence 10a, however, the situation is different. The terms *subject, verb,* and *object* still apply, but now there are additional words and Betty is no longer the topic of the sentence—the ball is. Also, there is some question as to whether the meaning of an active sentence changes if one switches it to the passive. In most cases the meaning doesn't appear to change, but in others a strange ambiguity arises:

11. Everyone at the party spoke a foreign language.

11a. A foreign language was spoken by everyone at the party.

Most students are told that they never should use passive constructions, that all sentences should be active, yet as this sentence demonstrates, passives are very useful constructions. They allow for a distancing among writer, object, and agent that is essentially mandatory in some forms of writing and that is tactful and polite in others. They also allow for greater sentence variety. In certain types of writing, lab reports, reports of data collection, and so forth, the passive is required by convention, and to fail to use it is to violate the writing conventions of the disciplines that produce lab reports.

The real problem with student writers is that they frequently use a passive construction when it isn't appropriate or necessary. They will hide subjects or delete them entirely, in part because they are insecure about their work and the passive allows them to equivocate. The role of teachers with respect to passive constructions therefore should not be to issue a universal ban against them but rather to help students understand when passive constructions are useful and necessary.

MISCONCEPTIONS ABOUT SENTENCE LENGTH

Another prevalent myth involves sentence length. Teachers generally tell students that short sentences are better than long ones—that's the myth. They then go on to tell students to make their sentences as short as possible. The basis for the myth as well as the command is shrouded in impenetrable mystery, but it may be connected to an effort on the part of teachers to help students avoid writing run-on sentences.

The research on writing maturity indicates that children's sentences increase in length and complexity as they grow older. Fourth graders in K. Hunt's (1965) study, for example, wrote very long sentences, averaging about 70 words each, because they compounded clauses, generally using the conjunction *and*. The following passage illustrates this sort of compounding. It comes from a sixth grader who was asked to write a response to a recent ban on gum chewing at his school:

> I think children at this school should be able to chew gum and I think it should be for fourth and up because those grades are the more mature grades and they would not spit it on the floor. If you were chewing gum you would not be able to talk but you must throw away your wrappers, and spit out your gum in the trash before recess, lunch, and Physical Education. This morning Rita Brown was chewing gum, the teacher caught her and she didn't get in trouble. You could only chew it, not throw it, or play with it and if it started getting out of hand you could abolish the priviledge.

The sentences in this passage are not especially long, but they tend to be run-on; that is, the student has joined independent clauses with conjunctions, without a comma at each joining. It is easy to see why one might be tempted to tell the student: "Write short sentences!" The student understands where to put a period, if not a comma, so dotting the essay with periods will take care of some of the run-on sentences. However, breaking each of these long sentences into shorter ones simply would trade one problem for another. If the change were made on the basis of independent clauses, the result would be choppy, at best, as we see in the altered version below of the "Rita Brown" sentence:

- This morning Rita Brown was chewing gum. The teacher caught her. She didn't get in trouble.

The effect is a Dick-and-Jane style that becomes virtually unreadable after a paragraph or two.

Francis Christensen (1967) observed that really good writers, professionals who make a living at writing, don't write short sentences. They write long ones, short ones, and some in between. Students, he noted, usually have little trouble with the last two categories, but they have serious difficulty with long sentences, because the tendency is to engage in compounding with *and* and subordinating with *because* until the sentence approaches gibberish. An important task of the writing teacher, in his view, is to help students master long sentences that truly reflect maturity in writing. The key, according to Christensen, lies in short independent clauses that have modifying constructions attached to them, usually following the clause. Sentence 12 illustrates this principle:

12. The misconceptions have existed for decades, being passed from teachers to students, year after year.

The independent clause in Sentence 12 is "The misconceptions have existed for decades," and it is followed by two modifying constructions: "being passed from teachers to students" and "year after year."

Several studies have found a relation between overall writing quality in student essays and sentences that fit the pattern of short independent clause followed by modifiers. These findings suggest that when working with students at the sentence level, teachers should not ask for shorter sentences, but for longer ones with short independent clauses.

CONCLUSION

The attitudes teachers bring to the classroom and the things they tell students have long-lasting effects on their lives. Students seem particularly susceptible to attitudes and assumptions about writing and writing ability. Teachers' attitudes and assumptions become students' attitudes and assumptions. Given the importance of writing, not only to students' education but to their work and place in society, teachers do them a terrible disservice if they perpetuate the misconceptions that prevent a clear understanding of what writing is about. One of the more difficult problems a teacher can face is the student who has come to believe that he or she can't write and, moreover, can't learn to write. Too often this false assumption is accompanied by a set of "rules" related to sentence structure that can lead to so much attention to form that ideas never have a chance to be developed. Nothing of worth gets written, and the student reinforces his or her own sense of defeat.

As stated at the outset, this appendix discusses only some of the myths that surround writing. The purpose here was not to be comprehensive but to provide a starting point for discussion and learning, to stimulate readers to examine critically their own understanding of what writing is about. It is often said that teachers teach just the way they themselves were taught, and this observation may explain in part why the myths in this appendix have been handed down from generation to generation. In trying to dispel them, this appendix dares readers to become risk takers, to challenge their preconceptions about writing.

Sample Essays

The following essays are offered for the purpose of practice evaluations. They were written in class by a group of high school seniors in
Southern California who had studied argumentative strategies in English class. They had 45 minutes to complete the task. For several weeks
before the assignment, the community and the campus had been talking about establishing a smoking area for students who smoke. The
proposal was controversial because it is illegal in California for anyone
under 18 to buy, possess, or use tobacco. Thus, the school would be
condoning an illegal activity were it to establish the smoking area.
 The writing assignment was as follows:

> The school principal is proposing to establish a smoking area on campus
> for students who smoke. In an argumentative essay, take a stand either
> for or against this proposal. Completed essays will be forwarded to the
> principal for his consideration. Be certain to state your position clearly
> after providing appropriate background information. Provide good rea-
> sons or support for your position, using convincing details. Finally, in-
> clude a conclusion that states the significance of the topic for the whole
> campus.

Essay 1

On Campus Smoking

[1] The fact that more students than ever before are smoking on campus has caused a lot of discussion among students and teachers. Our
school newspaper, The Scroll, even ran a series of articles about it. On
the one hand, smoking is illegal for anyone under 18, so students who
smoke, and teachers who let them, are breaking the law. On the other

hand, by the time a person reaches high school he/she is old enough to make some decisions on his own, so restricting smoking may be a limitation on his/her rights.

[2]   Now the district is toying with the idea of setting up a special area for smokers. The aim is to clear out the restrooms, which would reduce the fire hazard that comes from students lighting up around wastepaper bins that are often overflowing, and to put an end to the silly game of "hide and seek" played out between students and teachers. The students hide to have their cigarettes, and the teachers try to find them.

[3]   There's no doubt that the idea seems initially to make sense. Students could be open about their habit. They wouldn't have to sneak around behind the gym or in the restrooms to have a smoke. Non-smokers would really appreciate being able to walk into the restrooms without choking on the smoke-filled air. Smokers wouldn't have to dodge cars as they rush across the street to Paris Liqour to grab a quick one between classes, which means they would have fewer tardies. They could simply step over to the smoking area, have their cigarette, then go on about their business. Everyone would be happier: students, teachers, and administrators.

[4]   What all these good arguments ignore, however, is that existing California law prohibits minors from buying, possessing, or smoking cigarettes. That law isn't likely to change in the near future, considering the clear health problems tobacco causes. Until the law does change, the school district is really in no position to even propose a smoking area, unless administrators want to put themselves in the awkward position of aiding and encouraging criminal behavior among students. That's a bad position to be in, and it comes from their considering a bad idea.

Essay 2

[1]   Our school newspaper recently reported that the school district is thinking about setting aside a special area for smokers. I think this is good idea because so many students at W.H.S. smoke. They smoke out in the parking lot or in the restrooms. They smoke out behind the gym or across the street at the liqour store. There are probably more smokers at this school than there are nonsmokers.

[2]   The simple truth is that if a teenager wants to smoke there's no way to stop him/her. I know that a lot of parents don't want their kids to smoke, but the kids do it anyway. They are always willing to take a chance of getting caught whenever they want to smoke, because they are as addicted to their cigarettes as a junky is to heroine. Talking to them isn't going to help, neither is having teachers chase them out of the restrooms. All that does is make them resent their teachers more than they already do and make them dispise school more than they already do.

[3] In some ways it's like so many other things that adults do but don't want teenagers to do. Sex is a good example. Grown ups are all the time telling teenagers they shouldn't have sex, but we do anyway because it feels good and we figure we're old enough to make our own decision about it. And there sure aren't many adults who would give up sex. Sex isn't bad for us if we're in the Pill, so it's our decision regarding what we want to do with our bodies. Alcohol is another example. Adults are always telling us not to drink, that it's bad for us, but those same adults will have a drink before dinner, wine with their meal, and then a nightcap before going to bed.

[4] Smoking is a little more complex because it is bad for our health. But its our lungs and our health problems. In fact, the smoking area would let us smoke away from nonsmokers, so that our cigarettes don't pollute the air for them. All in all, it's a good idea. We are old enough to decide what to do with our bodies. We're going to do it anyway because we're addicted. And it would be good for nonsmokers.

Essay 3

I Don't Think There Should Be a Smoking Area

[1] It seems that everyday we hear another report on the news about how bad smoking is for smokers and nonsmokers around them. Now the principal's office is thinking about putting in a smoking area at Westminster High School. In my opinion, this would be a mistake, and in this essay I'll point out some of the reasons why.

[2] First, the school would in effect be encouraging students to smoke if it set aside this special area. Given the fact that smoking is illegal as well as the fact that it causes lung cancer, heart disease, and emfazima, smokers should be given help to kick their habit. They shouldn't be told by their school that it's o.k. to ruin their health and comit a crime.

[3] Second, we know that cigarette smoke is not only bad for smokers— it's bad for people. who don't smoke but who just happen to be standing around. If there was a spot on campus for smokers, what would their nonsmoking friends do? The smokers would probably smoke more freely and more often, which means that they would spend all their free time in the "smoking zone." Their nonsmoking friends sure wouldn't want to be around all that smoke, so they would stay away. The result would be that the smokers and the nonsmokers would rarely talk to each other. Friendships might end, and that wouldn't be good for anyone. As it is now, smokers have to sneak a quick smoke between classes or at lunch, so their nonsmoking friends have time to be with them.

[4] Finally, a lot of students probably wouldn't use the smoking zone because they would just go back to smoking where they usually do. A lot of students smoke at certain places where they can meet their friends be-

fore and after school. Most of them have been doing this for a long time. Why would they change now?

[5]   In this essay I have expressed my opinion on a smoking area on campus. As you can see, there are many different reasons why there shouldn't be a smoking spot. It's just a bad idea.

Essay 4

Smoking in the Schools

[1]   I think people have a right to smoke, as long as it doesn't bother others, and I would not mind if the schools set up a special place for smokers if the smoke did not effect the other people in the school. If a place for smokers was provided then smokers might stop smoking around people who don't smoke. This is important because many people are allergic to smoke and some of them could become sick.

[2]   The place set aside for smokers should in some way keep the smoke away from other areas so that it will not bother other people. We see this all the time in restaurants. In fact, it is now a law that restaurants must have a nonsmoking area for people who don't smoke. If someone comes in with a cigarette, they have to sit in the smokers area. If the smoke still bothers someone in the restaurant, the smoker has to put out the cigarette or leave the restaurant. I work at Denny's on weekends and we have this happen all the time. Sometimes the smoker gets mad and refuses to put out the cigarette, but then the manager comes and forces him to either put it out or to leave.

[3]   This is a good idea because smoke causes so many diseases and it smells so bad. When I have to work the smoking section I come home with cigarette smoke on my clothes and in my hair. It doesn't do any good to wear a nice perfume because the smoke kills the fragrance so that all anyone can smell is cigarettes. Well the same thing happens at school in the restrooms because of all the girls in there sneaking a smoke. I come out stinking.

[4]   As I say, people have the right to smoke, but only if it doesn't bother anyone else. If the place on campus is set up for smokers and the smoke bothers the nonsmokers, then the smoking area should be removed and smoking should be stopped in the school altogether.

Essay 5

[1]   Smokers seem to be everywhere on this campus. A person can't even go to the toilet without having to wade through clouds of smoke puffed into the air by all the guys hanging out in the restrooms sneaking a cigarette. A designated smoking area might put an end to this

problem, but in my opinion it would create more trouble than it's worth.

[2]   Let's face it, smoking is a dirty habit that's not only bad for the person smoking but that's bad for the health of any innocent bystanders. In addition, it's illegal for minors to smoke. They aren't even supposed to have cigarettes. So what is the school going to do, help students break the law? That's stupid.

[3]   Also, think of what a mess a smoking area would be. In my experience smokers are basically inconsiderate slobs. Rather than use an ashtray, most of them will just drop a butt on the floor. They also don't care where they put their ashes. They'll drop them anywhere. Concentrate a bunch of smokers in one small area, and you'll not only have ashes and butts to contend with, you'll have burned out matches and empty cartons everywhere. If you think convenient trash containers will help, you don't know many smokers. The result will be that our school will look trashy, which would bring the whole schools reputation down.

[4]   In all respects, of course, the area would be condouning the illegal possession and use of cigarettes by minors. Those who aren't of age are prohibited by law from buying cigarettes. So why should they be allowed to smoke them on campus? What would the parents of these children think if they didn't allow their son or daughter to smoke, only to find out later that the school districts not only allow them to smoke on campus, but even set up a reserved area for them? I don't think the parent would find this at all amusing.

[5]   And finally, there's the second hand smoke. Not only is smoke bad for the smoker but tests show that the second hand smoke is twice as bad for a person to breathe than what is going directly into the lungs of the smoker. If you concentrate all the smokers on this campus in one spot, you're going to generate a whole lot of smoke, and there's no way you're going to prevent it from affecting others. This means that the district would be endangering the lives and well being of innocent bystanders. Those who don't smoke would be getting a bad deal, and the school would be opening itself up to potential law suites.

[6]   Given all these reasons, I feel that to allow smoking on campus isn't right and shouldn't even be considered.

Essay 6

Smoking on Campus

[1]   The peer pressure applied on students in high school is very hard to cope with. Some people can ignore it, but most cannot. Those who are unfortunate get pulled into doing drugs, promiscuos sex, smoking, and other illegal acts. Probably the worst pressure would be to begin smoking, because unlike drugs it is more or less socially acceptable, and unlike

promiscuos sex it is harmful. Cigarette smoking is proven to cause cancer and heart disease. The problem is that teens either don't know this or they don't believe it, so they experiment. This is where the problem starts, because once they try it they get addicted. I therefore feel that giving students a place to smoke is wrong because it will only encourage more students to smoke because of the peer pressure. It may also encourage teens to loiter, and it may turn into a "hang out" where kids can sell and take drugs.

[2]   Teens are already under a lot of peer pressure and giving them a place to smoke is almost like saying, "smoking is what everybody does." Every time they get bored they'll go out to smoke a cigarette. This will probably be thier biggest reason for being tardy to class and for ditching or cutting class. It already is, of course, with teens hanging out in the restrooms and behind the gym. But it could be worse. Also, there is no guarante that this will stop students from smoking where they're not allowed.

[3]   Instead of adding to the problem, the school should be trying to do something about it. It should be trying to get teens off cigarettes. It should work on a way of controlling students urge to smoke, ending the addiction. Maybe then some of these students would concentrate more on learning rather than on sneaking another smoke.

Essay 7

Essay

[1]   I think it would be all right if we had a smoking area on campus. I think then the kids wouldn't go the liquor store and smoke there. It would be a good idea to get the smokers out in the open so the teachers could talk to them about quiting the habbit. This idea is to the bennafit of the people that smok, so they would support this idea.

[2]   On the other hand, I think that the smokers only smok to get atention. And having a smok area at school will only make it almost right for the High school kids to smoke Also they would incorage the people that don't smok to smok too. Then you would just have more of a problum with smoking at Westminster High school. I also think it's a fier hazzard and we shouldnt have that at our school We have enof to worrie about without this idea.

[3]   It is my opinion that there should be a smoking area on campus. If they want to muss up their lives by smoking it all right with me. I think it would be graet to teach the smokers the hard way just because they want to fit in. That way I think people suold be alowed to smok wereever they want or they suold stop selling cijrettes all together and take care of this problum once and for all!!

Essay 8

[1]   Upon entering high school students are faced with several important decisions. Among these decisions is whether or not to smoke. There
is much pressure put upon the adolescences by their peers to "light up"
with most parents having the oppisite veiws. Caught in the middle of this
heated battle are the schools. A recent proposition made by the schools is
to set aside an area for smoking on the schoolgrounds. Does this mean
the school is condoning smoking? Yes, to a very large degree it does. If
the students are given this area to use for smoking more students will begin "lighting up." There is no useful reason for such an area, and much
to the dismay of many parents this proposition may someday come into
affect.

[2]   With the awareness of the cancer-causing affects of the cigarettes
the schools should be condemning their use. On each package reads a
warning label to warn off that person from using the harmful product,
yet millions of teenagers and adults alike, are still smoking. Doctors
warn of serious results from smoking, such as lung cancer, deadening of
the cilia that line the throat, and several others as well. Yet still we keep
smoking. If areas are set aside in our schools we are leading our children
into an addiction from which some may never return. The cons far
outweight the pros in this situation, especially those from a medical
stand point.

[3]   The future of these smoking teenagers is a factor as well. Studies
have shown that smoking takes as much as five years off the life of a
smoker, and that of those who begun smoking in their teens fewer were
able to quit. Some of these students may die of cancer before attaining
their goals, and take away the contributions they might have put forth.

Essay 9

Smoking Area

[1]   I think setting aside an area on campus for students who smoke on
their break is the most absurd idea I have ever heard. Smoking is bad
enough already as it is and to even encourage it is something school administrators shouldn't be involved in. Most of the teenagers who smoke
are too young. A person cannot purchase cigarettes legally until they are
eighteen years of age, even though most liquor stores sell them to children well under the legal age.

[2]   By establishing this area on campus, smoking would be encouraged
more among teenagers because it would be accepted. In no way would
this eliminate smoke; high schoolers have thirty-five minutes of lunch to
go off campus and smoke to their heart's content. Being an occasional
smoker myself, I know that is plenty of time to have a few cigarettes.
When there is an urge, even though seldom, I get tempted to spend class
in a bathroom stall puffing on a cigarette, so somethimes I do. I never get

caught, and if I did it wouldn't be a big deal like possession of drugs such as marijuana, alcohol, cocain, etc.

[3]   Smoking is a major cause of many diseases, we all know. So why should teachers, administrators, and the campus police augment the growth and popularity of smoking by providing a "special" place for teens to practice their habit? Many people die each year of cigarette-related deaths. Smoking causes cancer, emphysema, high blood pressure and underweight babies at birth. These deadly diseases wouldn't show up in teenagers immediately, but in ten or twenty years from now, many more people would be dying because smoking was accepted so much in the one place where drugs and alcohol weren't. And that's saying to students that smoking is okay.

References

Abbott, V., Black, J., & Smith, E. (1985). The representation of scripts in memory. *Journal of Memory and Language, 24,* 179–199.

Abedi, J., Hofstetter, D., & Baker, E. (2001). *NAEP math performance and test accommodations: Interactions with student language background* (CSE Tech. Rep. No. 536). Los Angeles: National Center for Research on Evaluation, Standards, and Student Testing, University of California, Los Angeles.

Ackerman, J. (1993). The promise of writing to learn. *Written Communication, 10,* 334–370.

Adams, M., Treiman, R., & Pressley, M. (1998). Reading, writing, and literacy. In I. Sigel & K. Renninger (Eds.), *Handbook of child psychology: Child psychology in practice* (5th ed., Vol. 4, pp. 275–355). New York: Wiley.

Addison, R., & Homme, L. (1965). The reinforcement of event (RE) menu. *National Society for Programmed Instruction Journal, 5,* 89.

Albano, T. (1991). The effect of interest on reading comprehension and written discourse (Doctoral dissertation, Hofstra University, 1991). *Dissertation Abstracts International, 53,* 111A.

Allen, J. (1992). Discerning communities: Uniting theory and practice in the social epistemic composition class (Doctoral dissertation, University of South Carolina, 1992). *Dissertation Abstracts International, 53,* 2718A.

Amastae, J. (1981). The writing needs of Hispanic students. In B. Cronnell (Ed.), *The writing needs of linguistically different students.* Washington, DC: SWRL Educational Research and Development.

Amastae, J. (1984). The Pan-American Project. In J. Ornstein-Galicia (Ed.), *Form and function in Chicano English.* Rowley, MA: Newbury House.

Anastasi, A. (1980). Culture-free testing. In G. Lindzey (Ed.), *A history of psychology in autobiography* (Vol. 7). San Francisco: Freeman.

Aristotle. (1975). *The "art" of rhetoric* (J. Freese, Trans.). Cambridge, MA: Harvard University Press.

Artz, F. (1980). *The mind of the Middle Ages.* Chicago: University of Chicago Press.

Ashton, P. (1984). Teacher efficacy: A motivational paradigm for effective teacher education. *Journal of Teacher Education, 35,* 28–32.

Ashton-Warner, S. (1963). *Teacher.* New York: Simon & Schuster.

Austin, J. (1962). *How to do things with words.* Cambridge, MA: Harvard University Press.

Bain, A. (1866). *English composition and rhetoric.* New York: D. Appleton.

Baker, W., Prideaux, G., & Derwin, B. (1973). Grammatical properties of sentences as a basis for concept formation. *Journal of Psycholinguistic Research, 2,* 201–220.

Bamberg, B. (1983). What makes a text coherent? *College Composition and Communication, 34,* 417–429.

Bateman, D., & Zidonis, F. (1966). *The effect of a study of transformational grammar on the writing of ninth and tenth graders.* Champaign, IL: National Council of Teachers of English.

Bates, E. (1976). *Language and context.* New York: Academic Press.

Bates, E. (1979). *The emergence of symbols: Cognition and communication in infancy.* New York: Academic Press.

Bates, E., Camaioni, C., & Volterra, V. (1975). *Comunicazione nel primo anno di vita* [Communication in the first year of life]. Rome: Mulino.

Baudrillard, J. (1988). *America* (C. Turner, Trans.). London: Verso.

Baugh, J. (1983). *Black street speech: Its history, structure, and survival.* Austin: University of Texas Press.

Baugh, J. (1984). *Language in use: Readings in sociolinguistics.* Englewood Cliffs, NJ: Prentice-Hall.

Beach, R., & Liebman-Kleine, J. (1986). The writing/reading relationship: Becoming one's own best reader. In B. Petersen (Ed.), *Convergences: Transactions in reading and writing.* Urbana, IL: National Council of Teachers of English.

Beck, F. (1964). *Greek education, 450–359 B.C.* New York: Barnes & Noble.

Beers, D. (1996). *Blue sky dream: A memoir of America's fall from grace.* New York: Harcourt Brace.

Beesley, M. (1986). The effects of word processing on elementary students' written compositions: Processes, products, and attitudes (Doctoral dissertation, Indiana University, 1986). *Dissertation Abstracts International, 47,* 11A.

Belanoff, P. (1991). The myths of assessment. *Journal of Basic Writing, 10,* 54–67.

Benard, B. (1995). Fostering resiliency in urban schools. In B. Williams (Ed.), *Closing the achievement gap: A vision to guide change in beliefs and practice.* Oak Brook, IL: Research for Better Schools and North Central Regional Educational Library.

Berlin, J. (1982). Contemporary composition: The major pedagogical theories. *College English, 44,* 765–777.

Berlin, J. (1990). Writing instruction in school and college English, 1890–1985. In J. Murphy (Ed.), *A short history of writing instruction from ancient Greece to twentieth-century America.* New York: Hermagoras Press.

Berlin, J. (1992a). Freirean pedagogy in the U.S.: A response. *Journal of Advanced Composition, 12,* 414–421.

Berlin, J. (1992b). Poststructuralism, cultural studies, and the composition classroom: Postmodern theory in practice. *Rhetoric Review, 11,* 16–33.

Berthoff, A. (1981). *The making of meaning: Metaphors, models, and maxims for writing teachers.* Montclair, NJ: Boynton/Cook.

Berthoff, A. (1983). A comment on inquiry and composing. *College English, 45,* 605–606.

Berthoff, A. (1990). Killer dichotomies: Reading in/reading out. In K. Ronald & H. Roskelly (Eds.), *Farther along: Transforming dichotomies in rhetoric and composition.* Montclair, NJ: Boynton/Cook.

Bever, T. (1970). The cognitive basis of linguistic structures. In J. Hayes (Ed.), *Cognition and the development of language* (pp. 273–312). New York: Wiley.

Bilingual Education Act. (1968). *United States Statutes at Large, 81,* 817.

Bissex, B. (1980). Patterns of development in writing: A case study. *Theory Into Practice, 19,* 197–201.

Bizzell, P. (1982). Cognition, convention, and certainty: What we need to know about writing. *PRE/TEXT, 3,* 213–243.

Bizzell, P. (1984). William Perry and liberal education. *College English, 46,* 447–454.

Bizzell, P. (1987). What can we know, what must we do, what may we hope: Writing assessment. *College English, 49,* 575–584.

Bizzell, P. (1992). *Academic discourse and critical consciousness.* Pittsburgh, PA: University of Pittsburgh Press.

Blanding, M. (1997). A brief history of carnivals. *JINN.* Retrieved June 1, 2002, from www.pacificnews.org/jinn/stories/3.17/970814-carnival.html.

Bleich, D. (1995). Collaboration and the pedagogy of disclosure. *College English, 57,* 43–61.

Bloom, B. (1956). *Taxonomy of educational objectives: The classification of educational goals.* New York: David McKay.

Bloom, L. (1970). *Language development: Form and function in emerging grammars.* Cambridge, MA: MIT Press.

Bloom, L. (1973). *One word at a time: The use of single-word utterances before syntax.* The Hague, Netherlands: Mouton.

Bloomfield, L. (1933). *Language.* New York: Holt, Rinehart & Winston.

Bluck, R. (Ed.). (1947). *Plato's seventh and eighth letters.* Cambridge, England: Cambridge University Press.

Boas, F. (1911). *Handbook of American Indian languages.* Washington, DC: Smithsonian Institution.

Boethius. (1978). *De topicis differentiis* [Topics] (E. Stump, Ed. & Trans.). Ithaca, NY: Cornell University Press.

Bonner, S. (1977). *Education in ancient Rome: From the elder Cato to the younger Pliny.* Berkeley: University of California Press.

Booth, W. (1965). The revival of rhetoric. *PMLA, 80,* 139–145.

Borke, H. (1975). Piaget's mountains revisited: Changes in the egocentric landscape. *Developmental Psychology, 11,* 240–443.

Braddock, R., Lloyd-Jones, R., & Schoer, L. (1963). *Research in written composition.* Champaign, IL: National Council of Teachers of English.

Britton, J., Burgess, T., Martin, N., McLeod, A., & Rosen, H. (1975). *The development of writing abilities (11–18).* London: Macmillan Education Ltd.

Broad, B. (2000). Pulling your hair out: Crises of standardization in communal writing assessment. *Research in the Teaching of English, 35,* 213–260.

Broca, P. (1861). Remarques sur le siège de la faculté du langage articulé, suivies d'une observation d'amphemie (perte de la parole) [Remarks on the seat of the faculty of language articulation, following an observation of the loss of speech]. *Bulletin de la Société Anatomique, 36,* 330–357.

Brook, J., Nomura, C., & Cohen, P. (1989). A network of influences on adolescent drug involvement: Neighborhood, school, peer, and family. *Genetic, Social, and General Psychology Monographs, 115,* 303–321.

Brown, P. (1967). *Augustine of Hippo: A biography* (Reprinted 2000). Berkeley: University of California Press.

Brown, P. (1987). Late antiquity. In P. Ariès & G. Duby (Eds.), *A history of private life: Vol. 1. From pagan Rome to Byzantium.* Cambridge, MA: Harvard University Press.

Bruck, M., Lambert, W., & Tucker, G. (1974). Bilingual schooling through the elementary grades: The St. Lambert project at grade seven. *Language Learning, 24,* 183–204.

Bruffee, K. (1993). *Collaborative learning.* Baltimore: Johns Hopkins University Press.

Cairns, R. (1983). The emergence of developmental psychology: In P. Mussen (Ed.), *Handbook of child psychology: Vol. 1. History, theory, and methods.* New York: Wiley.

Callinicos, A. (1988). *Making history: Agency, structure, and change in social theory.* Ithaca, NY: Cornell University Press.

Caputo, J. D. (1996). *Deconstruction in a nutshell: A conversation with Jacques Derrida.* New York: Fordham University Press.

Carey, S. (1985). *Conceptual changes in childhood.* Cambridge, MA: MIT Press.

Carini, P. (1982). *The school lives of seven children: A five year study.* Grand Forks: University of North Dakota Press.

Carlson, N. (1994). *The physiology of behavior, 5th edition.* Needham Heights, MA: Allyn & Bacon.

Case, R. (1985). *Intellectual development: Birth to adulthood.* New York: Academic Press.

Case, R. (1991). *The mind's staircase: Exploring the conceptual underpinnings of children's thought and knowledge.* Hillsdale, NJ: Lawrence Erlbaum Associates.

Chall, J. (1996). American reading achievement: Should we worry? *Research in the Teaching of English, 30,* 303–310.

Chauvin, P. (1990). *A chronicle of the last pagans* (B. Archer, Trans.). Cambridge, MA: Harvard University Press.

Chomsky, N. (1957). *Syntactic structures.* The Hague, Netherlands: Mouton.

Chomsky, N. (1965). *Aspects of the theory of syntax.* Cambridge, MA: MIT Press.

Chomsky, N. (1972). *Language and mind.* New York: Harcourt Brace.

Chomsky, N. (1975). *Reflections on language.* New York: Pantheon.

Chomsky, N. (1979). *Language and responsibility.* New York: Pantheon.

Chomsky, N. (1980). *Rules and representations.* New York: Columbia University Press.

Chomsky, N. (1981). *Lectures on government and binding.* Dordrecht, Netherlands: Foris.

Chomsky, N. (1986). *Knowledge of language.* New York: Praeger.

Chomsky, N. (1988). *Generative grammar: Its basis, development, and prospects* [A special issue of *Studies in English Linguistics and Literature*]. Kyoto, Japan: Kyoto University of Foreign Studies.

Chomsky, N. (1992). *A minimalist program for linguistic theory.* Cambridge, MA: MIT Department of Linguistics.

Chomsky, N. (1995). *The minimalist program.* Cambridge, MA: MIT Press.

Christensen, F. (1967). *Notes toward a new rhetoric: Six essays for teachers.* New York: Harper & Row.

Christiansen, T., & Livermore, G. (1970). A comparison of Anglo-American and Spanish-American children on the WISC. *Journal of Social Psychology, 81,* 914.

Cicero. (1970). De oratore [On oratory]. In J. Watson (Ed. & Trans.), *Cicero on oratory and orators.* Carbondale: Southern Illinois University Press.

Cicero. (1978). *Letters to Atticus* (D. R. Shackleton Baily, Trans.). Harmondsworth, England: Penguin Books.

Cimbricz, S. (2002). State-mandated testing and teachers' beliefs and practice. *Education Policy Analysis Archives, 10.* Retrieved May 28, 2002, from http://epaa.asu.edu/epaa/v10n2.html.

Clark, A. (1993). *Associative engines: Connectionism, concepts, and representational change.* Cambridge, MA: MIT Press.

Clark, E. (1980). Here's the top: Nonlinguistic strategies in the acquisition of orientational terms. *Child Development, 51,* 329–338.

Clark, G. (1994). Rescuing the discourse community. *College Composition and Communication, 45,* 61–74.

Clark, H., & Clark, E. (1977). *Psychology and language.* New York: Harcourt Brace.

Clark, I. (2002). Reconsideration of genre. In J. Williams (Ed.), *Visions and revisions: Continuity and change in rhetoric and composition* (pp. 89–108). Carbondale: Southern Illinois University Press.

Cohen, E. (1994). Restructuring the classroom: Conditions for productive small groups. *Review of Educational Research, 64,* 1–35.

Colby, B., & Cole, M. (1976). Culture, memory and narrative. In R. Horton & R. Finnigan (Eds.), *Modes of thought.* New York: Academic Press.

Coles, W., & Vopat, J. (1985). *What makes writing good.* Lexington, MA: Heath.

Conley, T. (1990). *Rhetoric in the European tradition.* New York: Longman.

Connors, R., & Lunsford, A. (1993). Teachers' rhetorical comments on student papers. *College Composition and Communication, 44,* 200–223.

Conrad, R. (1972). Speech and reading. In J. Ravanaugh & I. Mattingly (Eds.), *Language by ear and eye.* Cambridge, MA: MIT Press.

Cooper, M. (1986). The ecology of writing. *College English, 48,* 364–375.

Corrigan, R. (1978). Language development as related to stage 6 object permanence development. *Journal of Child Language, 5,* 173–189.

Coulson, A. (1996). Schooling and literacy over time: The rising cost of stagnation and decline. *Research in the Teaching of English, 30,* 311–327.

Courts, P. (1991). *Literacy and empowerment: The meaning makers.* New York: Bergin & Garvey.

Crawford, J., & Haaland, C. (1972). Predecisional information seeking and subsequent conformity in the social influence process. *Journal of Personality and Social Psychology, 23,* 112–119.

Crowley, S. (1990). *The methodical memory: Invention in current–traditional rhetoric.* Carbondale: Southern Illinois University Press.

Cummins, J. (1976). The influence of bilingualism on cognitive growth: A synthesis of research findings and explanatory hypothesis. *Working Papers on Bilingualism, 9,* 143.

Cummins, J. (1988). The cross-lingual dimensions of language proficiency: Implications for bilingual education and the optional age issue. *TESOL Quarterly, 2,* 175–187.

Curwin, R. (1992). *Rediscovering hope: Our greatest teaching strategy.* Bloomington, IN: National Educational Service.

Day, P., & Ulatowska, H. (1979). Perceptual, cognitive, and linguistic development after early hemispherectomy: Two case studies. *Brain and Language, 7,* 17–33.

DeLoache, J., Miller, K., & Pierroutsakos, S. (1998). Reasoning and problem-solving. In D. Kuhn & R. Siegler (Eds.), *Handbook of child psychology* (Vol. 2, pp. 801–850). New York: Wiley.

Delpit, L. (1988). The silenced dialogue: Power and pedagogy in educating other people's children. *Harvard Educational Review, 58,* 280–298.

Dennis, M., & Kohn, B. (1975). Comprehension of syntax in infantile hemiplegics after cerebral hemidecortication: Left hemisphere superiority. *Brain and Language, 2,* 475–486.

Dennis, M., & Whitaker, H. (1976). Language acquisition following hemidecortication: Linguistic superiority of the left over the right hemisphere of right-handed people. *Brain and Language, 3,* 404–433.

Derrida, J. (1976). *Of grammatology* (G. Spivak, Trans.). Baltimore: Johns Hopkins University Press.

De Ste. Croix, G. (1981). *The class struggle in the ancient world.* Ithaca, NY: Cornell University Press.

Diaz, D. (1986). The writing process and the ESL writer: Reinforcement from second language research. *Writing Instructor, 5,* 167–175.

Diederich, P., French, J., & Carlton, S. (1961). *Factors in judgments of writing quality.* Princeton: Educational Testing Service. (ERIC Document Reproduction Service No. ED002172).

Dillard, J. (1973). *Black English: Its history and usage in the United States.* New York: Vintage Books.

Dillon, G. (1981). *Constructing texts: Elements of a theory of composition and style.* Bloomington: Indiana University Press.

Docker, J. (1994). *Postmodernism and popular culture: A cultural history.* Cambridge, England: Cambridge University Press.

Dodds, E. (1951). *The Greeks and the irrational.* Berkeley: University of California Press.

Donaldson, M. (1978). *Children's minds.* London: Fontana.

Dulay, H., Burt, M., & Krashen, S. (1982). *Language two.* New York: Oxford University Press.

Duncan, S., & DeAvila, E. (1979). Bilingualism and cognition: Some recent findings. *NABE Journal, 4,* 15–50.

Eco, U., Ivanov, V., & Rector, M. (1984). Frames of comic freedom. In T. Sebeok (Ed.), *Carnival!* Amsterdam: Mouton.

Edelsky, C. (1986). *Writing in a bilingual program: Había una vez.* Norwood, NJ: Ablex.

Edfelt, A. (1960). *Silent speech and silent reading.* Chicago: University of Chicago Press.

Edmonds, R. (1986). Characteristics of effective schools. In U. Neisser (Ed.), *The school achievement of minority children: New perspectives.* Hillsdale, NJ: Lawrence Erlbaum Associates.

Elbow, P. (1973). *Writing without teachers.* New York: Oxford University Press.

Elbow, P. (1981). *Writing with power.* New York: Oxford University Press.

Elbow, P., Berlin, J., & Bazerman, C. (1991). The second stage in writing across the curriculum. *College English, 53,* 209–212.

Elley, W., Barham, I., Lamb, H., & Wyllie, M. (1976). The role of grammar in a secondary school English curriculum. *New Zealand Journal of Educational Studies, 10,* 26–42. (Reprinted in *Research in the Teaching of English, 10,* 5–21).

Emig, J. (1971). *The composing process of twelfth graders.* Urbana, IL: National Council of Teachers of English.

Englehard, G., Gordon, B., & Gabrielson, S. (1992). The influences of mode of discourse, experiential demand, and gender on the quality of student writing. *Research in the Teaching of English, 26,* 315–336.

Enos, R. (1993). *Greek rhetoric before Aristotle.* Prospect Heights, IL: Waveland Press.

Enos, R. (1995). *Roman rhetoric: Revolution and the Greek influence.* Prospect Heights, IL: Waveland Press.

Erickson, F. (1984). Rhetoric, anecdote, and rhapsody: Coherence strategies in a conversation among black American adolescents. In D. Tannen (Ed.), *Coherence in spoken and written discourse* (pp. 81–154). Norwood, NJ: Ablex.

Eunapiaus. (1922). *Lives of the philosophers* (W. Wright, Trans.). London: Heinemann.

Everitt, A. (2001). *Cicero: The life and times of Rome's greatest politician.* New York: Random House.

Faigley, L. (1992). *Fragments of rationality: Postmodernity and the subject of composition.* Pittsburgh, PA: University of Pittsburgh Press.

Faigley, L., Cherry, R., Joliffe, D, & Skinner, A. (1985). *Assessing writers' knowledge and processes of composing.* Norwood, NJ: Ablex.

Farr, M., & Daniels, H. (1986). *Language diversity and writing instruction.* Urbana, IL: National Council of Teachers of English.

Farr, M., & Janda, M. (1985). Basic writing students: Investigating oral and written language. *Research in the Teaching of English, 19,* 62–83.

Farr Whitemann, M. (Ed.). (1981). *Variation in writing: Functional and linguistic-cultural differences.* Hillsdale, NJ: Lawrence Erlbaum Associates.

Fasold, R. (1972). *Tense marking in Black English: A linguistic and social analysis.* Washington, DC: Center for Applied Linguistics.

Faulconer, J. (1998). *Deconstruction.* Retrieved April 22, 2002, from http://jamesfaulconer.byu.edu/deconstruction.html.

Finnegan, R. (1970). *Oral literature in Africa.* London: Oxford University Press.

Fitts, K., & France, A. (Eds.). (1995). *Left margins: Cultural studies and composition pedagogy.* Albany: State University of New York Press.

Flavell, J., Botkin, P., Fry, C., Wright, J., & Jarvis, P. (1968). *The development of role-taking and communication skills in children.* New York: Wiley.

Flesch, R. (1955). *Why Johnny can't read—and what you can do about it.* New York: Harper.

Fleming, D. (2002). The end of composition–rhetoric. In J. Williams (Ed.), *Visions and revisions: Continuity and change in rhetoric and composition* (pp. 109–130). Carbondale: Southern Illinois University Press.

Flower, L., & Hayes, J. (1981). The pregnant pause: An inquiry into the nature of planning. *Research in the Teaching of English, 15,* 229–243.

Fodor, J. (1983). *The modularity of mind.* Cambridge, MA: MIT Press.

Fodor, J., Bever, T., & Garrett, M. (1974). *The psychology of language.* New York: McGraw-Hill.

Fodor, J., & Garrett, M. (1966). Some reflections on competence and performance. In J. Lyons & R. Wales (Eds.), *Psycholinguistics papers: Proceedings of the 1966 Edinburgh Conference.* Edinburgh, Scotland: Edinburgh University Press.

Foster, S. (1985, March). The development of discourse topic skills by infants and young children. *Topics in Language Disorders,* pp. 31–45.

Foucault, M. (1978). *The history of sexuality* (R. Harley, Trans.). New York: Pantheon.

Foucault, M. (1979). *Discipline and punish: The birth of the prison* (A. Sheridan, Trans.). New York: Vintage.

France, A. (2000). Dialectics of self: Structure and agency as the subject of English. *College English, 63,* 145–165.

Freire, P., & Macedo, D. (1987). *Literacy: Reading the word and the world.* South Hadley, MA: Bergin & Garvey.

Fukuyama, F. (1992). *The end of history and the last man.* New York: The Free Press.

Fukuyama, F. (1999). *The great disruption: Human nature and the reconstruction of social order.* New York: The Free Press.

Fukuyama, F. (2002). *Our posthuman future: Consequences of the biotechnology revolution.* New York: Farrar, Straus, and Giroux.

Furth, H. (1966). *Thinking without language: Psychological implications of deafness.* New York: The Free Press.

Gabarino, J., Dubrow, N., Kostelny, K., & Pardo, C. (1992). *Children in danger: Coping with the consequences of community violence.* San Francisco: Jossey-Bass.

Gale, I. (1968). An experimental study of two fifth-grade language-arts programs: An analysis of the writing of children taught linguistic grammar compared to those taught traditional grammar (Doctoral dissertation, Ball State University, 1967). *Dissertation Abstracts, 28,* 4156A.

Garcia, E. (1983). *Early childhood bilingualism.* Albuquerque: University of New Mexico Press.

Gardner, R. (1980). On the validity of affective variables in second language acquisition: Conceptual, contextual, and statistical considerations. *Language Learning, 30,* 255–270.

Gardner, R. (1983). Learning another language: A true social psychological experiment. *Journal of Language and Social Psychology, 2,* 219–239.

Garibaldi, A. (1979, March). *Teamwork and feedback: Broadening the base of collaborative writing.* Paper presented at the annual meeting of the Conference on College Composition and Communication. (ERIC Document Reproduction Service No. ED174994).

Gee, T. (1972). Students' responses to teachers' comments. *Research in the Teaching of English, 6,* 212–221.

Geiger, R. (1999). The ten generations of American higher education. In P. Altbach, R. Berdahl, & P. Gumport (Eds.), *American higher education in the twenty-first century: Social, political, and economic challenges* (pp. 38–69). Baltimore: Johns Hopkins University Press.

Genishi, C. (1981). Code switching in Chicano six-year-olds. In R. Duran (Ed.), *Latino language and communicative behavior* (pp. 133–152). Norwood, NJ: Ablex.

Gibson, E., & Levin, H. (1975). *The psychology of reading.* Cambridge, MA: MIT Press.

Gilbert, J. (1987). Patterns and possibilities for basic writers. *Journal of Basic Writing, 6,* 37–52.

Giroux, H. (1983). Theories of reproduction and resistance in the new sociology of education. *Harvard Educational Review, 53,* 257–293.

Giroux, H. (1987). Literacy and the pedagogy of political empowerment. In P. Freire & D. Macedo, *Literacy: Reading the word and the world* (pp. 1–28). South Hadley, MA: Bergin & Garvey.

Glass, A., Holyoak, K., & Santa, J. (1979). *Cognition.* Reading, MA: Addison-Wesley.

Glucksberg, S., & Danks, J. (1969). Grammatical structure and recall: A function of the space in immediate memory or recall delay? *Perception and Psychophysics, 6,* 113–117.

Goggin, M. (2000). *Authoring a discipline: Scholarly journals and the post-World War II emergence of rhetoric and composition.* Mahwah, NJ: Lawrence Erlbaum Associates.

Goldrick, M., & Rapp, B. (2001, November). *Mrs. Malaprop's neighborhood: Using word errors to reveal neighborhood structure.* Poster presented at the 42nd annual meeting of the Psychonomic Society, Orlando, FL.

Good, T., & Brophy, J. (1990). *Educational psychology: A realistic approach* (4th ed.). New York: Longman.

Goodman, K. (1967). Reading: A psycholinguistic guessing game. *Journal of the Reading Specialist, 6,* 126–135.

Goodman, K. (1973). Miscue analysis. Urbana, IL: ERIC Clearinghouse on Reading and Communication Skills.

Goody, J. (Ed.). (1968). *Literacy in traditional societies.* Cambridge, England: Cambridge University Press.

Goody, J. (1972, May 12). Literacy and the nonliterate. In *Times Literary Supplement.* (Reprinted in R. Disch (Ed.), *The future of literacy.* Englewood Cliffs, NJ: Prentice-Hall).

Goody, J. (1977). *The domestication of the savage mind.* Cambridge, England: Cambridge University Press.

Goody, J. (1987). *The interface between the oral and the written.* Cambridge, England: Cambridge University Press.

Goody, J., & Watt, I. (1968). The consequences of literacy. In J. Goody (Ed.), *Literacy in traditional societies.* Cambridge, England: Cambridge University Press.

Graff, H. (1987). *The legacies of literacy: Continuities and contradictions in western culture and society.* Bloomington: Indiana University Press.

Grant, M. (1992). *A social history of Greece and Rome.* New York: Macmillan.

Graves, D. (1975). Examination of the writing processes of seven year old children. *Research in the Teaching of English, 9,* 227–241.

Graves, D. (1979). Let children show us how to help them write. *Visible Language, 13,* 16–28.

Graves, D. (1981). The growth and development of first grade writers. In D. Graves (Ed.), *A case study observing the development of primary children's composing, spelling, and motor behaviors during the writing process: Final Report.* Durham: University of New Hampshire Press.

Green, S. (1992). Mining texts in reading to write. *Journal of Advanced Composition, 12,* 151–170.

Greenberg, K., Wiener, H., & Donovan, T. (Eds.). (1986). *Writing assessment: Issues and strategies.* New York: Longman.

Greenfield, P. (1972). Oral or written language: The consequences for cognitive development in Africa, the United States and England. *Language and Speech, 15,* 169–177.

Griswold del Castillo, R. (1984). *La familia: Chicano families in the urban Southwest 1848 to the present.* Notre Dame, IN: Notre Dame University Press.

Gumperz, J. (1982). *Discourse strategies.* Cambridge, England: Cambridge University Press.

Gunderson, B., & Johnson, D. (1980). Promoting positive attitudes toward learning a foreign language by using cooperative learning groups. *Foreign Language Annuals, 13,* 39–46.

Gundlach, R. (1981). On the nature and development of children's writing. In C. Frederiksen, M. Whiteman, & J. Dominic (Eds.), *Writing: The nature, development, and teaching of written communication* (pp. 133–152). Hillsdale, NJ: Lawrence Erlbaum Associates.

Gundlach, R. (1982). Children as writers: The beginnings of learning to write. In M. Nystrand (Ed.), *What writers know: The language, process, and structure of written discourse* (pp. 129–148). New York: Academic Press.

Gundlach, R. (1983). *How children learn to write: Perspectives on children's writing for educators and parents.* Washington, DC: National Institute of Education.

Guthrie, W. (1971). *The Sophists.* Cambridge, England: Cambridge University Press.

Hakuta, K. (1984). Bilingual education in the public eye: A case study of New Haven, Connecticut. *NABE Journal, 9,* 53–76.

Hakuta, K. (1986). *Mirror of language.* New York: Basic Books.

Hakuta, K., & Diaz, R. (1984). The relationship between bilingualism and cognitive ability: A critical discussion and some new longitudinal data. In K. Nelson (Ed.), *Children's language* (Vol. 5). Hillsdale, NJ: Lawrence Erlbaum Associates.

Hall, M. (1972). *The language experience approach for the culturally disadvantaged.* Newark, DE: International Reading Association.

Halliday, M. (1979). One child's proto language. In M. Bullowa (Ed.), *Before speech* (pp. 171–190). Cambridge, England: Cambridge University Press.

Halloran, M. (1993). Conversation versus declamation as models of written discourse. In T. Enos (Ed.), *Learning from the histories of rhetoric: Essays in honor of Winifred Bryan Horner.* Carbondale: Southern Illinois University Press.

Hardyck, C., & Petrinovich, L. (1967). Subvocal speech and comprehension level as a function of the difficulty level of reading material. *Journal of Verbal Learning and Verbal Behavior, 9,* 647–652.

Harris, J. (1987). The plural text/the plural self: Roland Barthes and William Coles. *College English, 49,* 158–170.

Harris, J. (1989). The idea of community in the study of writing. *College Composition and Communication, 40,* 11–22.

Harris, R. A. (1993). *The linguistics wars.* New York: Oxford University Press.

Harris, R. L. (1997). Forces and factors affecting Ohio Proficiency Test performance: A study of 593 Ohio school districts. Retrieved September 29, 2002, from www.cc. ysu.edu/~rlhoover/OPTISM/7-blackwhite.html.

Harrold, V. (1995). An investigation of faculty attitudes and oral communication programs for African American speakers of Black English at selected two-year private and public institutions of higher education in Michigan (Doctoral dissertation, Wayne State University, 1995). *Dissertation Abstracts International, 56,* 1676.

Harste, J., Burke, C., & Woodward, V. (1983). *Children's language and world: Initial encounters with print* (Final Rep. No. NIE-G-79-0132). Bloomington, IN: Language Education Departments.

Haswell, R., & Wyche-Smith, S. (1994). Adventuring into writing assessment. *College Composition and Communication, 45,* 220–236.

Hatch, E. (1978). *Second language acquisition: A book of readings.* Rowley, MA: Newbury House.

Haugen, E. (1966). *Language conflict and language planning: The case of modern Norwegian.* Cambridge, MA: Harvard University Press.

Hausner, R. (1976). Interaction of selected student personality factors and teachers' comments in a sequentially developed composition curriculum (Doctoral dissertation, Fordham University, 1975). *Dissertation Abstracts International, 36,* 5768A.

Havelock, E. (1982). *The literate revolution in Greece and its cultural consequences.* Princeton, NJ: Princeton University Press.

Hawisher, G. (1987). The effects of word processing on the revision strategies of college freshmen. *Research in the Teaching of English, 21,* 145–159.

Hawkins, T. (1980). The relationship between revision and the social dimension of peer tutoring. *College English, 40,* 64–68.

Hayes, B. (1992, August). *On what to teach the undergraduates: Some changing orthodoxies in phonological theory.* Paper presented at the International Conference on Linguistics, Seoul, Korea.

Healy, J. (1990). *Endangered minds: Why children don't think and what we can do about it.* New York: Simon & Schuster.

Heath, S. (1981). *Language in the USA.* Cambridge, England: Cambridge University Press.

Heath, S. (1983). *Ways with words.* Cambridge, England: Cambridge University Press.

Hegel, F. (1956). *The philosophy of history* (J. Sibree, Trans.). New York: Dover.

Herrnstein, R., & Murray, C. (1994). *The bell curve: Intelligence and class structure in American life.* New York: The Free Press.

Hertz-Lazarowitz, R., Kirkus, V., & Miller, N. (1992). An overview of the theoretical anatomy of cooperation in the classroom. In R. Hertz-Lazarowitz & N. Miller (Eds.), *Interaction in cooperative groups: The theoretical anatomy of group learning* (pp. 1–17). Cambridge, England: Cambridge University Press.

Hillocks, G. (1986). *Research on written composition: New directions for teaching.* Urbana, IL: National Conference on Research in English.

Hillocks, G. (2002). Rhetoric in classrooms: Prospects for the twenty-first century. In J. Williams (Ed.), *Visions and revisions: Continuity and change in rhetoric and composition* (pp. 219–248). Carbondale: Southern Illinois University Press.

Hirsch, E. (1977). *The philosophy of composition.* Chicago: University of Chicago Press.

Hoenigswald, H. (1978). The annus mirabilis 1876 and posterity. *Transactions of the Philosophical Society, 14,* 191–203.

Hoffer, B. (1975). Spanish interference in the English written in South Texas high schools. In E. Dubois & B Hofrer (Eds.), *Papers in Southwest English: Research techniques and prospects.* San Antonio, TX: Trinity University Press.

Howard, J. (1990). *Getting smart: The social construction of intelligence.* Lexington, MA: The Efficacy Institute.

Hudson, R. (1980). *Sociolinguistics.* Cambridge, England: Cambridge University Press.

Huff, R., & Kline, C. (1987). *The contemporary writing curriculum: Rehearsing, composing, and valuing.* New York: Teachers College Press.

Hughes, M. (1975). *Egocentrism in preschool children.* Unpublished doctoral dissertation, Edinburgh University, Edinburgh, Scotland.

Hunt, J. (1975). Reflections on a decade of early education. *Journal of Abnormal Child Psychology, 3,* 275–336.

Hunt, K. (1964). *Differences in grammatical structures written at three grade levels* (Cooperative Research Project No. 1998). Tallahassee: Florida State University.

Hunt, K. (1965). *Grammatical structures written at three grade levels* (NCTE Research Rep. No. 3). Champaign, IL: National Council of Teachers of English.

Huot, B. (1996). Toward a new theory of writing assessment. *College Composition and Communication, 47,* 549–566.

Hymes, D. (1971). Competence and performance in linguistic theory. In R. Huxley & E. Ingram (Eds.), *Language acquisition: Models and methods* (pp. 3–28). New York: Academic Press.

Jackendoff, R. (2002). *Foundations of language: Brain, meaning, grammar, evolution.* New York: Oxford University Press.

Jarratt, S. (1991). *Rereading the Sophists: Classical rhetoric refigured.* Carbondale: Southern Illinois University Press.

Jarvis, L., Danks, J., & Merriman, W. (1995). The effect of bilingualism on cognitive ability: A test of the level of bilingual hypothesis. *Applied Psycholinguistics, 16,* 293–308.

Jencks, C., & Phillips, M. (Eds.). (1998). *The black–white test score gap.* Washington, DC: Brookings Institution Press.

Jimenez, R. (2000). *Caesar against Rome: The great Roman civil war.* Westport, CT: Praeger.

Johnson, D. K. (1993). The relationship of reading, attitudes, and learning strategies to writing in college freshmen (Doctoral dissertation, University of Houston, 1992). *Dissertation Abstracts International, 53,* 3815A.

Johnson, D. W. (1980). Group processes: Influences of student-vs-student interaction on school outcomes. In J. McMillan (Ed.), *The social psychology of school learning.* New York: Holt, Rinehart & Winston.

Johnson, D. W., & Ahlgren, A. (1976). Relationship between students' attitudes about cooperation and competition and attitudes toward schooling. *Journal of Educational Psychology, 68,* 92–102.

Johnson, D. W., & Johnson, F. (2000). *Joining together: Group theory and group skills.* Needham Heights, MA: Pearson Education.

Johnson, D. W., Johnson, F., & Maruyama, G. (1983). Interdependence and interpersonal attraction among heterogeneous and homogeneous individuals: A theoretical formulation and a meta-analysis of the research. *Review of Educational Research, 53,* 554.

Johnson, T. R. (2001). School sucks. *College Composition and Communication, 52,* 620–650.

Johnson-Laird, P. (1983). *Mental models.* Cambridge, MA: Harvard University Press.

Jones, S., & Tetroe, J. (1983). Composing in a second language. In A. Matsuhashi (Ed.), *Writing in real time* (pp. 34–57). Norwood, NJ: Ablex.

Karmiloff-Smith, A. (1992). *Beyond modularity: A developmental perspective on cognitive science.* Cambridge, MA: MIT Press.

Kay, P., & Sankoff, G. (1974). A language-universals approach to pidgins and Creoles. In D. DeCamp & I. Hancock (Eds.), *Pidgins and Creoles: Current trends and prospects* (pp. 46–84). Washington, DC: Georgetown University Press.

Kelso, J. (1995). *Dynamic patterns: The self-organization of brain and behavior.* Cambridge, MA: MIT Press.

Kennedy, G. (1980). *Classical rhetoric and its Christian and secular tradition from ancient to modern times.* Chapel Hill: University of North Carolina Press.

Kennedy, G. (1991). *Aristotle on rhetoric: A theory of civic discourse.* New York: Oxford University Press.

Kent, T. (1991). On the very idea of a discourse community. *College Composition and Communication, 42,* 425–445.

Ketter, J., & Pool, J. (2001). Exploring the impact of a high-stakes direct writing assessment in two high school classrooms. *Research in the Teaching of English, 35,* 344–393.

Killian, L. (1971). WISC, Illinois test of psycholinguistic abilities and Bender Visual-Motor Gestalt test performance of Spanish-American kindergarten and first grade school children. *Journal of Consulting and Clinical Psychology, 37,* 383.

Kinneavy, J. (1971). *A theory of discourse.* Englewood Cliffs, NJ: Prentice-Hall. (Reprinted 1980. New York: Norton)

Kinneavy, J. (1982). Restoring the humanities: The return of rhetoric from exile. In J. Murphy (Ed.), *The rhetorical tradition and modern writing* (pp. 19–30). New York: Modern Language Association.

Kintsch, W., & van Dijk, T. (1978). Toward a model of text comprehension and production. *Psychological Review, 85,* 363–394.

Kirscht, J., Levine, R., & Reiff, J. (1994). Evolving paradigms: WAC and the rhetoric of inquiry. *College Composition and Communication, 45,* 369–380.

Kohl, H. (1967). *Thirty-six children.* New York: New American Library.

Kohn, B. (1980). Right-hemisphere speech representation and comprehension of syntax after left cerebral injury. *Brain and Language, 9,* 350–361.

Krashen, S. (1980). The input hypothesis. In J. Alatis (Ed.), *Current issues in bilingual education.* Washington, DC: Georgetown University Press.

Krashen, S. (1981a). *The role of input (reading) and instruction in developing writing ability* (Working paper). Los Angeles: University of Southern California.

Krashen, S. (1981b). *Second language acquisition and second language learning.* Oxford, England: Pergamon.

Krashen, S. (1982). *Principles and practice in second language acquisition.* Oxford, England: Pergamon.

Krashen, S. (1985). *Writing research, theory, and applications.* New York: Pergamon.

Kruse, M. (2001). Review of *The teacher's grammar book. Composition Studies, 29,* 139–142.

Labov, W. (1964). Phonological indices to social stratification. In J. Gumperz & D. Hymes (Eds.), *The ethnography of communication.* Washington, DC: American Anthropological Association.

Labov, W. (1966). *The social stratification of English in New York City.* Washington, DC: Georgetown University Press.

Labov, W. (1969). Contraction, deletion, and inherent variability of the English copula. *Language, 45,* 715–762.

Labov, W. (1970). *The study of nonstandard English*. Urbana, IL: National Council of Teachers of English.

Labov, W. (1971). The notion of system in Creole studies. In D. Hymes (Ed.), *Pidginization and creolization of language* (pp. 447–472). Cambridge, England: Cambridge University Press.

Labov, W. (1972a). *Language in the inner city: Studies in the Black English vernacular*. Philadelphia: University of Pennsylvania Press.

Labov, W. (1972b). *Sociolinguistic patterns*. Philadelphia: University of Pennsylvania Press.

Labov, W. (1980). The social origins of sound change. In W. Labov (Ed.), *Locating language in time and space* (pp. 251–266). New York: Academic Press.

Labov, W. (1994). *Principles of linguistic change: Internal factors*. London: Blackwell.

Lakoff, G. (1987). *Women, fire, and dangerous things*. Chicago: University of Chicago Press.

Langacker, R. (1987). *Foundations of cognitive grammar: Vol. 1. Theoretical prerequisites*. Stanford, CA: Stanford University Press.

Langacker, R. (1990). *Concept, image, and symbol: The cognitive basis of grammar*. New York: Mouton de Gruyter.

Laughlin, P., & McGlynn, R. (1967). Cooperative versus competitive concept attainment as a function of sex and stimulus display. *Journal of Personality and Social Psychology, 7*, 398–402.

Lee, J. (1987). Prewriting assignments across the curriculum. In C. Olson (Ed.), *Practical ideas for teaching writing as a process*. Sacramento, CA: State Department of Education.

Lenneberg, E. (1967). *Biological foundations of language*. New York: Wiley.

Levin, H (1988). Accelerated schools for disadvantaged students. *Educational Leadership, 44*, 19–21.

Levi-Strauss, C. (1966). *The savage mind*. Chicago: University of Chicago Press.

Lévy-Bruhl, L. (1926). *How natives think* (L. Clare, Trans.). New York: Knopf.

Lévy-Bruhl, L. (1975). *The notebooks on primitive mentality* (P. Riviere, Trans.). New York: Harper & Row.

Lindemann, E. (1985). At the beach. In W. Coles & J. Vopat (Eds.), *What makes writing good*. Lexington, MA: Heath.

Lindemann, E. (1993a). Freshman composition: No place for literature. *College English, 55*, 311–316.

Lindemann, E. (1993b). *A rhetoric for writing teachers* (3rd ed.). New York: Oxford University Press.

Livingston, S. (1980). *The effects of time limits on the quality of student-written essays*. (ERIC Document Reproduction Service No. ED286936).

Lloyd-Jones, R. (2002). Omnivorous study. In J. Williams (Ed.), *Visions and revisions: Continuity and change in rhetoric and composition* (pp. 13–31). Carbondale: Southern Illinois University Press.

Luges, A. (1994). A descriptive study of writing in a secondary ESL classroom (Doctoral dissertation, University of Colorado at Boulder, 1994). *Dissertation Abstracts International, 56*, 482.

Lunsford, A., Moglen, H., & Slevin, J. (1990). *The right to literacy*. New York: Modern Language Association.

Luria, A. (1976). *Cognitive development: Its cultural and social foundations* (M. Lopez-Morrillas & L. Solotaroff, Trans.). Cambridge, MA: Harvard University Press.

Lyons, G. (1976, September). The higher illiteracy. *Harper's,* pp. 33–40.

Lyons, J. (1970). *Noam Chomsky.* New York: Penguin.

Lyons, J. (1977a). *Semantics* (Vol. 1). Cambridge, England: Cambridge University Press.

Lyons, J. (1977b). *Semantics* (Vol. 2). Cambridge, England: Cambridge University Press.

Lyotard, J. (1985). *The postmodern condition: A report on knowledge* (B. Massumi, Trans.). Minneapolis: University of Minnesota Press.

Macaulay, R. (1973). Double standards. *American Anthropologist, 75,* 1324–1337.

Macnamara, J. (1972). Cognitive basis of language learning in infants. *Psychological Review, 79,* 1–13.

Macrorie, K. (1964). Composition as art. *College English, 15,* back cover.

Macrorie, K. (1968). *Writing to be read.* Rochelle Park, NJ: Hayden.

Macrorie, K. (1970). *Telling writing.* New Rochelle, NY: Hayden.

Malt, B. (1985). The role of discourse structure in understanding anaphora. *Journal of Memory and Language, 24,* 271–289.

Mano, S. (1986). Television: A surprising acquisition source for literacy. *Writing Instructor, 5,* 104–111.

Marcuse, H. (1941). *Reason and revolution: Hegel and the rise of social theory.* Boston: Beacon Press.

Marcuse, H. (1955). *Eros and civilization: A philosophical inquiry into Freud.* Boston: Beacon Press.

Marcuse, H. (1964). *One-dimensional man: Studies in the ideology of advanced industrial society.* Boston: Beacon Press.

Marcuse, H. (1965). Repressive tolerance. In R. Wolff, B. Moore, & H. Marcuse (Eds.), *A critique of pure tolerance.* Boston: Beacon Press.

Matsuhashi, A. (1981). Pausing and planning: The tempo of written discourse production. *Research in the Teaching of English, 15,* 113–134.

McClure, E. (1981). Formal and functional aspects of the code-switched discourse of bilingual children. In R. Duran (Ed.), *Latino language and communicative behavior: Advances in discourse processes* (Vol. 6, pp. 69–94). Norwood, NJ: Ablex.

McCrum, R., Cran, W., & MacNeil, R. (1986). *The story of English.* New York: Viking.

McGuigan, F. (1966). *Thinking: Studies of covert language processes.* New York: Appleton.

McGuigan, F. (1978). *Cognitive psychophysiology: Principles of covert behavior.* Englewood Cliffs, NJ: Prentice-Hall.

Mellon, J. (1969). *Transformational sentence-combining: A method for enhancing the development of syntactic fluency in English composition* (NCTE Research Rep. No. 10). Champaign, IL: National Council of Teachers of English.

Mencken, H. (1936). *The American language: An inquiry into the development of English in the United States.* New York: Knopf.

Michael, J. (1995). Valuing differences: Portnet's first year. *Assessing Writing, 2,* 67–90.

Michaels, B. (1982). *Black rainbow.* New York: Congdon & Weed.

Miller, C. (1993). Rhetoric and community: The problem of the one and the many. In T. Enos & S. Bron (Eds.), *Defining the new rhetorics* (pp. 79–94). Newbury Park, CA: Sage.

Miller, G. (1962). Some psychological studies of grammar. *American Psychologist, 17,* 748–762.

Miller, G., & McKean, K. (1964). A chronometric study of some relations between sentences. *Quarterly Journal of Experimental Psychology, 16,* 297–308.

Miller, J., Chapman, R., Branston, M., & Reichle, J. (1980). Language comprehension in sensorimotor stages V and VI. *Journal of Speech and Hearing Research, 23,* 284–311.

Miller, P. (1989). *Theories of developmental psychology* (2nd ed.). New York: Freeman.

Miller, S. (1982). Classical practice and contemporary basics. In James Murphy (Ed.), *The rhetorical tradition and modern writing* (pp. 46–57). New York: Modern Language Association.

Miller, S. D., & Meese, J. (1999). Third grader's motivational preferences for reading and writing tasks. *The Elementary School Journal, 100,* 19–36.

Moffett, J. (1968). *Teaching the universe of discourse.* Boston: Houghton Mifflin.

Moffett, J. (1985). Liberating inner speech. *College Composition and Communication, 36,* 304–308.

Moffett, J. (1990). Censorship and spiritual education. In A. Lunsford, H. Moglen, & J. Slevin (Eds.), *The right to literacy.* New York: Modern Language Association.

Munn, M. (2000). *The school of history: Athens in the age of Socrates.* Berkeley: University of California Press.

Murphy, J. (1974). *Rhetoric in the Middle Ages: A history of rhetorical theory from St. Augustine to the Renaissance.* Berkeley: University of California Press.

Murray, D. (1982). *Learning by teaching.* Montclair, NJ: Boynton/Cook.

Nelson, K. (1973). Structure and strategy in learning to talk. *Monographs of the Society for Research in Child Development, 38*(1–2, Serial No. 149).

Norris, C. (1993). *The truth about postmodernism.* London: Blackwell.

North, S. (1987). *The making of knowledge in composition: Portrait of an emerging field.* Upper Montclair, NJ: Boynton/Cook.

Nystrand, M., Gamoran, A., Kachur, R., & Pendergast, C. (1997). *Opening dialogue: Understanding the dynamics of language and learning in the English classroom.* New York: Teachers College Press.

Ober, J. (1989). *Mass and elite in democratic Athens.* Princeton, NJ: Princeton University Press.

O'Hare, F. (1972). *Sentence combining: Improving student writing without formal grammar instruction* (NCTE Committee on Research Report Series, No. 15). Urbana, IL: National Council of Teachers of English.

Olson, D. (1977). From utterance to text: The bias of language in speech and writing. *Harvard Educational Review, 47,* 257–281.

Olson, D. (1987). Development of the metalanguage of literacy. *Interchange, 18,* 136–146.

Ong, W. (1978). Literacy and orality in our time. *ADE Bulletin, 58,* 1–7.

Ong, W. (1982). *Orality and literacy: The terminologizing of the word.* London: Methuen.

Orr, J., Butler, Y., Bousquet, M., & Hakuta, K. (2000). *What can we learn about the impact of Proposition 227 from SAT-9 scores? An analysis of results from 2000.* Retrieved May 13, 2002, from http://www.stanford.edu/~hakuta/SAT9/SAT9_2000/analysis2000.html.

Ostwald, M. (1986). *From popular sovereignty to the sovereignty of law.* Berkeley: University of California Press.

Owens, D. (1994). *Resisting writings (and the boundaries of composition).* Dallas, TX: Southern Methodist University Press.

Parker, R. (1979). From Sputnik to Dartmouth: Trends in the teaching of composition. *English Journal, 68*(6), 32–37.

Patterson, O. (1991). *Freedom.* New York: Basic Books.

Peal, E., & Lambert, W. E. (1962). The relation of bilingualism to intelligence. *Psychological Monographs, 76*(27, Whole No. 546).

Peck, M. (1982). *An investigation of tenth-grade students' writing.* Washington, DC: United Press of America.

Pellegrino, J., Chudowsky, N., & Glaser, R. (2001). *Knowing what students know: The science and design of educational assessment.* Washington, DC: The National Academy of Sciences.

Penalosa, F. (1980). *Chicano sociolinguistics: A brief introduction.* Rowley, MA: Newbury House.

Perl, S., & Wilson, N. (1986). *Through teachers' eyes: Portraits of writing teachers at work.* New York: Heinemann.

Piaget, J. (1953). *The origins of intelligence in the child.* London: Routledge & Kegan Paul.

Piaget, J. (1955). *The child's construction of reality.* London: Routledge & Kegan Paul.

Piaget, J. (1962). *Plays, dreams, and imitation in childhood.* New York: Norton.

Piaget, J. (1974). *The language and thought of the child.* New York: New American Library.

Piaget, J., & Inhelder, B. (1969). *The psychology of the child.* New York: Basic Books.

Pinker, S. (1994). *The language instinct: How the mind creates language.* New York: Morrow.

Pinker, S. (2002). *The blank slate.* New York: Viking.

Plato. (1937a). Apology. In B. Jowett (Ed. & Trans.), *The dialogues of Plato* (Vol. 1). New York: Random House.

Plato. (1937b). Gorgias. In B. Jowett (Ed. & Trans.), *The dialogues of Plato* (Vol. 1). New York: Random House.

Plato. (1961). Letter VII. In E. Hamilton & H. Cairns (Eds. & Trans.), *The collected dialogues of Plato, including the letters.* Princeton, NJ: Princeton University Press.

Plutarch. (1958). *Fall of the Roman republic* (R. Warner, Trans.). Harmondsworth, England: Penguin.

Poe, E. A. (1962). To Helen. In K. Campbell (Ed.), *The poems of Edgar Allen Poe.* New York: Russell & Russell.

Proctor, C. (1984, March). Teacher expectations: A model for school improvement. *The Elementary School Journal,* pp. 469–481.

Putnam, H. (1975). The meaning of meaning. In H. Putnam (Ed.), *Philosophical papers: Vol. 2. Mind, language, and reality.* Cambridge, England: Cambridge University Press.

Quine, W. (1960). *Word and object.* Cambridge, MA: MIT Press.

Raimes, A. (1985). What unskilled ESL students do as they write: A classroom study of composing. *TESOL Quarterly, 19,* 229–258.

Raimes, A. (1986). Teaching ESL writing: Fitting what we do to what we know. *Writing Instructor, 5,* 153–166.

Raschke, C. (1996). *Fire and roses: Postmodernity and the thought of the body.* Albany: State University of New York Press.

Restak, R. (1979). *The brain: The last frontier.* New York: Warner.

Rice, M., & Kemper, S. (1984). *Child language and cognition.* Baltimore: University Park Press.

Rickford, J. (1975). Carrying the new wave into syntax: The case of Black English *been.* In R. Fasgold & R. Shuy (Eds.), *Analyzing variation in language* (pp. 162–183). Washington, DC: Georgetown University Press.

Robinson, J. (1990). *Conversations on the written word: Essays on language and literacy.* Portsmouth, NH: Boynton/Cook.

Rodriguez, R. (1982). *The hunger of memory: The education of Richard Rodriguez* (Reprinted 1983). New York: Bantam.

Rodriguez, R. (1997). *A view from the melting pot: An interview with Richard Rodriguez* (Insight & Outlook radio series, hosted by Scott London). Retrieved May 17, 2002, from http://www.scottlondon.com/insight/scripts/rodriguez.html.

Rosch, E. (1978). *Cognition and categorization.* Hillsdale, NJ: Wiley.

Rose, M. (1988). Narrowing the mind and page: Remedial writers and cognitive reductionism. *College Composition and Communication, 39,* 267–302.

Rumelhart, D., & McClelland, J. (1986a). *Parallel distributed processing: Explorations in the microstructure of cognition* (Vol. 1). Cambridge, MA: MIT Press.

Rumelhart, D., & McClelland, J. (1986b). *Parallel distributed processing: Explorations in the microstructure of cognition* (Vol. 2). Cambridge, MA: MIT Press.

Russell, D. (1987). Writing across the curriculum and the communications movement: Some lessons from the past. *College Composition and Communication, 38,* 184–194.

St. Augustine. (1958). *On Christian doctrine* (D. Robertson, Trans.). Indianapolis, IN: Bobbs-Merrill.

St. Augustine. (1962). *The confessions of St. Augustine* (R. Warner, Trans.). New York: New American Library.

Sanchez, N. (1987, June 10). Bilingual training can be a barrier to academic achievement for students. *Chronicle of Higher Education.*

Sanchez, R. (1983). *Chicano discourse: Socio-historic perspectives.* Rowley, MA: Newbury House.

Sanford, A., & Garrod, S. (1981). *Understanding written language.* New York: Wiley.

Scardamalia, M., & Bereiter, C. (1983). The development of evaluative, diagnostic, and remedial capabilities in children's composing. In M. Martlew (Ed.), *The psychology of written language: A developmental approach* (pp. 67–95). London: Wiley.

Schank, R., & Abelson, R. (1977). *Scripts, plans, goals and understanding.* Hillsdale, NJ: Lawrence Erlbaum Associates.

Schiappa, E. (1999). *The beginnings of rhetorical theory in classical Greece.* New Haven, CT: Yale University Press.

Schlesinger, I. (1971). The production of utterances and language acquisition. In D. Slobin (Ed.), *The ontogenesis of grammar.* New York: Academic Press.

Schroeder, C., Bizzell, P., & Fox, H. (Eds.). (2002). *Alt dis: Alternative discourses and the academy.* Upper Montclair, NJ: Boynton–Cook.

Schroeder, T. (1973). The effects of positive and corrective written teacher feedback on selected writing behaviors of fourth-grade children (Doctoral dissertation, University of Kansas, 1973). *Dissertation Abstracts International, 34,* 2935-A.

Scinto, L. (1986). *Written language and psychological development.* San Diego: Harcourt Brace.

Scollon, R., & Scollon, S. (1979). *The literate two-year-old: The fictionalization of self.* Austin, TX: Southeast Regional Laboratory.

Scribner, S., & Cole, M. (1981). *The psychology of literacy.* Cambridge, MA: Harvard University Press.

Searle, J. (1969). *Speech acts: An essay in the philosophy of language.* New York: Cambridge University Press.

Searle, J. (1992). *The rediscovery of the mind.* Cambridge, MA: MIT Press.

Searle, J. (1995). *The construction of social reality.* New York: The Free Press.

Seidman, S. (Ed.). (1994). *The postmodern turn: New perspectives on social theory.* Cambridge, England: Cambridge University Press.

Self, C. (1986). Reading as a writing strategy: Two case studies. In B. Petersen (Ed.), *Convergences: Transactions in reading and writing* (pp. 46–63). Urbana, IL: National Council of Teachers of English.

Shankweiler, D., & Crain, S. (1986). Language mechanisms and reading disorder: A modular approach. *Cognition, 10,* 139–168.

Shaughnessy, M. (1977). *Errors and expectations: A guide for the teacher of basic writing.* New York: Oxford University Press.

Shin, F. (1994). Korean parents' perceptions and attitudes of bilingual education (Doctoral dissertation, University of Southern California, 1994). *Dissertation Abstracts International, 56,* 850.

Skinner, B. (1957). *Verbal behavior.* New York: Appleton–Century–Crofts.

Slavin, R., Karweit, N., & Madden, N. (1989). *Effective programs for students at risk.* Boston: Allyn & Bacon.

Slobin, D. (1973). Cognitive prerequisites for the development of grammar. In C. Ferguson & D. Slobin (Eds.), *Studies of child language development* (pp. 175–208). New York: Holt, Rinehart & Winston.

Slobin, D. (1977). Language change in childhood and history. In J. Macnamara (Ed.), *Language, learning and thought* (pp.). New York: Academic Press.

Slobin, D. (1982). Universal and particular in the acquisition of language. In L. Gleitman & E. Wanner (Eds.), *Language acquisition: State of the art* (pp. 128–172). New York: Cambridge University Press.

Slobin, D., & Welsh, C. (1973). Elicited imitation as a research tool in developmental psycholinguistics. In C. Ferguson & D. Slobin (Eds.), *Studies of child language development* (pp. 485–497). New York: Holt, Rinehart & Winston.

Smith, F. (1972). *Understanding reading.* New York: Holt, Rinehart & Winston.

Smith, F. (1983). *Essays into literacy.* London: Heinemann.

Sokolov, A. (1972). *Inner speech and thought* (G. Onischenko, Trans.). New York: Plenum.

Sommers, N. (1982). Responding to student writing. *College Composition and Communication, 33,* 148–156.

Spear, K. (1993). *Peer response groups in action: Writing together in secondary schools.* Portsmouth, NH: Boynton/Cook.

Staats, A., & Butterfield, W. (1965). Treatment of nonreading in a culturally deprived juvenile delinquent: An application of reinforcement principles. *Child Development, 4,* 925–942.

Steinberg, D. (1993). *Introduction to psycholinguistics.* New York: Addison-Wesley.

Stephens, D. (1991). *Research on whole language: Support for a new curriculum.* Katonah, NY: Richard C. Owen Publishers.

Stiefel, L., Schwartz, A., Iatarola, P., & Fruchter, N. (2000). Academic performance, characteristics and expenditures in New York City elementary and middle schools. Condition report for the Education Finance Research Consortium. New York State Education Department.

Stotsky, S. (1999). *Losing our language: How multicultural classroom instruction is undermining our children's ability to read, write, and reason.* New York: The Free Press.

Straub, R. (1997). Students' reactions to teacher comments: An exploratory study. *Research in the Teaching of English, 31,* 91–119.

Supovitz, J., & Brennan, R. (1997). Mirror, mirror on the wall, which is the fairest test of all? An examination of the equitability of portfolio assessment relative to standardized tests. *Harvard Educational Review, 67,* 472–506.

Tannen, D. (1982). Oral and literate strategies in spoken and written narratives. *Language, 58,* 1–21.

Tannen, D. (1990). *You just don't understand: Women and men in conversation.* New York: Morrow.

Tarvers, J. (1988). *Teaching writing: Theories and practices.* Glenview, IL: Scott, Foresman.

Tate, G. (1993). A place for literature in freshman composition. *College English, 55,* 317–321.

Thucydides. (1986). *The Peloponnesian war* (R. Warner, Trans.). New York: Viking.

Trevarthen, C. (1974). Communication and cooperation in early infancy: A description of primary intersubjectivity. In M. Bullowa (Ed.), *Before speech: The beginnings of human communication* (pp. 321–347). Cambridge, England: Cambridge University Press, 1979.

Trimbur, J. (1987). Beyond cognition: The voices of inner speech. *Rhetoric Review, 5,* 211–221.

Trudgill, P. (2001). *Sociolinguistics: An introduction.* New York: Penguin.

Ullmann, J. (1963). *Semantics: An introduction to the study of meaning.* Oxford, England: Basil Blackwell & Mott.

U.S. Department of Education. (1995). *National Household Education Survey.* Washington, DC: Office of Educational Research and Improvement.

U.S. Department of Education. (1996). *NAEP 1996 trends in writing: Fluency and writing conventions.* Washington, DC: U.S. Government Printing Office.

U.S. Department of Education. (1999). *1998 writing: Report card for the nation and the states.* Washington, DC: U.S. Government Printing Office.

Vernant, J. (1982). *The origins of Greek thought.* Ithaca, NY: Cornell University Press.

Villamil, O., & DeGuerrero, M. (1999). Assessing the impact of peer revision on L_2 writing. *Applied Linguistics, 19,* 491–514.

Vygotsky, L. (1962). *Thought and language.* Cambridge, MA: MIT Press.

Vygotsky, L. (1978). *Mind in society* (M. Cole, V. John-Steiner, S. Scribner, & E. Souberman, Eds.). Cambridge, MA: Harvard University Press.

Wald, B. (1985). Motivation for language choice behavior of elementary Mexican-American children. In E. García & R. Padilla (Eds.), *Advances in bilingual education research* (pp. 71–95). Tucson: University of Arizona Press.

Walters, K. (1990). Language, logic, and literacy. In A. Lunsford, H. Moglen, & J. Sledd (Eds.), *The right to literacy* (pp. 173–188). New York: Modern Language Association.

Walvoord, B. (1996a). The future of writing across the curriculum. *College English, 58,* 58–79.

Walvoord, B. (1996b). *WAC in the long run: A study of faculty in three writing-across-the-curriculum programs.* Urbana, IL: National Council of Teachers of English.

Warren, R., & Warren, R. (1970). Auditory illusions and confusions. *Scientific American, 223,* 30–36.

Watson, R. (1985). Toward a theory of definition. *Journal of Child Language, 12,* 181–197.

Weber, H. (1968). The study of oral reading errors: A survey of the literature. *Reading Research Quarterly, 4,* 96–119.

Welch, K. (1990). Writing instruction in ancient Athens after 450 B.C. In J. Murphy (Ed.), *A short history of writing instruction from ancient Greece to twentieth-century America* (pp. 1–18). Davis, CA: Hermagoras Press.

Welsh, S. (2001). Resistance theory and illegitimate reproduction. *College Composition and Communication, 52,* 553–573.

Werner, E. (1990). Protective factors and individual resilience. In S. Meisels & J. Shonkoff (Eds.), *Handbook of early childhood intervention* (pp. 97–116). New York: Cambridge University Press.

Wernicke, C. (1874). *Der aphasische symptomenkomplex* [Aphasia]. Breslau, Poland: Cohen & Weigert.

White, E. (1986). *Teaching and assessing writing.* San Francisco: Jossey-Bass.

White, L. (1977). Error analysis and error correction in adult learners of English as a second language. *Working Papers in Bilingualism, 13,* 42–58.

White, R. (1965). The effect of structural linguistics on improving English composition compared to that of prescriptive grammar or the absence of grammar instruction (Doctoral dissertation, University of Arizona, 1964). *Dissertation Abstracts, 25,* 5032.

Whitehead, C. (1966). The effect of grammar diagramming on student writing skills (Doctoral dissertation, Montana State University, 1965). *Dissertation Abstracts, 26,* 3710.

Whorf, B. L. (1956). *Language, thought and reality: Selected writings of Benjamin Lee Whorf* (J. B. Carroll, Ed.). Cambridge, MA: MIT Press.

Wiersema, N. (2000). *How does collaborative learning actually work in a classroom and how do students react to it?* Retrieved April 17, 2002, from http://www.lgu.ac.uk/deliberations/collab.learning/wiersema.html.

Williams, J. (1983). Covert language behavior during writing. *Research in the Teaching of English, 17,* 301–312.

Williams, J. (1985). Coherence and cognitive style. *Written Communication, 2,* 473–491.

Williams, J. (1987). Covert linguistic behavior during writing tasks: Psychophysiological differences between above-average and below-average writers. *Written Communication, 4,* 310–328.

Williams, J. (1992). Politicizing literacy. *College English, 54,* 833–842.

Williams, J. (1993). Rule-governed approaches to language and composition. *Written Communication, 10,* 542–568.

Williams, J. (1999). *The teacher's grammar book.* Mahwah, NJ: Lawrence Erlbaum Associates.

Williams, J. (2000). Identity and reliability in portfolio assessment. In B. Sunstein & J. Lovell (Eds.), *The portfolio standard* (pp. 135–148). Portsmouth, NH: Heinemann.

Williams, J. (2001). *The LEA guide to composition*. Mahwah, NJ: Lawrence Erlbaum Associates.

Williams, J. (2002). Rhetoric and the triumph of liberal democracy. In J. Williams (Ed.), *Visions and revisions: Continuity and change in rhetoric and composition* (pp. 131–161). Carbondale: Southern Illinois University Press.

Williams, J., Gillett, J., & Temple, C. (2002). *Writing and language arts, K–6*. New York: SRA/McGraw-Hill.

Williams, J., & Snipper, G. (1990). *Literacy and bilingualism*. New York: Longman.

Willis, S. (1972). Formation of teachers' expectations of students' performance (Doctoral dissertation, University of Texas, Austin, 1972). *Dissertation Abstracts International, 33-09*, 4960.

Winterowd, W. (Ed.). (1975). *Contemporary rhetoric: A conceptual background with readings*. New York: Harcourt Brace.

Winterowd, W., & Blum, J. (1994). *A teacher's introduction to composition in the rhetorical tradition*. Urbana, IL: National Council of Teachers of English.

Witte, S. (1985). Revising composing theory and research design. In S. Freedman (Ed.), *The acquisition of writer language: Response and revision* (pp. 250–284). Norwood, NJ: Ablex.

Witte, S., & Cherry, R. (1986). Writing processes and written products in composition research. In C. Cooper & S. Greenbaum (Eds.), *Studying writing: Linguistic approaches*. Beverly Hills, CA: Sage.

Witte, S., & Faigley, L. (1981). Coherence, cohesion, and writing quality. *College Composition and Communication, 32*, 189–204.

Witte, S., Nakadate, N., & Cherry, R. (Eds.). (1992). *A rhetoric of doing: Essays on written discourse in honor of James L. Kinneavy*. Carbondale: Southern Illinois University Press.

Wittrock, M. (1977). The generative processes of memory. In M. Wittrock (Ed.), *The human brain*. Englewood Cliffs, NJ: Prentice-Hall.

Wolfram, W. (1969). *A sociolinguistic description of Detroit Negro speech*. Washington, DC: Center for Applied Linguistics.

Wolfram, W., Adger, L., & Christian, A. (1999). *Dialects in schools and communities*. Mahwah, NJ: Lawrence Erlbaum Associates.

Wright, R. (1998). *Black boy*. (1945). New York: Prentice-Hall.

Young, I. (1990). The ideal of community and the politics of difference. In L. Nicholson (Ed.), *Feminism/postmodernism* (pp. 300–323). New York: Routledge.

Zamel, U. (1983). The composing processes of advanced ESL students: Six case studies. *TESOL Quarterly, 17*, 165–187.

Zoellner, R. (1968). Talkwrite: A behavioral pedagogy for composition. *College English, 30*, 267–320.

Author Index

385

Subject Index

Note: An *f* after a page number denotes a figure; a *t* after a page number denotes a table.